STUDIES IN EARLY MODERN CULTURAL,
POLITICAL AND SOCIAL HISTORY

Volume 2

Restoration Scotland, 1660–1690

This new series of monographs and studies covers a wide variety of historical themes from the sixteenth through to the early nineteenth century. It aims to publish intellectually stimulating works of scholarship that will make a major original contribution to the field, whether through innovative conceptual, theoretical or methodological approaches or groundbreaking work on hitherto underexplored sources. By publishing work on cultural and social as well as political history, the series aims to break down some of the barriers that have traditionally existed between these various subfields. In addition, the series particularly welcomes studies which set the past in a more international or global context, such as for example works that link the histories of early-modern Britain and Ireland to Europe, to the Americas or to the British empire.

STUDIES IN EARLY MODERN CULTURAL, POLITICAL AND SOCIAL HISTORY

ISSN: 1476–9107

Series Editors

David Armitage
Tim Harris
Stephen Taylor

I

Women of Quality
Accepting and Contesting Ideals
of Femininity in England, 1690–1760

Ingrid H. Tague

Restoration Scotland, 1660–1690

Royalist Politics, Religion and Ideas

CLARE JACKSON

THE BOYDELL PRESS

First published 2003
The Boydell Press, Woodbridge

ISBN 0 85115 930 3

The Boydell Press is an imprint of Boydell & Brewer Ltd
PO Box 9, Woodbridge, Suffolk IP12 3DF, UK
and of Boydell & Brewer Inc.
PO Box 41026, Rochester, NY 14604–4126, USA
website: www.boydell.co.uk

A catalogue record of this publication is available
from the British Library

Library of Congress Cataloging-in-Publication data
Jackson, Clare, 1972–
    Restoration Scotland, 1660–1690 : royalist politics, religion and
ideas / Clare Jackson.
    p. cm. – (Studies in early modern cultural, political and
social history, ISSN 1476–9107 ; v. 2)
Includes bibliographical references (p.) and index.
  ISBN 0–85115–930–3 (alk. paper)
1. Scotland – History – 1660–1688.   2. Scotland – Politics and
government – 1660–1688.   3. Scotland – Church history – 17th century.
I. Title. II. Series.
DA804 .J33 2003
941.106'6 – dc21   2002153753

This publication is printed on acid-free paper

Printed in Great Britain by
St Edmundsbury Press Limited, Bury St Edmunds, Suffolk

Contents

List of Illustrations

Acknowledgements

In researching and writing this book, I have accrued a number of debts which it is now a pleasure to acknowledge. My greatest intellectual debt is to Mark Goldie who originally suggested this subject to me whilst I was an undergraduate and has remained a wonderful source of inspiration, counsel and support ever since. As this book has evolved from a doctoral thesis that was researched under his supervision, he has continued to supply patient forbearance, enthusiastic encouragement and candid caution in plentiful measure. At the same time, I have been fortunate to benefit not only from John Cairns' expertise on late-seventeenth century Scotland, but also from his friendship. For rendering numerous research trips to Edinburgh so enjoyable and stimulating, a particular debt is owed to John and to Donald Jardine.

I would also like to record my gratitude to a number of colleagues for their generous willingness to engage in discussions about Restoration Scotland, including James Burns, Tristram Clarke, Martin Fitzpatrick, Robert von Friedeburg, Tim Hochstrasser, Colin Kidd, Jon Parkin and David Stevenson. In common with a generation of Cambridge early modernists, I have derived great benefit from the continuing interest and refreshing keenness of John Morrill who, together with John Robertson, examined my doctoral thesis, and thereby offered perceptive and valuable advice. With reference to the institutions whose resources I have consulted, friendly and expert assistance has been supplied by the staff of the British Library, Cambridge University Library, Edinburgh University Library, the National Archives of Scotland and the National Library of Scotland. For granting permission to cite material from the Tollemache Papers held in the Buckminster Estate Office, I am grateful to Sir Lyonel Tollemache.

For their forbearance that has sustained me from the outset of this research, I am heavily indebted to my family and friends. I would especially like to thank my mother, Margaret Storrie, for her unstinting enthusiasm and enduring encouragement. An equally grateful debt is owed to my late grandmother, Louisa Storrie. Overlooking the Covenanting part of our family history, her generosity prevented this research incurring as many financial debts as personal obligations. Finally, within Cambridge, I am indebted to both the Master and Fellows of Sidney Sussex College and of Trinity Hall for providing two special and congenial intellectual atmospheres in which to contemplate and to write.

Clare Jackson
Trinity Hall
May 2002

Note

Throughout this book original orthography has been preserved and italicised texts have been romanised. Assistance in translating Robert Hamilton's *Schediesmata Libero-Philosophica* (Edinburgh, 1668) was supplied by Thomas Ahnert and in translating Hamilton's *Disputatio Juridica &c.* (Leiden, 1671) and Andrew Bruce of Earlshall's *Exercitatio Juridica &c.* (Franeker, 1683) by Helen Evans.

Amounts of money are given in Scots pounds unless otherwise specified. During the Restoration, £1 sterling was the equivalent of £12 Scots. The New Year is taken to begin on 1st January.

Abbreviations

AUL	Aberdeen University Library
Bodl.	Bodleian Library, University of Oxford
BL	British Library, London
CUL	Cambridge University Library
EUL	Edinburgh University Library
HMC	Historical Manuscripts Commission
Morrice Ent'ring Book	Roger Morrice's Ent'ring Book, Dr. Williams's Library, London
NAS	National Archives of Scotland, Edinburgh
NLS	National Library of Scotland, Edinburgh
PRO	Public Record Office, Kew
Tollemache MSS.	Tollemache Family Papers, Buckminster Park, Leicestershire

1

Introduction

In the twilight years of Stuart absolutism and Scottish independence, the Restoration period witnessed the apogee of royalist sentiment. This book provides the first reconstruction of late-seventeenth century Scottish intellectual culture, starting with the widespread popular royalism that accompanied Charles II's restoration in 1660 and closing with the collapse of royal authority that occurred when his brother, James VII & II, was driven from the throne in 1688. In doing so, this book restores to historical attention the richness and significance of the Restoration within Scottish history. For, until recently, historiographical orthodoxy tended to depict the entire seventeenth century as 'a sort of grotesque interlude between the great ages of Reformation and Enlightenment'.[1] Within that century, the Restoration period traditionally incurred particular opprobrium as an era of arbitrary government, state oppression, religious bigotry and fanatical rebellion. Situated between the excesses of the mid-century civil wars and the respectable settlement achieved by the 'Glorious' Revolution of 1688–89, it appeared an uncomfortable historical aberration. As the early-twentieth century Historiographer-Royal of Scotland, Peter Hume Brown, lamented, Charles II's return to power in 1660 marked 'the opening of the most pitiful chapter of the national history'.[2]

The causes of previous historiographical denigration are not difficult to elucidate. For although the Restoration was subsequently remembered by the eighteenth-century cultural connoisseur, Sir John Clerk of Penicuik, as an age in which 'religion and politics became totally confused', an entrenched historiographical preoccupation with ecclesiastical affairs has ensured that politics and religion have too often been studied discretely.[3] Secure in the knowledge that an

---

[1] David Stevenson, 'Twilight before night or darkness before dawn? Interpreting seventeenth-century Scotland', in Rosalind Mitchison ed., *Why Scottish History Matters* (Edinburgh, 1991), p. 37.
[2] Peter Hume Brown, *History of Scotland*, 3 vols. (Cambridge, 1899–1909), II, 379.
[3] John Clerk of Penicuik, *History of the Union of Scotland and England by Sir John Clerk of Penicuik*, Douglas Duncan trans. and ed. (Edinburgh, 1993), p. 80. Doctoral research that has produced narrative reconstructions of Restoration Scottish politics include Roy W. Lennox, 'Lauderdale and Scotland: A Study in Politics and Administration 1660–1682' (Columbia University, unpublished Ph.D. dissertation, 1977), Ronald Lee, 'Government and Politics in Scotland 1661–1681' (University of Glasgow, unpublished Ph.D. dissertation, 1995) and Kathleen M. Colquhoun, ' "Issue of the Late Civill [*sic*] Wars": James, Duke of York and the Government of Scotland 1679–1689' (University of Illinois at

episcopalian form of church government was abolished as a result of the Williamite Revolution in 1690, presbyterian apologists were quick to denigrate the Restoration religious settlement as flawed and tyranically erastian. As early as 1689, for example, the anonymous author of *The Scotish [sic] Inquisition* proclaimed his intention of speedily producing 'a Martyrology of these times' that juxtaposed the presbyterian Covenanters' courage alongside the 'Inhumanity, Illegality, and Severity of their Cruel and Bloody Persecutors'.[4] Successive chronicles of the Covenanters' sufferings amidst the carminated fields of Scotland between 1660 and 1690 soon followed. According to Robert Wodrow's exhaustive early-eighteenth century account, Restoration Scotland presented 'a very horrid scene of oppression, hardships and cruelty, which, were it not incontestably true, and well vouched and supported, could not be credited in after ages'.[5] Wodrow's work inaugurated a compelling tradition of presbyterian historical writing, imitated by numerous epigoni, often writing with less factual integrity than Wodrow, who had at least endeavoured to substantiate his attacks with documentary evidence, albeit selective. Since Wodrow had deliberately excluded analysis of the more extreme Covenanting sects, such as the Cameronians, less judicious successors remedied his omission and the tradition of penning hagiographic Covenanting martyrologies became entrenched. According to Lord Macaulay's mid-nineteenth century account, for example, the Covenanters were persecuted 'like wild beasts, tortured till their bones were beaten flat, imprisoned by hundreds, [and] hanged by scores' although they remained 'in a mood so savage that the boldest and mightiest oppressor could not but dread the audacity of their despair'.[6] It was not until the 1960s that historians such as Ian Cowan embarked on analyses of the Restoration Covenanters that were more discriminating and less emotive.[7]

Following the incorporating Anglo-Scottish Union of 1707, the Restoration period also came to symbolise the 'darkness before the dawn' of economic

Urbana-Champaign, unpublished Ph.D. dissertation, 1993). Ecclesiastical histories include two volumes by Julia Buckroyd entitled *Church and State in Scotland 1660–81* (Edinburgh, 1980) and *The Life of Archbishop James Sharp: A Political Biography* (Edinburgh, 1987).

[4] Anon., *The Scotish [sic] Inquisition; Or A Short Account of the Proceedings of the Scotish Privy-Counsel, Judiciary Court, and those Commissionated by them, Whereby the Consciences of good Men have been tortured, and the Peace of the Nation these several Years past exceedingly Disturbed, and Multitudes of Innocent People cruelly Opposed, and inhumanely Murdered* (London, 1689), p. 2.

[5] Robert Wodrow, *The History of the Sufferings of the Church of Scotland, from the Restoration to the Revolution*, Robert Burns ed., 4 vols. (Glasgow, 1828–30), I, 57.

[6] Thomas Babington Macaulay, *The History of England from the Accession of James II*, 2 vols. (London, 1849), I, 186.

[7] See, for example, Ian B. Cowan, 'The Covenanters: A Revision Article', *Scottish Historical Review*, 47 (1968), pp. 35–52 and *The Scottish Covenanters 1660–1688* (London, 1976); also Iain M. Smart, 'The Political Ideas of the Scottish Covenanters 1638–1688', *History of Political Thought*, 1 (1980), pp. 167–93; Margaret Steele, 'Covenanting Political Propaganda 1638–89' (University of Glasgow, unpublished Ph.D. dissertation, 1995). Hence this study seeks to correct an overly simplistic caricature suggested by William Ferguson in 1998 that, intellectually, 'new trends only affected Scotland *par ricochet*' because 'in Scotland the ecclesiastical strife raged away pretty much on the terms laid down in the 1640s' (William Ferguson, *The Identity of the Scottish Nation. An Historic Quest* (Edinburgh, 1998), p. 144).

prosperity and intellectual illumination generated by incorporating union. Since it was thereby accepted that Scottish society had historically been more backward and benighted than that of England, the period before 1707 was necessarily discredited and calumniated. As Colin Kidd has shown, new forms of 'conjectural history', which emphasised the significance of historical causality, were 'based on the insight that true liberty was a by-product of modernity'. Hence political freedoms in Scotland had not been acquired through native endeavour, but by incorporation into a sophisticated British polity.[8] To reinforce the innovative character of their critique, it thus served the interests of mid-eighteenth century Enlightenment *literati* to assume that seventeenth-century Scotland was a land of fanaticism, failure and ideological sterility, induced by parochial politics and ecclesiastical extremism. In his *General History of Scotland*, for example, William Guthrie judged the administration of Charles II 'one of the worst governments that ever existed in any civilized country'.[9] David Hume endorsed this description, contending that, although the Scottish people 'had but very imperfect notions of law and liberty' at the time of Charles II's restoration, the domestic experience of Stuart rule thereafter extinguished any 'genuine passion for liberty'. Following James VII & II's accession to the throne in 1685, Hume concluded that 'nothing could equal the abject servility of the Scottish nation during the period but the arbitrary severity of the administration'.[10] Another eighteenth-century Whig constitutionalist, Gilbert Stuart, declared that Charles II should 'be regarded as an enemy to the nation', observing the people of Scotland to have been 'sunk in langour and in sadness' during his reign, while the 'poise of the constitution was, in great measure, destroyed'.[11] A new culture of eighteenth-century politeness required a conscious rejection of the political partisanship and religious enthusiasm that had fostered the endemic violence and instability of the preceding century. As Regius Professor of History in Oxford in the 1960s, Hugh Trevor-Roper was therefore following a venerable historiographical tradition in relying on a form of 'intellectual alchemy' which could transform a barbarous province into a civilised European society by the beginning of the eighteenth century.[12]

The obloquy conventionally attached to assessments of the Restoration period also resonated with a broader lachrymose tendency of Scottish historians to gravitate towards studying subjects that elevated the darker and more deprived

---

[8] Colin Kidd, *Subverting Scotland's Past. Scottish Whig Historians and the Creation of an Anglo-British Identity, c.1689–c.1830* (Cambridge, 1993), p. 269. For more on conjectural history, see Harro Höpfl, 'From Savage to Scotsman: Conjectural History in the Scottish Enlightenment', *Journal of British Studies*, 17 (1978), pp. 19–40.

[9] William Guthrie, *A General History of Scotland, from the Earliest Accounts to the Present Time*, 10 vols. (London, 1767–8), X, 174.

[10] David Hume, *The History of England from the Invasion of Julius Caesar to The Revolution in 1688. In Six Volumes by David Hume Esq. Volume VI. Based on the Edition of 1778, with the Author's Last Corrections and Improvements*, William B. Todd ed. (Indianapolis, 1983), pp. 223, 415, 466–7.

[11] Gilbert Stuart, *Observations concerning the Public Law, and the Constitutional History of Scotland, with Occasional Remarks concerning English Antiquity* (Edinburgh, 1779), pp. 136, 133.

[12] Hugh Trevor-Roper, 'The Scottish Enlightenment', *Studies on Voltaire and the Eighteenth Century*, 63 (1967), p. 1636.

periods of national history. Rosalind Mitchison was, for example, one historian accused of advancing an excessively negative account of early-twentieth century Scottish industrial history that implicitly suggested the only influence the Scots people exerted over their historical destiny was 'such as to demonstrate their passivity in the face of conditions which more "developed" nations would consider unacceptable'.[13] But such a stance only echoed earlier historiographical convictions. Describing Restoration Scotland from a nineeenth-century perspective, for example, Henry Buckle denounced the years between 1660 and 1689 as representing 'a tyranny, so cruel and so exhausting, that it would have broken the energy of almost any other nation'.[14] A perceived background of unremitting government oppression and widespread popular distress thus rendered the very notion of Restoration Scottish intellectual culture a contradiction in terms.

Amidst the tremendous renaissance of activity experienced within all spheres of Scottish history in recent decades, however, such entrenched orthodoxies have begun to be challenged. Recognition has emerged of the need to revisit Restoration Scotland without the diverting imperative of tracing subsequent intellectual lineages. Surveying the state of Scottish historical studies in the mid-1990s, for example, Michael Lynch detected 'several lacunae – none more striking than the "black hole" in the Restoration period, although the Revolution of 1688–90 comes a close second'.[15] Focusing on the seventeenth century, Keith Brown likewise remarked that the 'literature on royalist ideas is very thin', while 'the 1688–90 revolution in Scotland is the least understood of the major events of this remarkable century'.[16] From the specific perspective of intellectual history, Glenn Burgess confirmed in the late-1990s that the 'whole subject of late-seventeenth-century Scottish political thought seriously demands attention'.[17] As much the victim of scholarly neglect as of historiographical misrepresentation therefore, it can be argued, with David Stevenson, that 'the "real darkness" comes from the lack of modern historical research'.[18]

Revisionist reappraisal of late-seventeenth century Scotland is nevertheless all the more urgently required as it has become increasingly acknowledged that anglocentric histories of historical events and ideological traditions can no longer remain as an unreflective synecdoche for 'British history'. Originally

---

[13] Craig Beveridge and Ronnie Turnbull, *Scotland after Enlightenment. Image and Tradition in Modern Scottish Culture* (Edinburgh, 1997), p. 23.

[14] Henry Buckle, *History of Civilisation in England*, 2 vols. (London, 1857–61), II, 281.

[15] Michael Lynch, 'Response: Old Games and New', *Scottish Historical Review*, 73 (1994), p. 47. An early attempt to reappraise this period, albeit briefly, was made by Henry W. Meikle in *Some Aspects of Later Seventeenth Century Scotland* (Glasgow, 1947).

[16] Keith Brown, *Kingdom or Province? Scotland and the Regal Union 1603–1715* (Basingstoke, 1992), pp. 202, ix. In 1992, Bruce Lenman denigrated the 'poverty of political theory' during the Williamite Revolution, albeit by overlooking the existence of a number of works which analysed revolutionary events in considerable detail and are examined in Chapter Eight (Bruce Lenman, 'The poverty of political theory in the Scottish Revolution of 1688–90', in Lois Schwoerer ed., *Changing Perspectives on the Revolution of 1688–89* (Cambridge, 1992), pp. 244–59).

[17] Glenn Burgess, 'Scottish or British? Politics and Political Thought in Scotland, *c.*1500–1707', *Historical Journal*, 41 (1998), p. 589.

[18] Stevenson, 'Twilight before night', p. 47.

stimulated in response to John Pocock's proposal in the mid-1970s for a 'new subject' that accurately reflected the British historical experience, investigation of the ways in which the distinct, but interdependent, histories of early modern Scotland, England, Wales and Ireland successively interacted with one another subsequently became a particularly lively and productive focus of historical research.[19] Changing contemporary political priorities have also served to promote pluralist understandings of early modern state formation and the construction of national identities.[20] Within a British framework, however, attention remained largely focused on tracing the breakdown of political and religious authority that occurred in the early seventeenth century, meaning that analysis of the Restoration throughout the Stuart multiple monarchy has only recently formed the subject of renewed study. Hence, despite resurgent interest in the Restoration process in England, late-seventeenth century Scotland and Ireland have hitherto remained relatively uncharted historiographical territory.[21]

Similar objectives have been articulated in the realm of intellectual history in a series of systematic attempts to enquire into the nature and character of 'British political thought' by discovering the distinctive characteristics of early modern Scottish, English, Welsh and Irish political discourse. As several specialist studies have shown, archipelagic and Continental interaction with the Stuart multiple monarchy decisively shaped the idiomatic political and religious discourses current in particular polities.[22] Yet despite the impressive expansion of knowledge produced by such initiatives, even Pocock himself has felt obliged to rue the apparent lack of 'literature, either contemporary or modern, on Restoration and its failure in Scotland', leaving historians 'uncertain how far to regard it as a provincial variation on an otherwise English theme'.[23] Further afield, revisionist reappraisal of late-seventeenth century Scottish intellectual culture is

[19] See J. G. A. Pocock, 'British History: A Plea for a New Subject', *Journal of Modern History*, 47 (1975), pp. 601–28 and 'The limits and divisions of British History', *American Historical Review*, 87 (1982), pp. 311–34.
[20] For responses to Pocock's initiative, see Ronald Asch ed., *Three Nations? – A Common History?* (Bochum, 1992); Brendan Bradshaw and Peter Roberts eds., *British consciousness and identity. The making of Britain, 1533–1707* (Cambridge, 1998); Glenn Burgess ed., *The New British History. Founding a Modern State 1603–1714* (London, 1999); Steven Ellis and Sarah Barber eds., *Conquest and Union: Fashioning a British State, 1485–1720* (Harlow, 1995); Alexander Grant and Keith Stringer, *Uniting the Kingdom: The Enigma of British History* (London, 1995); Brendan Bradshaw and John Morrill eds., *The British Problem, c.1534–1707. State Formation in the Atlantic Archipelago* (Basingstoke, 1996) and Jim Smyth, *The Making of the United Kingdom 1660–1800* (Harlow, 2001).
[21] See, however, Toby Barnard, 'Scotland and Ireland in the later Stewart Monarchy', in Ellis and Barber eds., *Conquest and Union*, pp. 250–75; Mark Goldie, 'Divergence and Union: Scotland and England 1660–1707', in Bradshaw and Morrill eds., *The British Problem*, pp. 220–45; Tim Harris, 'What's New About the Restoration?', *Albion*, 29 (1997), pp. 187–222 and 'Critical Perspectives: The Autonomy of British History?' in Burgess ed., *The New British History*, pp. 266–86 and Clare Jackson, 'Restoration to Revolution 1660–1690', in Burgess ed., *The New British History*, pp. 92–114.
[22] See J. G. A. Pocock ed., *The Varieties of British Political Thought 1500–1800* (Cambridge, 1993); Roger Mason ed., *Scots and Britons. Scottish Political Thought and the Union of 1603* (Cambridge, 1994); John Robertson ed., *A Union for Empire. Political Thought and the Union of 1707* (Cambridge, 1995) and Jane Ohlmeyer ed., *Political Thought in Seventeenth-Century Ireland* (Cambridge, 2000).
[23] J. G. A. Pocock, 'Empire, State and Confederation: The War of American Independence as a Crisis in Multiple Monarchy', in Robertson ed., *A Union for Empire*, p. 324.

also urgently required at a time when historiographical trends are encouraging the integration of 'national' intellectual histories within a wider European understanding of the early Enlightenment period. Jonathan Israel's *Radical Enlightenment*, for example, surveys a dazzling clash of competing ideologies that flourished across Europe from around 1650 to 1750. For Israel, the intellectual dynamism was such that 'the real business' of Enlightenment was over by 1740 as philosophy emancipated itself from its theological background while rationalist and secularist forces ran counter to the established teachings of traditional political and ecclesiastical authorities.[24] With relatively little known about the intellectual history of early modern Scotland, particularly before 1707, evaluations of any characteristically Scottish contributions have, however, necessarily been absent from such historiographical enquiries.

I

Considerable care is, however, required in adopting an appropriate conceptual framework to investigate the mental world of Restoration Scotland. According to J. H. Burns, political ideas in late medieval and early modern Europe were 'preponderantly, and inevitably, about kings and kingship',[25] while a recent study of political thought in seventeenth-century Ireland has likewise emphasised 'the central role played by kingship'.[26] As this study reveals, a similar case can be made for Restoration Scotland, although concepts of kingship and the formation of royalist ideology often remain elusive. For if the antonym of a 'royalist' is assumed to be a 'republican', then the absence of virtually any discrete republican discourse effectively renders 'royalist' intellectual discourse synonymous with the intellectual culture of Restoration Scotland. Even the most savage and uncompromising attacks on Charles II's regime were largely predicated on presbyterian royalist principles, rather than on notions of humanist republicanism that still survived, for example, in Restoration England. As Thomas Sydserf's royalist newsletter, *Mercurius Caledonius*, affirmed at the outset of the Restoration, 'the Blasphemers, Rumpers, and other Antimonarchical Vermin in England' would henceforth find scant sympathy for their cause in Scotland.[27] Notwithstanding Sydserf's satirical caricature, an individual's theoretical attachment to the Stuart monarchy was not, however, necessarily regarded as illative of his practical support for a particular monarch or for that monarch's government in Restoration Scotland. As this study reveals in detail, crucial distinctions prevailed between theoretical attachment to monarchy and practical political

---

[24] Jonathan Israel, *Radical Enlightenment. Philosophy and the Making of Modernity 1650–1750* (Oxford, 2001), p. 7.
[25] J. H. Burns, *The True Law of Kingship. Concepts of Monarchy in Early Modern Scotland* (Oxford, 1996), p. 1.
[26] Jane Ohlmeyer, 'Introduction: for God, king or country?', in Ohlmeyer ed., *Political Thought in Seventeenth-Century Ireland*, p. 18.
[27] Quoted by William Couper, *The Edinburgh Periodical Press*, 2 vols. (Stirling, 1908), II, 179–80.

obedience. Bishop Andrew Honyman of Orkney, for example, self-consciously aligned himself with those he regarded as 'judicious Royalists', recognising that 'as to the point of Alledgiance or Fidelity, that is another matter than Obedience'.[28] While the phenomenon of constitutional, or moderate, royalism is familiar to historians of early modern England, little attempt has been made to investigate parallel ideas in Scotland. Notwithstanding, a royalist is henceforth assumed to be someone who regarded loyalty to the monarch as their primary civil allegiance and this book focuses on the manifold ways in which such royalism was both theoretically conceptualised and practically revealed.

For if nothing else, the effects of the mid-century civil wars had conspired to render this a generation whose sense of the political was, above all, highly practical. Hence this study necessarily considers systematic analyses of contemporary political and religious authority, as well as sources documenting the practical effect of such power. An anonymous *Letter from Scotland* published in 1681 drew attention to the unprecedented levels of popular interest in political affairs, observing that since 'now every man calls himself the People', whenever controversy arose, proponents and opponents of a policy 'both cry out, that if this or that be done the People is betray'd'.[29] Politics was no longer confined to the Privy Council Chamber or Parliament Hall. Observing how specific proposals were 'as soon puplick [*sic*] at the cross of Edinburgh as they uer proposed in the closet', the Treasurer-Depute, John Drummond of Lundin, dismissed rumours circulating in 1683 that the Scottish Treasury was to be put into commission, but deemed it imperative that 'people hav both ther ears and eyes open'.[30] Among Restoration politicians, considerable consequence was thus placed on achievements within the sphere of practical politics as much as on abstract philosophical speculation. In 1678, for instance, the Lord Advocate, Sir George Mackenzie of Rosehaugh, dedicated a treatise on criminal law to the duke of Lauderdale as parliamentary High Commissioner acclaiming him as 'the greatest States-man in Europe, who is a Schollar; and the greatest Schollar, who is a States-man'.[31] The legacy of a consummate politician, Lauderdale's extensive correspondence vividly illuminates the constitutional framework within which contemporary political commentaries were framed. As Lauderdale's erstwhile colleague, Sir Robert Moray, once directed him, 'leave no Lacunas in

---

[28] [Andrew Honyman], *A Survey of the Insolent and Infamous Libel entituled Naphtali &c. Wherein several things, falling in debate in these times are considered, and some Doctrines in Lex Rex and the Apolog. Narration . . . are brought to the touch-stone. Part I* ([Edinburgh], 1688), pp. 12, 7. For historiographical discussions of the difficulty of devising an accurate taxonomy for royalist ideas, see Paul Seaward, 'Constitutional and unconstitutional Royalism', *Historical Journal*, 40 (1997), pp. 227–39 and David L. Smith, *Constitutional Royalism and the Search for Settlement, c.1640–1649* (Cambridge, 1994).

[29] Anon., *A Letter from Scotland* (Edinburgh, 1681), p. 1.

[30] 'John Drummond of Lundin to William, duke of Queensberry, 2 June 1683', HMC *Report on the Buccleuch & Queensberry Manuscripts (Fifteenth Report, Appendix, Part VIII)*, 2 vols. (London, 1897), II, 114.

[31] Sir George Mackenzie, *The Laws and Customes of Scotland, in Matters Criminal. Wherein is to be seen how the Civil Law, and the Laws and Customs of other Nations do agree with, and supply ours* (Edinburgh, 1678), 'Epistle Dedicatory'.

your letters . . . it is fitt that evry particular be under your hand, that your letters put together may make up a complete story; remember this'.[32]

As Moray's advice suggests, an exploration of both the philosophical and the practical articulations of Restoration intellectual discourse involves the collation and analysis of an extensive range of historical sources. First to be considered is the output of Scottish printing presses between 1660 and 1690, to which is added investigation of works composed by Scots or written about Scottish ideas that were published in England and throughout Continental Europe. Considered alongside such printed material are also products of scribal publication in Restoration Scotland, including detailed memoranda that circulated among the members of the political and ecclesiastical establishments as well as more ephemeral matter, such as the anonymous lampoons produced by Edinburgh scriptoria that circulated illegally and eluded government suppression.[33] In addition, a scattered range of anonymous memoranda, legal depositions, sermon notebooks, commonplace-book reflections, diary entries and private correspondence further reveal the intellectual preoccupations of the late-seventeenth century Scottish establishment. For in addition to bridging political and ecclesiastical history, this study also demonstrates the extent to which late-seventeenth century Scottish intellectual culture encompassed not only political theory, but also devotional writings, moral and natural philosophy, legal theory and imaginative literature. Addressing the reasons for an effective historiographical vacuum subsisting between accounts of the late-fifteenth century Renaissance and the mid-eighteenth century Enlightenment, Michael Lynch cited previous failures to appreciate the breadth of the early modern Scottish intellectual tradition. For Lynch, an essentially multidisciplinary approach is required to reflect accurately 'the challenges posed by the characteristic eclecticism of the Scottish intellect in the period 1550–1720'.[34]

By embracing a characteristically extensive and diffuse range of sources, this book seeks to reconstruct as rich a qualitative understanding of Restoration intellectual discourse as possible. While eschewing the production of a primarily enumerative and quantitative account, it nevertheless considers the literary remains of a generation of Scottish statesmen, divines, lawyers, polemicists and contemporary commentators. In 1681, the episcopalian writer, James Craufurd, could only identify two Scots authors worthy of note: the Lord Advocate, Mackenzie of Rosehaugh, and the divine, Gilbert Burnet, the latter of whom had recently departed to reside in England, despite 'having gratefully sacrificed the

---

[32] Osmund Airy ed., *The Lauderdale Papers*, 3 vols. (London, 1884–5), I, 183–4.

[33] In 1686, for example, the Scottish Privy Council formed a committee to investigate the circulation of critical accounts of government policy and satirical lampoons in manuscript form (*The Register of the Privy Council of Scotland. Third Series. Volume XII (1686)*, H. Paton ed. (Edinburgh, 1930), pp. 194 and 204–5). For analysis of the importance of scribal publication in early modern England, see Harold Love, *Scribal Publication in Seventeenth-Century England* (Oxford, 1993) and D. F. Mackenzie, 'Speech-Manuscript-Print', *Library Chronicle*, 20 (1990), pp. 87–109.

[34] Lynch, 'Response: Old Games and New', p. 61.

first-fruits of his labours' to the land of his birth.[35] In the 1960s, Trevor-Roper distinguished only three figures 'managing to operate as a leaven in the presbyterian lump', being the politician and natural philosopher, Sir Robert Moray, and the mathematicians, David and James Gregory.[36] While recognising that sheer quantity does not necessarily equate with ideological innovation or conceptual sophistication, the extensive and heterogeneous range of contributions considered throughout this study suggests that earlier verdicts castigating the dearth of intellectual activity in Restoration Scotland have been unduly severe.

Hence this study evokes a range of shared intellectual sensibilities alongside more detailed forms of textual exegesis. Methodologically, the history of ideas has been strongly influenced since the 1960s by a concern to interpret political and philosophical ideas within a framework of historical contextualisation. As well as shifting the focus of intellectual history from the confines of textual analysis in philosophical isolation, greater importance has also been attached to examining the wider character of public discourse at specific historical junctures, extending the range of texts under consideration far beyond canonical classics. As the arguments in this book indicate, such an approach is particularly appropriate for studying an intellectual culture such as late-seventeenth century Scotland where the source materials are of an essentially disparate nature and where the focus necessarily encompasses a large number of writers and texts.[37]

For although it has been suggested by John Pocock that, for the period between 1560 and 1640, 'scholars are now in a position to organize (should they decide to do so) a "history of Scottish political thought" around a canon or succession of prominent authors', little attempt has been made to produce a similar canon for the second half of the seventeenth century.[38] As will become evident in this study, however, this is partly because Restoration Scots did not always expound political, religious and philosophical commentaries in systematic form, but articulated their ideas within the context of their quotidian avocations, from which the more diffused nature of their thought must be extracted. So destabilising was the ideological legacy of the mid-century civil wars that political sensitivities remained uniquely acute. As the former Covenanting leader, the marquis of Argyll, warned in 1661, for instance, whatever 'hath been said by me and others . . . you must repute and accept them as from a distracted Man, of a distracted Subject, in a distracted Time wherein I lived'.[39] Bereft of

---

[35] [James Craufurd], *The History of the House of Esté, From the time of Forrestus until the Death of Alphonsus, the last Duke of Ferrara* (London, 1681), 'Preface'.

[36] Trevor-Roper, 'The Scottish Enlightenment', p. 1644.

[37] For more on methodological issues, see J. G. A. Pocock, 'Texts as Events: Reflections on the History of Political Thought', in Kevin Sharpe and Stephen Zwicker eds., *Politics of Discourse: The Literature and History of Seventeenth-Century England* (Berkeley, 1987), pp. 21–34; Quentin Skinner, 'Meaning and Understanding in the History of Ideas', *History and Theory*, 8 (1969), pp. 1–69 and James Tully ed., *Meaning and Context: Quentin Skinner and his Critics* (Cambridge, 1988).

[38] J. G. A. Pocock, 'Two kingdoms and three histories?: Political thought in British contexts', in Mason ed., *Scots and Britons*, p. 294.

[39] Archibald Campbell, marquis of Argyll, *Instructions to a Son* (London, 1661), p. 7.

9

his own former intellectual certainties, the Quaker apologist, Robert Barclay, likewise dedicated a treatise to Charles II in 1678, acknowledging that 'no age furnisheth us with things so strange & marvellous' as those which had 'faln out within the compass of thy time'.[40] Meanwhile, Mackenzie of Rosehaugh began his political memoirs of the Restoration by acknowledging that although he was not presenting 'an account of the fate of great monarchies', the events he sought to describe 'were the products of as much hate, and of as many thoughts in the actors, as actions of much greater splendour'.[41]

Ideas of historical causality unsurprisingly also assumed central importance as heightened national anxieties encouraged Restoration Scots to subject past political and religious experiences to detailed scrutiny. In 1683, for instance, George Scott of Pitlochie insisted that it was the potential to 'discover those hidden Springs of Affairs, which give motion to all the vast Machines and stupendous Revolutions of Princes and Kingdoms' that had inspired him to edit and publish the political memoirs of his grandfather, the Jacobean Privy Councillor, Sir James Melville of Hallhill. In doing so, he hoped to supply additional sagacity enabling Restoration politicians to avoid treading 'the same Precipices, whereby others have shipwrackt both their Masters and themselves'.[42] An equally didactic purpose underpinned Gilbert Burnet's twin biography of a former Scottish Secretary, William, second Duke of Hamilton, and his brother, James, which he published in 1677. Insisting that 'nothing does more clear the Prospect of what is before us, than a strict Review of what is past', Burnet deemed it essential to reveal 'the secretest Causes and Beginnings of great Changes or Revolutions' and 'open up things fully, so as to be easily understood by every Reader'.[43]

Burnet's confidence that the fruits of his historical researches would be widely read indicates that he envisaged a suitably erudite audience for such material. In 1670, Burnet had participated in an episcopalian evangelising tour of south-west Scotland, pronouncing himself 'amazed to see a poor commonalty so capable to argue upon points of government, and on the bounds to be set to the power of princes in religion'. Wherever Burnet and his clerical colleagues visited, they had encountered crowds who had 'texts of scripture at hand, and

---

[40] Robert Barclay, *Apology for the True Christian Divinity, As the same is held forth, and preached by the People, Called, in Scorn, Quakers. Being a full explanation and vindication of their Principles and Doctrines, by many Arguments deduc'd from Scripture and right Reason, and the Testimony of famous Authors, both ancient and modern, with a full answer to the strongest objections usually made against them* ([Aberdeen], 1678), sig. Av.

[41] Mackenzie, *Memoirs*, p. 4. His enthusiasm was not, however, universally shared by subsequent generations. In 1822, for example, Sir Walter Scott complained that Mackenzie's *Memoirs* were so 'immersed in little political detail, and the struggling skirmish of party' that they 'seemed to have lost sight of the great progressive movement of human affairs' (John Gibson Lockhart, *The Life of Sir Walter Scott*, 10 vols. (London, 1902–3), VII, 11).

[42] George Scott ed., *The Memoires of Sir James Melvil of Hal-Hill: Containing An Impartial Account of the most remarkable Affairs of State, During the last Age, not mentioned by other Historians* (London, 1683), sig. A2r.

[43] Gilbert Burnet, *The Memoires of the Lives and Actions of James and William, Dukes of Hamilton and Castleherald &c.* (London, 1677), 'To the King' and sig. Av.

were ready with their answers to anything that was said of them', even including 'the meanest of them, their cottagers and their servants'.[44] Burnet's impressions had been shared by the pioneer of the evangelising mission, Archbishop Robert Leighton of Glasgow, who later confirmed that 'every pedlar and mechanic who should be occupied in the business of their calling' instead 'must be handling the helm of Government, and canvassing all the affairs of Church and State'.[45] Amidst such contentious times, an Edinburgh merchant, Thomas Kincaid, advised his sister in 1687 always to 'carie a pockett bible and a compend of the Councell of Trent always about with you', so that both testimonies could 'be readily produced in any dispute you happen in'.[46] As this book confirms, polemic remained pervasive and disputation ubiquitous throughout the Restoration.

II

This introductory chapter indicates the historiographical and conceptual scope of this study, together with the methodological approach adopted and the range of source materials employed. The following chapter supplies a conspectus of the institutional and social milieux within which intellectual debate occurred in late-seventeenth century Scotland, together with an overview of the official constraints placed on the domestic and foreign dissemination of ideas. Chapter Three outlines the different types of political theory current during the Restoration. Since Scotland was widely regarded as being the oldest monarchy in the world, seventeenth-century political thought was, to a considerable extent, predicated on establishing the alleged manner in which the Scottish monarchy had been originally founded in 330 BC. Hence the chapter investigates not only the polemical role of such nationalist historiography, but also differing notions about the ways in which monarchical succession was regulated. Correspondingly, it also discusses the manner in which contrary accounts of the origins and nature of the Scottish monarchy generated divergent notions regarding rights of resistance and the dissolution of government in the event of monarchical misrule.

Chapter Four focuses on the first two decades of the Restoration to show how such concepts of monarchy translated into practice and considers the extent to which theoretical support for monarchy could be combined with practical opposition, as perceptions of misgovernment arose. In doing so, it draws particular attention to the emergence of a vibrant constitutional opposition within the Scottish Parliament, whose activities served as a crucial check on the potentially arbitrary inclinations of Charles II's administration. Among the arguments

[44] Gilbert Burnet, *The History of My Own Time*, Osmund Airy ed., 2 vols. (Oxford, 1897–1900), I, 524.
[45] Robert Leighton, 'The Rule of Conscience', in William West ed., *Remains of Archbishop Leighton* (London, 1875), p. 281.
[46] Henry W. Meikle ed., 'An Edinburgh Diary 1687–1688', *The Book of the Old Edinburgh Club*, 27 (1949), p. 143.

advanced by members of this opposition was a paramount attachment to notions of fundamental law which upheld the reciprocal duties incumbent on monarch and subject alike. The following chapter examines the relationship between political loyalty and religious conformity. Historiographical concerns to emphasise sectarian struggles between episcopalian conformists and presbyterian nonconformists during the Restoration have hitherto served not only to undermine the importance of presbyterian loyalism, but also to associate ecclesiastical episcopalianism with political Jacobitism from a misleadingly defeatist and proleptic perspective. By contrast, this chapter draws attention to the predominantly anticlerical climate which determined the nature of the Restoration religious settlement, together with the conspicuous failure of the re-established episcopalian church to develop any convincing account of its own *iure divino* status. Consequently, it is argued that the political leaders of late-seventeenth century Scotland were much less constrained in their ability to impose ecclesiastical erastianism by the absence of the type of theocratic episcopalian discourse that existed in Restoration England.

Amidst the escalating civil unrest that extended across Scotland from the late-1670s onwards, political and religious debate increasingly polarised. Chapter Six studies the increasing use of arguments championing a 'super-eminent law', namely that of reason of state, together with the practical effect that this imperative exerted on issues such as oath-taking and treason trials. It then turns to consider the increasingly destabilising effects of James VII & II's brief rule between 1685 and 1688 on those sections of the political and ecclesiastical establishment traditionally regarded as the natural allies of the Stuart monarchy. Despite the increasing polarisation of political and religious affairs during the 1680s, the following chapter discusses the remarkable degree of intellectual convergence discernible between moderate episcopalians and presbyterians on issues deemed 'indifferent' to true religion, such as ceremonial forms and the externals of church government. It outlines the epistemological implications of such debates by exploring how moderate episcopalians and presbyterians defended notions of 'true religion' from both sceptical and puritan attacks by upholding notions of universal justice and incorporating contemporary developments in natural philosophy.

Chapter Eight presents an account of the ideological context of the Revolution of 1688–89 by outlining the different types of theoretical explanations generated by James' flight to France in December 1688. Despite the immense support that had been expressed for James by the Scottish political nation at the time of his accession, by 1688 most royalists were prepared to support arguments that James had unequivocally forfeited his right to occupy the Scottish throne through irredeemable misgovernment. The chapter also describes the various combinations of arguments for resistance *in extremis*, providentialism and notions of *ius gentium* that were subsequently deployed to account for the accession to power of William and Mary.

This study concludes with an evaluation of the distinctive character of intellectual discourse in Restoration Scotland. Paradoxically, it argues that far from being enervated by the conspicuous absence of a resident monarch, concepts of monarchy in late-seventeenth century Scotland became sufficiently enduring and inclusive to command near-universal acceptance. Freed from the need to frame their political and religious ideas to reflect the actions of the monarch in their midst, Restoration Scots formulated a highly idealised conception of monarchy that also allowed them to remain shrewdly vigilant as to the merits of its practice. Moreover, the lack of any severe critiques emanating from the established church also enabled political leaders to assuage the contumacious and destructive nature of mid-century religious invective. Seeking to procure the civil allegiance of as many late-seventeenth century Scots as possible, the political leaders of Restoration Scotland embraced a combination of ideological latitude with practical schemes of religious indulgences ultimately aimed at the preservation of civil order. Following the breakdown of civil authority that occurred in 1688, however, the legacy of former ideological latitude in ecclesiastical affairs generated a characteristically flexible and accommodating mentality that enabled a relatively erastian form of presbyterianism to be re-established in 1690 with relatively minimal political and social dislocation.

2

Restoration Scotland

The restoration of Charles II as King of Scotland, England, Ireland and Wales on 29 May 1660 presented an occasion for universal celebration and rejoicing throughout Scotland. According to the minister of the Tolbooth Church in Edinburgh, James Kirkton, no 'accident in the world altered the disposition of a people more' than the arrival of news proclaiming the monarch's return to power.[1] Witnessing the popular reaction at the Mercat Cross in Edinburgh, the diarist, John Nicoll, recorded how the 'haill bellis in Edinburgh and Cannongait did reing, the drumes did beatt, trumpettis soundit', while 'the spoutes of the Croce rynnand all that tyme with abundance of clareyt wyne'.[2] After nightfall, the festivities continued with bonfires throughout the city streets and fireworks launched from the Castle ramparts. A London barber, Thomas Rugg, heard oral accounts of events in Edinburgh, confirming that the Mercat Cross had been covered 'with arteficual vines loaden with grapes, both good clarit wines plentifully springing out from all its chanels', with a statue of Bacchus bestride a hogshead. A sumptuous banquet had also been served to over a hundred 'persons of eminensey', after which was observed 'the dances of our magistrates and citizans about the bonfiers'.[3]

Public and private jubilation reverberated throughout the country. As one Dundee minister, Andrew Auchinleck, confessed in October 1660, 'the joy and rejoycing of my heart upon the account of his royall Majesties returne and re-establishment is such as I cannot expresse'. Despite having suffered eighteen months' imprisonment for his royalist sympathies during the civil wars, Auchinleck was now, aged sixty-seven, celebrating not only Charles II's return to power, but also the subsequent and safe arrival of his twenty-seventh child,

---

[1] James Kirkton, *A History of the Church of Scotland 1660–1679*, Ralph Stewart ed. (New York, 1992), p. 34.

[2] John Nicoll, *A Diary of Publick Transactions and other Occurrences chiefly in Scotland. From January 1650 to June 1667*, David Laing ed. (Edinburgh, 1836), p. 293. Elsewhere, an allegorical account of events in Edinburgh published in 1660 similarly described how 'the people kindled innumerable bonfires . . . both bells and people did both sing and dance all at once . . . wine was sent in abundance to the earth, that it might drink his Majesties health also, and the glasses capreoled in the air, for joy to hear his name' (George Mackenzie, *Aretina, or the Serious Romance* (London, 1660), pp. 322–3).

[3] William L. Sasche ed., *The Diurnal of Thomas Rugg 1659–1661* (London, 1961), p. 96.

fittingly named Charles. Writing to John Maitland, earl of Lauderdale, Auchinleck observed how 'trees, flowers and herbes sprout and spring and floorish in the summer' and from 'the radiant beames flowing from his Majesty even at this distance', he felt 'like the eagle who by casting her bill reneweth her age'. Were he one day able to pay court to Charles II in person 'and have my lips perfumed with a kisse of his royall hand', Auchinleck concluded that 'I shall be in some measure like a Moses comming [*sic*] doune from the mount'.[4]

In sermons preached throughout Scotland in the weeks and months following the Restoration, ministers enthusiastically acclaimed Charles II's return to power, sharing Auchinleck's interpretation of events as a certain manifestation of divine favour analogous to that bestowed on the Old Testament Jews by Moses' eventual return from his Midian exile. In Linlithgow, for instance, James Ramsay reminded his congregation that although Charles and Moses had both been unjustly 'driven to exile, and put to great pinches under it', both had 'remained constant in the Truth', patiently awaiting divine deliverance.[5] Amidst the prolonged revelry, the Stirling minister, Matthias Symson, wished 'the noise and sound of your triumphant Rejoycing, to be heard in all the places of our Soveraigns solitary and tedious exile' to demonstrate 'to all the world, that he was never cast out of the hearts of his Subjects'.[6] In Eccles, John Jameson apprised his listeners that 'after such earth-shaking intervals of time', Charles' return should not only be generally celebrated throughout the Stuart multiple monarchy, but also by every Scottish 'Shire, City, Burgh, Incorporation, Paroch, Village, Family, [and] Person' of whatever social rank.[7]

The widespread exuberance that greeted Charles II's restoration encapsulated a more profound popular anticipation of release from the chaotic disorientation of the civil war period. The efficacy of Providence in safely delivering the prodigal monarch thus appeared to vindicate the miseries wrought upon Scotland by the same divine Providence over the last twenty years. Hence although the Scottish populace did not witness the carefully-choreographed pageantry that accompanied Charles II's triumphant arrival in London in May 1660, the news of the return to monarchical government alone seemed sufficient to promote widespread confidence.

---

[4] 'Mr. Andrew Auchinleck, minister of Dundee, to the Earl of Lauderdale, 20 October 1660', HMC, *Report on the Laing Manuscripts (Seventh Report)*, 2 vols. (London, 1914), I, 312–13.

[5] J[ames] R[amsay], *Moses Returned from Midian; Or, God's Kindnesse to a Banished King: His Office and His Subjects Duty* (Edinburgh, 1660), p. 8.

[6] Matthias Symson, *Mephiboseth; Or, the Lively Picture of a Loyal Subject* (Edinburgh, 1660). After preaching his thanksgiving address on 19 June 1660, Symson received a sum of £52 from Stirling Town Council the following January to assist with the costs incurred by the sermon's subsequent publication (R. Renwick ed., *Extracts from the Records of the Royal Burgh of Stirling A.D. 1519–1666* (Glasgow, 1887), p. 234). For an account of similar sermons in England, see Carolyn A. Edie, 'Right Rejoicing: Sermons on the Occasion of the Stuart Restoration, 1660', *Bulletin of the John Rylands University Library of Manchester*, 62 (1979–80), pp. 61–86.

[7] John Jameson, *Rebellio Debellata, Et Scota Rediviva* (Edinburgh, 1661), sig. A2v.

I

Yet Restoration Scotland thereafter remained under the rule of an absentee monarch. Following Charles I's execution by members of the English Parliament on 30 January 1649, Scottish enthusiasm for the Stuart monarchy had been vividly demonstrated by the speed with which the decision was taken to crown his son, king not only of Scotland, but also of England, Wales and Ireland, together with the euphemistic addition of France. Although Charles II's subsequent coronation as a 'Covenanted' king at Scone on 1 January 1651 marked the last coronation of a British monarch in Scotland, subsequent military defeat at Worcester ensured that Charles quickly returned to his Continental exile. Scotland was thereafter subjected to military occupation and an incorporating union with the English Republic, while the memories of his hapless Scottish experiences evidently deterred Charles from venturing north of the border again as king. Nor did his brother, James VII & II, visit Scotland as king between 1685 and 1688, although he did reside in Edinburgh during his two terms as High Commissioner to the Scottish Parliament between 1679 and 1682.

This chapter considers the range of institutional and intellectual environments within which political and religious debate were conducted in an absentee monarchy, while also drawing attention to the practical limitations and ideological restrictions that collectively conspired to constrain such activity. Historiographical attention has recently drawn attention to the crucial importance of Caroline court culture, both in terms of providing not only a political space where personal rivalries and patronage networks flourished, but also a political theatre that endowed the constitutional absolutism of Stuart monarchy with iconographic and ritualistic representation.[8] In Edinburgh, the lack of a royal presence and attendant court culture was certainly bemoaned repeatedly throughout the seventeenth century by Scots of all social rank. In the late-1630s, for instance, the poet, William Lithgow, had lamented that 'bravest Wits turn dull, Poets singe dumbe, Pen-men grow deafe, and best spirits slumber' when deprived of the cultural focus provided by royal court.[9] Preaching a thanksgiving sermon to celebrate Charles II's restoration in 1660, one Edinburgh minister, Robert Lawrie, wistfully extolled the manifest benefits of a resident monarchy, including the alleged extent to which 'Industrie, Learning, Arts, Trade, Traffick, are encouraged and advanced, and a people prosper, even in externall things'.[10] In 1663, an Edinburgh lawyer, William Clerke, wrote a play,

---

[8] With reference to the later Stuart period, see, for example, Alan Marshall, *The Age of Faction. Court Politics, 1660–1702* (Manchester, 1999).

[9] William Lithgow, *A True and Experimentall Discourse upon the Beginning, Proceedings, and Victorious Event of this Last Siege of Breda* (London, 1637), p. 51.

[10] Robert Lawrie, *God Save the King, or, The loyal and joyfull Acclamations of Subjects to their King. As it was opened in a Sermon, preached in one of the Congregations of the City of Edinburgh, upon the day of Solemn Thanksgiving for the King's Majesty his happy Return and Restauration to his Dominions; Kept, June 19. 1660* (Edinburgh, 1660), p. 6.

entitled *Marciano*, about the happy restoration of a legitimate monarchy in Florence after many years of miserable civil war, that was performed at the Tennis-Court Theatre at Holyrood before the parliamentary High Commissioner, the earl of Rothes. In the preface to the published version, Clerke expressed his hope that the fortunes of Scottish drama would henceforth correspond with those of monarchy, 'upon whom they have such a dependance'. As Clerke argued, watching dramatic plays served to 'divert the current of our otherwayes melancholly imaginations, and hinder people from dreaming on rebellion'.[11] In 1681, an episcopalian cleric, James Craufurd, composed an elegy on the parlous state of Scottish intellectual culture, identifying the greatest obstacle to cultural flourishing as being the absence of 'the great incitements, which a Courts residing among us would afford'. As Craufurd conceived, the reason why the Scots intelligentsia was inclined to 'languish in Virtue' and watch 'the Muses grow barren among us' was attributable to the cessation of royal patronage. The nation's sense of international isolation was also inevitably increased since Scotland was also deprived of the need to maintain foreign emissaries. Without the attraction of a royal court, Scotland thereby attracted fewer foreign visitors, ensuring that, as Craufurd concluded, 'we seem to be in all respects cut off from the Society of Mankind'.[12]

Two years after Craufurd wrote his treatise, the arrival in Edinburgh of James, duke of York and his court prompted scenes of enthusiastic merriment. The first royal personage to reside for a prolonged period in Scotland since the departure of James VI & I for London in 1603, James stayed in Edinburgh as parliamentary High Commissioner for two separate terms between 1679 and 1682. Dedicating a legal treatise to the duke of York in 1683, Andrew Bruce of Eccleshall recalled the reception James had received in Scotland 'as if arriving in a theatre', venerated by 'the unified voice of the gentry and the common people, of every rank, of our Scotland'.[13] Newspaper accounts reported Bacchanalian scenes in Edinburgh where, again, wine flowed freely and the streets were filled with bonfires that 'were so great and numerous that the whole Town seemed one fire' as Scots rejoiced 'to see a Prince so nearly related to His Majesty and the Crown among them'.[14] When James returned from a brief visit

---

[11] [William Clerke], *Marciano, or The Discovery. A Tragi-Comedy. Acted with great applause, before His Majesties High Commissioner, and others of the Nobility, at the Abby of Holyrud-House, on St. Johns night: By a company of gentlemen* (Edinburgh, 1663), p. 4. For more information about other plays performed in Scotland during the Restoration, see A. Cameron, 'Theatre in Scotland 1660–1800', in Andrew Hook ed., *The History of Scottish Literature. Volume 2: 1660–1800* (Aberdeen, 1987), pp. 191–204 and Terence Tobin, 'Plays presented in Scotland, 1660–1705', *Restoration and Eighteenth Century Theatre Research*, 12 (1973), pp. 51–9 and by the same author, *Plays by Scots 1660–1800* (Iowa, 1974).

[12] Craufurd, *History of the House of Esté*, 'Preface', sig. A2r, A3r, A2v. For more on this theme, see David Allan, 'Prudence and Patronage: The Politics of Culture in Seventeenth-Century Scotland', *History of European Ideas*, 18 (1994), pp. 467–80.

[13] Andreas Bruce, *Exercitatio Juridica de Constitutionibus Principium* (Franeker, 1683), sig. A3r.

[14] *The London Gazette. No. 1465 (1–4 December 1679)* (London, 1679), p. 2. When the duke returned again to Scotland the following year, similar scenes were recorded in Anon., *A True Narrative of the Reception of their Royal Highnesses at their Arrival in Scotland* (Edinburgh, 1680), p. 3.

to London the following summer, the Under-Keeper at Holyrood Palace, Robert Kennedy, received a grant from the Scottish Treasury to light bonfires at Holyrood and on Arthur's Seat to celebrate both the anniversary of Charles II's restoration on 29 May and the duke of York's safe arrival in Edinburgh on 1 June. Kennedy was also given £44 to cover the expenses of the 'wine drunk and glasses broken at the bonfire' by the nobles, town magistrates and soldiers in attendance.[15] Such public endorsements of royal authority staged in Scotland could not, however, entirely elevate Charles II and his brother above more contingent and potentially disruptive political realities. For this reason, historians such as Keith Brown have suggested that the Stuart kings had become so estranged from the majority of the Scottish populace that official accounts of public thanksgiving instead reflected the extent to which late-seventeenth century Scottish royalism was

> ... reduced to sporadic and unenthusiastic outbursts of bells and bonfires, prayers for the royal family, a scattering of portraits and medals held by noblemen in their houses, and a coinage which increasingly served to remind Scots of their relative poverty.[16]

In the monarch's absence, the Scottish nobility might have been expected to expand their traditionally high levels of civic consciousness and political participation. As the marquis of Argyll mischievously remarked in 1661, 'the Nobility of Scotland, have always bickered with their Princes'.[17] Certainly, the powerful martial strain within early modern Scottish monarchical theory conspicuously emphasised the binding duty of noble members of the *primores regni* to call to account the frequently wayward and misguided actions of individual monarchs. Periods of intense civil strife necessarily renewed interest in the qualities required for virtuous leadership. In this context, the historian, Arthur Williamson, has drawn attention to the nobility's genealogical role in defining early modern Scottish national identity by contrasting the ways in which contemporary Scots 'wrote histories of great families as general histories of Scotland' while their English counterparts adopted a more institutional approach by seeking to 'devise parliamentary histories which served as general histories of England'.[18]

During the Restoration, however, the absence of royal patronage and

---

[15] NAS, GD 90/2/115, 'Receipt by Robert Kennedy, Under-Keeper of Holyroodhouse from Sir William Sharp, 1 June 1682'. The grant was for £10 (sterling). When the duchess of York was confined to bed with child in August 1682, Kennedy received £5 (sterling) to light bonfires in the Abbey Close and on Arthur's Seat (GD 90/2/117, 'Receipt by Robert Kennedy, Under-Keeper of Holyroodhouse from Sir William Sharp, 22 August 1682'). In September 1683, £60 (Scots) was awarded for bonfires celebrating the discovery of the Rye House Plot as well as £40 (Scots) for the 'wines, glasses and bottles broken at the bonfire' (GD 90/2/112, 'Receipt by Robert Kennedy, Under-Keeper of Holyroodhouse from Sir William Sharp, 30 September 1683').
[16] Keith Brown, 'The vanishing emperor: British kingship and its decline 1603–1707', in Mason ed., *Scots and Britons*, p. 87.
[17] Argyll, *Instructions*, pp. 4–5.
[18] Arthur H. Williamson, *Scottish National Consciousness in the Age of James VI: The Apocalypse, the Union and the Shaping of Scotland's Political Culture* (Edinburgh, 1979), p. 7.

widespread indebtedness conspired to render noble priorities more immediate and personal. The enthusiastic alliance between theocratic presbyterian Covenanters and noble opponents of Charles I had quickly collapsed, as the majority of nobles eventually took up arms for the king, thereby incurring forfeiture and sequestration during the 1650s. As the Saxon philosopher, Samuel Pufendorf, observed, although the martial race of noble Scots had been 'always bickering with the English', if not their own monarchs, he noticed that after 1603, they 'grew careless of Warlike Exercises', while 'their ancient Glory was quite obscur'd' following the Cromwellian subjugation.[19] From a domestic perspective, Robert Baillie graphically recorded in 1658 how the 'Countrey lyes very quiet; it is exceeding poor; trade is nought; the English hes all the money'. Consequently, as Baillie rued, 'Scotland's Noble families are almost gone; Lennox hes little in Scotland unsold, Hamilton's estate, except Arran and the Baronie of Hamilton, is sold . . . the Gordons are gone, the Douglasses little better, Eglintoun and Glencairn on the brink of breaking, many of our chief families Estates are cracking.'[20] Mindful of the destabilising effects of previous noble intervention, in 1660 the former bishop of Galloway, Thomas Sydserf, privately advised Charles II to exploit such propitious conditions for a reassertion of the royal prerogative, observing that many Scots nobles were 'young in yeares and aspire after his Ma[ties] favour', while others were 'thrald with debt, and will need his Ma[ties] support by some extraordinary remedy in law'. Aware, moreover, that many nobles were also nervously reviewing their past allegiances and thus 'in hope of Imunity will not rashly adventure on new Invitations to hasten their own ruine', Sydserf recommended Charles to 'use this opportunity well, not knowing if the like may ever offer againe'.[21]

In the event, however, noble debt, debilitation and dependence were not as easily effaced as Sydserf had predicted. The destabilising potential for financial insolvency to generate political disaffection was recognised by the first Restoration Parliament that convened in Edinburgh in 1661. Six years' grace was allowed for repayments, if certain loyal duties were fulfilled and if debtors could prove before a member of the judiciary that their debts exceeded the equivalent of four years' rent on their estates.[22] But according to a manuscript account of the state of Scotland that was written in the mid-1670s, the nobility remained 'generallie broken & poor', to the extent that 'as they are att present staited under his Ma[ties] absence', instead of being 'serviceable to him their decay and povertie renders them obnoxious' while their lack of territorial and political influence rendered them 'useless & unprofitable, to the King and Countrie'.[23]

[19] Samuel Pufendorf, *An Introduction to the History of the Principal Kingdoms and States of Europe* (second edition, London, 1697), p. 154.
[20] Robert Baillie, *Letters and Journals of Robert Baillie A. M., Principal of the University of Glasgow, M.DC.XXXVII.–M.DC.LXII.*, David Laing ed., 3 vols. (Edinburgh, 1841–2), III, 387.
[21] Bodl. Clarendon MSS. 75, '[Thomas Sydserf], Information for his sacred Ma[tie] in order to the setling of the Church of Scotland [1660]', f. 427.
[22] 'Act for crediting the payment of Debts betuixt Creditor and Debtor', Thomas Thomson and Cosmo Innes eds., *The Acts of the Parliament of Scotland*, 12 vols. (Edinburgh, 1814–75), VII, 317–20.
[23] NAS GD 406/2/636/6(ii), 'A short accompt of the affaires of Scotland [1674]'.

The Restoration thus remained not only a period of noble retrenchment, but also one of continued re-negotiation of the political relationship between monarch and aristocracy. For example, although the powers associated with heritable jurisdictions that had been abolished in 1652 were restored to members of territorial baronage in 1660, ministers recognised that it would 'certainly [be in] the intrest of the Crowne, by degrees to gett in to their hands all the heritable offices.'[24] Furthermore, the Lyon King of Arms Act passed in 1672 established a 'Public Register of All Arms and Bearings in Scotland' obliging all armigerous families to present their heraldic arms and noble genealogies for official confirmation. Over a decade later, on the anniversary of his brother's restoration in 1687, James VII & II issued a set of statutes reviving 'the Most Ancient and Noble Order of the Thistle', and specifying the various insignia, habits and oaths that would henceforth be associated with the premier chivalric honour that could be awarded for personal loyalty to the monarch in Scotland. The most prominent feature of the splendid attire prescribed for the eight Knights of the Thistle newly-appointed by James in 1687 was an oval badge, bearing the image of St. Andrew and the chivalric motto: *nemo me impune lacesset* ('let no one assail me with impunity').[25] The increased extent of royal control patronage subsequently ensured, however, that traditional noble attributes of martial valour and civic patriotism were dismissed by eighteenth-century critics, such as William Robertson, who denounced seventeenth-century Scottish history as 'singular' in that its 'kings were despotic; its nobles were slaves and tyrants; and the people groaned under the rigorous domination of both'.[26]

The enervated condition of the Scots nobility also diminished the potential for the unicameral Scottish Parliament to serve as a focus for intellectual debate and political influence during the Restoration. Deprived of the spectacles provided by courtly ceremonial, Edinburgh citizens nevertheless witnessed instead the official 'riding of Parliament' at the beginning of each parliamentary session when its members symbolically processed through the city's streets. According to Sir John Clerk of Penicuik, the panoply made 'a very grand appearance . . . such as I never saw the like in any foreign place'.[27] A detailed illustration of the pageantry occasioned by the summoning of the Parliament in 1681 was included in Nicolas du Guedeville's early-eighteenth century *Atlas Historique* and is shown in the accompanying engraved image.[28] As

---

[24] 'James, Duke of York to William Douglas, first Duke of Queensberry, 24 June 1683', HMC, *Buccleuch and Queensberry*, I, 192.

[25] For more on this revival, see Charles J. Burnett and Helen Bennett, *The Green Mantle. A Celebration of the Revival in 1687 of the Most Ancient and Most Noble Order of the Thistle* (Edinburgh, 1987). The revival of the Order was, however, somewhat compromised by the partisan purposes it served to promote since all the Knights initially appointed were Catholic co-religionists of James himself.

[26] Quoted by Kidd, *Subverting Scotland's Past*, p. 183.

[27] Sir John Clerk of Penicuik, *Memoirs of the Life of Sir John Clerk of Penicuik, Baronet, Baron of the Exchequer, Extracted by Himself from his own Journals 1676–1755*, John Gray ed. (Edinburgh, 1892), p. 46.

[28] Nicolas de Guedeville, *Atlas Historique, ou Nouvelle Introduction à l'Histoire, à la Chronologie & à la Géographie Ancienne & Moderne*, 3 vols. (Amsterdam, 1708), II, Plate No. 56: 'The Procession from Holyroodhouse to the Parliament; scene inside the Parliament House'.

Guedeville's commentary explained, however, rhetorical allusions to the notion of 'three estates' were commonplace in early modern Scotland denoting the original legislative divisions that had subsisted among prelates, nobles and burgesses. Following the admission to Parliament of shire commissioners in 1587, however, there were, in fact, four separate estates, as indicated by the standard form of address used by Charles II to 'the lords spirituall and temporall, the commissioners of shires and burrows assembled in our Parliament of Scotland'.[29] Inspired by municipal building works in Louis XIV's France, a programme of civic improvements was also undertaken during the late-1670s and 1680s to create an impressive *'place royale'* in Edinburgh's Parliament Close. Forming the focus of this dignified public space was a lead replica of the bronze equestrian statue of Charles II that had been designed by Grinling Gibbons for Windsor and which represented the first depiction of a British monarch in classical dress as a Roman Emperor.[30] Viewing the statue shortly after it had been unveiled, however, the judge, Sir John Lauder of Fountainhall, reported in April 1685 how 'the vulgar peeple, who had never seen the like before, ware much amazed at it', some comparing it to 'Nebuchadnezar's image, which all fell doune and worshipped', while others feared it represented 'the pale horse in the Revelation, and he that sate theiron was Death.'[31]

Despite its impressive ceremonial aspect, the Scottish Parliament was by no means a regular constitutional entity. During the Restoration, Charles II convened three Parliaments and his brother only one, meaning that for half of the years between 1661 and 1689, no Parliament was held.[32] Procedural constraints also circumscribed Parliament's potential to serve as a forum either for unimpeded debates about monarchy or for independent political action. All legislative initiative was regulated by a committee of royal appointees known as

---

[29] Thomson and Innes eds., *Acts of the Parliament of Scotland*, VIII, 467. For more information on terminological debates, see Julian Goodare, 'The Estates in the Scottish Parliament, 1286–1707', *Parliamentary History*, 15 (1996), pp. 11–32.

[30] For more information about these civic improvements, see Aonghus MacKechnie, 'Housing Scotland's Parliament, 1603–1707', *Parliamentary History*, 21 (2002), pp. 99–130; E. J. MacRae, 'Charles II. Statue, Parliament Square', *Book of the Old Edinburgh Club*, 17 (1930), pp. 82–90 and David Howarth, 'Sculpture and Scotland 1540–1700', in Fiona Pearson ed., *Virtue and Vision: Sculpture and Scotland 1540–1990* (Edinburgh, 1991), pp. 27–44.

[31] Sir John Lauder of Fountainhall, *Historical Notices of Scotish [sic] Affairs, Selected from the Manuscripts of Sir John Lauder of Fountainhall, Bart., one of the Senators of the College of Justice*, David Laing ed., 2 vols. (Edinburgh, 1848), II, 635. According to Sir John Fountainhall, the cost of the statue amounted to over £1000 (sterling).

[32] Under Charles II, the first Parliament had three sessions: (i) 1 January to 12 July 1661; (ii) 8 May to 9 September 1662; (iii) 18 June to 8 October 1663. The second had four sessions: (i) 19 October to 23 December 1669; (ii) 22 July to 22 August 1670; (iii) 12 June to 11 September 1672; (iv) 12 November 1673 to 3 March 1674. The third comprised only a single session from 28 July to 17 November 1681. Under James VII, only one Parliament was held which had two sessions: (i) 23 April to 16 June 1685 and (ii) 29 April to 15 June 1686. For more details, see G. W. Iredell, 'The Law, Custom and Practice of the Parliament of Scotland with particular reference to the period 1660–1707' (University of London unpublished Ph.D. dissertation, 1966). An account of the material ceremonies associated with the parliamentary sessions of 1669 and 1670 is provided in Iain MacIvor and Bent Petersen, 'Lauderdale at Holyroodhouse, 1669–70', in David J. Breeze ed., *Studies in Scottish Antiquity, Presented to Stewart Cruden* (Edinburgh, 1984), pp. 249–68.

Plate 1 The ceremonial progression occasioned by the summoning of Parliament in 1681 as depicted in Nicolas de Guedeville's *Atlas Historique, ou Nouvelle Introduction à l'Histoire, à la Chronologie & à la Géographie Ancienne & Moderne...* (Amsterdam, 1708), Plate No. 56. © The Trustees of the National

Plate 2 John Elphinstone's 'Perspective View of the Parliament House and Exchequer' from Hugo Arnot's *History of Edinburgh* (Edinburgh, 1788). © The Trustees of the National Museums of Scotland.

the 'Lords of the Articles' drawn from shire and burgh commissioners, representatives of the established church and officers of state. Aware of its practical benefits for Charles II's personal control, one parliamentary Commissioner, the duke of Lauderdale, celebrated the system as 'one of the best flowries in his Crowne of Scotland' in 1674.[33] The number of individual commissioners elected tended to be slightly over two hundred, many of whom often objected to the inappropriate haste with which legislation was introduced and the relative impotence of members to influence the outcome of royal proposals. During the 1681 session, for instance, Lauder of Fountainhall complained that 'by surprise', draft acts were 'brought in upon the Parliament, past in Articles that morning, and very seldom delayed, but put to a vote that same dyet'. Members were thus denied any 'leisure to prepare themselfes for argueing, nor to deliberat, combine, or take joynt measures', rendering the majority of enacted legislation 'so raw and indigested'.[34] Communications between government ministers in London and their Edinburgh counterparts were also frequently unreliable and confused. In 1685, for example, remonstrations were lodged regarding the ambitious scope of James VII & II's legislative instructions for his Parliament. As various Privy Council members protested, the king might 'consider that affairs persons and actions will have a different aspect at 300 myles distance' from that envisaged at Whitehall.[35] Two years earlier, James had himself similarly questioned reports that the Scottish Parliament had actually been adjourned, denying that 'by the accident of the losse of a letter a Parliament should be disolved which I thinke cannot be done but by his Majestys order or proclamation'.[36]

Notwithstanding such difficulties, the considerable extent to which the Scottish Parliament served as an arena for national debate during the Restoration should not be underestimated, particularly in the absence of an equivalent ecclesiastical forum being convened, such as an episcopalian national synod or a presbyterian General Assembly. Not least, the very existence of an independent legislature in Scotland had important implications for the Stuart multiple monarchy. As the Lord Advocate, Sir George Mackenzie of Rosehaugh, subsequently reasoned in his Restoration memoirs, while England and Scotland retained sovereign independence, 'his Majesty had two Parliaments, whereof the one might always be exemplary to the other, and might, by a loyal emulation, excite one another to an entire obedience'.[37] In 1689, the author of a manuscript

---

[33] John Dowden ed., *Thirty-four letters written to James Sharp, Archbishop of St Andrews by the Duke and Duchess of Lauderdale and by Charles Maitland, Lord Hatton 1660–1677* (Edinburgh, 1893), p. 270. Under Lauderdale's direction, the procedure for selecting the composition of the Lords of the Articles changed in 1663. Previously, the clergy and nobility had together selected the gentry and burgess members, but, after 1663, the clergy chose the eight noble members while the nobles selected the eight bishops. The group of sixteen nobles and bishops then appointed representatives from the remaining estates assuring greater noble and clerical control over the individuals chosen.

[34] Lauder of Fountainhall, *Historical Notices*, I, 313–14.

[35] 'Instructions . . . to the Duke of Queensberry as Treasurer, to make representations to his Majesty on a variety of subjects concerned with Scotland', HMC *Buccleuch and Queensberry*, I, 132.

[36] 'James, duke of York, to Marquis of Queensberry, 21 July 1683', *Ibid.*, I, 194.

[37] Mackenzie, *Memoirs*, p. 138.

memorial addressed to William of Orange likewise warned him that 'the maine thing that kept Ingland in peace' during the Restoration was the harmonious understanding Charles II had reached with the Scottish Parliament 'which being allwayes fixt to his enterest did overaw Ingland into a continowall peace dureing his tyme'.[38] In non-revolutionary times, domestic parliaments could, however, be regarded as a costly, divisive and unnecessary extravagance. Doubting the effectiveness of the first parliamentary session of the Restoration, for instance, its High Commissioner, the earl of Rothes, called for Charles II to adjourn the assembly in 1663 and return instead to 'the good old forme of government' whereby executive authority was vested in the Scottish Privy Council and judicial authority exercised by the Lords of Session.[39] A similar scenario was suggested by Lauder of Fountainhall in 1681, since it was widely felt that 'our civil rights and interests [are] as well and safely lodged' in the Session as in Parliament, since the latter 'judge more with a biass and in a hurry, and with less regard to law'.[40]

As such views imply, the legal community in late-seventeenth century Scotland not only continued to exert considerable political power and influence, but also supplied a lively forum for intellectual debate and disputation. If nothing else, the mid-century civil wars had ended forever the days when James VI & I had been confidently able to enjoin that 'the absolute Prerogatiue of the Crowne, that is no subject for the Tongue of a Lawyer, nor is it lawfull to be disputed'.[41] By contrast, it was one Restoration Lord Advocate, Mackenzie, who produced what has subsequently been acclaimed as 'the most powerfully argued of all seventeenth-century expositions of the theory of absolute monarchy'.[42] In stark contrast to Mackenzie's political stance, however, his successor, Sir James Steuart of Goodtrees, anonymously penned works later regarded as 'unquestionably the most strident revolutionary tracts of the Restoration . . . explicit justifications of rebellion and tyrannicide'.[43]

---

[38] NAS GD 406/M9/200/10, 'A memoriall discussing past relations between the Scots parliament and England and advising King William of the benefits and necessity of maintaining good relations with the Scots parliament'.

[39] Airy ed., *Lauderdale Papers*, I, 172. Elsewhere, Robert Baillie formed a similar impression of the first parliamentary session of the Restoration, declaring that 'it had sitten long for no very pleasant purposes. The most desired it to rise without adjournment, and choiced rather to be governed simply by the King's good pleasure' (Baillie, *Letters and Journals*, III, 469).

[40] Quoted by Æ. J. G. Mackay, *Memoir of Sir James Dalrymple, First Viscount Stair* (Edinburgh, 1873), p. 116.

[41] James VI & I, 'A Speech in the Starre-Chamber, the XX of June, Anno 1616', in *Political Writings*, Johann P. Sommerville ed. (Cambridge, 1994), p. 214.

[42] J. H. M. Salmon, *The French Religious Wars and English Political Thought* (Oxford, 1959), p. 144. The tract in question was Mackenzie's *Jus Regium: Or, the Just and Solid Foundations of Monarchy In General; and more especially of the Monarchy of Scotland: Maintain'd against Buchannan [sic], Naphtali, Dolman, Milton &c.* (London, 1684).

[43] Mark Goldie, 'John Locke and Anglican Royalism', *Political Studies*, 31 (1983), p. 79. The tracts in question were, first, one that Steuart co-authored with the Covenanting minister, John Stirling, entitled *Naphtali, Or The Wrestlings of the Church of Scotland for the Kingdom of Christ; Contained in A true and short Deduction thereof, from the beginning of the Reformation of Religion, until the Year 1667* ([Edinburgh], 1667) and also Steuart's own tract entitled *Jus Populi Vindicatum. Or, The People's Right to Defend Themselves and their Covenanted Religion* ([Edinburgh], 1669).

For although Mackenzie upheld the divine right of kings on Scriptural, as well as on pragmatic grounds, in 1684 he declared that he had composed his major work of royalist political theory, *Jus Regium*, primarily to demonstrate that 'if these points be clear by our positive Law, there is no further place for debate'. Despite acknowledging the sixteenth-century contributions of Adam Blackwood and William Barclay, Mackenzie stressed the need for a correct understanding of current laws, deeming it 'absolutely necessary for Mankind' that in political matters 'they at least acquiesce in something that is fix'd and certain'.[44] Such claims became even more imperative during the Williamite Revolution. As one young advocate, Francis Grant, perceived in 1689, since Providence had ordered political events such that each individual 'must find his own opinion' regarding the legitimacy of allegiance, it was now essential that 'Law must determine your incertainty.'[45] The same point was made by an anonymous commentator on the revolutionary proceedings, presumed to have been Sir James Dalrymple, Viscount Stair, who pronounced that 'the Right of a Prince over his Subjects is a political Question' which could not be determined 'by the Law of God, but by the Fundamental Laws of each Constitution'.[46]

Seeking to defend the rights and integrity of the Scottish crown from its internal and external detractors alike, Restoration legal theorists also became involved in broader jurisprudential endeavours to establish the sources of authority in Scots law. For his part, Mackenzie maintained in 1686 that no individuals were 'so much obliged to Laws as Monarchs', having previously recognised statutes as pre-eminent from the competing sources of legal authority available in his *Institutions of the Law of Scotland* of 1684.[47] A radically divergent construction had been presented three years earlier, when Stair had produced his own, much larger, *Institutions of the Law of Scotland* which propounded a realist theory of natural law and favoured custom as a source of law in contrast to Mackenzie's voluntarism.[48] Both Stair and Mackenzie were, however, concerned to render the different sources of Scots law as publicly accessible as possible. Hence Stair received permission from Charles II to publish the first printed collection of judicial decisions from the Court of Session which appeared in two volumes in 1683 and 1687, while an exclusive government licence was granted in 1681 to the

---

[44] Mackenzie, *Jus Regium*, pp. 5–6.
[45] F[rancis] G[rant], *The Loyalists Reasons. For his giving Obedience, and swearing Allegiance to the present Government* (Edinburgh, 1689), sig. A2r.
[46] Anon., *A Vindication of the Proceedings of the Convention of Estates in Scotland &c.* (London, 1689), p. 16.
[47] Sir George Mackenzie, *Observations on the Acts of Parliament, Made by King James the First &c.* (Edinburgh, 1686), 'To the King', sig. A2r.
[48] Sir James Dalrymple, Viscount Stair, *The Institutions of the Law of Scotland, Deduced from the Originals and Collected with the Civil, Canon, and Feudal-Laws, and with the Customs of Neighbouring Nations* (Edinburgh, 1681). For more on the status accorded to institutional writings in Scotland, see John W. Cairns, 'Institutional Writings in Scotland Reconsidered', in Albert Kiralfy and Hector L. MacQueen eds., *New Perspectives in Scottish Legal History* (London, 1984), pp. 76–117 and by the same author, 'The Moveable Text of Mackenzie: Bibliographical Problems for the Scottish Concept of Institutional Writing', in John W. Cairns and Olivia F. Robinson eds., *Critical Studies in Ancient Law, Comparative Law and Legal History* (Oxford, 2000), pp. 233–48.

Clerk Register, Sir Thomas Murray of Glendook, to produce a new edition of the Scottish statutes from 1424 onwards, adorned with handsome engravings of each Scottish monarch with emblematic regalia.[49]

In addition to producing formal legal commentaries on the substantive law itself, Restoration Scots lawyers were also energetically involved in promoting a broadly humanist cultivation of learning within their profession. The lively legal culture that evolved was partly due to the changing social composition of the Faculty of Advocates, as men from the upper echelons of peers and landed gentry became dominant during the Restoration.[50] Endowed with increasing social prestige, the advocates also developed an enhanced corporate identity through the election of Faculty office-holders, together with the institution of a private entrance examination for entrants seeking admission to the Faculty prior to being publicly examined by members of the Court of Session. Having been elected Dean of the Faculty in 1682, Mackenzie also assumed responsibility for pioneering the foundation of the Advocates' Library, subsequently insisting that successful new entrants be required to donate volumes to the Library, thus ending the 'bad custome' which had hitherto prevailed whereby successful petitioners held feasts for their examiners.[51] In March 1689, Mackenzie disregarded the surrounding political maelstrom to compose a speech for the Library's public inauguration, envisaging that it would become 'a modern Lyceum and a new Stoa'.[52]

The successful establishment of the Advocates' Library reflects the royalist 'virtuoso' culture that has previously characterised accounts of Restoration Scotland. Historians such as Hugh Ouston and Roger Emerson have shown how late-seventeenth century Scots enthusiastically sought to establish various institutions to expand knowledge, both secular and divine, through the collection of empirical data.[53] A similar spirit of virtuoso pansophism was elsewhere evinced by members of the late-seventeenth century medical profession, the most prominent of whom was the physician, Sir Robert Sibbald. Believing that 'the

---

[49] *The Decisions of the Lords of Council and Session . . . Observed by Sir James Dalrymple of Stair*, 2 vols. (Edinburgh, 1683, 1687) and *The Laws and Acts of Parliament made by King James the First . . . [to] King Charles the Second Who now presently reigns, Kings and Queens of Scotland. Collected, and Extracted, from the Publick Records of the said Kingdom, by Sir Thomas Murray of Glendook, Knight, and Baronet, Clerk to His Majestie's Council, Register and Rols, by his Majestie's special warrand* (Edinburgh, 1681).

[50] Thomas I. Rae, 'The Origins of the Advocates' Library', in Patrick Cadell and Ann Matheson eds., *For the Encouragement of Learning: Scotland's National Library 1619–1989* (Edinburgh, 1989), p. 4.

[51] John M. Pinkerton ed., *The Minute Book of the Faculty of Advocates, Volume 1, 1661–1712* (Edinburgh, 1976), pp. 75–6.

[52] Sir George Mackenzie, *Oratio Inauguralis in Aperienda Jurisconsultorum Bibliotheca*, John W. Cairns and A. Cain eds. (Edinburgh, 1989), p. 64. For more on Mackenzie's vision, see John W. Cairns, 'Sir George Mackenzie, the Faculty of Advocates and the Advocates' Library', in Cairns and Cain eds., *Oratio Inauguralis*, pp. 18–35. The holdings of the Advocates' Library duly formed the basis of the National Library of Scotland established in 1925.

[53] See Hugh Ouston, 'York in Edinburgh: James VII and the Patronage of Learning in Scotland 1679–1688', in John Dwyer, Roger Mason and Alexander Murdoch eds., *New Perspectives on the Culture and Society of Early Modern Scotland* (Edinburgh, 1982), pp. 135–55 and 'Cultural Life from the Restoration to the Union' in Hook ed., *History of Scottish Literature*, pp. 11–32 and Roger L. Emerson, 'Scottish Cultural Change 1660–1707 and the Union of 1707', in Robertson ed., *Union for Empire*, pp. 121–44.

Plate 3 The title-page from the folio edition of Sir Thomas Murray of Glendook, *The Laws and Acts of Parliament made by King James the First . . . [to] King Charles the Second Who now presently reigns &c.* (Edinburgh, 1681). By permission of the Trustees of the National Library of Scotland.

Plate 4 An engraving of Charles II in classical attire that appeared in the folio edition of Sir Thomas Murray of Glendook, *The Laws and Acts of Parliament made by King James the First . . . [to] King Charles the Second Who now presently reigns &c.* (Edinburgh, 1681). By permission of the Trustees of the National Library of Scotland.

simplest method of Physick was the best', Sibbald's interest in the cultivation of indigenous plants and medicinal herbs encouraged him to undertake the establishment of the first botanical garden in Scotland in 1670.[54] A catalogue of the plants grown in the Edinburgh Physic Garden, entitled *Hortus Medicus Edinburgensis*, was published by the Keeper, James Sutherland, in 1683 and cited over 2,000 different species collected 'from the Levant, Italy, Spain, France, Holland, England, east and west Indies; and by many painful Journeys in all the Seasons of the year' throughout Scotland.[55] In addition to his endeavours to promote the Physic Garden, Sibbald also served his profession by obtaining the duke of York's support in founding the Royal College of Physicians in 1681, as demarcation disputes between Scottish physicians and surgeons had become increasingly protracted and litigious.[56] The following year, Sibbald received a patent from Charles II to become the Royal Physician in Scotland.

The influence of Sibbald's 'virtuoso' activities extended nationally when he was appointed Scottish Geographer-Royal in 1682, commanded by Charles II to research and publish a geographical description and natural history of the kingdom. Conceiving the project within the framework of service to the state, Sibbald advertised for assistance, declaring the project to be especially necessary since the period of peace which had accompanied the Restoration had so improved the physical appearance of the country that 'we begin to contend with the happiest of our Neighbours'.[57] But, as he added, although most Scots had 'a great desire to travell', Sibbald deemed it 'an inexcusable fault to be ignorant of what concerneth our own Countrey'.[58] Although the collapse of royal authority which occurred under James VII & II in the late-1680s conspired to ensure that Sibbald's atlas was never produced, topographical descriptions of nearly eighty localities were undertaken by a network of corresponding individuals who

---

[54] Francis Hett ed., *The Memoirs of Sir Robert Sibbald (1641–1722)* (Oxford, 1932), p. 64. For more on Sibbald's involvement, see John M. Cowan, 'The History of the Royal Botanic Garden, Edinburgh', *Notes from the Royal Botanic Garden Edinburgh*, 19 (1933–8), pp. 1–62.

[55] James Sutherland, *Hortus Medicus Edinburgensis, or a Catalogue of all the Plants in the Physic Garden at Edinburgh* (Edinburgh, 1683), 'Dedication'. In 1684, Sutherland was granted £20 (sterling) by Edinburgh Town Council to assist with costs incurred in publishing the catalogue.

[56] See A. D. C. Simpson, 'Sir Robert Sibbald – The Founder of the College', in R. Passmore ed., *Proceedings of the Royal College of Physicians of Edinburgh Tercentenary Congress 1981* (Edinburgh, 1982), pp. 59–91. Surgeons in Edinburgh had been formally incorporated as a craft guild by the Town Council in 1505. For an account of the ways in which similar professional rivalries persisted in Glasgow, see Johanna Geyer-Kordesch and Fiona Macdonald, *Physicians and Surgeons in Glasgow. The History of the Royal College of Physicians and Surgeons of Glasgow*, 2 vols. (Hambledon, 1999), I, 21–5.

[57] Sir Robert Sibbald, *An Account of the Scottish Atlas, Or the Description of Scotland Ancient and Modern, By His Sacred Majestie's special Command To be published presently* &c. (Edinburgh, 1683), p. 4. For more on Sibbald's endeavours, see Charles W. J. Withers, 'Geography, Science and National Identity in Early Modern Britain: The Case of Scotland the Work of Sir Robert Sibbald (1641–1722)', *Annals of Science*, 53 (1996), pp. 29–73; 'How Scotland came to know itself: geography, national identity and the making of a nation, 1680–1790', *Journal of Historical Geography*, 21 (1995), pp. 371–97 and *Geography, Science and National Identity: Scotland since 1520* (Cambridge, 2001).

[58] Sibbald, *Account of the Scottish Atlas*, p. 3.

responded to the project's instigation.[59] Simultaneously, Sibbald collaborated with the cartographer, John Adair, who produced a series of regional maps of Scotland during the 1680s.[60] Other fields of geographical and chorographical enquiry initiated during the Restoration generated the navigational information provided in James Paterson's *Geographical Description of Scotland* of 1681 and the gazeteer of Scottish place-names supplied by Christopher Irvine's *Scoticae Historiae Nomenclatura* which was published the following year.[61] Elsewhere, in his capacity as Chief Engineer for Scotland, the German artillery officer, John Slezer, began the series of perspective images of Scottish urban 'prospects' that eventually appeared in the *Theatrum Scotiae* of 1693.[62]

II

While the activities of Sibbald and his colleagues served to enhance Restoration Scots' appreciation of their own country, Sibbald's recognition that most of his contemporaries also evinced 'a great desire to travell' was indicative of the extent to which Scottish intellectual discourse was rendered cosmopolitan by frequent foreign travel. Throughout the Restoration, the benefits of exposure to foreign mores were indeed widely extolled. As the marquis of Argyll put it in 1661, 'he that hath lived lock'd up in one Kingdome' was 'but a degree beyond a Country-man, who was never out of the bounds of his parish'.[63] Intellectual, political, religious and commercial associations combined, however, to promote regular contact between Restoration Scots and an extensive overseas diaspora.

At the very least, the reality of being ruled by an absentee monarch ensured that considerable political activity and intellectual debate concerning Scottish affairs was conducted in London. In the late-1650s, a future English Historiographer-Royal, James Howell, remarked that the regal union between Scotland and England in 1603 'did not a little conduce to make this union 'twixt London and Westminster', since the Scots 'multiplying here mightily, nested themselves about the Court', greatly improving and extending the districts of Charing Cross and Aldywch.[64] In institutional terms, the increasingly sizeable nature of the expatriate community not only prompted the foundation by charter

---

[59] These accounts are listed by Withers in 'Geography, Science and National Identity', pp. 69–73. For an indication of the use subsequently made of these accounts, see Stan Mendyk, 'Scottish Regional Historians and the *Britannia* Project', *Scottish Geographical Magazine*, 101 (1985), pp. 165–73.

[60] See Allen Simpson, 'John Adair, cartographer, and Sir Robert Sibbald's Atlas', *The Map Collector*, 62 (1993), pp. 32–6 and J. N. Moore, 'Scottish Cartography in the later Stuart era, 1660–1714', *Scottish Tradition*, 14 (1986–7), pp. 28–44.

[61] James Paterson, *A Geographical Description of Scotland* (Edinburgh, 1681) and Christopher Irvine, *Scoticae Historiae Nomenclatura Latino-vernacular* (Edinburgh, 1682).

[62] See Keith Cavers, *A Vision of Scotland: The Nation observed by John Slezer 1671–1717* (Edinburgh, 1993) and James Cameron, 'A Bibliography of Slezer's *Theatrum Scotiæ*', *Papers of the Edinburgh Bibliographical Society*, 3 (1895–8), pp. 141–7.

[63] Argyll, *Instructions*, p. 72.

[64] James Howell, *Londinopalis; An Historicall Discourse, or Perlustration, On the City of London, The Imperial Chamber, and chief Emporium of Great Britain* (London, 1657), p. 346.

of the Royal Scottish Corporation in 1665, but also required the construction of the first Scottish Hospital near Blackfriars in 1672. In 1667, Thomas Sydserf's play, *Tarugo's Wiles*, became the first play by a Scot to be performed in London as playwrights like Sydserf moved south, frustrated by the paucity of domestic literary activity in Scotland.[65] While Sydserf's play, sub-titled *The Coffee-House*, was published the following year, the first actual 'Scottish Coffee-house' opened near Newgate during the 1670s. On occasion, however, the activities of 'London-Scots' drew criticism from their fellow countrymen, including one visitor to the English Parliament in 1675 who commented on the large numbers of Scots daily attending 'the Commons doores, lyke as many porters, ambitious to be slaves to them, to betray their own cuntrey and cuntreymen'.[66]

Scottish interest in English ideas was also stimulated by the large numbers of London stationers who not only frequently dispatched book catalogues to their counterparts north of the border, but also supplied Scots purchasers with items on their regular book-buying trips to the English capital.[67] Temporarily resident in London in 1689, the episcopalian minister of Aberfoyle, Robert Kirk, remarked upon the considerably more sophisticated and extensive nature of English political culture, identifying the 'great Advantage' as being that, despite 'the Changes continually occurring in Church or State', there were 'so many learnd men who immediatly publish their Advice pro & con that each may see & quickly chuse what is safest and best to do without much study'.[68] Other Scots clerics were, by contrast, less than impressed. In 1681, for instance, James Craufurd acknowledged that popular interest in political affairs in London had 'come to that pitch' that 'the Curious must be with their Bookseller once a day to see what new things are come out that morning'. Despite regretting the comparative poverty of literary activity in Scotland, he concluded that the large majority of publications produced in England resembled 'Mushrooms, are they are hatched in one day or week at the most, so they seldom survive another'.[69]

Throughout the Restoration, Scottish curiosity about English affairs was, however, reciprocated by a keen English interest in events north of the border. Members of Charles II's administration were unlikely to return to the state of affairs that had evidently prevailed in England at the outbreak of the Bishops' Wars in the late-1630s. For, according to Edward Hyde, earl of Clarendon, although 'the whole nation was solicitous to know what passed weekly in

---

[65] For more on this subject, see Adrienne Skullion, ' "Forget *Scotland*": Plays by Scots on the London stage, 1667–1715', *Comparative Drama*, 31 (1997), pp. 105–28. Sydserf was the son of the Caroline bishop of Galloway, also called Thomas Sydserf.

[66] 'Alexander Murray to Charles Murray, 11 November 1675', HMC, *Twelfth Report, Appendix, Part VIII. The Manuscripts of the Duke of Athole, Kt. and the Earl of Home* (London, 1891), p. 33.

[67] See, for instance, John Grant, 'Archibald Hislop, Stationer, Edinburgh, 1668–1678', *Papers of the Edinburgh Bibliographical Society*, 12 (1921–5), pp. 35–51.

[68] EUL MSS. La.III.545, Robert Kirk, 'Sermons, Conferences, Mens Opinions, of the late Transactions, with a Description of London, Ann. 1689', f. 137v.

[69] Craufurd, *History of the House of Esté*, 'Preface', sig. [A]2r. As Craufurd opined, in England, the 'Politicks are so in vogue' that 'so much money and time is consumed in them, that any thing of more valuable Learning is too much laid aside' (*Ibid.*, sig. [A]v).

Germany and Poland and all other parts of Europe', no interest had been shown in Scottish affairs and 'nor had that kingdom a place or mention in one page of any gazette, so little the world heard or thought of that people'.[70] During the Restoration, a thrice-weekly mail service ensured that a letter posted in London took around five days to arrive in Edinburgh and incoming Scottish mail arrived in the English capital on Mondays, Wednesdays and Fridays.[71] English journalists reported a variety of official ceremonies taking place in Scotland including, for instance, a military 'wapinshaw', or general muster, of around two thousand tradesman and merchants, staged by Edinburgh Town Council on 29 May 1677 to commemorate the anniversary of Charles II's restoration. Although it was later claimed that 'many things ware [sic] advanced a litle beyond what was true' in printed accounts of the day's festivities,[72] the London Gazette described a magnificent distribution of 'Confections and Fruits' while 'by several Conduits the Cross did run several sorts of Wines for many hours together'. Amidst further bonfires and general rejoicing, the citizens of Edinburgh had publicly re-affirmed their gratitude for Charles' restoration, considering themselves blessed by his peaceful protection 'whilst the rest of the World lies bathed in bloud, and distracted by a thousand Confusions'.[73]

Furthermore, the lapse of the English Licensing Act proved an unexpected consequence of the political tensions generated by the so-called 'Exclusion Crisis' which occurred when a series of unsuccessful parliamentary attempts were launched to prevent James, duke of York, succeeding to the English throne on account of his Roman Catholicism between 1679 and 1681. A variety of new and unlicensed newspapers thus appeared, including Benjamin Harris' Domestick Intelligence; Or, News both from City and Country, Nathaniel Thompson's Loyal Protestant and John Smith's Currant Intelligence. Within the section devoted to 'country news', such newspapers relied on Edinburgh correspondents to supply their English readership with reports of Scottish affairs which were of especial interest since the period coincided with the duke of York's two terms as parliamentary High Commissioner to the Scottish Parliament between 1679 and 1682.[74] Perusing reports that the duke of York had 'certainly arrivd in Scotland' in November 1680, however, the English Puritan diarist, Roger Morrice, confessed that 'we are not agreed (notwithstanding the directions) whether his reception was very magnificent, or but indifferent and cool'.[75]

The politics of multiple monarchy alone ensured that supporters and opponents alike of the Stuart monarchy frequently discovered that political allegiance

---

[70] Edward Hyde, earl of Clarendon, The History of the Rebellion and Civil Wars in England, W. Macray ed., 6 vols. (Oxford, 1888), I, 145–6.
[71] Thomas Gardiner, A General Survey of the Post Office 1677–1682, Foster W. Bond ed. (Postal History Society, 1958), p. 65.
[72] Lauder of Fountainhall, Historical Notices, I, 157.
[73] The London Gazette, 7 June 1677.
[74] See James Sutherland, The Restoration Newspaper and its Development (Cambridge, 1985), pp. 106–7.
[75] Morrice Ent'ring Book, 'P', f. 274.

transcended national loyalties. Particularly amidst increasing tensions generated by Charles II's involvement in Continental hostilities, Scots and English royalists feared the recurrence of another British crisis. Writing to Archbishop Gilbert Sheldon of Canterbury shortly before the outbreak of the second Anglo-Dutch war in 1665, for instance, Archbishop Alexander Burnet of Glasgow confirmed that although 'at present we may possibly prevent domestike disorders and insurrections', he feared that 'the least commotion in England or Ireland, or encouragement from forraigners, would certainly engage ws [*sic*] in a new rebellion'.[76] Burnet's concerns were justified when the withdrawal of troops from the south-west of Scotland, necessitated by the Dutch hostilities, created conditions propitious for the outbreak of the Pentland Rising in the autumn of 1666. Receiving news of the Rising in London, Samuel Pepys recorded how, 'contrary to practice', the English Parliament decided to sit in session on St. Andrew's Day, 30 November, 'people having no mind to observe that Scotch saint's day till they hear better news from Scotland'.[77]

The potential for concerted action was keenly appreciated by those responsible for maintaining domestic security in Scotland. In a later rebellion, a declaration issued on behalf of the armed Covenanters in 1680 explicitly recognised a 'formed and universal plot' to establish popery and arbitrary government by 'secret undermining and murderous practices in England', together with 'the open introduction of slavery and tyrannical government in Scotland'.[78] These opportunities were certainly appreciated by those individuals suspected of seditious and treasonable tendencies by the Scottish authorities, such as James Fraser of Brea, who in 1682 elected to suffer banishment to England rather than imprisonment in Scotland. Although headed for a 'strange country', Fraser remained confident that 'a godly man in England or Ireland, is more my countryman than a wicked Scotsman' since he regarded 'wicked folk, though Scotsmen, as the greatest aliens, foreigners, and strangers'.[79] Across the Irish Sea, the Irish authorities were likewise alarmed by the steady influx of disaffected Covenanters fleeing Scotland from the mid-1670s onwards. Arriving in Dublin in 1683, for instance, another exiled Covenanter, James Renwick, announced that 'the Lord has a special hand in my coming to this place', having 'kindled a fire which I hope Satan shall not quench'.[80] Renwick joined a growing community of Scots presbyterians, the majority of whom resided in Ulster. As the Irish magnate, Sir George Rawdon, had earlier observed in 1678, the government's policy of persecution and repression had 'blown over the

---

[76] Airy ed., *Lauderdale Papers*, II, Appendix, p. xxxi.
[77] R. C. Latham and W. Matthews eds., *The Diary of Samuel Pepys 1660–1669*, 10 vols. (London, 1970–83), VII, 391.
[78] 'A declaration of the oppressed protestants now in arms in Scotland, 1680', in Wodrow ed., *Sufferings*, III, 97.
[79] Alexander Whyte ed., *Memoirs of the Rev. James Fraser, of Brea, A.D. 1638–1698* (Inverness, 1889), p. 290.
[80] Quoted by Phil Kilroy, *Protestant Dissent and Controversy in Ireland 1660–1714* (Cork, 1994) at p. 111.

greatest bigots' whose vociferous presence and 'insolent demands' prompted Rawdon to suggest that 'the counties near the sea coast may well be renamed Nova Scotia'.[81]

Concerned that discontented elements might indeed seek to exchange ideas and make common cause with one another throughout the multiple monarchy, members of the Stuart administration subjected Anglo-Scottish communication to constant scrutiny. As early as 1661, for example, the English Postmaster-General, Henry Bishop, denied charges of 'opening the Scotch letter bags', having already adopted measures 'to prevent that abuse which has been generally practised'.[82] Despite such assurances, interception evidently continued throughout the Restoration. When the Scots Parliament refused to sanction James VII & II's proposals for religious toleration in 1686, for example, Lauder of Fountainhall recorded how 'letters ware one post all broken up and searched' as officials sought to establish 'if any correspondence or intelligence could be discovered betuen Scotland and England'.[83] Within Scotland, the Glasgow postmaster and news agent, Robert Mein, was paid by Glasgow Town Council to obtain news and gazettes from London during the 1660s and 1670s. Although he subsequently undertook to provide a similar service for the magistrates of Edinburgh during the 1680s, Mein and another news agent, Thomas Comley, had been censured by the Scottish Privy Council for dispersing 'false news' obtained from London in January 1680 and Mein was also briefly imprisoned for the same offence the following September.[84] News became a prize accorded the highest premium. The Borders laird, Sir William Scott of Harden, managed to receive an uninterrupted series of weekly printed gazettes and newsletters from London, despite being warned that such publications were often 'false and uncertaine', containing many items 'otherwise represented than reallie they are, by purpose to satisfie the people'. As his son, James Scott, recognised, controls on the spread of news were so stringent that 'none adventurs to give any true account of the present occasiones'.[85] The English diarist, Roger Morrice, was likewise moved to complain in June 1679 that 'letters out of Scotland are so inconsistent and irreconcilable' that he could not ascertain whether civil commotions there 'be dissipated or whether they encrease'.[86]

The government's fears that Anglo-Scottish combinations might succeed in synchronising their subversive enterprises were by no means unjustified.

[81] 'Sir George Rawdon to Viscount Conway, 13 October 1678', in *Calendar of State Papers, Domestic Series, March 1st, 1677 to February 28th, 1678*, F. H. Blackburne Daniell ed. (London, 1911), p. 398; see also R. M. Young, 'News from Ireland: Being the Examination and Confession of William Kelso, 1679', *Ulster Journal of Archaeology*, 2 (1895), pp. 274–9.
[82] Answer of Hen. Bishop, postmaster general', *Calendar of State Papers, Domestic, of the Reign of Charles II. 1661–2*, M. Everett-Green ed. (London, 1861), p. 57.
[83] Lauder of Fountainhall, *Historical Notices*, II, 735.
[84] See account in Alastair J. Mann, *The Scottish Book Trade 1500–1720. Print Commerce and Print Control in Early Modern Scotland* (East Linton, 2000), p. 174.
[85] NAS 157/2673/2, 'Sir James Scott to Sir William Scott of Harden, 20 January 1680'.
[86] Morrice Ent'ring Book, 'P', f. 196.

Following the discovery in June 1683 of the English Whig conspiracy to murder Charles II and the duke of York, known as the 'Rye House Plot', for example, the earl of Aberdeen, as Scottish Chancellor, was immediately instructed to 'discover iff any strangers from Ingland com into any place in Scotland'. Deeming it 'very probable that some of this helishe plotinge crew may goe ther', orders were summarily dispatched to apprehend all Englishmen currently in Scotland in order to establish their individual identities. Aberdeen had already received warnings from London about the proliferation of subversive publications 'which daylie swarm heir' on the grounds that works such as Samuel Johnson's *Julian the Apostate* (1682) might 'fall into the hands of our blind and bloody phanaticks' and thereby exert a destabilising influence.[87] Meanwhile, the English authorities were equally alarmed by those 'several Scotchmen in London they call confederates'.[88] For late-seventeenth century Anglo-Scottish co-operation also extended overseas through various colonial ventures as schemes to establish Scottish settlements in New Jersey and South Carolina in the 1680s attracted enthusiastic support from the duke of York. His elder brother, however, questioned the probity of such enterprises. In the aftermath of the disclosure of the Rye House Plot, Charles II issued a statement claiming that, since 'correspondency by letters was thought dangerous', English opposition leaders had invited disaffected Scottish magnates to London 'under pretence of purchassing [*sic*] lands in Carolina, but, in truth, to concert with them, the best means of carrying on the design jointly in both kingdoms'.[89] Scots delegates sent to confer with leading Whigs, such as Lord Russell and the duke of Monmouth, had indicated that 'the Scotch were ready at an hour's warning', to rebel across the country, leaving the English Whigs 'sure of Scotland and did not question they would be masters of it in 24 hours whenever they began'.[90] Responsible for maintaining civil order in Scotland in his capacity as Lord Advocate, Mackenzie of Rosehaugh thus concluded in 1685 that the Stuart multiple monarchy was divided 'not in nations, but Opinions, the old Animosities amongst Scots, English and Irish' being 'forgot and buried'. As Mackenzie conceived, 'the modern Differences' were 'between the Episcopal and Fanatick, Cavalier and Republican, or as some term it, Whig and Tory'.[91]

Beyond British shores, both the administrations of Charles II and James VII & II were equally anxious to detect signs of ideological or practical sedition

[87] John Dunn ed., *Letters Illustrative of Public Affairs in Scotland, Addressed by Contemporary Statesmen to George, earl of Aberdeen, Lord High Chancellor of Scotland, MDCLXXXI–MDCLXXXIV* (Aberdeen, 1851), pp. 133, 27.
[88] 'Alexander Gordon of Earlston to the Lord Chancellor of Scotland, 20 June 1683', in *Calendar of State Papers, Domestic Series, January 1 to June 30, 1683*, F. H. Blackburne Daniell ed. (London, 1933), p. 329.
[89] 'Narrative of the plot for the assassination of His Majesty and the Duke of York', *The Register of the Privy Council of Scotland. Third Series. VIII (1683–1684)*, P. Hume Brown ed. (Glasgow, 1915), p. 214.
[90] 'The deposition of Ezekiel Everest', *Calendar of State Papers Domestic Series, October 1, 1683 – April 30, 1684*, F. H. Blackburne Daniell and Francis Bickley eds. (London, 1938), p. 226.
[91] Sir George Mackenzie, *A Defence of the Antiquity of the Royal Line of Scotland, With a true Account When the Scots were Govern'd by Kings in the Isle of Britain* (London, 1685), p. iii.

emanating from the Netherlands, where several hundred Scots exiles obtained political asylum and freedom from religious persecution during the Restoration. In 1680, for instance, members of the Scottish Privy Council intimated to the duke of Lauderdale their concern that the Scots 'people are much influenced by [those] rebells and fugitives, who live in Holland, to all their madd and dangerous practices'. As the Councillors conceived, the exiled 'rebells are as dangerous to ye government as if they kept their caballs here'.[92] Ostensibly writing 'from Amsterdam' in 1678, one English Tory pamphlet had likewise ironically observed how 'our Scotish [sic] friends trace the old method of 1640', having 'walkt hand in hand like brethren' with English republicans now seeking 'to revive and rake that phoenix, the Covenant, out of his ashes'.[93] Following the discovery of the Rye House Plot in 1683, legal depositions confirmed how nonconformist presbyterian ministers had long been observed 'passing to and fro betwixt Holland and Scotland', remaining incognito through 'being clad in seaman's cloths, and working in the ships as sea-men'.[94]

Sustained endeavours were made during the Restoration to take action against individual Scots exiles regarded as undermining domestic peace. In July 1670, for instance, the English Ambassador to the Netherlands, Sir William Temple, unsuccessfully attempted to persuade the Dutch States-General to banish three presbyterian ministers, Robert Trail, Robert MacWard and John Nevay, for writing and publishing anti-monarchical material. Complex diplomatic negotiations ensued when Temple tried again in 1676 to insist that MacWard, together with John Brown of Wamphray and James Wallace of Auchens, should be banished as rebels under the provisions of the 1660 Treaty of Breda, having been previously convicted of treasonable activity in Scotland. Although the trio was temporarily expelled, the ambiguities involved in determining whether or not exiled ministers were indeed political malcontents, or legitimate religious refugees, deterred further action by Charles II's ministers. For their part, in 1676, the Dutch authorities at the Scottish staple port of Campvere formally agreed to obstruct the sale or purchase of 'all manner of ammunition of warre, weapons, offensive and defensive, unto or by any fugitives, rebells, enimies or others disaffected to His Majesties royall persone and government'. A guarantee was also provided that the authorities would seek to hinder the publication of any seditious books or pamphlets within their

---

[92] Airy ed., *Lauderdale Papers*, III, 203. For a detailed study of the personnel who comprised the Scottish exile community in the Netherlands during this period, see G. J. Gardner, 'The Scottish Exile Community in the United Provinces, 1660–1690' (University of Oxford unpublished D.Phil. dissertation, 1998).

[93] Anon., 'A Letter from Amsterdam to a Friend in England', in *A Collection of Scarce and Valuable Tracts on the most interesting and entertaining Subjects, but chiefly such as relate to the History and Constitution of these Kingdoms. Selected . . . [from the library] of the late Lord Somers*, Walter Scott ed., 13 vols. (London, 1809–15), VIII, 88.

[94] 'Introduction to the Trials for the Rye House Plot' in T. B. Howell ed., *A Complete Collection of State Trials and Proceedings for high Treason and other Crimes and Misdemeanours from the Earliest Period to the Present Time*, 33 vols. (London, 1816–28), IX, 431.

jurisdiction as well as to impede the transport of such material to any of Charles II's dominions.[95]

Concerns over the dissemination of subversive political and religious ideas thus remained paramount since the Dutch press supplied 'the crucible for Scottish non-conformist polemic'.[96] Included among numerous Covenanting works published in the Netherlands during the Restoration were John Brown of Wamphray's *Apologeticall Relation* (1665), James Steuart and John Stirling's *Naphtali* (1667) and Robert MacWard's *Poor Man's Cup of Cold Water* (1678). Numerous Scottish titles were also translated into Dutch by sympathetic divines such as Jacobus Koelman in Rotterdam. From Holland, the earl of Argyll launched an unsuccessful invasion force that landed on the west coast of Scotland in May 1685, arriving 'so conceitty' as to import not only arms and ammunition, but also a Dutch printing press which published Argyll's *Declaration* at Campbeltown in Kintyre.[97] Keen interest in Scottish affairs was also evident within the Dutch newspaper press. Amidst the heated debates being held to discuss James VII & II's controversial proposals to enact religious toleration in Scotland during 1686, for example, Lauder of Fountainhall remarked how 'the Harleem Gazet from Holland boor also a good account of what past in our Scots Parliament.'[98]

Equally eager for news of Scottish affairs were the large numbers of Scots students attracted to studying at the renowned Dutch universities of Franeker, Groningen, Leiden and Utrecht. Particularly popular among students of medicine and law, it has been estimated that around two-fifths of lawyers joining the Faculty of Advocates during this period had studied in the United Provinces.[99] The dissemination of ideas was also promoted by regular overseas travel that provided Restoration Scots with opportunities to procure foreign imprints of political and religious works. Purchasing extensively during his various sojourns in Poitiers, Paris, Brussels, Amsterdam and Leiden between 1667 and 1679, for instance, the judge, Lauder of Fountainhall, amassed a collection of approximately 500 titles. In similar manner, whilst his sons were enjoying a Continental tour in 1680, the earl of Queensberry urged their tutor, James Fall, 'upon all occasions [to] give me an account of publique newes and transactions therein so

---

[95] 'Articles of Agreement for settling the Staple-port at Campheer, ratified by the Convention 9th July 1675 and 12th October 1676', in M. Rooseboom, *The Scottish Staple Port in the Netherlands* (The Hague, 1910), Appendix, p. ccxvii.

[96] Mann, *Scottish Book Trade*, p. 172.

[97] Sir John Lauder of Fountainhall, *Historical Observes of Memorable Occurrents in Church and State from October 1680 to April 1686 by Sir John Lauder of Fountainhall*, David Laing and A. Urquhart eds. (Edinburgh, 1840), p. 195. For more on the complicated publishing history of Argyll's *Declaration*, see R. H. Carnie, 'The Campbeltown Declaration and its Printer', *The Bibliotheck*, 10 (1980), pp. 59–67.

[98] Lauder of Fountainhall, *Historical Notices*, II, 735.

[99] See Robert Feenstra, 'Scottish-Dutch Legal Relations in the 17th and 18th centuries', in Hilde de Ridder Symoens and John M. Fletcher eds., *Academic Relations between the Low Countries and the British Isles 1450–1700* (Ghent, 1989), pp. 25–45. Regarding the influence of Dutch legal education in this sphere, see John W. Cairns, 'Importing our Lawyers from Holland: Netherlands Influences on Scots Law and Lawyers in the Eighteenth Century', in Grant G. Simpson ed., *Scotland and the Low Countries 1124–1994* (East Linton, 1996), pp. 136–53.

far as safely you can'.[100] Subsequently appointed Historiographer-Royal on his return to Scotland, Fall was himself a keen bibliophile with liberal and catholic tastes, who engaged Continental book agents to obtain titles unavailable domestically. Referring to the works of the Dutch freethinker, Benedict de Spinoza, for example, Fall informed the earl of Tweeddale in 1678 of reports that 'there is lately come out a piece writne [sic] by that Famous author of Tractatus Theologico-Politicus'. While Fall confessed to being 'sorry such books are printed', he admitted that 'since they are they my curiosity leads me to desire a sight of them'.[101]

Imbued with a similarly cosmopolitan spirit, the episcopalian cleric, James Cockburn, aimed to advise and inform Scots about the best of contemporary literature by founding a new periodical entitled *Bibliotheca Universalis* in 1688. While his editorial proudly declared that 'the Republick of Letters has flourished more in this last Age, than perhaps in any of the former', Cockburn acknowledged that although learning was not 'totally a Stranger to this Nation; yet it were to be wisht, that it were more universally spread'. Seeking to foster suitable fora for intellectual pursuits, Cockburn intended to supply monthly accounts of 'what is doing Abroad, by the Learned World' as well as to include reports of 'what the Virtuoso's and Learned among our selves are pleased to communicate'.[102] Amidst the sectarian sensibilities of the late-1680s, however, such endeavours were not universally construed as innocuous. After only one issue, the periodical was closed down by the newly-converted Catholic Chancellor, the earl of Perth, who allegedly objected to some of the anti-Catholic sentiments expressed in the journal, but was sufficiently impressed by the enterprise to add that he would 'cause his own churchmen to do it better'.[103]

III

As the earl of Perth's actions categorically demonstrated, while the appetites of Scots for new information and ideas remained keen, the intellectual culture of Restoration Scotland was subject to stringent regulation which placed numerous official and unofficial constraints upon the dissemination of ideas. According to *A History of Scotland* published by 'T. S.' in 1690, when the duke of Lauderdale's authority in Scotland was at its height in the 1670s, 'Informing were a

---

[100] James Fall, *Memoires of My Lord Drumlanrig's and His Brother Lord William's Travells Abroad for the Space of Three Yeares beginning Sept' 13th 1680*, Hew Dalrymple ed. (Edinburgh, 1931), p. 8.
[101] Quoted by Murray Simpson, 'Some Aspects of Book Purchasing in Restoration Scotland: Two Letters from James Fall to the Earl of Tweeddale, May 1678', *Edinburgh Bibliographical Society Transactions*, 6 (1990), p. 7.
[102] James Cockburn], *Bibliotheca Universalis, or an Historical Accompt of Books, and Transactions of the Learned World* (Edinburgh, 1688), 'Preface'.
[103] Sir John Lauder of Fountainhall, *The Decisions of the Lords of Council and Session from June 6th, 1678 to July 30th, 1712*, 2 vols. (Edinburgh, 1759), I, 502.

Trade then more encourag'd then in the Reign of Tyberius'.[104] In 1698, the republican writer, Andrew Fletcher of Saltoun, celebrated a new climate encouraging freedom of expression, recalling earlier 'tyrannical reigns in which it was a crime to speak of publick affairs' or to suggest 'that the king had received bad counsel in any thing'.[105] Deprived of the benefit of hindsight, in 1687, the radical Covenanter, Alexander Shields, despaired of the increasingly harsh and paranoid controls, complaining that 'reason, if roundly written' was usually 'read with a stammering mouth, which puts a T before it, and then it is stumbled at as Treason'.[106]

From the outset of the Restoration, equally stringent control was also exercised over political views expressed in private correspondence. Even Lauderdale himself had formerly been obliged to devise devious routes for his own private correspondence. In 1664, he informed his intimate confidante, Lady Margaret Kennedy, that he was sending letters for his brother under cover to her, since although 'some people had the curiosity to intercept his letters to me', he hoped that they would not be 'so uncivill as to open yours'.[107] Lauderdale's optimism was, however, misplaced. During the 1670s, for example, Jean, countess of Tweeddale, wrote to her husband objecting to 'that base and barbarous practice' of intercepting private letters that impelled her to make 'sure to write nothing that I cared who see it'.[108] The dangers of sensitive communications falling into unintended hands was confirmed by Lord Advocate Mackenzie who complained to Lauderdale in 1679 that he had seen copies of his own letters being passed to his professional and political rival, Sir George Lockhart of Carnwath. Regarding a particular letter which Mackenzie had evidently desired to 'keep most secret', he insisted to Lauderdale that it had been 'taken out of your pockets by one of your servants', despite Lauderdale's assumption that it must have been 'dropt careleslie in the privie garden' by Lauderdale himself.[109]

In the absence of a centralised mechanism for press regulation along the lines of the English Stationers' Company, it was the Scottish Privy Council, in association with the burgh councils of Edinburgh, Glasgow and Aberdeen, which

---

[104] T.S., *The History of the Affaires of Scotland from the Restauration of King Charles the 2d in the year 1660 &c.* (London, 1690), p. 17.

[105] Andrew Fletcher, 'Two Discourses Concerning the Affairs of Scotland; Written in the Year 1698', in *Political Works*, John Robertson ed. (Cambridge, 1997), p. 34.

[106] [Alexander Shields], *A Hind let loose: Or, An Historical Representation of the Testimonies of the Church of Scotland, for the Interest of Christ; With the true State thereof in all its Periods* ([Edinburgh], 1687), sig. A4v.

[107] Charles Sharpe ed., *Letters from the Lady Margaret Kennedy to John, Duke of Lauderdale* (Edinburgh, 1828), p. 26.

[108] CUL Add. MSS. 9362/8, 'Jean, countess of Tweeddale to the earl of Tweeddale, 28 April [1670s]'.

[109] BL Add. MSS. 23,243, f. 9, 'Sir George Mackenzie to the earl of Lauderdale [1679]'. In an age when political information and intelligence was highly prized, the royalist soldier and author, Sir James Turner, concluded that although advice might be 'written in Cyphers, yet the art of finding Keys for Cyphers is now common; and though a Cypher be unlockt, yet he to whom it is directed, will rationally conclude it was unlockt, and therefore will find it needful to fall upon new resolves. Other manner of writing with illegible ink, are soon found out with fire and water' (Sir James Turner, *Pallas Armata. Military Essayes of the Ancient Grecian, Roman and Modern Art of War. Written in the Years 1670 and 1671. By Sir James Turner, Knight* (London, 1683), p. 263).

exercised the greatest controlling influence on the circulation of ideas by printed and other means within Scotland. Underpinned by long-established laws against both heresy and *lèse-majesté*, legislation against unlicensed printing of political and religious material was passed in November 1661, threatening sanctions of the 'highest peril' unless permission was first obtained. For those who dared to disregard this form of *a priori* censorship, retribution was thorough. In 1664, for instance, the Privy Council received reports that copies of the speech delivered on the scaffold by the condemned Covenanter, Archibald Johnston of Wariston, had been illicitly 'published in print, and publickly vented and sold by booksellers and boyes in the streetts' of Edinburgh. Consequently, orders were given to imprison as many booksellers and vendors as necessary until the Council was able to 'examin how these pamphletts coms to be sold without authority or warrand'.[110] Such constraints even extended to those publications of an overtly royalist disposition. Acting on Charles II's directions in March 1661, the burgh authorities in Edinburgh intervened to close down the first regular newspaper to be produced in Scotland, the *Mercurius Caledonius*, when its irreverent, satirical and anticlerical stance was deemed dangerously controversial.[111]

Government vigilance also extended to cover all forms of news circulation, irrespective of whether or not such material was printed. For although the first public coffee-houses in Scotland were opened in 1673 by John Row in Edinburgh and by Colonel Walter Whiteford in Glasgow, the Edinburgh establishment was closed down within four years when the Privy Council became suspicious of its potential to foster subversive discussion.[112] Following the subsequent re-opening of coffee-houses, the Privy Council instead insisted in 1680 that all 'Gazettes and News-letters read in Coffee-houses' must first be submitted for inspection to the Bishop of Edinburgh or a Council official to ensure that 'false and seditious news and slanders may be prevented'.[113] Such rigorous watchfulness continued in James VII & II's reign when the Privy Council fined and imprisoned several Edinburgh booksellers and printers in 1687, after ordering all stationers to supply catalogues of their stock and to declare on oath the titles of books they had printed, imported or sold during the previous year.[114]

In addition to monitoring the output of individual printers, the Privy Council

---

[110] 'Warrant to Sir Robert Murray of Cameron', *The Register of the Privy Council of Scotland. Third Series. Volume I (1661–1664)*, P. Hume Brown ed. (Edinburgh, 1908), p. 584. For a full account of press censorship during this period, see Mann, *Scottish Book Trade*.

[111] See Julia Buckroyd, '*Mercurius Caledonius* and its immediate successors, 1661', *Scottish Historical Review*, 54 (1975), pp. 11–21.

[112] James Grant, *Cassell's Old and New Edinburgh*, 3 vols. (London, [c.1890]), I, 178 and George Eyre-Todd, *History of Glasgow. Volume II: From the Reformation to the Revolution* (Glasgow, 1931), p. 365.

[113] Lauder of Fountainhall, *Decisions*, I, 73. Regarding the influence of coffee-houses in late-seventeenth century England, see Steve Pincus, ' "Coffee Politicians Does Create": Coffeehouses and Restoration Political Culture', *Journal of Modern History*, 67 (1995), pp. 807–34.

[114] As Fountainhall noticed, however, James Watson, the King's Roman Catholic printer at Holyrood Palace was exempted from this requirement (Lauder of Fountainhall, *Historical Notices*, II, 816).

also adopted a range of *a postiori* measures to regulate the transmission of ideas. Over thirty individual titles were specially banned during the Restoration, some of which were also ordered to be publicly burned, such as the Covenanting manifesto entitled *The Causes of God's Wrath against Scotland*, which had been co-authored by James Guthrie and Johnston of Wariston.[115] After ordering the work to be burned at the Mercat Cross in Edinburgh in October 1660, the Privy Council further proceeded to forbid any persons who possessed or condoned the book from entering within ten miles of Edinburgh while Parliament was sitting between January and July 1661.[116] In 1667, the imposition of fines of up to £2,000 were levied on any individuals who refused to surrender copies of James Stewart and John Stirling's anonymous *Naphtali* to the Edinburgh magistrates by the following February, while the Council not only threatened similar penalties if copies of Steuart's anonymous *Jus Populi Vindicatum* in 1671 were found, but also offered rewards of £100 for information leading to the author's identification. For their part, members of the Stuart administration defended such restrictions on the grounds that 'Licentiousness of the Press' inevitably tended to 'weaken all Government, corrupt all Intelligence, and blast so unavoidably the Reputation of the best, and most Innocent'. As Mackenzie insisted, those subjects who attempted to deny Charles II the 'most necessary Privilege and Prerogative of restraining the Press' were to be equated with those who would seek 'to refuse to the Master of a Ship, the power to prevent its leaking'.[117]

Government policy was, however, equally as proactive as reactive, as government ministers sought to edify the populace to promote loyalism. In July 1680, Charles II ordered that the Covenanters' 'new, villainous and treasonable' declaration issued at Sanquhar be officially printed, so that the people 'may have a just abhorrence of the principles and practises of those villaines'.[118] A similar ambition of seeking to tarnish presbyterian nonconformity with subversive radicalism underpinned the decision to publish particularly extravagant Covenanter manifestoes, such as the 'Queensferry Paper', in London in 1680. Alarmed by the extent of presbyterian extremism, Lauderdale's Anglican chaplain, George Hickes, reproduced a number of Covenanters' dying speeches in London. Seeking to dissuade English nonconformists from making common cause with their Scottish counterparts, Hickes hoped to demonstrate that English dissenters had erroneously assumed the Covenanters to be 'a more rational, and innocent sect' than such testimonies revealed.[119]

---

[115] For a list of these titles, see Mann, *Scottish Book Trade*, pp. 255–7.

[116] Thomson and Innes eds., *Acts of the Parliament of Scotland*, VII, 12.

[117] Sir George Mackenzie, *A Vindication of His Majesties Government and Judicatures in Scotland; from some Aspersions thrown on them by Scandalous Pamphlets and News-books: and Especially with relation to the late Earl of Argyle's Process* (Edinburgh, 1683), p. 1.

[118] 'Letter from his Majesty ordering the Council to print and publish the Declaration and Covenant of Sanquhar', *The Register of the Privy Council of Scotland. Volume VI (1678–1680)*, P. Hume Brown ed. (Edinburgh, 1914), p. 495.

[119] [George Hickes], *The Spirit of Popery speaking out of the Mouths of Phanatical Protestants, or the last Speeches of Mr. John Kid and Mr. John King, Two Presbyterian Ministers, who were Executed for High-Treason and Rebellion, at Edinburgh, August the 14th, 1679* (London, 1680), 'Preface'.

In 1671, the Stuart government had also restricted the Scottish printing trade by granting a monopoly to one printer, Andrew Anderson, which conferred the 'privilege of secluding and debarring all others' from publishing freely.[120] Following Anderson's death in 1679, the exclusive licence passed to his widow, preserving the monopoly until 1712. Although conceived within a spirit of economic protectionism, it was subsequently alleged that by this action 'the Art of Printing in this Kingdom got a dead Stroke', for 'no Printer could print any thing from a Bible to a Ballad' without permission from the Anderson family.[121] Having survived a series of legal challenges seeking to rescind the monopoly during the 1670s and 1680s, representatives of the Anderson family remained convinced that their powerful position was crucial to the maintenance of public order. Were the printing trade to be deregulated, it was thus argued that perfidious individuals would immediately 'import and reprint those scandalous and seditious books whereof they have most gain and advantage', including copies of the Solemn League and Covenant, *Naphtali* and *Jus Populi Vindicatum*.[122] On James VII & II's authority, special dispensation from the monopoly was, however, granted to an Aberdeen Catholic, James Watson, allowing him to establish a printing press within the precincts of the Palace of Holyroodhouse 'so he and his son may print or sell what they please against the Protestants.'[123]

The imposition of press censorship not only curtailed the spread of political and religious ideas throughout Restoration Scotland, but also served to retard the development of the domestic printing industry. During the civil wars, the royalist author, Sir Thomas Urquhart of Cromarty, had alleged that '[m]any learned books written in Scotland, for want of able and skillful printers and other necessaries requisite for works of such liberal undertaking have perished'.[124] Within Scotland, the monopoly powers granted to the Anderson family came under further criticism in 1671 when the Privy Council was obliged to confess that 'great danger may ensue to the christian religion' from Andrew Anderson's recent publication of a version of the New Testament found to contain 'many grosse errours and faultes'. To avoid the imposition of a substantial fine, all copies in circulation were immediately ordered to be

---

[120] Thomson and Innes eds., *Acts of the Parliament of Scotland*, VIII, 206–7.
[121] William Couper ed., *Watson's 'Preface' to the 'History of Printing', 1713* (Edinburgh, 1913), p. 49. For more on this monopoly, see William Couper, 'Mrs. Anderson and the Royal Prerogative in Printing', *Proceedings of the Royal Philosophical Society of Glasgow*, 48 (1916–17), pp. 79–102 and Alastair Mann, 'Book Commerce, Litigation and the Art of Monopoly: The Case of Agnes Campbell, Royal Printer, 1676–1712', *Scottish Economic and Social History*, 18 (1998), pp. 132–56.
[122] 'Answers for James Anderson, His Majesty's Printer, and Agnes Campbell, his mother, to the petition of Robert Sanders, printer in Glasgow', in *The Spottiswoode Miscellany: A Collection of original Papers and Tracts, illustrative chiefly of the Civil and Ecclesiastical History of Scotland. Volume I*, James Maidment ed. (Edinburgh, 1844), p. 308.
[123] Lauder of Fountainhall, *Historical Notices*, II, 816. For more on the output of this press, see William Cowan, 'The Holyrood Press, 1686–1688', *Edinburgh Bibliographical Society Transactions*, 6 (1904), pp. 83–100. In February 1681, a similar monopoly granting the sole right of issuing playing cards had been conferred upon Watson's eventual successor, the German Catholic, Peter Bruce, who owned a paper factory at Canonmills, near Edinburgh.
[124] Sir Thomas Urquhart, *The Jewel*, R. D. S. Jack and R. J. Lyall eds. (Edinburgh, 1983), p. 173.

recalled and corrected.[125] When the Anderson monopoly expired, the printing trade was eventually released from government control. As the son of the erst-while Holyrood printer, James Watson, contended in 1713, since Scotland has 'at present so many good Spirits and Abundance of more Authors than in any former Age', it was imperative that the domestic printing trade be rendered equally professional. Were that to be the case, Watson remained confident that Scots authors would then 'need not, as many of our former Authors have been forc'd to do, go to other Countries to publish their Writings, lest a learn'd Book, should be spoil'd by an ignorant or careless Printer'.[126]

Forms of government restriction in late-seventeenth century Scotland were not, however, designed to eliminate all forms of political criticism or to promote the adoption of a uniform ideology. With reference to early modern England, Glenn Burgess has argued that censorship was only exercised in 'circumstances where words were likely to incite people to particular actions'. Hence official sanctions were deployed not against 'words as such, but words used in contexts where they could create political and social disobedience'.[127] Even so, not all Restoration Scots were convinced about the practical effectiveness of govern-ment stringency. In 1667, for instance, the Privy Council ordered the public burning of Steuart and Stirling's anonymously-issued *Naphtali* which had been described by one appalled reader as 'displaying all that a Toung set on fire by hell can say'.[128] But as Bishop Andrew Honyman of Orkney acknowledged, 'one fire cannot destroy all the copies', nor serve to 'satisfie the minds of these who carry them about as Books of devotion'.[129] Having observed another public burning of a copy of the mid-century 'Solemn League and Covenant' at the Mercat Cross in Edinburgh in 1682, for example, Lauder of Fountainhall simi-larly questioned the political prudence of 'reviving the memory of so old and buried a legend', surmising that it only served to 'set peeple now a-work to buy it, and read it'.[130] Having surveyed the tightly-controlled environment within which royalist ideas found expression in Restoration Scotland, the next chapter looks in more detail at those very ideas to which Honyman and Lauder of Fountainhall referred.

---

[125] 'Prohibition of the sale of copies of the New Testament &c.' in *The Register of the Privy Council of Scotland. Third Series. Volume III (1669–1672)*, P. Hume Brown ed. (Edinburgh, 1910), p. 292.
[126] Couper, *Watson's Preface*, p. 44.
[127] Glenn Burgess, *Absolute Monarchy and the Stuart Constitution* (New Haven, 1996), p. 7.
[128] Airy ed., *Lauderdale Papers*, II, 88.
[129] Andrew Honyman], *Survey of Naphtali. Part II. Discoursing of the Heads proposed in the Preface of the former. Together with an examination of the Doctrines of the Apolog. Narration concerning the King's Supremacy in and about Ecclesiastick Affairs, and the Obligation of the Covenants* (Edinburgh, 1669), p. 2.
[130] Lauder of Fountainhall, *Historical Notices*, I, 346.

3

The Origins and Nature of the Scottish Monarchy

Charles II's return to power was accompanied by a widespread determination that political authority should never again be allowed to disintegrate in the fatal manner that had unleashed the miseries of the recent civil wars. A renewed political Augustinianism dictated that government was essential to 'bridle the Extravagancies of restless Mankind', in the words of Mackenzie of Rosehaugh.[1] Preaching a thanksgiving sermon to celebrate the restoration in 1660, the Aberdeen minister, Alexander Scrougie, confirmed that magistracy was so indispensable that 'better no Creation, then no Government; better not to be at all, then not to be under Rule'.[2] Since government represented the 'vital spirits of humane Societies', Bishop Andrew Honyman of Orkney therefore insisted that keen attention be paid to those 'Nerves and Sinews' in the body politic 'without which there could be no right motion'.[3]

Believing themselves to be subjects of the most ancient monarchy in the world, early modern Scots universally identified the monarch as the political authority to whom obligation was owed. In the 1580s, the absolutist lawyer, Adam Blackwood, had celebrated the Scottish monarchy's antiquity and integrity by wondering if any other royal dynasty existed in the world that, having begun 'nineteen hundred years ago in one nation, survives among them even today?'[4] Charles II's restoration prompted the reiteration of such claims by royalist pamphleteers, eager to extol the fact that monarchy had been 'the form of State Policy in Scotland neer these 2000 yeers'.[5] In similar vein, Sir James Dalrymple, Viscount Stair, dedicated his weighty *Institutions of the Law of Scotland* to Charles in 1681, acknowledging that although Scotland might not rank

---

[1] Mackenzie, *Jus Regium*, p. 123.
[2] Alexander Scrougie, *Mirabilia Dei, or Britannia Gaudio Exultans. Opened in a Congratulatory Sermon for the safe Return of our Gracious Soveraign and happy Restitution to the full and free exercise of His Royall Authoritie Preached on the 14th June, 1660* (Edinburgh, 1660), 'Dedication'.
[3] [Honyman], *Survey of the Insolent and Infamous Libel entituled Naphtali*, p. 1.
[4] Quoted by J. H. Burns, 'George Buchanan and the antimonarchomachs', in Mason ed., *Scots and Britons*, p. 152.
[5] J. I., *Short Treatise*, 'Dedication', p. 2.

among the most rich and potent kingdoms in the world, he doubted that any nation could rival the Scots' adherence to 'one blood and lineage, without any mixture . . . above 2000 years'.[6]

Attachment to the Stuart monarchy could thus be perceived as axiomatic. As Mackenzie later observed of the Scots nation in his Restoration memoirs, 'so remarkable was our loyalty to the world', that it was 'believed and presumed in all places where our nation travelled, whither in England or beyond Sea, that a Scot was still a Royalist'.[7] In 1682, Alexander Mudie published an account of Scottish political affairs that he dedicated to Charles II's natural son, the ten-year-old duke of Richmond, who had been appointed Governor of Dumbarton Castle the previous year. As Mudie sought to impress upon Richmond, 'no King in Christendom, nor other Potentate received from His Subjects more Reverence, Honour and Respect' than the monarch of Scotland.[8] Preaching in St. Giles' Cathedral on James VII & II's birthday in 1687, John MackQueen likewise reminded his congregation that the Scots nation was so 'fam'd all the World over for its Loyalty and Courage', that 'until our late unhappy Times; a Scots Traytor was of Old as contradictory, as a Drunken Christian, or an Innocent Robber'.[9]

The historical evidence required to sustain such claims derived from a medieval myth of national origin, largely created by the fourteenth-century chantry priest, John of Fordun, who had systematised various contradictory myths concerning the elopement of the eponymous heroine, the Greek princess, Scota. The daughter of an Egyptian Pharoah, Scota and her successors had allegedly travelled through Spain and Ireland before finally settling in Scotland. The first Scottish monarchy had thereafter been founded in 330 BC by their descendant, the mythical Fergus MacFerquhard. Fordun's narrative later formed the basis for Scotland's first humanist history, Hector Boece's *Scotorum Historiae* (1527) which elaborated Scotland's mythic history since the arrival of Gathelus and Scota, by inventing a succession of kings who delivered lengthy speeches to describe the intervening political events. In addition to providing an account of the origins of the Scottish monarchy, the Gathelus-Scota myth also became the polemical device by which medieval and early modern Scots rebutted English claims that the Scots had traditionally paid homage to their English superiors. The English, in turn, derived such notions of historical superiority from their rival 'Brutus' myth which claimed that, on his original founding of Britain, Brutus the Trojan had divided the island among his three sons, giving England

---

6   Dalrymple, Viscount Stair, *Institutions*, 'Dedication'.
7   Sir George Mackenzie, *Memoirs of the Affairs of Scotland from the Restoration of King Charles II A.D.M.DC.L.X.*, Thomas Thomson ed. (Edinburgh, 1822), p. 27.
8   [Alexander Mudie], *Scotiæ Indiculum: or the Present State of Scotland. Together with divers Reflections Upon the Antient State thereof* (London, 1682), p. 36.
9   John MackQueen, *God's Interest in the King, set forth in forth in a Sermon Preached in the Cathedral of Edinburgh, October the 14th, At the Anniversary Commemoration of his Majesties Birth* (London, 1687), pp. 29–30.

to his eldest son, Locrinus, Wales to his second son, Kamber, and Scotland to his youngest son, Albanactus.[10]

Scottish attachment to the Stuart monarchy was thus distinctively Scottish, although Mackenzie granted that 'every honest man in Scotland rejoyces, when they hear of the Prosperity of the Royal Family in England . . . a Union in Principles, being stronger than that of Kingdoms'.[11] The negative legacy of the Cromwellian occupation had also discredited formal unionism, considerably eroding Scots' enthusiasm for closer associations with their English neighbours. As the earl of Lothian observed in May 1660, for instance, while 'we are in another world againe and there are people newe modelling this land', he insisted that 'we must be a free Independent nation, brethren and Good friends . . . under one soveraigne and Head, but no parte of England'.[12] Charles II apparently agreed. According to his chief political advisor in England, Edward Hyde, earl of Clarendon, Charles had declared that he 'would not build according to Cromwell's models', apparently preferring to keep Scotland 'within its own limits and bounds, and sole dependence on himself'.[13] Nevertheless, the practical manner in which the Restoration had been accomplished may have served to increase Scottish suspicions of English intentions. For as Clarendon recognised, the Scots had long feared that an eventual consequence of absentee monarchy might result in their gradually being 'reduced to but a province of England'.[14] Hence, although the future Scottish Chancellor, the earl of Rothes, confessed with relief in April 1660 that 'our redemption from slavery is very near', other Scots were more circumspect.[15] Preaching a thanksgiving sermon in Aberdeen later that year, John Paterson wondered 'that an English Generall, an English Army, an English Parliament, should have been the Instruments of Scotland's Deliverance'. Such a sequence of events was indeed 'lyke a Dreame'.[16]

This chapter examines theories of monarchical government current in late-seventeenth century Scotland to illustrate the different ways in which Charles II's restoration to power was conceptualised. For although the Stuart monarch was universally identified as the source of political authority to whom obligation was owed, fundamental differences surrounded the nature and extent of this

---

[10] See Roger Mason, 'Scotching the Brut: Politics, History and the National Myth of Origins in Sixteenth-century Britain', in Roger Mason ed., *Scotland and England 1286–1815* (Edinburgh, 1987), pp. 60–84. For more on the Gathelus-Scota myth, see William Skene ed., *John of Fordun's Chronicle of the Scottish Nation*, 2 vols. (Lampeter, 1993); E. Cowan, 'Myth and Identity in early medieval Scotland', *Scottish Historical Review*, 53 (1984), pp. 11–25 and W. Matthews, 'The Egyptians in Scotland: The Political History of a Myth', *Viator*, 1 (1970), pp. 289–306.
[11] Mackenzie, *Vindication of his Majesties Government & Judicatures*, p. 2.
[12] Tollemache MSS., MS. 1041, 'Earl of Lothian to the Earl of Lauderdale, 8 May 1660'.
[13] Quoted by Godfrey Davies and Paul H. Hardacre, 'The Restoration of the Scottish Episcopacy, 1660–1661', *Journal of British Studies*, 1 (1960), p. 34.
[14] Hyde (Earl of Clarendon), *History*, I, 113.
[15] EUL MSS. Dc.4.46, 'Earl of Rothes to Earl of Lauderdale, 6 April 1660'.
[16] John Paterson, *Post nubila Phoebus. Or, A Sermon of Thanksgiving For the safe and happy return of our gracious Soveraign, to his Ancient Dominions, and Restauration to His just and Native Dignity, Royalties and Government* (Aberdeen, 1660), p. 15.

sovereignty. Understanding the manner in which Fergus MacFerquhard had been crowned king of Scotland in 330 BC thus remained pivotal to political philosophising as adherents and opponents alike of the Restoration monarchy derived theoretical inspiration from the prescriptive character of Scottish historical ideology.

I

When James VI acceded to the English throne as James I in 1603, his claim of hereditary right triumphed over the obstacles of a statutory bar and his legally 'alien' status as a Scot. His accession thus ensured that, in England at any rate, hereditary right became increasingly synonymous with monarchical legitimacy. Since many seventeenth-century Scots considered themselves members of the most ancient monarchy in the world, sustaining the defence of the hereditary Stuart monarchy was, however, inextricably associated with expressions of national identity. Describing how the heir to the throne immediately assumed power 'at the very moment of the expiring of the king reigning', James had denounced as invalid attempts to preclude hereditary succession by statutory means or by allegations of heresy in his *Trew Law of Free Monarchies* of 1598.[17] At the time of his accession to the English throne, James' case was strongly supported in a manuscript treatise composed by the Scots lawyer, Thomas Craig of Riccarton, who accounted hereditary succession to be 'Natural Justice, or the Natural Law', since it was superior to any other legal rights and was itself 'the Fountain and cause of all Laws'.[18]

During the Restoration, the pre-eminence of hereditary succession was comprehensively defended by Mackenzie of Rosehaugh who likewise insisted that 'this Right of Succession flows from the Law of Nature' and was thus discernible by every rational individual. Citing Craig extensively, Mackenzie defined the principle of hereditary succession as that 'which gives life and authority' to Scottish statutes, thus bearing 'the undeniable Marks and Characters of a Fundamental Right in all Nations'.[19] During the 1670s, Mackenzie sought to arrange for the posthumous publication of Craig's Latin manuscript, but was frustrated in his attempts when informed by Edinburgh printers that 'the English Stationers hav assurd them they will not vent many Latin books printed in Scotland'. For Mackenzie, this obstructive attitude merely revealed

---

[17] James VI & I, 'The Trew Law', in *Political Writings*, p. 82.

[18] Thomas Craig, *The Right of Succession to the Kingdom of England. In Two Books; Against the Sophisms of Parsons the Jesuite, Who assum'd the Name of Doleman, By which he endeavours to overthrow not only the Rights of Succession in Kingdoms, but also the Sacred Authority of Kings themselves*, J. Gatherer ed. (London, 1703), pp. 108, 111. For a fuller account of seventeenth-century English succession debates, see Howard Nenner, *The Right to be King: The Succession to the Crown of England 1603–1714* (Basingstoke, 1995).

[19] Sir George Mackenzie, *That the Lawful Successor Cannot be Debarr'd from Succeeding to the Crown: Maintain'd against Dolman, Buchannan [sic], and others* (London, 1684), p. 149. This treatise was appended to Mackenzie's *Jus Regium* and hence the pagination runs continuously.

characteristic English 'malice & ignorance' and a recognition that 'we exceed them by farre in latin as they doe us in English' that arose 'from ther not understanding that language'.[20]

Theoretical debates concerning monarchical succession acquired particular urgency during the late-1670s and early-1680s, when unsuccessful attempts were made by Whig members of the English Parliament to debar the hereditary heir, James, duke of York, from succession to the English crown on account of his Roman Catholicism. On two separate occasions between 1679 and 1682, Charles II sent his brother to Edinburgh, in the capacity of parliamentary High Commissioner, to remove him from the volatile political atmosphere in England generated by exclusionist endeavours. Nevertheless, members of the English Parliament remained keenly aware of the dangers posed by dynastic uncertainty within the multiple monarchy. As a secretary to the duke of York, Sir William Coventry informed the House of Commons in May 1679 that if the Scots 'set him up for a king, whom you acknowledge not', then the Scots would thus 'set up such a thorn in your sides, by the help of France, that you will never be able to get it out'.[21] Under York's presidency in 1681, the Scottish Parliament accordingly apprised Charles II of its intention to 'let your other Kingdoms and all the World see' that any attempt to divert the hereditary succession would necessarily incur 'the utter Subversion of the Fundamental Laws of this your Majesties Ancient Kingdom'.[22] To this end, the assembly proceeded to confirm fully the indefeasibility of hereditary succession by passing a Succession Act which held that since Scottish kings derived 'their Royall power from God almightie alone', their succession was solely governed by proximity of blood and could not be altered by parliamentary statute.[23]

The implications of this legislation were indeed clearly intended to travel beyond Scotland. Not only did the Act serve to reinforce recognition that the crown of Scotland was independent and distinct from the crowns of England and Ireland, but the effective creation of a reversionary interest served an unambiguous warning to exclusionist members of the English Parliament. As the duke of York's biographer later recorded, the 'world was surprised' at this testimony of loyalty, since Scotland had 'been alwayes looked upon as the fountain of Presbiterie', but had now chosen to assert the royal prerogative 'when England it self flew so furiously in its face'.[24] With hindsight, subsequent generations of Scottish pamphleteers drew attention to the significance of the Parliament's

---

[20] EUL MSS. La.III.354, 'Sir George Mackenzie to the earl of Lauderdale, 8 April [1670s]', f. 70.

[21] Anchitell Grey ed., *Debates of the House of Commons, from the Year 1664 to the Year 1694*, 10 vols. (London, 1768), VII, 257.

[22] Charles II, *His Majesties Gracious Letter to His Parliament of Scotland. With the Speech of His Royal Highness the Duke, His Majesties High Commissioner, At the Opening of Parliament at Edinburgh, the 28th Day of July, 1681. Together with The Parliaments most Loyal and Dutiful Answer to his Majesties Letter* (London, 1681), p. 7.

[23] Thomson and Innes eds., *Acts of the Parliament of Scotland*, VIII, 238–9.

[24] J. S. Clarke, *The Life of James the Second, King of England, &c. Collected out of Memoirs writ of his own hand. Together with the King's Advice to his Son, and his Majesty's Will*, 2 vols. (London, 1816), I, 697.

actions. As a manuscript pamphleteer informed William of Orange in 1689, for example, maintaining harmonious relations with the Edinburgh legislature was imperative, for had James been unable to rely on 'the countenance & concurrence of Scotland' during this critical juncture, it was 'very probable that the bill of exclusione [*sic*] had gone against him'.[25] Pressing for an incorporating union between Scotland and England in 1707, the presbyterian lawyer, Sir Francis Grant, therefore deemed it essential that, henceforth, no monarch should be allowed to 'play one of the Kingdoms against the other', recalling the way in which 'Scotland did almost nail Ruine on England' by enacting the Succession Act of 1681.[26]

Scottish concern for the sanctity of hereditary succession could, however, be interpreted more cynically. In 1682, an English pamphlet entitled *Scotch Politicks* attacked 'the usual Obscurity of Scotch Integrity and Principles', claiming that it was a maxim of state that the political actions of smaller countries were never governed by first principles. The Scottish decision to pass the Succession Act was not, therefore, to be understood as representing a permanent commitment to the principle of hereditary succession, but merely as an opportunistic device that would enable the Scots to retain such a 'variety of Prospects' as would maximise room for future manoeuvre.[27] The efficacy of such tactics was duly proven in the early-1700s, when the Scottish Parliament exploited its potential to adopt an uncompromising and independent stance over the same issue of dynastic succession within the multiple monarchy.

Despite such English casuistry, Restoration royalists in Scotland who sought to vindicate the duke of York's hereditary claim returned to the arguments earlier advanced by James VI & I and Craig. Arguing that succession itself purged the successor of all constitutional impediments, including a different confessional persuasion, alien status, treason or bastardy, Mackenzie pointed out that it would be 'absurd that he who can restore all other men' from such defects could not be restored himself. Recalling the capricious manner in which members of the English Parliament had decided to dethrone the piously Protestant monarch, Charles I, he insisted that advancing such arguments would serve only to 'allow that Arbitrariness against our Kings, which we would not allow in them to us'. As far as Mackenzie himself was concerned, an impious Protestant monarch remained 'a worse Governor, and less Gods Viceregent and Image' than a devout Roman Catholic monarch.[28]

Such loyalist sentiments were also echoed in Gaelic literature. As parliamentary High Commissioner in the early 1680s, the duke of York had attempted to abolish feudal jurisdictions, earning popularity among smaller Highland clans

---

[25] NAS GD 406/M9/200/10, 'A Memorial discussing past relations between the Scots parliament and England and advising King William of the benefits and necessity of good relations with the Scots parliament [1689]'.

[26] [Sir Francis Grant], *The Patriot Resolved. To an Addresser, from his Friend; of the same Sentiments with himself; concerning the Union* ([Edinburgh], 1707), p. 22.

[27] ['J.S.'], *Scotch Politicks, In a Letter to a Friend* (London, 1682), pp. 2, 7.

[28] Mackenzie, *Lawful Successor*, pp. 169, 175–6.

and enhancing traditional notions of clan fidelity to the monarch. Attachment to the indefeasibility of hereditary monarchical succession was expressed, for instance, by the Glencoe bard, Aonghus MacAlasdair Ruaibh:

> Chan eil e ceadaicht' dhiunn claonadh,
> No 'n righ saoghalta mhùchadh,
> 'S gur e 'n t-oigre fior dhlgheach,
> O'n a ghineadh o thùs e;
> Chan fhaod deifir an creidimh,
> No neo-chreidimh ar taladh,
> 'S gun ùghdaras laghail,
> Is gniomh foilleil dhuinn àicheadh.

(It is not permissible for us to turn aside from, or suppress our temporal king, for, from the moment he was first conceived, he was the true rightful heir. No difference of faith, or (even) lack of faith, may draw us away; without lawful authority it is a treacherous thing for us to renounce him).[29]

From a jurisprudential perspective, it could also be argued that altering the hereditary succession contravened notions of equity since the monarch only enjoyed the same right to possess the throne as the hereditary heir did to succeed. Similarly, in Scots private law, although an individual could alter the succession of his own estates by application to Parliament, he could not alter the succession in his own individual capacity. Neither the Scottish nor the English Parliament was, however, competent to alter monarchical succession since the monarch's estate was not at the disposal of either nation. The care and attention traditionally paid to legal issues of posterity had been observed by Craig as reflecting the instinctive human tendency to 'affect or covet Diuturnity; which Christians call immortality'. Hence there was no reason why children of the Stuart dynasty should be 'defrauded of the Just reward of their Fathers merits and virtues' or of their right to succeed them any more than the descendants of private individuals.[30]

Increasingly sophisticated means were employed to celebrate what was widely regarded as the 'uninterrupted Obedience', given by the Scots 'to an Hundred and Ten Kings, in two Thousand Years Time, by exact Calculation'.[31] At the restoration, for instance, one ardent royalist, Walter Chieslie, arranged for a Latin motto declaring *nobis haec invicta miserunt 108 proavi* ('to us these things unimpaired 108 ancestors have sent') to adorn the drawing-room ceiling of his residence at Dalry House, near Edinburgh.[32] In 1683, this universal interest in the history of the venerable Scottish monarchy was given iconographic status

---

[29] Archibald J. Macdonald and Angus Macdonald eds., *The Macdonald Collection of Gaelic Poetry* (Inverness, 1911), p. 80.
[30] Craig, *Right of Succession*, pp. 109–10.
[31] Sir George Mackenzie, 'A Discourse concerning The three Unions between Scotland and England', in *The Works of that Eminent and Learned Lawyer, Sir George Mackenzie of Rosehaugh &c.*, [Thomas Ruddiman ed.], 2 vols. (Edinburgh, 1718–22), II, 650.
[32] J. Smith, 'Dalry House: Its Lands and Owners', *Book of the Old Edinburgh Club*, 20 (1935), p. 27.

by Charles II who commissioned the Dutch painter, Jacob de Wet, to produce 111 portraits of the entire line of Stuart kings to hang in the palace at Holyrood. Deeming the impressive series to be 'a very pretty show', Lauder of Fountainhall pointed out how de Wet had 'guessed at the figure of ther faces' for monarchs before the seventeenth century by drawing inspiration from images used at Charles I's coronation in 1633.[33] Since a similar public pageant of 'all the kings heertofore of Scotland' had been mounted when James VI's new wife, Anne of Denmark, had entered Edinburgh in 1590, the Holyrood display drew on a familiar and venerable traditional of iconographic royalism.[34]

Apart from the visual message vividly displayed, a considerable amount of intellectual energy was devoted during the Restoration to proving the historical validity of the hereditary line depicted in the Holyrood portraits. One of the more disputed events was, for instance, the succession of Robert III in 1390. Those who sought to challenge hereditary succession cited a range of historical authorities, including Boece, to claim that the succession had been diverted when Robert II's elder lawful sons by his first marriage had been passed over by Act of Parliament, in preference to the issue of his second marriage, the future Robert III. Dismissing such allegations, Mackenzie jettisoned Boece's account as flawed, opining that in such an important case, 'Historians should be little credited, except they could have produc'd very infallible Documents', since it was common for one erroneous historical claim quickly to assume authoritative status. Burgeoning interest in suggestions that, historically, the Scottish monarchy had perhaps been sporadically elective was reflected by an enquiry made to Mackenzie in 1681 by Archbishop William Sancroft of Canterbury. Expressing concern that 'ye Licentiousness of your English press should allow such debates to be cryed up and down your streets', Mackenzie quickly reassured Sancroft that, from the evidence available, it appeared that the Scots Parliament had not altered the succession, but had only acknowledged the true successor formally in order to thwart 'the usurping hopes of an illegall pretender'.[35]

In the mid-1680s, Mackenzie also became involved in a protracted pamphlet dispute with another Anglican bishop, William Lloyd of St. Asaph, whose researches into the ancient origins of the Welsh episcopate had obliged him to conclude that the Scots could not have settled Scotland until the sixth century. Seeking to demonstrate, as Lauder of Fountainhall put it, 'how injurious the

33 Lauder of Fountainhall, *Historical Observes*, p. 156. An accompanying regnal history was published by William Alexander in 1685 entitled *Medulla Historiæ Scoticæ. Being a Comprehensive History of the Reigns of the Kings of Scotland from Fergus I to Charles II* (London, 1685). For more on the Holyrood portraits, see S. Bruce and S. Yearley, 'The Social Construction of Tradition: The Restoration Portraits and the Kings of Scotland', in David McCrone, Stephen Kendrick and Pat Straw eds., *The Making of Scotland: Nation, Culture and Social Change* (Edinburgh, 1989), pp. 175–87.
34 Quoted by Roger A. Mason, 'George Buchanan, James VI and the presbyterians', in Mason ed., *Scots and Britons*, p. 119. More than a century later, Daniel Defoe was touring Glamis Castle where he observed four brass garden statues of James VI, Charles I, Charles II and James VII. According to Defoe, Charles I was 'booted and spurr'd, as if going to take horse at the head of his army', while Charles II was 'habited a la Hero, which the World knows the nothing of about him' (Daniel Defoe, *Tour of Great Britain*, 1727 edition, p. 700).
35 BL Add. MSS. 4297, 'Sir George Mackenzie to Archbishop Sancroft, September 1681', f. 13r.

Bischop is, not only to our wholle nation, but to our kings', in 'loping of 45 of ther royall ancestors', Mackenzie published *A Defence of the Antiquity of the Royal Line of Scotland* in 1685.[36] Producing his own account of the foundations of the Scottish monarchy, Mackenzie confessed his surprise that the majority of English subjects did not regard the bishop's attempts to curtail the extent of Charles II's royal ancestry as treasonable. Following the entry of Bishop Edward Stillingfleet of Worcester into the debate on Lloyd's side, Mackenzie was, however, compelled to issue another treatise in 1686 acknowledging that both clerics were 'angry at me, tho' the King's Advocate, for daring to say that this was a kind of Lèse-Majesté', conceding that he had intended the term 'in a rhetorical, and not in a legal Sense'.[37] Mackenzie's ideological stance subsequently supplied irresistible inspiration for Sir Walter Scott's novel, *The Antiquary* (1816), in conveying the passions that could be provoked by rival antiquarian interpretations of the ancient Fergusian constitution. Effectively paraphrasing Mackenzie, the Jacobite character, Sir Arthur Wardour, claimed he would have 'deemed himself guilty of the crime of leze-majesty had he doubted the existence of any single individual of that formidable bead-roll' of Stuart monarchs 'whose portraits still frown grimly upon the walls of the gallery of Holyrood.'[38]

II

The iconographic apotheosis of Stuart loyalism depicted in the Holyrood portraits was accompanied by a concomitant triumph of royalist political ideology. In his *Two Treatises of Government*, published in 1689, John Locke had witnessed how in England, 'a generation of men has sprung up among us' intent on seeking to 'flatter princes with an Opinion, that they have a Divine Right to absolute Power'.[39] This phenomenon was also apparent north of the border, where one anonymous observer agreed that the same 'Doctrine, in this last Age, has been so importunately obtruded upon People both from the Pulpit and the Press' that the majority of Scots 'believed it to be a Truth, without ever examining it'.[40]

Accompanying Charles II's restoration in Scotland was thus considerable support for belief in the divine right of kings, whereby God appointed rulers as his representatives on earth, meaning that the laws enacted by such rulers derived from their God-given right and could effectively be regarded as God's laws. In the first Scots Parliament of the Restoration, the notorious Rescissory

---

[36] Lauder of Fountainhall, *Historical Observes*, p. 155.
[37] Sir George Mackenzie, 'The Antiquity of the Royal Line of Scotland, further cleared and defended, against the Exceptions lately offered by Doctor Stillingfleet, in his Vindication of the Bishop of St. Asaph', in *Works*, II, 400.
[38] Sir Walter Scott, *The Antiquary*, David Hewitt ed. (Edinburgh, 1995), p. 38.
[39] John Locke, *Two Treatises of Government*, Peter Laslett ed. (Cambridge, 1988), p. 142.
[40] Anon., *Vindication of the Proceedings of the Convention of the Estates*, p. 15.

Act of 1661 was passed, effectively rescinding all parliamentary legislation enacted since 1633. According to the wording of the Act, such legislation could be retrospectively declared illegal since the Covenanting Parliaments had ignored the 'sacred right inherent to the imperiall Croun' which 'his Majestie holds imediately of God Almighty alone'.[41] The unambiguous purpose of Mackenzie's *Jus Regium*, published in 1684, was likewise to prove that 'our Monarchs derive not their Right from the People, but are absolute Monarchs, deriving their Royal Authority immediately from God Almighty'.[42] The divine character of monarchy was lauded by numerous clerics, such as the Edinburgh minister, John MackQueen, who observed in 1687 that 'as Monarchy hath its Original from God' who directly settled that political model among the Jews, so it also bore 'more lively Vestigies of his Government of the World, than any other'.[43] Dismissing all suggestions that the government of Scotland was based on the unstable constitutive power of the community, this theory of the divine right of kings had been most clearly articulated at the end of the sixteenth century by James VI & I, for whom kingship represented the 'trew paterne of Diuinitie'.[44]

Associated with such ideas of the monarch as God's Vicegerent were notions which sought to identify royal with patriarchal power and adhered to beliefs in natural subjection by attacking rival theories of natural freedom which endowed men with the ability to determine particular governmental forms. As James VI & I had insisted, by natural law, 'the King becomes a naturall Father to all his Lieges at his Coronation'.[45] Patriarchalist theory had been most conspicuously advanced in Scotland during the 1640s by the former bishop of Ross, John Maxwell, who, in upholding the view that '*Monarchia fundatur in paterno jure*' supported the notion that political power was identical with the natural power exercised by a father over his children.[46] During the Restoration, Mackenzie likewise postulated that 'if we consider exactly our Historians, we shall find, that our Kings reign over us by this Paternal Power'.[47] Since God had intended Adam's children to remain subject to Adam, as all future offspring would remain subject to their parents, notions of original freedom were thus spurned. In 1689, the university authorities at St. Andrews similarly affirmed their allegiance to James VII & II by asserting that indefeasible hereditary monarchy remained natural, being a 'Draught of the Paternal or Patriarchall Power from which it had its Original'. Dismissing naturalistic arguments to the contrary, the University's address also made clear that men were 'not dropt from the clouds',

---

41 Thomson and Innes eds., *Acts of the Parliament of Scotland*, VII, 86–7.
42 Mackenzie, *Jus Regium*, p. 13.
43 MackQueen, *God's Interest in the King*, p. 4.
44 James VI & I, 'The Trew Law of Free Monarchies: or, The Reciprock and mutuall duetie betwixt a free King and his naturall Subjects', in *Political Writings*, p. 64.
45 *Ibid.*, p. 65.
46 [John Maxwell], *Sacro-Sancta Regum Majestas; Or, The Sacred and Royall Prerogative of Christian Kings* (Oxford, 1644), p. 85.
47 Mackenzie, *Jus Regium*, p. 26.

but born and raised within families, providing sufficient evidence 'to destroy the vain pretence' of men's original freedom and equality.[48]

Notwithstanding the potency of such ideas, it was increasingly accepted by divine-right theorists that, whilst in Scripture, God had intervened directly by appointing a king for the Israelites, divinely-endowed kings elsewhere acquired their thrones by more indirect means. Despite the affinity for patriarchal theories of writers like Maxwell and Mackenzie, there was no attempt in Scotland to imitate the controversies surrounding the ideas of the seventeenth-century English patriarchalist, Sir Robert Filmer, whose political works were often misrepresented as implying that the authority of the Stuart kings derived in lineal descent from God's dominion of the world to Adam.[49] While Honyman, for example, perceived a 'full parity and agreement' between paternal powers and those of magistrates and kings, he acknowledged that 'Kings are not Fathers of our flesh, or by generation, neither can they truly be called so'.[50] For while paternal and political powers remained distinct from one another, Honyman recognised that they could coincide in one individual, as had probably been the case in those forms of government described in the Old Testament. During the civil wars, Maxwell had outlined a form of designation theory by explaining that, while there could be some signal act that involved, for example, election, succession or conquest, such human intervention only extended to designation. Hence although the king might appear to be appointed by the people, 'the reall constitution, the collation of Soveraignty and Royalty is immediately from God'.[51] Preaching in a similar vein before the first Parliament of the Restoration on 1 January 1661, the former Moderator of the presbyterian General Assembly, Robert Douglas, reminded the legislature that royal power originally resided in God, 'though conveyed and derived from God to the man, Judge or King, with the consent and agreement of the people'.[52]

In place of Adamite descent therefore, several monarchical theories were underpinned by an interpretation of Boece's Scottish history that accorded prime importance to military conquest. At the time when Scota and her followers settled in Ireland, their neighbours across the Irish Sea were being oppressed by the Picts and Britons. A deputation was sent from Scotland to seek Irish military help from one Ferquhard, who dispatched his son, Fergus, to assist the beleaguered tribes and successfully secured them against their enemies. According to Mackenzie therefore, after Fergus' victory, the heads of the Scottish tribes not only acknowledged him as king, but also 'swore that they should never admit of any other Form of Government then Monarchy; and that they

---

[48] *The Addres* [*sic*] *of the University of St. Andrews to the King* (London, 1689), p. 12.
[49] See Sir Robert Filmer, 'Patriarcha: A Defence of the Naturall Power of Kinges Defended against the Unnatural Liberty of the People', in *Patriarcha and other Writings*, Johann P. Sommerville ed. (Cambridge 1991) and W. H. Greenleaf, 'Filmer's Patriarchal History', *Historical Journal*, 9 (1966), pp. 157–71.
[50] [Honyman], *Survey of the Insolent and Infamous Libel entituled Naphtali*, p. 29.
[51] [Maxwell], *Sacro-Sancta Regum Majestas*, p. 22.
[52] Robert Douglas, *Master Dowglasse his Sermon, Preach'd at the Down-sitting of this last Parliament of Scotland, 1661* (London, 1661), p. 4.

should never obey any except Him and his Posterity'.[53] A similar version of conquest theory had earlier been employed by James VI & I who had maintained that Fergus had arrived in Scotland from Ireland, 'making himself master of the countrey, by his owne friendship and force'.[54] In this manner, 330 BC was regarded as the decisive moment in Scottish history when authority was vested in the Fergusian line through divine designation manifested by military conquest. Emphasis upon divine designation also reduced the possibility that such claims could be nullified should the historical records regarding this alleged conquest subsequently be proved inaccurate.

Ideas of divine designation also accorded well with legal understandings of the Roman *lex regia* whereby total authority was irrevocably surrendered to the ruler. Addressing this theme, an aspiring Scots lawyer, Andrew Bruce of Earlshall, embarked on a 'juridical investigation into the decrees of princes' which he defended publicly at the Dutch university of Franeker before the renowned natural jurist, Ulrich Huber, in 1683. Characterising the indivisible, irresistible and inalienable sovereignty possessed by an absolute monarch as the same as that vested in Roman Emperors by the *lex regia*, Bruce argued that 'the simple transfer of power from the people nonetheless remains certain and fixed', irrespective of whether this authority was bestowed on one individual or on an assembly.[55] In the late sixteenth century, another lawyer, Adam Blackwood, had specifically claimed that, in Scotland, the *lex regia* rested not on any form of popular election, but simply on the original oath of allegiance sworn by the Scots to Fergus I and to his posterity in perpetuity. Nevertheless, this argument contained an inherent tension, since it could imply that the Scots people were in the position to confer such power irrevocably. As J. H. Burns has shown, Blackwood's insistence that ' "kings inherit, not from [previous] kings, but from the realm [itself]" ' suggested 'that the realm subsists in some sense independently of the king'.[56]

Within Restoration Scotland, however, there was an additionally formidable reason why justifications for divine-right monarchy, grounded chiefly upon Fergus' conquest, were usually perceived as insufficient during the Restoration. Although exempt from the usurping power of William I in England in 1066, Restoration Scots had nevertheless just experienced military conquest and occupation from English Cromwellian forces during the 1650s. As such, divine-right arguments which seemed to derive their greatest validity from conquest theory ran dangerously close to offering legitimations of *de facto* power. Hence it was by no means clear how the Fergusian conquest differed from *de facto* notions which collapsed distinctions between right and power. During the seventeenth century, the most common Biblical text used by royalists to deny the legality of political resistance was Romans 13:1–2: 'Let every soul be subject unto the

---

[53] Mackenzie, *Jus Regium*, p. 27.
[54] James VI & I, 'The Trew Law', in *Political Writings*, p. 73.
[55] Bruce, *Exercitatio Juridica*, p. 14.
[56] Burns, *The True Law of Kingship*, p. 226.

higher powers. For there is no power but of God: the powers that be are ordained by God.' The injunction regarding non-resistance was explicit, but what was less clear was the notion of obedience unto 'the powers that be'.

The practical implications of this theoretical liability became evident in 1661 when the marquis of Argyll was placed on trial for his political activities in the 1650s. During his trial, Argyll himself deemed the crime of compliance as 'the epidemical sin of the nation'.[57] As a newly-qualified advocate, Mackenzie of Rosehaugh acquired early prominence for his courageous pleading as a member of Argyll's defence counsel, reiterating the argument that such 'Compliance was so customary, and so universal, that it was thought no more a Crime, than the living in Scotland was criminal.' Moreover, since no Act of Indemnity had yet been passed in Scotland, Mackenzie conceived that regarding Argyll's former compliance as perfidious established a dangerous precedent, since all Scots had been 'forc'd to be the idle Witnesses' of the usurpation, even by paying Cromwellian taxes.[58] Such arguments were, however, rejected by the restored monarchy of Charles II and Argyll's execution was ordered by the same monarch on whom Argyll had himself placed the crown of Scotland at Scone a decade earlier in 1651. Nevertheless, the nonconformist presbyterian divine, John Brown of Wamphray, later regarded Argyll's conviction as 'strange considering what the principle of Royallists is'. If one accepted the royalist principle that conquest had historically conferred a legitimate right to govern, then Cromwell could be regarded as 'the lawfull supreme Governour of the Kingdome of Scotland'. Following Argyll's conviction for treason on the grounds of compliance, Brown thus challenged 'all the Royallists [to] answer this, without contradicting themselves, if they can'.[59]

Similarly ambiguous was the other Biblical text most frequently cited to enjoin non-resistance which came from the second chapter of St. Peter's first epistle: 'Submit your selves unto every Ordinance of man for the Lord's sake, whether it be to the King as supreme, Or unto governors, as unto them that are sent by him for the punishment of evil-doers, and for the praise of them that do well.' Aware of the potential for casuistical interpretation, the Restoration archbishop of Glasgow, Robert Leighton, markedly denied the need to establish conclusively the origins of civil power in a posthumously-published commentary on the Petrine text. Regarding the legitimacy of most monarchical titles, Leighton ventured that were all such claims to be investigated thoroughly, there would be 'few crowns in the world' wherein there would not be 'found some crack or other'.[60]

Despite the existence of such theoretical inconsistencies regarding the origins

---

[57] Burnet, *History of My Own Time*, II, 221.
[58] Sir George Mackenzie, 'Pleadings, in some Remarkable Cases, Before the Supreme Courts of Scotland, Since the Year, 1661', in *Works*, I, 82, 80.
[59] [John Brown of Wamphray], *An Apologeticall Relation, Of the particular Sufferings of the faithfull Ministers & professours of the Church of Scotland, since August 1660* (n.p., 1665), p. 81.
[60] Robert Leighton, *A Practical Commentary upon the Two first Chapters of the first Epistle General of St. Peter* (York, 1693), p. 373.

of the Scottish monarchy, consensus about its absolute nature was deemed imperative in the aftermath of the civil wars, dubbed the recent 'great State-quake' by John Paterson in 1660.[61] Arguing that if sovereignty was indivisible, monarchy was, by corollary, absolute, Bodinian theories of unified sovereignty had influenced earlier generations of civil war royalists, such as Lord Napier, whose 'Letter to a Friend on Sovereign Power' was composed in 1643. According to Napier, since the essential attributes of sovereignty were that it could not be divided, transferred or alienated, it could not 'subsist in a body composed of individuities', for were it to be 'divided among several bodies, there is no government'.[62]

During the Restoration, similar ideas were articulated by those royalists such as Honyman who declared that all political societies founded by God possessed a supreme source of magistratical power, whether vested solely in one person or in more than one person 'in a united way'. To ensure order, it was essential 'to arrive at something that is first, before which, or above which, there is nothing in that order'.[63] In the 1680s, Mackenzie reiterated that if monarchy was the form of government whereby the king was supreme, he could not share his power with the nobility, since that implied an aristocracy, nor could he share his rule with the people, for that denoted a democracy. Hence since 'the very Essence and Being of Monarchy' consists in its possessing a supreme and absolute power, Mackenzie insisted that 'in allowing our King to be an absolute Monarch, we have only allow'd him to be a Monarch, and to have what naturally belongs to him'. By such reasoning, just as every man was presumed to be a rational creature, since reason was the essence of man, so a king was presumed to be absolute, except in those instances whereby a monarch was restrained by specific limitations 'prov'd by an express Contract'.[64] Addressing James VII & II in 1689, the university authorities in St. Andrews similarly pointed out that 'even bigot Republicans cannot deny' that the democratic governors of classical Athens as much as the representative assemblies or Renaissance republican governments 'were all as Supreme, Absolute and incontrollable, as the Persian, Assyrian, or whatsoever Monarchie in the World'.[65]

In the aftermath of the mid-century civil wars, absolute monarchy received further endorsement as the form of government which appeared to present the most effective bulwark against civil disorder. Recalling events that had ostensibly occurred in 330 BC, Mackenzie thus commended the actions of the Scots tribal leaders for having decided to place themselves under an absolute monarchy, for 'though a mixt Monarchy may seem a plausible thing to

[61] Paterson, *Post Nubila Phoebus*, 'Dedication'.

[62] Lord Napier, 'Letter to a Friend on Sovereign Power', in *Memoirs of the Marquis of Montrose*, Mark Napier ed., 2 vols. (Edinburgh, 1856), I, 281–2. See David Stevenson, ' "The Letter on Sovereign Power" and the Influence of Jean Bodin on Political Thought in Scotland', *Scottish Historical Review*, 61 (1982), pp. 25–43 which establishes Napier's authorship of the 'Letter', following previous attributions to Napier's brother-in-law and former pupil, Montrose.

[63] [Honyman], *Survey of the Insolent and Infamous Libel entituled Naphtali*, p. 72.

[64] Mackenzie, *Jus Regium*, p. 38.

[65] *Addres* [sic] *of the University of St. Andrews*, p. 8.

Metaphysical Spirits and School-men, yet to such as understand Government and the World, it cannot but appear impracticable'.[66] The conviction with which Mackenzie consistently defended his monarchical ideas subsequently moved the Victorian constitutional historian, Frederic Maitland, to declare that nowhere in the history of political thought was the belief 'that we perceive intuitively that hereditary monarchy is at all times and in all places the one right form of government' defended more vigorously or extensively than in Mackenzie's *Jus Regium* of 1684.[67]

At a civic level, approval of absolute kingship also co-existed alongside support for Aristotelian ideas of mixed government. As Sir Francis Grant recalled in 1707, the governance of Scotland had traditionally 'maintained a Monarchical Form of Government in Shires, and an Aristocratical Model in Burghs', both of which worked effectively for the common good.[68] During the Restoration, the Aberdeen baillie, Alexander Skene, endorsed this vision, acknowledging that, at a national level, the Scottish people lived under 'the Power and Protection of a Potent Monarch' whose rule was assisted by the 'advantage of the best Laws of any Kingdom in Europe'. Within Scottish towns, however, Skene discerned 'a well mixed Government' made up of nobles, gentry, lairds and burgesses benevolently instituted by the absolute monarch.[69]

III

The articulation of absolutist theories in the late seventeenth century was, however, by no means uncontested. Embarking on his canonical defence of monarchical absolutism in the late-1670s, the tutor to the French dauphin, Jacques-Bénigne Bossuet, observed that political opponents had sought to render the concept of absolute power 'odious and insupportable' by nefariously seeking 'to confuse absolute government and arbitrary government'.[70] In Scotland, Mackenzie made a similar point in 1684 when he acknowledged that 'our Fanaticks and Republicans, will be ready to misrepresent absolute Monarchy, as Tyranny'.[71] But by no means did theorists of absolute monarchy envisage the seventeenth-century absolute monarch of Scotland to be despotic. As much in moral as in constitutional terms, clear distinctions prevailed between monarchy and tyranny. For although the monarch was *legibus solutus*, he was not freed

---

[66] Mackenzie, *Jus Regium*, p. 48.
[67] Frederic Maitland, 'A Historical Sketch of Liberty and Equality as Ideals of English Political Philosophy from the Time of Hobbes to the Time of Coleridge', in H. Fisher ed., *The Collected Papers of Frederic William Maitland*, 3 vols. (Cambridge, 1911), I, 8.
[68] [Grant], *Patriot Resolved*, p. 12.
[69] Alexander Skene, *Memorialls for the Government of the Royall Burghs in Scotland* (Aberdeen, 1685), p. 20.
[70] Jacques-Bénigne Bossuet, *Politics Drawn from the Very Words of Holy Scripture*, Patrick Riley ed. (Cambridge, 1990), p. 81.
[71] Mackenzie, *Jus Regium*, p. 49.

from all laws, since the laws of God, of nature and of nations still bound the absolute king as much as his subjects. A clear distinction thus prevailed between the sovereign's absolute liberty of action and his mere immunity from civil laws; although God's revealed law bound the king absolutely, he was accorded full scope for creative action by human laws. Before proceeding to consider issues of resistance, therefore, recognition of the limitations which served to circumscribe the absolute power of the monarch is required.

The distinction between monarchy and tyranny had been made explicit during the civil wars when, for instance, Bishop Maxwell had confirmed that although monarchical power was indeed *legibus solutus*, this did not signify that kings were free from divine or natural law, but only from any form of 'Coercion humane, or any humane coactive power to punish, censure, or dethrone'.[72] Consequently when Charles II was restored in 1660, royalist pamphleteers contended that monarchical rule alone ensured the preservation of Scottish lives, liberties and estates and deplored notions of original freedom by insisting that *sine rege, sine lege*. Since the monarch remained subject to the laws of God, of nature and of nations, the subject's liberty remained secure. By contrast, as Mackenzie reiterated, 'whoever thinks he may Dispense with Law' must conceive 'that he is ty'd by no Law; and that is to be truly Arbitrary'.[73]

The conduct of monarchical absolutism was thus conceived within a framework of divine limitation that protected both the ruler and the ruled. In the 1590s, James VI had subtitled his *Trew Law of Free Monarchies* 'the reciprock and mutuall duetie betwixt a free king and his naturall subjects' and had consistently emphasised a king's duties over his rights. Writing at the same time, Craig of Riccarton characterised all earthly kingdoms and empires as 'feus proceeding from the ultimate Lord Superior', rendering it unlawful for princes, however absolute, to 'turn their feudal rights to abuse by oppressing their subjects' or by imposing their authority 'more heavily upon them than the safety of the state requires'.[74] Emphasising the symbiosis that subsisted between the royal prerogative and liberty of the subject, Napier likewise insisted in 1643 that 'one can never stand unless supported by the other'.[75]

Fundamental to the correct operation of this symbiosis between monarch and people was, however, a correct understanding of the iniquity of popular resistance. Having established the divinely-ordained, hereditary and absolute nature of Stuart kingship, the concomitant commands of passive obedience and non-resistance could be deduced. For if, as Mackenzie put it, the monarch was supremely powerful, he was not to be held accountable by his subjects 'for no man is judg'd but by his Superior'.[76] The limitations of divine and natural law

---

[72] [Maxwell], *Sacro-sancta Regum Majestas*, p. 140.
[73] Mackenzie, *Vindication of his Majesty's Government & Judicatures*, p. 12.
[74] Thomas Craig, *The Jus Feudale by Sir* [sic] *Thomas Craig of Riccarton with an Appendix Containing the Books of the Feus*, 2 vols., Lord Clyde ed. (Edinburgh, 1934), I, 204.
[75] Napier, 'Letter . . . on Sovereign Power', in *Memoirs of . . . . Montrose*, I, 287.
[76] Mackenzie, *Jus Regium*, p. 78.

which served to restrict the absolute monarch's scope for action remained unenforceable by temporal authorities.

For those who sought to uphold divinely-ordained, hereditary and absolute monarchy, all forms of political resistance were thus to be condemned wholesale even in the event of manifest monarchical misrule. Preaching before the Scottish Parliament in March 1661, the Stirling minister, Matthias Symson, advised strengthening the royal prerogative as far as possible, warning that if 'the Kingdom be headlesse, the Subjects will be brainless'.[77] The following year, the Scottish Parliament deemed it 'rebellious treasone' for subjects to 'put limitations upon their due obedience and allegiance'.[78] Maintaining an inviolable duty of obedience to one's superiors, resistance was denounced on Scriptural grounds as likely to incur eternal damnation. Addressing the first two verses of Romans 13, for instance, Bishop Honyman warned that 'Christian patience and violent resistance are incompatible'. Those who advocated resistance in God's name thus sinned by their actions, since to preserve order God had ordained that 'such as are in supreme Power by lawful calling' were to be honoured and obeyed 'even although in the main things they pervert the ends of Government'. The formal reason underpinning individual subjection and non-resistance was thus the divine nature of the magistratical power, rather than its correct use by the earthly magistrate. As Honyman reminded his readers, although 'Caesar give not God his due, yet it is Christs mind that we give Caesar his due'.[79] Endorsing this argument, another member of the Scottish episcopate, Archbishop Leighton of Glasgow, explained that the main reason why human obedience to earthly powers was ordained derived from the divine nature of their authority. Hence although Leighton accepted that governors 'did many things unjustly', God's institution of political authority on earth 'puts upon inferiours an obligation to obedience'.[80] From a legal perspective too, the scope for action enjoyed by an absolute monarch brooked no civil obstacle. As Andrew Bruce publicly acknowledged in his defence of kingly power at the University of Franeker in 1683, 'princes simply have the right, that is the power, of treating their citizens badly' and it was the subjects' duty to recognise this power.[81]

Hence non-resistance theorists unequivocally rejected the principle of defensive arms which could be raised against a magistrate who appeared to be ruling in his own interest, rather than that of his subjects. In the aftermath of the Covenanters' Pentland Rising of 1666, Honyman denied that any legitimating authority could be invoked to justify such action. Individual rights of resistance instead represented a 'Doctrine point-blank contrary to reason' that only served

---

[77] Matthias Symson, *Yehoveh ve melek, or God and the King. Being the Good Old Cause. As it was stated and discussed in a Sermon preached before his Majesties High Commissioner, and the Honourable Estates of the Parliament of the Kingdome of Scotland, at Edinburgh, on the 17th day of March 1661* (London, 1661), p. 15.

[78] 'Act for the Preservation of his Majesty's Person, Authoritie and Government', Thomson and Innes eds., *Acts of the Parliament of Scotland*, VII, 377–9.

[79] [Honyman], *Survey of the Insolent and Infamous Libel entituled Naphtali*, pp. 34, 8.

[80] Leighton, *Practical Commentary*, pp. 374–5.

[81] Bruce, *Exercitatio Juridica*, p. 37.

to dissolve human society and opened 'a door to all seditious confusions'. Although reluctant to engage in a detailed refutation of the ideas promoted by the anonymous authors of the resistance tract, *Naphtali* (1668), Honyman deemed it imperative to ensure that 'the gangrene of his words may not creep further to the consumption and subversion of Church and State'. If nothing else, he conceded that the author should be thanked for revealing 'the malitious bloody and cruel designs of his party'. Those in authority 'being fore-warned, may be fore-armed' and thus become sufficiently vigilant to 'keep our eyes in our head'.[82] As Covenanting violence escalated in the 1680s, Mackenzie similarly wondered, in his role as Lord Advocate, 'how can Defensive Arms be distinguished from Offensive Arms?' For even under those governments which had been established on a contractarian basis, Mackenzie denied that subsequent resistance to the ruler was permissible, since this was 'after Vows to make Inquiry' and all oaths and vows would be rendered ineffectual 'if the giver were to be Judge how far he were ty'd', and convenience made the measure of obligation.[83]

As Professor of Divinity in the University of Glasgow in 1673, Gilbert Burnet distinguished between natural laws and natural rights to refute claims that resistance was justified by the fundamental human imperative of self-preservation. Deeming resistance to be 'the matter of the greatest Importance', Burnet insisted that laws of nature were 'certain notions of Truth' impressed by God on the souls of rational individuals to endow them with the ability to discern good from evil.[84] His reasoning was supported by another episcopalian cleric, James Craufurd, who confirmed in 1682 that 'the great Fallacy is here, Men are apt to confound Natural Rights, and the Law of Nature, which vastly differ'. Far from providing a legitimating lexicon of resistance, individuals surrendered such rights on assuming membership of a civil society, which natural law had convinced them was 'the wisest Bargain they could make'. But having abdicated such rights, Craufurd was unequivocal in declaring that no 'severity in the Prince can cancel the obligation that lies upon Subjects' since that would imply that the subjects were rejecting an authority which they had previously owned as supreme.[85]

Despite such clarion injunctions to obedience, the possibility of moral restraint was not removed entirely. Although subjects were required to display active obedience to godly commands, ungodly orders were only to be met with passive obedience. The Scriptural text most frequently cited in this context was

---

82 [Honyman], *Survey of the Insolent and Infamous Libel entituled Naphtali*, pp. 57, Preface, pp. 12–13.
83 Mackenzie, *Jus Regium*, pp. 95, 40.
84 Gilbert Burnet, *A Vindication of the Authority, Laws and Constitution of the Church and State of Scotland. In Four Conferences. Wherein the Answer to the Dialogues betwixt a Conformist and a Nonconformist, is Examined* (Glasgow, 1673), pp. 6, 9.
85 [James Craufurd], *A Serious Expostulation with that Party in Scotland, Commonly known by the Name of Whigs. Wherein is modestly and plainly laid open the inconsistency of their Practices* (London, 1682), pp. 6, 12. In defending this line of reasoning, Burnet and Craufurd were echoing the distinction stridently made by Thomas Hobbes in *Leviathan* who had insisted that 'Law, and Right, differ as much, as Obligation and Liberty' (Thomas Hobbes, *Leviathan*, Richard Tuck ed. (Cambridge, 1991), p. 91.

Acts 5:29, 'We ought to obey God rather than man.' Since kings were God's divinely-appointed lieutenants on earth, James VI & I had made clear that subjects were to act in no other manner than by 'following and obeying his lawfull commands, eschewing and flying his fury in his unlawfull, without resistance, but by sobbes and teares to God'.[86] As Robert Douglas explained in a sermon to the Scottish Parliament in 1661, although a subject may decide he is unable to obey the magistrate without sinning, he should nevertheless continue to obey that magistrate's authority: 'if he cannot give active obedience (as others speak) he should give passive'.[87] This view was endorsed by Leighton who conceded that divine injunctions to obedience subsisted only so long as rulers observed divine law, 'but if they go out of that even line, follow them not'.[88] Distinguishing between allegiance to the monarch and obedience to his commands, Honyman readily envisaged situations whereby loyal subjects retained their fidelity to the king, but were unable to obey his orders 'because of Gods countermand'. Countering allegations that passive obedience to an ungodly and tyrannical magistrate was sinful, he reassured his readers that since 'no man goes to hell, for the sin of another', individuals would not be held accountable for the misdemeanours of their magistrates or fellow subjects.[89]

This argument concerning the culpability of subjects forced to choose between compliance with an ungodly magistrate or passive obedience to his ungodly commands was also raised with respect to military discipline in Restoration Scotland. In a collection of martial essays entitled *Pallas Armata*, the royalist soldier, Sir James Turner, attacked the 'just war' arguments of Hugo Grotius' *De Jure Belli ac Pacis* of 1625. Insisting that 'Obedience is the very Life of an Army', Turner denied that individual soldiers were always capable of determining the justice of the cause, legitimacy and ultimate intention of every conflict. While accepting that soldiers should obey God before man, Turner contended that soldiers were 'not so strictly to examine the quarrel', since the sin involved in commanding soldiers to fight for an unjust cause was sufficient to render 'the Souldier's obedience in fighting, blameless and innocent'. Invoking Tacitus' authority, Turner thus declared that 'we should suffer the wrongs of Princes, as we do Rain, Tempests, Hail, Thunder, Lightning, and other injuries of the Air'.[90]

Embracing non-resistance, therefore, did not necessarily imply incipient political disloyalty. In 1689, Francis Grant considered the etymology of the word 'loyalty', showing that it derived from the French word '*loi*' denoting law. From this, he concluded that loyalty must always conform with legality indicating that 'Allegiance is an Obedience according to Law; and goes not a foot farther'.[91] Similarly, although the animus behind much Gaelic bardic poetry was

---

[86] James VI & I, 'The Trew Law', in *Political Writings*, p. 72.
[87] Douglas, *Master Dowglasse His Sermon*, pp. 8–9.
[88] Leighton, *Practical Commentary*, pp. 375–6.
[89] [Honyman], *Survey of the Insolent and Infamous Libel entituled Naphtali*, pp. 7, 51.
[90] Turner, *Pallas Armata*, pp. 167, 371, 256.
[91] Grant, *Loyalists Reasons*, sig. A2r.

directed towards obedience to the supreme and divinely-ordained magistrate, there were those, such as the Clan Maclean bard, Iain MacAilein, who held that submission was only necessary so long as the magistrate's commands were consonant with divine law:

> Gu m'bharail féin, ge beag mo reusan
> Gheibh mi cead g' a chòmhdach,
> Ge b'e tì dhe 'n dean Dia rìgh,
> Gur còir 'bhith strìochdte dhàsan;
> 'S ged théid e ceum de lan thoil féin,
> 'S gun e 'cur éiginn oirnne,
> 'N saoil sibh an lagh no reusan
> Dol a leum 'na sgròban?

(In my opinion – I may have little understanding, but I shall take leave to express it – whoever God appoints king, we ought to submit to him. And, though he follow his own free will, so long as he does not oppress us, do you think it is either lawful or reasonable to jump at his throat?)[92]

IV

In contrast to the political ideas examined above, alternative monarchical theories held that sovereignty resided in the Scottish community. Such opinions enjoyed a long pedigree, having been conspicuously articulated in the Declaration of Arbroath of 1320. Rediscovered during the Restoration, the Declaration powerfully vindicated the rights of the *communitas regni* to regulate the actions of deviant monarchs, on the grounds that political authority was legitimate only in so far as it accorded with the consent of those who created it. Hence active opposition to the Scottish monarch was permissible, if it could be proved that Fergus I had been elected king in such a manner as allowed his subjects considerable rights of resistance in the event of his subsequent misrule. Both the historical materials and methodology remained the same as for theorists of divinely-ordained, absolute and irresistible monarchy, only this time the stated objective was to discover 'from those dark and odious Historical Accounts we have' that Fergus had instead been 'chosen and set up by the People'.[93] Ironically, responsibility for the translation and publication of the Declaration of Arbroath in 1680 had been undertaken by Mackenzie to demonstrate that if ever a misguided Scottish king 'should offer to submit to England', the *communitas regni* 'would disown him and chuse another'. As Mackenzie had added by way of hasty commentary, this clause by no means implied that 'the power of Electing Kings, was ever thought to Reside in our Nobility', but solely

---

[92] A. Maclean Sinclair, *The Maclean Bards*. Volume I (Charlottetown, 1908), p. 94.
[93] Anon., *Vindication of the Proceedings of the Convention of the Estates*, p. 15.

signified that a king was not entitled to alienate his kingdom to a foreign prince.[94]

At the end of the sixteenth century, James VI & I's vigorous defence of unconditional political obligation and natural subjection had been consciously framed to counter the political philosophy of his childhood tutor, George Buchanan. For although the monarch was universally recognised as the source of sovereign power in Scotland, the Protestant Reformers had established the Scottish kirk in 1560 and deposed the Catholic monarch, Mary Stuart, in 1567, crowning her infant son, James VI, in her place. Buchanan had provided the fullest theoretical justification for this display of popular resistance in his tract, *De Jure Regni apud Scotos* which had originally been published in 1579 and was to appear in a printed English translation for the first time in 1680 amidst debates generated by the Exclusion Crisis.[95]

In his *De Jure Regni*, Buchanan had denied the autonomous or inherent right of any individual to rule, arguing that magistracy and kingship were instead human constructs. Alleging that the whole body of a people would instinctively appoint a ruler for the purposes of mutual protection and the welfare of the body politic in a pre-political society, Buchanan had contended that by understanding 'the duty of a Physician . . . we shall not much mistake the duty of a King'. It was, nevertheless, important to remember that such a ruler was not only a king, but 'also a man, erring in many things, through ignorance, often failing willingly, doing many things, by constraint'.[96] If the *salus populi* remained the *suprema lex*, however, virtuous kings could remain confident that their position was secure so long as they acted legally, since only wicked kings risked being called to account by the elective community. To substantiate his claims, in 1582 Buchanan had produced a version of Scottish history entitled the *Rerum Scoticarum Historia*, vividly describing the violent manner in which nefarious Scottish monarchs had regularly been deposed. Identifying the coronation oath as the means by which the original elective contract sworn by the people of Scotland was historically perpetuated, Buchanan's works thus presented a radically different interpretation of the allegedly seamless history of monarchical succession depicted in the Holyrood portraits.

During the mid-century civil wars, Buchanan's ideas had been developed and extended by adherents of the Scottish National Covenant formulated in

---

[94] Mackenzie, *Observations*, p. 19. For more on the Declaration, see Grant G. Simpson, 'The Declaration of Arbroath revitalised', *Scottish Historical Review*, 56 (1977), pp. 11–33.

[95] Buchanan's treatise appeared as *De Jure Regni apud Scotos. Or, A Dialogue, concerning the Due Privilege of Government in the Kingdom of Scotland, Betwixt Buchanan And Thomas Maitland, By the said George Buchanan. And Translated out of the Original Latine into English. By Philalethes* (n.p., 1680). Concern had, however, earlier been expressed about the possible clandestine circulation of other vernacular translations. In April 1664, for example, the Privy Council reported that 'some seditious and illaffected [*sic*] persons [who] indevour to infuse the principalls of rebellion in the myndes of many good subjects of purpose to dispose them to new trowbles, and for that end have adventured to translate in the English tongue ane old seditious pamphlett entituled *De Jure Regni apud Scotos*, whereof Mr George Buchanan was the authour [*sic*]' ('Proclamation prohibiting the circulation of George Buchanan's *De Jure Regni apud Scotos*', Hume Brown ed., *Register of the Privy Council . . . I (1661–1664)*, p. 527.

[96] Buchanan, *De Jure Regni*, pp. 16, 22.

opposition to the imposition of Laudian Anglicanism in the late-1630s. Described by the legal historian, John Cairns, as a characteristically 'clever, ambiguous and legalistic' document, the Covenant's signatories denied they sought 'the diminution of the kings greatnesse and authority', but declared they were nevertheless 'obliged to detest & abhorre recent novations in religion'.[97] With regard to the origins of the Scottish monarchy, committed mid-seventeenth century Covenanters, such as Samuel Rutherford, believed that God had once designated rulers himself, but did not comprehend 'how God, in our daies, when there are no extraordinary revelations' could fix the succession in one dynasty rather than another. Instead, Rutherford concluded that since kings were now selected 'without any Propheticall Unction', they emanated from 'the free choice of the people'.[98]

Similar ideas were expounded by the next generation of Restoration Covenanters. James Steuart of Goodtrees, for example, denied the exclusive claims of monarchy, arguing that although God had instituted government, the determination of its precise structure was entrusted to the people who were 'at liberty to walke here on rational grounds and to consult their owne advantage'. Given the natural equality that subsisted among mankind, Steuart rejected individual claims to kingly titles: 'no man coming out of the womb into this world, with a crowne on his head, and a sceptre in his hand'. Without seeking to derogate from the divinely-endowed nature of government, he affirmed that 'the People create the Magistrate' by making 'this man King, and not that man'. Since Steuart thus accepted that 'Subjects can destroy the Monarch and choose another', he rejected as inappropriate metaphors which sought to render the health of the body politic analogous to the health of the physical body.[99] For while James VI & I had accepted that kings might frequently have reason to 'cut off some rotten member' of the body politic, he had prophesied its certain death 'if the head, for any infirmitie that fall to it, be cut off'.[100]

Concomitant with such reasoning was also a commitment to notions of original freedom. Drawing on the Buchananite inheritance, such arguments proposed that although men were born with a natural power of self-determination, they subsequently discovered it was in their common interest to contract together and form a society based on mutual protection. In 1687, for instance, the radical Covenanter, Alexander Shields, insisted that 'as to Civil & Politick Subjection: man by nature is born free as beasts'. Consequently, just as 'No Lyon is born King of Lyons', kingship remained the product of human selection. While societies remained free to choose whichever system of government they pleased, Shields declared that even where strict hereditary succession

[97]   John Cairns, 'Historical Introduction', in Kenneth Reid and Reinhard Zimmerman eds., *A History of Private Law in Scotland*, 2 vols. (Oxford, 2000), p. 80; 'The National Covenant of 1638', in Gordon Donaldson ed., *Scottish Historical Documents* (Edinburgh, 1970), pp. 201, 200.
[98]   [Samuel Rutherford], *Lex, Rex: The Law and the Prince. A Dispute for the just Prerogative of King and People, &c.* (London, 1644), p. 17.
[99]   [Steuart], *Jus Populi Vindicatum*, pp. 83, 85, 146.
[100]   James VI & I, 'Trew Law', in *Political Writings*, p. 78.

was observed, it should be recognised that 'originally and radically' the lineal heir 'is constitute, and chosen by the People'.[101] A similar claim was made in the *Queensferry Paper*, issued on behalf of an extreme Covenanting faction in 1680, wherein it was alleged that kingship was not to be regarded as 'an inheritance that passes from father to son without the consent of tenants', but was instead an office bestowed '*ad culpam, non ad vitam*'.[102]

More generally, the widespread and significant use of bonds, oaths and covenants in Scottish history provided a firm basis for contractarian understanding of the formation of government. For an earlier period, it has been estimated that around eight hundred documents are still extant recording agreements made by members of the Scottish nobility and gentry from around 1450 to 1603, the majority representing bonds of maintenance and manrent.[103] In addition to such legalistic understandings, mid-seventeenth century engagements such as the National Covenant and Solemn League and Covenant were also vigorously defended on the grounds of their binding religious obligations. Denouncing the government's attempt to persuade subjects to forswear such oaths during the Restoration, Steuart declared that such asseverations remained 'Covenants, and National tyes perpetually binding' before God, obliging the monarch, nobility and people 'so long as Scotland is Scotland'.[104]

Within this contractarian tradition, there were, however, ways in which theories of a social contract could be combined with a form of designation theory which precluded individual rights of resistance, similar to those examined earlier which enjoined non-resistance to the divinely-endowed magistrate. In 1668, for example, a young philosophy lecturer, Robert Hamilton, published a set of graduation theses entitled *Schediesmata Libero-Philosophica* that were intended for disputation by students at St. Salvator's College in St. Andrews. Following ideas expounded in Thomas Hobbes' *Leviathan* (1651), Hamilton not only argued that man was not 'a political animal from native mutual love, but by accident is made suitable to enter society through fear and education', but also deduced a politically absolutist state from a seemingly conventional and contractualist position. Acknowledging that there was often likely to be 'an uncertain dominion by two persons over the same thing', Hamilton also recognised *de facto* rights of conquest from an illegal war as a valid title to government.[105] Particularly contentious in the aftermath of the Cromwellian occupation, he enjoined, as a further corollary, that subjects were obliged to support their sovereign in war, irrespective of their opinion about the legality of such wars. This unconventional stance, combined with numerous unorthodox postulates pertaining to natural philosophy, were sufficient for the university authorities to request that Hamilton's theses be immediately rescinded 'upon the account they were erronious', containing many precepts 'not aggrieabell to the

---

[101] [Shields], *A Hind let loose*, pp. 303, 86.
[102] 'The Queensferry Paper [1680]', in Wodrow, *Sufferings*, III, 209.
[103] See Jenny Wormald, *Lords and Men in Scotland: Bonds of Manrent, 1442–1603* (Edinburgh, 1985).
[104] [Steuart], *Jus Populi Vindicatum*, p. 5.
[105] Robert Hamilton, *Schediesmata Libero-Philosophica* (Edinburgh, 1668), p. 17.

common tenets of philosophie'.[106] After leaving St. Andrews soon afterwards, Hamilton studied law at the University of Leiden where in 1671 he defended a doctoral dissertation within which he developed his account of the origins of government. Indebted to the political ideas of Samuel Pufendorf, Hamilton identified two different and discrete contracts operating simultaneously. First, individuals combined to form a popular contract, or *pactum unionis*, by which 'each individual must agree, together with the other individuals, to subject himself to one rule'. This was followed by a second rectoral contract, or *pactum subjectionis*, whereby 'everyone commits themselves, giving their will up to one man alone to use their money and their power for the public good', ensuring that 'they by no means want to resist his orders'.[107]

This double-contract framework was also sufficiently flexible to accommodate accounts provided by theorists who adhered to the divinely-ordained nature of government, such as the young advocate, Francis Grant, who had also just returned from studying at Leiden when he published his *Loyalists Reasons* in 1689. For his part, Grant accepted that divine sovereign power had been originally vested in fathers over their families, but held that this patriarchal power had been lost when it had been transferred by consent. In all civil societies, Grant thus also identified the *pactum unionis* enabling families to combine to form political society for the purposes of union, commerce and defence, followed by the *pactum subjectionis* which devolved authority on the ruler. The latter contract involved the representatives or sovereign head of the people arranging a constitution, succession and other matters relating to government, as eventually enshrined in the coronation oath. According to Grant's analysis, the divine nature of the authority remained intact since the process was analogous to that by which ecclesiastical chapters elected bishops, who could not thereafter be removed. For this reason, the *pactum subjectionis* could be broken while the *pactum unionis* remained in place. As Grant explained, while a king could break his part of the rectoral contract with his subjects by a series of notorious injuries, the popular contract remained, rendering it high treason for subjects to rebel against the king or state. For even if the king had severed his contract with the kingdom, the people could not declare the anterior contract broken, since 'Divine and Humane Laws oblige us morally, to keep Sacredly a Valid Contract.'[108]

This line of reasoning was, however, dismissed by those who followed Buchanan in maintaining that in all civil societies, the collectivity of the people remained more powerful than a single ruler. For while a people might fervently venerate their monarch, Buchanan deemed it incredible that subjects 'should endure to be in a worse case than formerly they were in'.[109] During the Restoration, the same point was made by Steuart who deemed it 'a firme truth, that the

---

[106] G. Kinloch ed., *The Diary of Mr. J[ohn] L[amont] of Newton* (Edinburgh, 1830), p. 207.
[107] Robert Hamilton, *Disputatio Politico-Juridica Inauguralis, de Ærarii Publici Necessitate, ac Pleno Principum vectigalia, &c. imponendi Jure* (Leiden, 1671), p. 12.
[108] Grant, *Loyalists Reasons*, p. 3.
[109] [Buchanan], *De Jure Regni*, pp. 81–2.

condition of a people modelled into a civil state, is not worse then it was before, but rather better'. Since government was predicated on an original contract, when a king violated a major part of that agreement, 'the Subjects are *de Iure* freed from subjection to him, and at liberty to make choice of another'. More-over, Steuart conceived it to be the fundamental right of every subject to 'know, and be distinct in the knowledge, and perswaded of the lawfullnesses' of their right to resist.[110] To justify his defence of individual rights of resistance, Steuart also drew on a wealth of Continental Protestant scholarship, most prominently from Johannes Althusius' *Politica* of 1606. In his application of Althusius' political ideas to a Scottish context, Steuart not only chose to ignore Althusius' emphasis on the crucial role of intermediary representative institutions within the Holy Roman Empire, but also disregarded the prevalent hierarchical assumptions upon which the imperial resistance debate was predicated. When applied to a Scottish context, Steuart's selective use of Althusian ideas in *Jus Populi Vindicatum* produced what has been regarded by Robert von Friedeburg as 'a new framework of rights, an inflated case of necessity and a rhetoric of religious crusade'.[111]

Distinguishing between the person and the office of a monarch, active resis-tance was nevertheless construed as lawful against a king who perverted the ends of protection for which his office had been instituted. Consequently, the theological distinction between a king's civil office and his natural person became increasingly significant as suspicions arose that the *salus populi* might no longer be guaranteed. Regarding the sovereign's power as 'properly a fidu-ciary power', Steuart pointed out that since 'Royalists grant he may be dethroned' if he alienated his kingdom to a foreign power, the Scottish monarch enjoyed no more power than that 'of a Tutor, Publick Servant, or Watchman'.[112] Nor could the transactions of previous generations be regarding as binding since 'they did not buy their liberty and conquest with our thraldome and slavery' as the Covenanting manifesto entitled *The Queensferry Paper* made clear in 1680.[113] Since men were only bound to that administration which best secured their current lives and liberties, if the government failed in that objective, its subjects had recourse to elect an alternative authority.

Such interpretations of the ends of government also generated contrasting notions of tyrannous rule based upon the distinction between the illegal usurper of a throne (a *tyrannus absque titulo*), and a legitimate ruler who wielded authority in a tyrannical manner (or a *tyrannus administratione*). The conven-tional royalist position had been stated in the early seventeenth century by Thomas Craig, for example, who defined a tyrant as 'one who brought no right to

[110] [Steuart], *Jus Populi Vindicatum*, pp. 83, 117, 'Epistle to the Christian Reader'.
[111] Robert von Friedeburg, 'From collective representation to the rights of individual defence: James Steuart's *Ius Populi Vindicatum* and the use of Johannes Althusius' *Politica* in Restoration Scotland', *History of European Ideas*, 24 (1998), p. 29.
[112] [Steuart], *Jus Populi Vindicatum*, p. 149.
[113] 'The Queensferry Paper [1680]', in Wodrow, *Sufferings*, III, 209.

the kingdom, but only violence, and not him who rules tyrannically'.[114] In similar vein, Mackenzie of Rosehaugh characterised a tyrant as one without legitimate title to govern who 'may be oppos'd, as the common Enemy of all the Society'. In this context, Mackenzie rejected Hobbesian claims that the duty of obedience was solely grounded upon the sovereign's ability to protect, observing that this 'were to invite men to torment us, and to justifie Crimes by success'.[115] By contrast, Buchanan and his intellectual heirs considered that the correct definition depended upon a ruler's moral conduct as opposed to the constitutional legality of his accession. As Buchanan explained, rulers who governed in the national interest, despite having obtained their office unlawfully, were to be tolerated 'as we do endure some bodily diseases rather than throw our life into the hazard of a doubtsome cure'. Real tyrants were those who ruled in their own interest rather than that of the nation becoming 'a publick enemy, with whom all men have a perpetuall warfare'.[116] The enduring influence of Buchanan's ideas had been vividly demonstrated in 1649 when Oliver Cromwell allegedly 'entered into a long discourse of the nature of regal power according to the principles of [Juan de] Mariana and Buchanan' in an unsuccessful attempt to persuade the Scots to acquiesce in the execution of Charles I.[117]

For this reason, Covenanting ministers, such as John Brown of Wamphray justified their armed resistance to Charles II's administration on the grounds that it was only divinely-ordained powers which were irresistible. By contrast, 'Magistrates turning tyrants, and exercising tyranny, cannot be called the ordinance of God' although their 'office abstracted from tyranny' remained divinely-ordained.[118] The radical Cameronian Covenanter, Alexander Shields, echoed such sentiments, denying that tyrannical powers were derived from God and deeming it 'Blasphemie to assert they were of the Lords Authorization'.[119] The injunction of the Petrine text prescribing obedience to earthly superiors was also rejected by the anonymous author of a pamphlet published in 1689, often assumed to have been Stair. For as the writer explained, although most assumed that St. Peter had indicated divinely-ordained power 'in the Abstract', what he had really intended was the exercise of power 'in the Concrete, as it relates to the Person or Persons vested with this Power'.[120]

Royalist injunctions to non-resistance and passive obedience thus came under increasingly sustained attack during the Restoration. Referring, for instance, to a commemorative sermon preached on the anniversary of Charles I's execution by Archbishop James Sharp of St. Andrews in 1669, James Steuart of Goodtrees wondered incredulously how 'men of common sense . . . could sit and heare

[114] Craig, *Right of Succession*, p. 186.
[115] Mackenzie, *Jus Regium*, p. 49.
[116] [Buchanan], *De jure regni*, pp. 69, 127.
[117] Quoted by Roger Mason, 'George Buchanan, James VI and the presbyterians', in Mason ed., *Scots and Britons*, p. 137.
[118] Brown, *Apologetical Relation*, p. 154.
[119] [Shields], *A Hind let loose*, pp. 272–3.
[120] Anon., *Vindication of the Proceedings of the Convention of the Estates*, pp. 20–1.

such a base flattering claw-back depressing them and all persons of all ranks and qualities in the land, in a condition, below the Bestial?'[121] Almost two decades later, Shields was likewise moved to ponder that the world might 'never be awakned out of this Dream & dotage, of Dull & stupid subjection to every Monster that can Mount a Throne'. The entire notion of passive obedience, Shields deemed to be 'in-intelligible Non-sense, & a meer contradiction in terms' since, by definition, obedience denoted a positive action.[122]

Notwithstanding such sentiments, resistance theorists needed to remain vigilant to prevent their arguments from being dangerously construed as offering an unlimited licence for complete disorder. As Shields recognised, although tyranny presented 'a destructive plague', the anarchy it usually generated was 'no less pernicious, bringing a Community into a Paroxysme as deadly & dangerous'.[123] Citing Samuel 15:23, Steuart of Goodtrees and John Stirling judged that unlawful opposition was 'indeed Rebellion, and as the sin of witchcraft'. Such misguided disobedience was, however, entirely different from the actions of those who resisted 'persons Abusing sacred Authority, and rebelling against God the Supream' thus acting in God's name in vindication of his sacred authority.[124] As will be seen in the sixth chapter, the escalation of civil unrest which occurred across Scotland during the Restoration was, however, accompanied by a simultaneous radicalisation of resistance theory. With the memories of Charles I's regicide still vivid, Steuart explicitly declared in 1669 that he was 'not speaking of doing violence unto the persons of Sovereigns, or of committing parricide'. According to Steuart, 'the matter of resistance' was only one of 'natural sinlesse selfe-defence, which is far different from the Killing of Kings'.[125] By contrast, however, the contents of the radical *Sanquhar Declaration*, publicised in June 1680, advocated regicide as the due punishment for Charles II's treachery in betraying his status as a 'Covenanted' king. Similarly alarming degrees of conviction prevailed among those insurgents arrested in the same month by the authorities in the aftermath of the Covenanters' military defeat at Bothwell Brig. As Lauder of Fountainhall recorded, even after suffering torture, three accused rebels, Robert Hamilton, John Spreul and Archibald Stewart, would give 'no positive categorick answer' when questioned about the legality of regicide, but 'would nather call it lawfull nor unlawfull'.[126]

Following the accession of James VII & II in February 1685, even more committed opposition was voiced in a determined attempt to prevent Scotland 'from drowning in popish idolatry and slavery'.[127] Three ships commanded by the earl of Argyll arrived in the west of Scotland from Holland in May 1685, and

---

[121] [Steuart], *Jus Populi Vindicatum*, p. 471.
[122] [Shields], *A Hind let loose*, pp. 272, 291.
[123] *Ibid.*, pp. 300–1.
[124] [Steuart and Stirling], *Naphtali*, p. 157.
[125] Steuart, *Jus Populi Vindicatum*, p. 270.
[126] Lauder of Fountainhall, *Historical Observes*, p. 8.
[127] W. Macleod ed., *Journal of the Hon. John Erskine of Carnock 1683–7* (Edinburgh, 1893), pp. 113–14.

were intended to coincide with an armed uprising commanded by the duke of Monmouth in the West Country of England. While a popular manifesto of Argyll's ultimately unsuccessful uprising was provided in his printed *Campbeltown Declaration*, a fuller account of Argyll's political ideas can be gleaned from a contemporaneous manuscript tract on monarchical power that was possibly penned by Argyll himself.[128] Predicated on the belief that 'no particular government is of Nature', the author argued that although monarchs have traditionally been endowed with advisory councils, 'Monarchs now gen^lly shune all limitations as much as they can.' Nevertheless, since monarchical power originally resided in the people, the author deemed it 'Abject & wicked flattery' to declare that princes were 'subject to no law or limitation at all either in Authority liffe [*sic*] or succession'. Denying that hereditary proximity alone conferred the right to govern the ship of state, the author counselled full discussion among the people about the most suitable monarchical candidate. As he reasoned, passengers on a normal ship were not concerned whether a ship's captain owned the individual ship or not, but 'rather whether he be skillful valiant and like to bring them in safly to ther ways end or to droune them among the waves'. Providing explicit justification for Argyll's decision to rise in arms against a Catholic successor, the author concluded that failure to resist an unsuitable monarch rendered each individual 'guilty of all the evils hurts miseries & calamities both temporall and spiritual which afterwards by his evill government may ensue'.[129]

In this manner, theoretical precepts were of direct consequence for the contemporary practicalities of kingship. Referring to the Covenanters' Pentland Rising of 1666, James Steuart of Goodtrees regarded the disturbances as 'the defence of innocents' in extreme circumstances 'against illegal commissioners, contrary to the Law of God'. If *salus populi* was accepted as the essential foundation of civil society, it was irrational to 'condemne them as Traitors, seing they were noble Patriots and loyall to that Supreame law'.[130] As opposition intensified during the so-called 'Killing Times' of the 1680s, Shields likewise declared himself unconcerned whether Scotland was a monarchy, aristocracy or democracy. For as he explained, the 'dispute at present is not levelled against Monarchy' or 'the Institution of the Species', but only against 'the constitution of this individual Monarchy established among us'.[131] It is now time to see how theories of monarchical government translated into practice in Restoration Scotland.

---

[128] For the printed Declaration, see Carnie, 'The Campbeltown Declaration'. For the manuscript, see Inverary Castle Argyll Manuscripts, NRA(S) 1209 Inventory, p. 29, Bundle 56, 'Discussion of the nature of monarchy and right to allegiance of the subjects'. I am most grateful to Professor James Burns for generously supplying me with a copy and transcript of this document.

[129] Argyll Manuscripts NRA(S), p. 29, Bundle 56, ff. 32, 34, 26, 12, 17.

[130] [Steuart], *Jus Populi Vindicatum*, pp. 172, 160.

[131] [Shields], *A Hind let loose*, p. 301.

4

Constitutional Monarchy

In November 1678, the leading English Whig politician, the earl of Shaftesbury, delivered a speech to the House of Lords, remarking on the political and constitutional state of late-seventeenth century Europe. In his opinion, although subjects of all the northern countries enjoyed 'an undoubted and inviolable right to their liberties and properties' by law, he observed that the Scots had 'outdone all the eastern and southern countries' by having their 'lives, liberties and estates sequestered to the will and pleasure of those that govern'.[1] At a time when fears of popery and arbitrary government were being increasingly articulated in England, Scotland seemed to offer firsthand evidence of what might be expected, should the absolutist propensities of the Stuarts be allowed to proceed unchecked. Shaftesbury ensured that forty printed copies of his speech were immediately dispatched to Edinburgh, where, according to the English Tory, Roger North, their arrival provided 'a Trumpet Signal' to disaffected factions in Scotland, giving them 'cause to think there was a Party in Parliament, already formed to assist and sustain them'.[2]

News of Shaftesbury's speech penetrated widely within Scotland. At home in Brodie Castle in the Highlands in April 1679, the presbyterian laird, Alexander Brodie of Brodie, recorded how a recent visitor had 'raisd my spirit a litl' by showing him a copy of the speech, drawing attention to 'the tyranni and arbitrari gouernment usd and exercisd in Scotland' and indicating that 'they could expect noe better in England'.[3] Alarmed by the impact of Shaftesbury's address, the

---

[1] Anthony Ashley Cooper, earl of Shaftesbury, 'Speech made in the House of Peers, by the Earl of Shaftesbury, November 1678, upon Consideration of the State and Condition of England, Scotland and Ireland', in Scott ed., *A Collection of scarce and valuable tracts*, VIII, 49. The following year, a similar view was propounded in the House of Commons by the presbyterian M.P., John Birch, who contended that if there was 'any arbitrary power in the World, it is in Scotland' (Grey ed., *Debates of the House of Commons*, VII, 194).

[2] Roger North, *Examen: Or, An Enquiry into the Credit and Veracity of a Pretended Complete History: Showing the Perverse and Wicked Design of it, and the Many Falsities and Abuses of Truth contained in it: Together with some Memoirs Originally inserted* (London, 1740), p. 87. As North explained, Shaftesbury's timing had been carefully planned. The fact that copies of the speech had been 'dispatched that very Night of the Speech spoke' suggested that the speech had been 'designed probably on a Post Day for the very purpose' and was thus not 'made and timed by Accident' (*Ibid.*).

[3] David Laing ed., *The Diary of Alexander Brodie of Brodie MDCLII–MDCLXXX and of his Son, James Brodie of Brodie, MDCLXXX–MDCLXXXV* (Aberdeen, 1863), p. 411.

duke of Lauderdale's Anglican chaplain, George Hickes, doubted whether the speech had in fact ever been delivered, but contended that even if it had, Shaftesbury would have desisted from doing so 'had he known the true state of Scotland, which few Englishmen do'. For, as Hickes alleged, Shaftesbury's ignorance prevented him from foreseeing 'the evil effects, which it immediately had, in encouraging the Covenanters to Assassinate, Massacre and Rebel'.[4] Such apprehensions intensified the following year, when James, duke of York, was sent to Scotland to remove him from the volatile political atmosphere generated by Whig parliamentary attempts to remove him from the line of succession on account of his Roman Catholicism. Among English commentators, it was widely feared that the purpose of Charles' having dispatched 'the Popish Duke to King it over them' was to 'let us timely know that if Laws may be broken by a Popish Duke, how much more they may be violated by a Popish King'.[5]

Shaftesbury's polemical perspective was evidently aimed at a particularly receptive constituency within Scotland. But as one Scots observer, Matthew Mackaile, informed a correspondent in London in 1678, regarding 'the present state of Scotland . . . the kingdom is divided in three several interests'. According to Mackaile, these three interests were discernible among nobles and gentry alike, comprising 'the Episcopal and Court interest, the interest for liberty and privileges now followed by [the duke of] Hamilton and his party and the interest of religion and presbytery'.[6] While Shaftesbury's speech was enthusiastically welcomed among the latter group, historians of the Restoration, as much as partisan contemporaries, have often been inclined to overlook the second moderate 'interest for liberty and privileges'. Historiographical interpretations have accordingly focused on juxtaposing a minority despotic court tyrannising over a majority of persecuted presbyterians, whose prime concerns about church government precluded any possible reconciliation to the Restoration regime. As Mackaile was aware, however, not only were the realities of Restoration Scottish politics considerably more intricate than some English observers believed, but the origins of such complexities could be traced back to the civil wars. Despite the efforts of English contemporaries, such as the earl of Clarendon, to apply quasi-'Cavalier' and 'Roundhead' appellations to mid-seventeenth century Scottish political groupings, this taxonomy was fundamentally inappropriate. For by 1660, virtually all Scots nobles over the age of forty had taken up arms against the monarch on at least one occasion. Furthermore, although the civil wars had begun as a revolt against the perceived imposition of Laudian Arminianism, most nobles were not committed opponents of episcopalian church government. Accepting that some form of state control of the church was necessary, the majority thus refused to join forces with those more extreme presbyterian elements who would only countenance the adoption of purely

4   [Hickes], *Spirit of Popery speaking*, pp. 72–3.
5   Anon., *A Letter sent to D. L.* (London, 1679), p. 3.
6   'Matthew Mackaile to Sir John Frederick, 19 June 1678', in F. Blackburne Daniell ed., *Calendar of State Papers Domestic, March 1st 1678 to December 31st, 1678, with Addenda 1674 to 1679* (London, 1913), p. 232.

theocratic models. By 1660, therefore, a large degree of consensus could be discerned amongst the majority of the Scottish political elite who were ready to yield their foremost allegiance to a constitutional monarch and were thus also prepared to support whichever form of church government that monarch thought fit to institute. In the years after 1660, however, the subsequent political and ecclesiastical history of Restoration Scotland inevitably generated different reactions within this large body of moderate opinion, to the extent that, by 1678, Mackaile was able to discern his three distinct groupings.

By reconstructing the institutional structure of Restoration politics, this chapter explores the ways in which differing notions of how monarchical government should operate in principle were applied to practical situations. The chapter focuses on the first two decades of the Restoration, illustrating the paramount importance attached by most members of the political establishment to observing constitutional proprieties, together with the various methods employed to register opposition when irregularities occurred during the 1660s and 1670s. While the Restoration is acknowledged to have been the period that witnessed the emergence of 'party politics' in England, one of the most significant political developments north of the border was likewise the increasingly apparent breach between officials appointed by the Stuart administration and members of a nascent and unofficial parliamentary 'opposition'.[7] As Restoration Scots increasingly identified a range of shared political principles, the considerable extent to which royalist sympathies in theory could coherently be combined with practical opposition became evident. During the 1670s, these tensions were characterised most vividly by the personal struggle that evolved between the duke of Lauderdale, who represented what Mackaile termed the 'Episcopal and Court interest' in his capacity as High Commissioner to the Scottish Parliament from 1669 to 1679, and the influential magnate, William Douglas, duke of Hamilton, who vociferously defended 'the interest for liberty and privileges'.

Bridging political theory and practice therefore, this chapter begins by outlining the character of the Restoration political settlement. It then considers the range of practical political grievances identified by contemporaries in the years immediately following the Restoration, together with a discussion of the several methods employed to register discontent with the policies of the executive. Historiographically, eighteenth-century critics evidently shared 'a universal embarrassment' regarding 'the corruption of parliaments to the point of uselessness during the Restoration period'.[8] By contrast, this chapter challenges such tendencies to dismiss the Restoration Parliament as a servile and impotent institution by revealing instead how late-seventeenth century Parliaments continued to play a crucial role in supplying a forum within which a vibrant political opposition could develop. The chapter concludes by placing

---

[7] For a discussion of Restoration party politics in England, see Tim Harris, *Politics under the Later Stuarts. Party Conflict in a Divided Society 1660–1715* (Harlow, 1993).

[8] Kidd, *Subverting Scotland's Past*, p. 138.

such practical political opposition to Charles II's government within an ideolog-ical context of constitutional royalism and attachment to notions of natural and fundamental law.

I

Despite claiming to be the most ancient independent monarchy in the world, Restoration Scotland was nevertheless ruled by an absentee monarch. This ines-capable reality determined not only the nature of political controversies that arose under Charles II and his brother, but more crucially, the manner in which they were confronted and resolved. In 1661, it had been mooted that the govern-ment of Scotland should largely be conducted by a Scottish council, which would convene at Whitehall and would include any members of the Scottish Privy Council who happened to be in London, together with six members of the English Privy Council. In return, the Scots would be entitled to send two repre-sentatives from the Scottish Privy Council to meetings of its English counterpart. This proposal was, however, immediately opposed by some of Charles II's closest Scottish advisors, including Lauderdale, who despite being an ex-Covenanter, had subsequently changed sides and suffered imprisonment in England for nearly nine years during the Interregnum for his royalist sympa-thies.[9] According to Gilbert Burnet, Lauderdale objected to the idea of a Scottish Council on the grounds that 'to all Scottishmen, this would make Scotland a province to England', by subjecting its governance to English councillors who 'neither knew the laws nor interests of Scotland', but would wield absolute authority, ensuring that Scottish wealth would also 'be employed to bribe them'. Despite such advice, Charles had assented to the proposal, evidently trusting the earl of Clarendon's reassurance that should the Scots decide to rebel again, Charles 'must have the help of England to quiet them'.[10]

Such arrangements proved only temporary, however, and the Scottish Council was disbanded in 1663. Effective political power was thereafter increas-ingly vested in the office of parliamentary High Commissioner, ensuring that opposition was no longer constrained to criticism of the monarch himself. Under ministerial government, officers of state were supposedly responsible in law to the king, enabling rival political factions likewise to appeal to that king. Political opposition thus shifted from older notions of attacks on the crown to newer modes of attack on the executive. Approving such arrangements, the presbyte-rian Principal of Glasgow University, Robert Baillie, informed Lauderdale in 1661 that the 'old maxim in the Stat of Ingland is wyse & good' in guaranteeing

---

[9]   In the early-1650s, Lauderdale had appeared to represent a body of moderate opinion prepared to support the restoration of a constitutional monarchy in Scotland. Together with two political colleagues, he had composed a memorial identifying 'but two pairties in Scotland, those who stand for the right and liberties, the Laws and Government of Scotland, and those who have protested and acted against those good ends. The last we doe not looke on as Scotsmen' (Airy ed., *Lauderdale Papers*, I, 8).
[10]   Burnet, *History of My Own Time*, I, 203.

that 'the king can do no fault, but the hiest ministers of state aught in reason to aunsuer on ther hiest pains for all miscariages'.[11]

Former divisions between supporters of a restored constitutional monarchy and irreconcilable presbyterian opponents had, moreover, been complicated by the emergence of a group of Scottish allies of the earl of Clarendon, led by John, earl of Middleton, appointed by Charles II as the first Restoration parliamentary High Commissioner to Scotland. The power struggle that quickly evolved between Middleton and Lauderdale was observed by the royalist soldier, Sir James Turner, who predicted that 'great Pompey will endure no equall, and greater Caesar will acknowledge no Superior'.[12] Clear differences of opinion among the Scottish political establishment also emerged when Charles' first Scottish Parliament opened in Edinburgh on 1 January 1661. Although it was later claimed that 'never any parliament was so obsequious to all that was propos'd to them', particularly contentious were the debates surrounding the controversial passing of the Act Rescissory later that year.[13] The motivation for the Act derived from a growing consensus that some form of legislation was necessary to render illegal certain innovations of the civil war years, in order to restore the legal basis of Charles II's authority. As Clarendon put it, Scottish laws could not be restored to their former integrity as long as Covenanting 'extravagancies remayne declared Lawfull' since 'posterity may reasonably enough resorte to the same councells'.[14]

Disagreement quickly arose, however, over the appropriate extent of such retrospective legislation. Although the Act Rescissory was eventually issued on Middleton's authority, Burnet later claimed that its original scope had been suggested by the Clerk Register, Archibald Primrose, 'but half in jest'.[15] Such a controversial proposal did not encounter universal approbation and Lauderdale was only one dissenting voice in what was effectively a legislative attempt to imagine away the entire Covenanting revolution. While acknowledging his commitment to restoring the royal prerogative in full, Lauderdale privately warned the earl of Glencairn, as Scottish Chancellor, that 'to swipe away all the acts' of civil war legislatures, including those passed by assemblies at which Charles I and Charles II had been present was unsafe. As Lauderdale recognised, since such an act would undermine all previous indemnities, 'yow may judge how dangerous that may be . . . if the people shall see acts of oblivion made so little binding'.[16] Although he later became a committed opponent of Lauderdale's administration in the mid-1670s, the duke of Hamilton recalled

[11] Airy ed., *Lauderdale Papers*, I, 95.
[12] Thomas Thomson ed., *Memoirs of his own Life and Times by Sir James Turner, M.DC.XXXII–M.DC.LXX* (Edinburgh, 1829), p.134.
[13] Mackenzie, *Memoirs*, p. 19.
[14] Bodl., Clarendon MSS. 74, '[Clarendon] to [Middleton], March 26th, 1660', f. 292r.
[15] Burnet, *History of My Own Time*, I, 214.
[16] Bodl., Clarendon MSS. 75, 'Ld Lauderdale to the Earl of Glencairn, Lord High Chancellour of Scotland, 1661', ff. 400r–v. In similar vein, Baillie likewise questioned the security that would remain to Charles II if 'treaties confirmed by King and Parliament, in all due form, are not binding, but so easily ranversed' (Baillie, *Letters and Journals*, III, 464–5).

that, at the Restoration, he had also insisted that 'to take away absolutlie' the actions of the 1641 Parliament which had been 'as legally (for any thing I knew) constitute by the Laues of the kingdome, as any parl: could be' was unlikely to strengthen Charles II's power, but would instead 'occasion fears & grumbling to the people'.[17] Although the Act is generally assumed to have annulled all legislation passed by any Parliament since 1633, the precise wording of the Act only rendered 'voyd and null' acts passed in 'the pretendit Parliaments' held between 1640 and 1648.[18] Nevertheless, the repeal of the Triennial Act in 1661 also presumably removed the validity of the Parliaments held in 1650 and 1651 when Charles II had been in attendance.

Although the Act Rescissory became law, Middleton's tenure as High Commissioner ended abruptly in 1663, however, when he unsuccessfully attempted to pass legislation precluding former Covenanters, such as Lauderdale, from holding offices of public trust. Lauderdale had himself denounced such a stratagem as misplaced, given that its precedent was the 'oystershell billeting' practised by 'the Athenians, who were governed by that cursed Sovereign Lord the People'.[19] Middleton's demise in the aftermath of the so-called 'Billeting Affair' was accompanied by a parliamentary prorogation and no Parliament convened again in Scotland until 1669. As Samuel Pepys recorded, by early 1664, Lauderdale had 'got the whole power of Scottland [sic] into his hand'.[20] Although two conventions were held solely for taxation purposes in 1665 and 1667, effective control over the evolution of royal policy in Scotland during this period was exercised by a select group of ministers normally resident at Whitehall. As Charles II's Scottish Secretary, Lauderdale was certainly the most influential, but he received committed assistance from Sir Robert Moray, who subsequently became Lord Justice Clerk, and John Hay, second earl of Tweeddale, who was later appointed Treasurer. To replace Middleton, John Leslie, earl of Rothes, was appointed parliamentary High Commissioner, largely on the assumption that his presence would be required when a national synod was convened to discuss ecclesiastical affairs. Writing to Lauderdale from Edinburgh in 1667, however, Moray questioned the expensive need to maintain a parliamentary High Commissioner, particularly since Rothes also chaired the Scottish Privy Council, presided over the Treasury and was General of the Scots military. Concerned that in the absence of a national synod, the 'vast and indeed unknown power of such a commission' was potentially prejudicial to the common interest, Moray reasoned that 'there can be no need of an

---

[17] NAS GD 406/M9/148, '1661, March 28, Memorandum in the hand of the 3rd duke of Hamilton, discussing what he said in parliament about the rescinding of the acts made by the parliament in the 1640s'. A similarly retrospective argument was articulated before a Dutch university audience by Andrew Bruce of Earlshall in 1683, who compared Charles II's passing of the Rescissory Act to the abolition of the Perpetual Edict in the Netherlands. According to Bruce, both actions confirmed not only the suspicious character of revolutionary ideological models held to transcend time and place, but also demonstrated their long-term impotence (Bruce, *Exercitatio Juridica*, p. 15).

[18] Thomson and Innes, *Acts of the Parliament of Scotland*, VII.

[19] Mackenzie, *Memoirs*, p. 87.

[20] Pepys, *Diary*, V, 57.

unlimited power', given the combined authority of monarch and Privy Council.[21] For, as Moray recognised, the office of parliamentary High Commissioner was relatively unpopular in Scotland, being both costly and lacking specific powers during parliamentary adjournments. Moreover, it thereby offered the potential to establish a quasi-perpetual dictatorship that operated outside the normal framework of government and was only responsible to the Crown. When the office of parliamentary High Commissioner was subsequently removed from Rothes in September 1667 therefore, Lauderdale explained to a sceptical Rothes that Charles II had resolved to return Scottish government 'to the old channel without the place of Commissioner'.[22]

Ironically, however, identical lines of reasoning were later turned against Lauderdale himself, following his own appointment as parliamentary High Commissioner in 1669. His failure to demit office whilst in London for the intervening periods between Parliaments proved highly unpopular and provoked a number of anonymous writers to pen memoranda to Charles II. Accompanied by affirmations of loyalty to Charles himself, one writer complained in 1674, for example, that Lauderdale's 'very place & power is [i]n effect, soe extraordinarie that we cannot bear it . . . ane deputie King is as absurd in ane place as ane deputie father in nature'. Even if Lauderdale were to be made a proper viceroy and thus obliged to reside in Scotland, the author contended that 'the evill would be mor tollerable', but Lauderdale seemed to be as absent from Scotland as the monarch himself.[23] When it was subsequently mooted in 1681 that the title of 'viceroy', rather than that of 'parliamentary High Commissioner', should be conferred on the duke of York, however, opposition was entrenched. As Lauder of Fountainhall objected, for instance, the appointment of a viceroy was unsuitable for 'a free kingdom as Scotland is', since commissioners were 'tyed up to instructions', while a viceroy's power remained unlimited. Viceroys were thus conventionally sent to 'debelled and conquered kingdomes, as to Naples, Ireland &c., but never to independent crounes.'[24]

Whether commissioner or viceroy, the politics of absentee monarchy nevertheless placed an increased onus on the personal character and political conduct of such individuals. With reference to Lauderdale, one anonymous author denied in 1674 that, since there 'was never ane person of sutch qualities and trust more vexing and disobliging to the Country and more generalie dislyked', he advised Charles II to admit other Scottish members 'free of ane Lauderdellian dependance to give their opinion both of the evills and of their

---

[21] 'Sir Robert Moray, Lord Justice Clerk . . . to John, Earl of Lauderdale', *HMC Laing*, I, 360–1.

[22] NLS MS. 7003, 'Earl of Rothes to earl of Lauderdale, 19 August 1667', f. 56r. Although Rothes duly became Chancellor, his handling of the Covenanters' Pentland Rising the previous year is assumed to have contributed to his being deprived of the role of parliamentary High Commissioner, as well as the Treasureship, command of the army and the presidency of the Privy Council.

[23] NAS GD 406/2/635/6(ii), 'Ane short accompt'. According to the author, Lauderdale 'in fine doth all things at his will, so that the Counsell though it hath the name of his Ma[ties] Counsell yet in effect is not so much his as Lauderdailles' (*Ibid.*).

[24] Lauder of Fountainhall, *Historical Observes*, p. 42.

Remedies'.[25] At the highest political levels, Lauderdale's increasingly satrapic style of government ultimately also served to alienate several of his former political supporters, such as Moray and Tweeddale. Sojourning at Charles II's court in 1668, the Italian diplomat, Lorenzo di Magalotti, acknowledged Lauderdale as parliamentary High Commissioner, but regarded him as 'in essence the Viceroy or Governor' of Scotland. Dubbing him 'the serpent among the eels', Magalotti observed how 'everyone wishes him ill and he wishes well to few', admiring his particular ability 'to form parties and destroy them according to his own purposes'.[26] Meanwhile, amongst English politicians, his imperious influence at Whitehall was regarded as sufficiently destabilising for the Secretary of State, Sir Joseph Williamson, to be informed that although Lauderdale was residing at his Surrey home, Ham House, in August 1673, there were many who 'wish him hamstringed there, that he never come further'.[27]

Within Scotland, printed attacks on Lauderdale became increasingly savage and personal. The author of an anonymous *Letter sent to D. L.* in 1679 accused the High Commissioner of such 'Mischievous Subtilty, Hellish Machination, Violence and Cruelty' that he had arguably 'outdone Machiavel, Caesar Borgia his Prince, if not the Spanish Inquisition it self.'[28] Attacking Lauderdale's treatment of presbyterian nonconformists in particular, another manuscript tract casuistically alleged that Lauderdale had 'taken all ye ways he could fall on to force them into Rebellion' as evinced by the many false accusations, illegal imprisonments and barbaric sentences suffered by nonconformists during the 1670s, including the banishment of 'shipfulls to be slaves in English plantations'.[29] In the aftermath of the Williamite Revolution, a presbyterian pamphleteer confirmed that the government's military rout of the Covenanters at Bothwell Bridge in June 1679 had indeed represented another 'piece of L[auderdale]'s Matchiavilianism', in successfully provoking an uprising 'which the severity of their Persecution after the Defeat sufficiently justified'.[30]

[25] NAS GD 406/2/635/6 (ii), 'Ane short accompt'.
[26] W. E. Knowles Middleton ed., *Lorenzo Magalotti at the Court of Charles II* (Waterloo, Ont., 1980), pp. 31, 55.
[27] 'Sir N. Armorer to Sir Joseph Williamson, August 1, 1673', *Calendar of State Papers, Domestic Series, March 1st to October 31st, 1673*, F. H. Blackburne Daniell ed. (London, 1902), p. 475. The opulent splendour of Lauderdale's residence at Ham was described by John Evelyn in 1678 as 'indeede inferiour to few of the best Villas in Italy itselfe', since it was 'furnishd like a greate Princes' and surrounded by 'Gardens, Orangeries, Groves, Avenues, Courts, Statues, Perspectives, fountaines, Aviaries, and all this at the banks of the sweetest river in the World' (E. S. de Beer ed., *The Diary of John Evelyn* (London, 1959), p. 653).
[28] Anon., *Letter Sent to D. L.*, p. 1.
[29] BL Add. MSS. 23,938, 'That the Duke of Lauderdale concurred in the Design for bringing in of Popery as appears by these following particulars [1679]', f. 12v.
[30] T. S., *History of the Affairs of Scotland*, p. 8. Other appraisals of Lauderdale's contribution were, however, less ferocious. Despite being ejected from his parish in 1662, the Covenanting minister, Robert Law, deemed Lauderdale 'a man of great spirit, great parts, a most daring man, and a man of great success . . . [who] did more without the sword than did Oliver Cromwell, the great usurper, did with it; was a man very national, and truely the honour of our Scots nation for witt and parts' (Charles Sharpe ed., *Memorialls; Or, the Memorable Things that fell out within this Island of Britain from 1638 to 1684, by the Rev. Mr. Robert Law* (Edinburgh, 1818), p. 65). Another gracious construction placed on Lauderdale's character was that offered by his former Anglican chaplain, John Gaskarth, in a sermon preached

II

Political opposition during the 1660s and 1670s was not, however, confined to attacks upon the personal character or constitutional office of the parliamentary High Commissioner. Considerable concern was increasingly articulated about a range of other perceived constitutional abuses and injustices, ranging from the collection of excise dues to the independence of the justiciary. The process of political restoration also presented the challenge of addressing the economic dislocation suffered by Scotland during years of civil war and subsequent Cromwellian occupation. Confirming the fervid protestations of loyalty that greeted Charles II's return to political power, in 1661 the Scottish Parliament voted the monarch a lifetime annuity of £480,000 to be raised by excise dues. As Mackenzie of Rosehaugh recalled, on hearing the news, Charles had allegedly 'admired how, after so many troubles, so poor a people, exhausted by many oppressions could have made so liberal offer' and, in doing so, 'seemed rather to pity than thank them'.[31] Although it may have been preferable for Scots ministers to calculate a fixed annuity, rather than await the capricious and unknown amounts demanded by royal supply, the burden remained considerable since the Scottish budget had amounted to just over £300,000 under Cromwell, most of which financed the heavy military resources required by an occupying army.

Once the series of Anglo-Dutch wars commenced in the mid-1660s, it became evident that the annuity was, moreover, insufficient and further fiscal burdens were imposed by a land tax in 1665 and by the reintroduction of direct taxation in the form of the cess in 1667. Such demands not only frustrated attempts to restore national prosperity, but the obligation to pay for military hostilities against Holland was specifically resented, since Dutch markets continued to represent a major source of Scottish mercantile business excluded from English markets. In March 1665, for instance, Rothes reported discontented 'toun talck [talk]' among Edinburgh merchants. Since the war was being fought to secure markets from which English traders alone could benefit, merchants objected to being obliged to raise the requisite funds and rued how 'this war brings distruxion upon us'. As Treasurer, Rothes was also increasingly concerned about the scarcity of specie in circulation. To this end, he even contemplated publishing the nation's accounts if their inspection could be

---

soon after the duke's death in 1682. According to Gaskarth, Lauderdale had always possessed 'a strange Apprehension to discern Good, not only present, but in the remote Consequence of things, and the long effects of them'. Hence Gaskarth contended that this attribute was 'one great Reason, why so many were dissatisfied with his Proceedings, and turned Adversaries to him, because he understood [state affairs] better than they . . . This is the only Account that can be given of those loud Clamors against him, as one that was bringing in Popery and Arbitrary Government' (John Gaskarth, *A Sermon Preached upon the first occasion, After the Death of His Grace, John Duke of Lauderdale, In the Chappel at Ham* (London, 1683), p. 26).
31 Mackenzie, *Memoirs*, p. 31.

restricted to Scots merchants alone, so 'that our pouertie might not be bleased [blazed] throu the world'.[32]

Complaints about economic dislocation also extended to domestic finances. Since it was envisaged that the royal annuity would be raised through a combination of inland excise and foreign customs, protectionist legislation had been devised to exact dues on a range of foreign commodities and to forbid the importation of certain items. As one anonymous political observer complained in 1674, 'the true cause of o[r] discontents is o[r] grievances, w[ch] print allreadie hes made but too publick'.[33] Acting in response to English protectionist measures such as the Irish Cattle Acts, Scots officials placed absolute embargoes upon the importation of foreign salt. Angry opposition regarding the consequent economic dislocation was, however, compounded by the official decision to allow the relevant tax 'farms' to be appropriated personally by ministerial associates, thus eliminating the possibility for Scottish merchants to receive impartial government compensation. Collection difficulties were compounded by incipient corruption ensuring that annual customs and excise receipts rarely exceeded £300,000.[34] Newly-elected as a parliamentary Commissioner for Ross-shire in 1669, Mackenzie consistently opposed what he perceived as unlawful extensions of the government's prerogative, denouncing such fiscal gifts as 'against express standing Lawes to the great detriment of the Crown' confirming suspicions that the system of personal monopolies was defrauding the Scottish Treasury to the detriment of royal revenue.[35] Another anonymous writer conjectured that if the excise revenues and receipts were to be calculated separately, a substantial annual surplus remained, 'whereof noe good account can be given'.[36] Although the major items affected by the monopolies system were salt, brandy and tobacco, it was widely feared that similar arrangements could be devised to cover other commodities, such as iron, pitch and tar, thereby enriching a few court favourites at the rest of the nation's expense.

In drafting successive memoranda to Charles II, discontented observers remained careful to couch their criticism in terms of unswerving loyalty to the monarch himself. Public abuses were thus construed to be all the more unacceptable within the context of Scotland's record of steadfast loyal support to the Crown. As Mackenzie commented in 1670, each Parliament since the Restoration had endowed Charles II with 'more prerogatives than all His predecessors' together with 'all the Money we had and have obeyed him and his servants to the greatest degrees [that] could be imagined'. Opposition to Lauderdale's policies was not therefore to be interpreted as an attempt to undermine royal

---

[32] EUL MSS. Dc.4.47, 'Earl of Rothes to Earl of Lauderdale, 14 March [1665]'; 'Earl of Rothes to Earl of Lauderdale, 13 May 1665'.
[33] NAS GD 331/18/1–2, 'Paper addressed to the King on current political affairs, 7 December 1674'.
[34] For more on government finances, see 'Chapter 3. The cost of repression: government finances, 1661–c.1681', in Lee, 'Government and Politics' and Lennox, 'Lauderdale and Scotland', *passim*.
[35] NAS GD 406/2/635/16, 'A Representation of the State of Affairs in Scotland, drawn by Sir Georg [*sic*] Mackenzie, His Ma[ties] Advocat [1670]'.
[36] NAS GD 406/2/635/6 (ii), 'Ane short accompt'.

authority, but instead 'to secure our Country against the violence of one Minister and the overturning of our fundamental Lawes'.[37] Although he later became a fierce critic of Mackenzie's actions as Lord Advocate in the 1680s, Sir James Steuart of Goodtrees echoed similar concerns. As Steuart argued in 1672, for example, although 'the soundest policie hath allwayes judged, the power in the Prince and purse with the people to be the justest balance of government', this system had been jeopardised by the Restoration financial settlement wherein 'all that was dearest to us was to him surrendered'.[38]

Scrutiny was further construed as being all the more imperative since a major corollary of the parliamentary High Commissioner's lengthy residences at Whitehall was that the political importance of civil servants in Scotland was enhanced and the potential for fiscal corruption expanded. Financial abuses were therefore symptomatic of wider misgivings about the ways in which court favourites of debatable competence and aptitude were increasingly being appointed to replace those summarily dismissed from offices 'whereunto they had Legall right without hearing'.[39] In 1672, Lauder of Fountainhall had observed how members of the 'old nobility cannot but repute them selfes slighted' when they saw 'great offices of State conferred upon upstarts.' But as he concluded, it was 'part of the absolute power of kings to raise men from the dunghill and make them their oune companions.'[40] Two years later, Charles II received a similar protest on the anniversary of the Restoration from an anonymous correspondent calling himself 'Jocke a Bread Scotland'. Wishing that 'the sun of your Royall favour could shyne and warm' his subjects in a less partisan manner, the writer warned Charles that 'men fear your Minions power' more than any obligations enjoined by the monarch himself.[41]

In addition to perceived injustices within the fiscal and financial spheres, increasing disquiet also emerged with regard to the administration of justice. In the late sixteenth century, James VI had deemed a monarch's knowledge of law to be essential, advising his heir, Prince Henry, 'to haunt your Session, and spie carefully their proceedings; taking good heede, if any briberie may be tried among them'.[42] His grandson, Charles II, was, however, confronted by a series of angry Scots missives, provoked by the unprecedented appointment of

---

[37] NAS GD 406/2/635/16, 'A Representation of the State of Affairs in Scotland'. Mackenzie's point was confirmed by the anonymous author of another memorandum in 1674 which likewise denied 'that a Nation loyall to such heights could have undertaken any thing that ther prince could blame or that they could have refuised any thing wch reasonable men could suffer' (NAS GD 406/2/635/6 (iii), 'A Representation of the present affaires of Scotland [1674]').

[38] [James Steuart of Goodtrees], *An Accompt of Scotlands Grievances By reason of the D. of Lauderdales Ministrie, Humbly tendred to his sacred Majesty* ([?Edinburgh, 1672]), pp. 5–6, 7.

[39] NAS GD 406/2/640/5, 'Address to his Majesty giving a rep^{n} of the state and interest of Scotland and listing the chief causes of complaint [c.1665]'.

[40] Sir John Lauder of Fountainhall, *Journals of Sir John Lauder of Fountainhall with his Observations on Public Affairs and other Memoranda 1665–1676*, Donald Crawford ed. (Edinburgh, 1900), p. 222.

[41] NAS GD 30/1716, 'Letter to Charles II from Jock a Bread Scotland, 29 May 1674'. In Fountainhall's *Journals*, cited above, a reference made to 'our Jock of bread Scotland' is taken to denote Lauderdale himself (Lauder of Fountainhall, *Journals*, p. 213).

[42] James VI & I, 'Basilicon Doron', in Sommerville ed., *Political Writings*, p. 45.

members with no legal training or experience to serve as judges hearing civil cases in the College of Justice. In 1674, one anonymous writer claimed that Lauderdale had elevated 'men all of them so unskilled in Law' that if professional examinations discussed in Parliament 'had been seriouslie gone about', this would have 'debarred them in ther entrie'. The promotion of Lauderdale's brother, Charles Maitland of Hatton, as an extraordinary Lord of Session in 1670, was especially resented, since he was not only accused of 'exerting ane absolute sway', but also of setting an 'evill example' to other judges in tending to 'favour bryberie and other direct practices [which] doth sadly prevaill to the unsettling of right and propertie'.[43] Judges were not, however, unique in their opposition to Hatton, for the following year, the earl of Shaftesbury received an account of Hatton's controversial attempts to influence town council elections in Edinburgh. Acknowledging that he could have 'wearied yow with a thousand passages of the Impertinent, passionat Carriage' of Hatton 'in whom there is as much folly, Insolency and bossines as ever met in one breast', Shaftesbury's correspondent was moved to wonder why Lauderdale 'will needs mak a Statesman of him . . . tho God and nature had made him a mad foole'.[44]

While concern surrounded the allegedly incompetent state of the Session, the increasing corporate confidence of the advocates became increasingly evident during the Restoration. Following a regulation enjoining that legal fees were to vary according to the social status of the client, the advocates staged a two-month strike in 1669. They particularly objected to the manner in which the fees regulation had been imposed by nobles without legal training, conceiving that 'soldiers, salt or coal masters, would think it imprudence in such as are not bred up in their profession' to regulate payment requirements.[45] Although the fees regulation was not rescinded until 1681, a more serious constitutional dispute arose in 1674 when a large proportion of the Faculty of Advocates again decided to withdraw their services after Charles II had refused to allow an appeal from a judgement of the Session to Parliament. There was an added element of political partisanship to the controversy, since the judgement concerned an appeal pursued by Lauderdale's uncle, the earl of Dunfermline, against Hamilton's son-in-law, the earl of Callendar.

Entailing the effective cessation of judicial proceedings for almost a year, the advocates' petition for parliamentary appeal not only indicated that the Session had forfeited the nation's confidence in its competence, but also reflected a wider desire to remove the final decision of justice from appointed judges to an elected assembly. For if established as the ultimate court of appeal, the Scots Parliament would need to have become a permanent constitutional feature. The

---

[43] NAS GD 406/2/635/6 (ii), 'Ane short accompt'. Although Lords of Council and Session met regularly to dispense justice from the late fifteenth century, papal dispensation to establish the College of Justice in 1532 saw the first appointment of Senators of the College of Justice. Distinctions between Ordinary and Extraordinary Lords subsequently emerged as Ordinary Lords held permanent salaried appointments as judges and Extraordinary Lords were unpaid royal appointees.

[44] PRO, SP 30/24/5, 'T. Wilson to the earl of Shaftesbury, 10 September 1675'.

[45] Mackenzie, *Memoirs*, p. 235.

legal position remained obscure, since there was neither a clear ruling on a writ of error in Scots law, nor a regular system of appeal. In 1663, a previous parliamentary appeal attempted by a commissary court judge, Nathaniel Eldred, against the M.P. for Haddington, Sir Thomas Hamilton of Preston, had failed. As the Lords of the Articles informed Charles II, reversing a decision of the Session was 'never done by any Parliament authorized be your Majestie or any of your Majesties so numerous progenitors'.[46] Interestingly, as a native Englishman, Eldred had then attempted to appeal against the seizure of his Scottish properties by taking his case to the English House of Lords where the committee on petitions narrowly dismissed the appeal on a tied 4–4 vote 'on the ground that it related to a judgment given in Scotland'.[47] The question of whether or not Scots peers should be allowed to hear English appeals in a united Parliament if no correlative system of parliamentary appeal was allowed in Scots law resurfaced during negotiations held to discuss greater political union between Scotland and England in 1670. According to one of the Scots commissioners, the earl of Kincardine, 'the point being so ticklish', the debate was adjourned and resolution of this legal issue was averted by the breakdown of the union negotiations.[48] Following the Williamite Revolution, however, the advocates' argument was upheld by the Claim of Right in 1689 which deemed it 'the right and privileges of subjects' to appeal against Session judgements to the monarch and Parliament.[49]

Although the advocates strenuously maintained that they were only concerned to preserve the right of appeal, for Lauderdale their actions represented 'no less than the Overthrow of ye goverment [sic] & ye disturbance of the people'.[50] Writing from Edinburgh, the earl of Kincardine complained to Lauderdale that it was unimaginable 'to what a height of malice & discontent people's spirits are raised', believing that the advocates 'contribute more to this then any body', since clients remained dependent on their goodwill, while the advocates 'have opportunity to influence evry body by their informations'.[51] Looking wider afield, Archbishop James Sharp of St. Andrews also considered it 'fitt wee have as much quyet as can be in all affairs here', since the English Parliament was also sitting, within which 'some ly at catch to make and improve clamours of great animositie and discomposure in Scotland at that critical epoch'.[52] When Charles II subsequently insisted that all advocates take an oath disowning such appeals, around fifty refused and were immediately debarred from practice. Although one such 'outed' advocate, Mackenzie wondered

[46] Thomson and Innes eds., *Acts of the Parliament of Scotland*, VII, 500.
[47] 'The Manuscripts of the House of Lords', HMC *Eighth Report of the Royal Commission on Historical Manuscripts, Report and Appendix (Part I)* (London, 1881), p. 115. A brief account of Eldred's case is cited in Richard S. Thompson, *Islands of Law: A Legal History of the British Isles* (New York, 2000), p. 41.
[48] NLS MS. 7004, 'Earl of Kincardine to the marquis of Tweeddale, 24 September 1670', f. 162r.
[49] Innes and Thomson eds., *Acts of the Parliaments of Scotland*, IX, 40.
[50] BL Add. MSS. 23,136, 'The earl of Lauderdale to Charles II, 7 February 1674', f. 80.
[51] Airy ed., *Lauderdale Papers*, III, 61.
[52] NAS CH 12/12/1370, 'Archbishop James Paterson to Archbishop James Sharp, 11 March 1675'.

whether it was 'an affront to be wyser then our enimies or to submitt to our prince', internal divisions among the recalcitrant advocates subsequently prompted their eventual deference to Charles II's authority.[53] In 1677, any remaining pretensions to integrity on the judicial bench vanished completely when all commissions were made for 'the duration of the king's pleasure', rather than for life. Ironically, the terms of the commission were changed to facilitate Mackenzie's appointment as Lord Advocate to replace Sir John Nisbet of Dirleton, who was described by Lauderdale's Anglican chaplain, George Hickes, as one who 'either loves or fears the Fanatical Faction too much'.[54]

III

The prominence of the Scottish Parliament was not only significant in terms of its juridical status as the supreme civil and criminal court in the nation, but also in terms of its function as a forum for political debate. Since the majority of personal appeals submitted to Charles II were composed during periods when Parliament was not sitting, continual parliamentary prorogations evidently created a significant constitutional void. Historically, parliament's political potential could, however, be denigrated by arguing that since parliament was a royal creation, gifted to the body politic to assist with government, it was never intended to be representative of the nation and thus should not be accorded an inflated constitutional status. In his *Trew Law of Free Monarchies*, James VI & I had defined a parliament as 'nothing else but the head Court of the king and his vassals'.[55] Hence it remained impossible for Parliament to enact a statute without the royal sceptre endowing the act with legal force, despite the confusions and delays that inevitably occurred by an absentee monarch delegating such legislative authority to a High Commissioner. One of the very first actions of the Parliament that convened in 1661 was to reassert Charles II's right to call and dissolve parliaments at will. Opposing Middleton's 'billeting' proposal as an innovation that exceeded the royal instructions, Lauderdale reminded Charles II that 'Your Majesty hath alone the negative vote' since it was 'your Assent that turns the consultations of Parliament into laws, and your dissent reduces them into nothing'.[56]

Similarly, in the mid-1670s, Gilbert Burnet acknowledged 'the Constitution of Parliaments to be a rational and excellent Model', but denied their existence compromised the Scottish monarch's absolute sovereignty. For although the king became 'a Tyrant when he violates their Privileges and governs without law', Burnet later distinguished between the hortative role of Scottish

---

[53] NLS MS. 14,407, '[Sir George Mackenzie] to the earl of Tweeddale [n.d.]', f. 322r.

[54] [George Hickes], *Ravillac Redivivus, being a Narrative of the late Tryal of Mr. James Mitchel a Conventicle Preacher* (London, 1678), p. 6.

[55] James VI and I, 'The Trew Law', *Political Writings*, p. 74.

[56] BL Add. MSS. 23,118, 'A Speech concerning the Act of Billeting . . . before his Majesty, 5 February 1663', ff. 15–16, 23–4.

Parliaments and English constitutional theory where supreme legislative authority was shared between the monarch and Parliament.[57] Confirming that the Scots monarch retained the 'Legislative and Architectonick' power of making laws, Mackenzie of Rosehaugh regarded Parliaments as extensions of the tenth-century *proceres regni*, or group of nobles, who traditionally gathered to offer the king counsel. Since Scotland had been ruled by kings for much longer than by parliaments, in no sense could Parliament have 'a Co-ordinate power with the King, when no man could sit in it but by a Privilege from the King'.[58] Similar controversies regarding the origins of parliament raged in England during the 1680s when the Tory historian, Robert Brady, countered claims of ancient constitutionalism by arguing that the English Parliament was no more than a royal concession yielded after the Norman Conquest in the thirteenth century.[59]

Hence the constitutional welfare of the Scottish Parliament remained of central importance for both political theory and practice. James VI & I's vigorous defence of monarchical supremacy in late-sixteenth century Scotland had been largely framed in response to Buchanan's insistence that the monarch be excluded from the legislative process.[60] The majority of the Restoration political establishment likewise construed the summoning of the Scottish Parliament as an essential mechanism for the operation of legitimate monarchical government. The anonymous author of a manuscript memorandum penned during the 1670s specifically denied the Privy Council's right to make laws and redress grievances, 'these being the proper workes of parl[ts]' since the Council was comprised of nominated political favourites whose 'reports cannot be looked on as the sense of the nation'.[61] While also recognising its limited sphere of competence theoretically, Mackenzie composed a memorial to Charles II in 1670, imploring him to maintain a parliament at a time when he perceived that 'the Lawes are too high'. For not only were the 'Fanaticks' thereby encouraged to agitate for reform, but the bishops remained vulnerable 'when a Kingdome is said to be against them which nothing but a parliament can clear'. As Mackenzie

---

[57] Burnet, *Vindication*, p. 156. Burnet's discussion of English constitutional theory was articulated in his *Vindication of the Ordinations of the Church of England* (London, 1677).

[58] Mackenzie, *Jus Regium*, pp. 67, 69.

[59] See J. G. A. Pocock, 'The Brady Controversy' in *The Ancient Constitution and the Feudal Law. A Study of English Historical Thought in the Seventeenth Century* (second edition, Cambridge, 1987), pp. 182–228.

[60] Despite being frequently credited with advocating popular, or at least full, parliamentary sovereignty, Buchanan himself protested that he had never claimed that such matters should be left 'to the judgement of the whole people in general'. Although his wording is ambiguous, Buchanan can be read as effectively endorsing the established Lords of the Articles system by contending that 'a select number' from each of the estates be appointed to convene with the king to discuss prospective legislation, after which such initiatives were to be submitted for full parliamentary approval (see Roger Mason, '*Rex Stoicus*: George Buchanan, James VI and the Scottish Polity', in Dwyer, Mason and Murdoch eds., *New Perspectives*, pp. 9–33 and Hugh Trevor-Roper, 'George Buchanan and the Ancient Scottish Constitution', *English Historical Review*, Supplement 3 (1966)).

[61] NAS GD 406/2/635/6 (iii), 'A representation of the present affaires'. As the author reminded Charles II, similar arguments had been used by Lauderdale in the 1660s 'against Middleton, when the true sense of the parl[t] was contraverted' (*Ibid.*).

reflected, it was 'strange to think that any thing can cure a National Rupture but a National Meeting'. In the absence of open parliamentary debate, Mackenzie further charged that Charles II was undoubtedly the victim of continual political misinformation from councillors who 'may say what they please having his Maties ear and they may safely also show his Matie letters which they make up in our names'.[62] As he argued elsewhere, the Scots nation had historically been 'more forward then our Neighbours, and consequently more inclined to ruin one another when wee enter into faction, and our Parliam^ts were the scenes wherein our Factions appear'd most'.[63] Meanwhile, in 1672, Mackenzie's colleague, Steuart of Goodtrees published an anonymous tract beseeching Charles II to call a new parliament on the grounds that the 'arbitrarie and frequent long adjournments' represented a 'manifest violating of the ancient and natural constitution of our government'. Steuart denied that such a meeting would serve to weaken or undermine royal authority. For although a free discussion of affairs 'might stirre up, and raise every ingenious spirit, to the highest degree of indignation', he insisted that, ultimately, Parliament's royal sanction did 'farr more powerfullie encline, to a dutifull regret'.[64]

Such sentiments thus reflected a fairly widespread belief that the king's refusal to make parliament a regular constitutional fixture was not only unjust, but detrimental to the efficient government of the country as well as to his own royal authority. Disquiet inevitably intensified when such anxieties were automatically misconstrued as denoting incipient political disloyalty. As one anonymous writer complained, 'nothing will dissuade o^r king but we all designe rebellion' while 'nothing will dissuade us but his Matie intends the way of arbitrary government in this kingdom', thereby establishing 'the ground work of all Tiranny & oppression'. The author warned that the crown's continued allegations that the Scots were inherently rebellious and seditious could rebound dangerously since 'experience hes observed this to be a sure maxime y^t to persuade princes w^tout just cause to suspect their subjects of either is to provock them to be both'. Although the writer feared that Charles II might resent such uninvited personal communications as 'too plain & peremptor', he trusted that from such 'rude ingenuitie might easilie be found the true pulse of affairs in Scotland at this tym'.[65] As violence escalated in the late-1670s, another writer petitioned for a parliament to be summoned on the grounds that it was 'the onlie Court that can understand the true nature of this Epidemick distemper'. Remembering how the Roman Emperor, Nero, had 'wished all the Romanes in one hand that he might cut it off', the author prophesied, however, that 'Lauderdale would by one stroke cut off this comon head of the nation' by endowing the Lords of the Articles with a power of veto, contrary to 'all the

---

[62] NAS GD 406/2/635/16, 'A Representation of the State of Affairs in Scotland'.

[63] BL Add. MSS. 18,236, Sir George Mackenzie of Rosehaugh, 'A Discourse on the 4 First Chapters of the Digest to Shew the Excellence and usefullnesse of the Civill Law [1691]', f. 24v.

[64] [Steuart], *Accompt of Scotland's Grievances*, pp. 32, 51.

[65] NAS GD 331/18/1–2, 'Paper addressed to the King'.

reason, practice, and records of our parliament, & opposite to the verie essence & life of this great Court'.[66]

As already indicated by the issue of legal appeals, preserving the independent integrity of the Scottish Parliament acquired particular importance when the prospect of an incorporating union being enacted between Scotland and England was mooted in 1670. In a letter sent to the Parliament that had convened in Edinburgh in October 1669, Charles II articulated his intention to pursue the glorious objective that his grandfather, James VI & I, had 'attempted as the greatest thing he could devise'.[67] Although parliamentary union would also serve to remove hostile trade restrictions between the two countries, Charles' proposals to appoint commissioners to negotiate a political and economic union encountered immediate resistance. Vociferous opposition was lodged, for example, by Mackenzie of Rosehaugh who argued that the appointment of commissioners entrusted to embark on such a momentous course of action should be the separate responsibility of the English and Scottish Parliaments, rather than the monarch. As Mackenzie conceived, any 'Union should be a national Act; and the way to make it so is, that all its steps should be nationally concluded'. Keenly aware that any 'allowances from parliaments soon become a prerogative', Mackenzie urged caution, indicating that it was imperative that 'England may know, that we are not so weary of our liberties as not to think them worthy of our exactest pains'.[68]

Although Mackenzie's procedural protestations regarding the appointment of commissioners went unheeded, mutual Anglo-Scottish suspicions ultimately conspired to render the union proposals abortive when formal negotiations were held during the autumn of 1670. Fourteen commissioners from England and seventeen from Scotland met at Whitehall and discussed the possibility of uniting the two kingdoms into one monarchy 'inseparately', dissolving the Scottish and English Parliaments and creating a bicameral British Parliament in London, preserving the independent integrity of each country's legal system and ecclesiastical structures and removing all trade restrictions between the two kingdoms.[69] Proposals to apportion thirty seats to Scottish representatives within the bicameral British Parliament revived particularly unwelcome memories of Cromwellian precedents. As Mackenzie later observed, no proposal of greater integration with England 'could have been less acceptable to the people at this time, than at this, in which the remembrance of their Oppresion [*sic*] from the Usurper was yet fresh with them'.[70] Separate suspicions were also voiced

---

[66] NAS GD 406/2/635/14, 'A short information of some few of the Grievances of the Kingdome of Scotland and their causes'.

[67] Charles II, *His Majesties Gracious Letter to His Parliament in Scotland, assembled October 19. 1669, Together with the Speech of his Grace the Earl of Lauderdaill, His Majesties High Commissioner; As Also The Answer of the Parliament of Scotland to His Majesties Gracious Letter* (London, 1669), p. 2.

[68] Mackenzie, *Memoirs*, pp. 152–3, 149.

[69] C. Sandford Terry ed., *The Cromwellian Union: Papers Relating to the Negotiations for an Incorporating Union Between England and Scotland, 1651–1652, with an Appendix of papers Relating to the Negotiations in 1670* (Edinburgh, 1902), p. 197.

[70] Mackenzie, *Memoirs*, p. 141.

regarding Charles II's motives in wishing to enlarge the size of a future British legislature. Recognising that the power of the English House of Commons lay 'verie heavy upon his loines [*sic*] and the loins of his predecessors . . . especially of his brave father', the judge, Lauder of Fountainhall, detected a royal attempt to 'wrest this excessive power out of the commons' as an 'unspeakable impairment of his soveraintie'.[71] Furthermore, even if the union negotiations could have been concluded satisfactorily, Mackenzie denied the right of Scottish parliamentary commissioners to assent to a proposal that would 'extinguish, or innovate the Constitution of the Parliament' unless unanimous agreement was obtained, since each commissioner's right 'cannot be taken away without his own Consent, tho' all these who are in the Society with him should Renounce what is theirs'.[72] This argument that the Scottish Parliament was not entitled to legislate itself out of existence by a majority vote acquired especial resonance amidst subsequent parliamentary debates regarding Anglo-Scottish union in 1706 when Mackenzie's opinions were published by anti-unionist pamphleteers.[73]

Within the domestic sphere, traditional Scottish parliamentary privileges, such as freedom of speech, were also defended energetically during the Restoration. In September 1661, for instance, the earl of Tweeddale was imprisoned in Edinburgh Castle for objecting to the sentence of death pronounced at the treason trial of the Covenanter, James Guthrie, on the grounds that punishment for similar crimes had hitherto been banishment. In response, Tweeddale confessed his incredulity that 'words spoke in Parliament were censurable to that height', since freedom of parliamentary speech was 'not only there allow'd, but is also advantageous to his Majesty's service'. Such reasoning had always explained why commissioners were 'expressly indemnified by our law for what is spoke by them in Parliament'.[74] Although Tweeddale was released from the Castle, his subsequent confinement under house arrest for over eight months was widely regarded as an unacceptable affront to a prominent Scottish earl. Legislation passed by the Scottish Parliament in 1662 further precluded anyone from holding civil, ecclesiastical or military office if they sought to provoke 'hatred or dislyk' of Charles II's royal prerogative in temporal and spiritual matters and, unlike legislation passed at the same time in England, did not contain a clause preserving freedom of speech in Parliament.[75] In 1665, another anonymous memorial insisted that 'freedome in voteing, speakeing and

---

[71] Lauder of Fountainhall, *Journals*, pp. 229–30.
[72] Sir George Mackenzie, 'Discourse Concerning The three Unions', in *Works*, II, 669.
[73] See Anon., *A Letter concerning the Union, with Sir George Mackenzie's Observations and Sir John Nisbet's Opinion upon the same Subject* ([Edinburgh], 1706). As the tract indicates, this argument had also been articulated during the negotiations by Mackenzie's predecessor as Lord Advocate, Sir John Nisbet of Dirleton. Regarding Nisbet's objections as 'exceeding troublesome, & impertinently peremptorie', Lauderdale reported to Tweeddale that Nisbet had declared that even to debate reducing the two Parliaments into one British Parliament 'was treason' since 'even the [Scottish] parlᵗ hath no power to do it' (NLS MS. 7023, 'Earl of Lauderdale to the marquis of Tweeddale, 27 September 1670', f. 246r.
[74] Mackenzie, *Memoirs*, p. 60.
[75] Thomas and Innes eds., *Acts of the Parliament of Scotland*, VII, 378.

reasoning be most necessar' in all judicial courts, particularly the 'High Court of Parlia[t]'. By contrast, the recent experience of members was that they had been 'overawed and Interupted' in speaking, or challenged for using that freedom 'contrair to express standing Lawes, and to the great scandall and contempt of that Supream Court'.[76] When another Commissioner, William Moir, urged that before the assembly approved the cess in 1672, members should be given time to consult their constituents, he was also imprisoned for 'some words vttered tending to the subversion of the constitution of Parliament'.[77] The incident was recorded by Mackenzie of Rosehaugh as one whereby 'a member was punisht shamefully in Parliament', but without parliamentary 'consent or concurrence'.[78] More generally, the anonymous author of a manuscript memorial considered it 'strange that it should be thought Irregular' for members to propose grievances in Parliament which was 'both necessar & ordinar', rendering it 'much stranger that the priviledges of parlia[t] should be thus quarrelled by private subjects'.[79]

Allegations of further parliamentary abuses were recorded privately by William Douglas, third duke of Hamilton, during excise debates in 1669. According to Hamilton, when it was proposed that some staple foods, such as cured herring, be exempted from the import tax on salt, they were apprised by Lauderdale 'in a threatning way', that 'if they refuised it, his Ma[tie] wold do it by his prerogative'. When accusations of voting improprieties subsequently surfaced and requests for a recount were refused, Hamilton further recorded that 'this incroachment upon the priviledg of parl: was much resented by most of the members', as was the fact that 'particular members were threatned & reproched as was my self'. The portents of such abuses for royal authority were foreseen by Hamilton when the act in question was passed without debate, such 'strang & unusuall actings [as] this did much disgust the generallitie of all ranks of people & discouraged them in ther dutie & service to his Ma[tie]'.[80] Commissioners were similarly intimidated the following year, when they voiced discontent regarding proposals that obliged heritors to sign bonds guaranteeing the religious conformity and peaceable behaviour of their tenants. When members were prevented from voicing their disquiet, Hamilton observed 'how little service such insolen[t] carreing on of affairs is to his Ma[tie] time will show'.[81] When attempting to explain why the government enjoyed such assured and regular victories, however, Mackenzie of Rosehaugh attributed partial reason to the fact that Commissioners failed to regard themselves as a united entity. As he

---

[76] NAS GD 406/2/640/5, 'Address to his Majesty giving a rep[n] of the state and interest of Scotland'.
[77] Thomson and Innes eds., *Acts of the Parliament of Scotland*, VIII, 63.
[78] Mackenzie, *Memoirs*, p. 231.
[79] NAS GD 406/2/635/6(iii), 'A representation of the present affaires'.
[80] NAS GD 406/2/640/3, 'Memorandum of some passages in parl: begune in October 1669 and first session'. Mackenzie of Rosehaugh also criticised Lauderdale's authoritarian style of parliamentary management, recalling that 'he never consulted what was to be done; nor were the members of Parliament solicited by him . . . on the contrary, he would oftimes vent at his table, that such Acts should be passed in spight of all oppositions' (Mackenzie, *Memoirs*, p. 181).
[81] NAS GD 406/2/640/3, 'Memorandum of some passages in parl:'.

observed, those who were 'not concern'd in their immediate interest' instinctively tended to vote for the government, thereby ensuring that 'oftimes the whole country is, by parcels, prejudg'd'.[82]

IV

By the mid-1670s, Hamilton's dire predictions regarding the limited potential for full and free constitutional debate within the Scots Parliament appeared likely to be fulfilled. With all individual attempts at opposition systematically frustrated, discontented elements within the political establishment increasingly combined to form an organised parliamentary opposition of the type that had been deemed absent by Mackenzie. Despite evincing a broad plurality of political interests, those who opposed Lauderdale's administration increasingly came to follow a shared political agenda. Hence although relatively brief and of limited success, the members of this parliamentary opposition succeeded in placing the workings of constitutional monarchy at the centre of political debate while again demonstrating the difficulties of combining ideological support for an absentee absolute monarch with practical opposition to his executive government.

Prior to the formal opening of Parliament on 12 November 1673, Mackenzie detected the growth of an identifiable 'confederacy' that served to 'heighten the courage' of those opposed to Lauderdale's administration.[83] Lauderdale himself noticed a group of 'Lords who keep there constant meetings at Mastersons' tavern' where proposals for Middleton's billeting scheme had also been secretly drafted in 1663.[84] Observing the manner in which they 'meet day & night publickly', Lauderdale identified his erstwhile ally, Tweeddale, as 'the head & heart' of the assembly, while Hamilton seemed 'content to appear the Leader and the Dryver'.[85] From what he could gather, the connivers were intending to petition for a committee to be established to debate national grievances which Lauderdale construed would not only 'make the [Lords of the] Articles insignificant', but also lay a foundation 'for perpetuall trouble'.[86] Such a strategy was, however, defended by lawyers such as Steuart of Goodtrees on the grounds that it followed traditional Scottish practice. According to Steuart, historically there had been a 'more ancient meeting ordained' by Parliament called the '*domini ad querulas*, or (if you will) the Committee of Grievances'.[87]

---

[82] Mackenzie, *Memoirs*, p. 172. Referring to the excise debates of 1669, for instance, Mackenzie observed how 'those who have salmond [*sic*], care not how much is impos'd on beef, &c., wheras when it comes to their share to be concern'd, they who have the other commodity do, out of revenge, or at least by the same reason, desert them' (*Ibid.*).

[83] *Ibid.*, pp. 252–3. For more detail, see John Patrick, 'The origins of the opposition to Lauderdale in the Scottish Parliament of 1673', *Scottish Historical Review*, 53 (1974), pp. 1–21.

[84] Tollemache MSS. 2413, 'Earl of Lauderdale to ?, 18 November 1673'.

[85] Airy ed., *Lauderdale Papers*, III, 3.

[86] Tollemache MSS. 2413, 'Lauderdale to ?, 18 November 1673'.

[87] [Steuart], *Accompt of Scotlands Grievances*, p. 16.

Encountering 'such a spirit as I thoght never to have seen heir', Lauderdale nevertheless opened the assembly, but found its proceedings immediately obstructed by Hamilton, who refused to allow a reply to the royal letter to be formulated until a full and free parliamentary debate about the nation's discontents had occurred. Following Lauderdale's refusal, it was then moved that a debate should be conducted as to 'whither they were a free parlᵗ or not' at which point the assembly itself was precipitately suspended. As Lauderdale later recalled, many 'set speeches were prepared, but my soddaine adjourning made them be kept cold'.[88] Amidst this charged political atmosphere, particular objection was also lodged against the opening sermon, preached by the dean of Edinburgh, John Paterson. In his address, Paterson had claimed that, to punish the sins of the people, God would sometimes send up 'a fawning Absolom' who 'under protest of grievances for their oune ends wold studie to alienat the peoples affections from their obedience and loyaltie' and would 'therby insinuat himself in the peoples favour and obtaine a popular applause'. When Paterson drew on Biblical parallels to claim that the outcome of such nefarious activity was always unlawful rebellion, members of Parliament remonstrated.[89] In defending his actions to Hamilton, Paterson claimed that he had 'made no manner of application to anie present person or affair', but had deliberately 'made the historie look backwards to our late civill wars'.[90] When Parliament reconvened, however, Lauderdale subsequently consented to acts discharging specific excise impositions on salt, brandy and tobacco, but further trouble erupted over the maintenance of unpopular officials such as Andrew Ramsay, the allegedly corrupt Provost of Edinburgh. Not only did members of the Convention of Royal Burghs combine with parliamentary commissioners for the first time over this issue, but when Ramsay's removal was specifically requested, the use of the English term 'impeachment' was heard for the first time in Scottish politics.[91]

There was, however, another dimension to domestic affairs within the Parliament. From the outset, Lauderdale himself suspected that there were 'industrious tamperings from London heir', evident from the way in which Hamilton 'who desires brouillerie . . . brags what great friends he hath at London'. Anticipating that members of the Scottish opposition might travel to London to present their case to Charles II in person, Lauderdale consoled himself by acknowledging that they might journey south, but would never be granted authority to depute parliamentary commissioners to negotiate with the monarch 'as the

---

88 Airy ed., *Lauderdale Papers*, II, 243, 246.
89 NAS GD 406/1/2691, 'Summary of sermon provided by John Paterson, November 1673'.
90 NAS GD 406/1/2690, 'John Paterson to the duke of Hamilton, 2 November 1673'. Elsewhere Robert Law confirmed that Paterson's sermon had allegedly insinuated that 'the giving in of grievances was the first thing began the warrs against King Charles the First, and that many now a-dayes were lyk Absalom sitting in the gate, and saying "O if I were ruler" ' (Law, *Memorialls*, p. 55).
91 See Mackenzie, *Memoirs*, p. 261. The impeachment and subsequent dismissal of the earl of Clarendon for mismanaging the Anglo-Dutch War by the English House of Commons in 1667 had represented a direct challenge to the monarch's prerogative to choose his own ministers.

Rebells did during the Covenanters rebellion'.[92] His reasoning ultimately proved correct, for although Hamilton and an accompanying deputation travelled to Whitehall in 1674, Charles II's response was only to charge them with having attempted 'to undermine the very foundation of his authority', by trying to initiate debates in Parliament and bypassing the Lords of the Articles 'which Articles he lookt upon as the securest fence of his government'.[93]

Hamilton's visit to London in 1674 coincided, however, with a series of unsuccessful English parliamentary attempts to remove Lauderdale permanently from Charles II's presence on the grounds of his attempting to introduce arbitrary government by allegedly informing the Scottish Privy Council that Charles II's edicts were to be accorded higher authority than standing law. In addition, English M.P.s also drew attention to the Scottish Militia Act of 1663 that had established a sizeable army of 2,000 cavalry and 20,000 foot soldiers for use in Charles II's service throughout the multiple monarchy. Although this act had been passed before Lauderdale became parliamentary High Commissioner, fears remained regarding the potential for such forces to be deployed in England. In January 1673, for instance, Sir Thomas Littleton had insisted that a 'cloud hangs over us, and 'tis high time it was scattered'. Two years later, the former Speaker, Henry Powle, likewise voiced his own frustration that 'all our Addresses cannot remove an obnoxious person', doubting that England 'can be in security, if these Scotch Acts be continued as a scourge to hang over us'.[94] Ironically, fears that Scottish troops would be used against English dissidents were ultimately reversed when the duke of Monmouth was appointed to command the Anglo-Scottish army that defeated the Covenanters at Bothwell Bridge in June 1679.

The activities of the Scottish parliamentary opposition to Lauderdale during the mid-1670s were therefore keenly observed south of the border. As the earl of Kincardine confirmed to Lauderdale in December 1673, the earl of Shaftesbury 'did guesse before the Parliament of Scotland sat doune of all that has been done since at it'.[95] Meanwhile, in London, the Scottish deputation were observed 'daily concerting a correspondence with Buckingham, Shaftsbury and others who were discontented' and the English M.P., Thomas Ross, confirmed that 'at this great baiting, one of the bears intended to be brought to the stake' was indeed Lauderdale. Moreover, Ross alluded to the enormous contrast in physical size and bearing between Lauderdale and his principal antagonist, Shaftesbury, adding that although the former was boasting that he 'would crush the little worme with his great toe', English political consensus believed that Shaftesbury would 'wriggle from under him and trip up his heeles'.[96]

---

[92] Airy ed., *Lauderdale Papers*, II, 241, 244, 247.
[93] Mackenzie, *Memoirs*, pp. 263–4.
[94] Grey ed., *Debates of the House of Commons*, II, 238, III, 214.
[95] Airy ed., *Lauderdale Papers*, III, 18. Evidence that Shaftesbury and his Whig colleagues were engaged in drawing up lists of Scots politicians with whom they could concert over opposition to Lauderdale is supplied in John Patrick, 'The Scottish Constitutional Opposition in 1679', *Scottish Historical Review*, 37 (1958), pp. 37–41.
[96] William Christie ed., *Letters from London addressed to Sir Joseph Williamson while Plenipotentiary at the Congress of Cologne*, 2 vols. (London, 1874), II, 29.

Attempts at impeachment were ultimately frustrated, however, when key witnesses such as Kincardine refused to testify either for or against Lauderdale, on the grounds that the English House of Commons 'could pretend no jurisdiction over Scotland'.[97] Hence the duchess of Lauderdale was able to record her satisfaction at what she perceived as the objectionably 'longing desire' of English politicians to achieve 'such a conquest as would be the cantonising of Scotland'.[98] Instead, English M.P.s such as the presbyterian, John Birch, were ironically obliged to observe how Lauderdale 'grows fat upon the displeasure of the House of Commons', after Lauderdale was created baron of Petersham and earl of Guildford in 1674, for which he received an additional annual pension of £3,000 (sterling). An anonymous manuscript tract meanwhile alleged that Lauderdale had 'upon all occasions spoken of the house of Com[m]ons and their magna Carta with the greatest Contempt calling the latter magna farta', warning that if 'they would Addresse against him, he would fart against them'.[99] A similarly cynical and scatological humour later characterised Lauderdale's response to the presentation of the 'Monster Petition' by the citizens of London to Charles II in 1680. According to a court observer, having witnessed Charles gather over a hundred signed sheets under his arm, Lauderdale allegedly informed Charles, in 'his drolling maner', that 'yow have sufficient provision for yo[r] sacred arse for neare yo[r] lyfetyme' whereupon 'all present fell in a greatt laughter'.[100]

Although Charles II consented to another parliamentary sitting in Edinburgh during the following spring of 1674, the session was adjourned immediately after prayers. While Hamilton and others remonstrated, Lauderdale declared himself unwilling to receive 'representations made by men in such a ferment', adding that they 'were no more a court of Parliament, and so could not act as such'.[101] When Charles then prorogued Parliament by proclamation, Lauderdale applauded his ending an assembly 'where mad motions were prepared against yo[r] Service'. By the postponement, he informed Charles that he had 'dasht them in a moment, and laid a foundation for restoreing your authority here, w[ch] was industriously shaken in all the corners of the kingdome'. Anticipating his imminent return to Charles' presence in London, Lauderdale eagerly pronounced that 'yow shall find me readier than all your Enemies to rid yow of the trouble of Scots Parliaments, w[ch] I swear are now useles at the best'.[102]

Within Scotland, however, such sentiments were not universally echoed. As Hamilton's heir, the earl of Arran, protested from Glasgow, news of the parliamentary adjournment came 'like a thunder boult' at which 'wee wer all put to a

[97] Airy ed., *Lauderdale Papers*, III, 32.
[98] Sharpe ed., *Letters from the Lady Margaret Kennedy*, Appendix, p. 105.
[99] BL Add. MSS. 28,938, 'That the Duke of Lauderdale concurred in the Design', f. 13r.
[100] NAS GD 157/2673/2, 'Sir James Scott to Sir William Scott of Harden, 20 January 1680'. For more about the petition, see Mark Knights, 'London's "Monster Petition" of 1680', *Historical Journal*, 36 (1993), pp. 39–67.
[101] Mackenzie, *Memoirs*, p. 265.
[102] Airy ed., *Lauderdale Papers*, III, 36.

non plus ultra'.[103] The nonconformist minister, Robert Law, confirmed that '[a]ll men are troubled at the adjurnment of the parliaments and all loyal men are truely grieved for it', notwithstanding a small minority 'who love to fish in moddy [*sic*] waters, and look after changes of the government'.[104] Nevertheless, the inherent strength of the opposition's tactics ensured that no Parliament was convened again in Scotland whilst Lauderdale remained either Secretary or parliamentary High Commissioner, although a Convention was held for taxation purposes in June 1678.[105] Moreover, following James', duke of York's, appointment as parliamentary High Commissioner in 1681, Charles II explicitly warned his brother to 'take speciall care, to suppres [*sic*] all motions for proposeing, votinge or carrieing on anie things in parlament, in an unparlamentarie method . . . upon the verie first appearance of them'.[106]

V

Although the activities of Hamilton and his supporters indicate vibrant constitutional opposition to Lauderdale's administration in the mid-1670s, such activity was hampered by a number of weaknesses of which the greatest was the unswerving support bestowed upon Lauderdale by Charles II. As Mackenzie of Rosehaugh concluded, by 1678 Scottish parliamentary defiance against Lauderdale's administration was construed as virtually impossible by most of the nobility 'seeing the King own him against all opposition'.[107] Continuing to interpret all grievances as unwarranted invasions on the royal prerogative, Charles thereafter refused to countenance any complaint put forward by the opposition unless it was presented in written form, fully aware that to do so would immediately lay individuals open to charges of treasonable slander. Unsurprisingly, Hamilton rejected such constructions of political disloyalty, maintaining in 1674 that his only intention had been to reveal 'to the world how his Majestie in his particulare reveneus [*sic*] has been abused and his subjects opressed'. Had it not been for the prorogation, Hamilton was confident that the Parliament would have 'made as high and full offers of there lives and fortunes to his Majesties service as ever any was done befor'.[108]

During the Convention subsequently held for taxation purposes in June 1678, however, Hamilton's repeated attempts to obstruct political business by

---

[103] NAS GD 406/1/2786, '[Earl of Arran] to James Johnston, 10 March 1674'.
[104] Law, *Memorialls*, p. 64.
[105] A Convention was identical to a Parliament in composition, but possessed restricted powers, being only able to discuss specific subjects, such as the grant of taxation. Conventions were not preceded by the ceremonial 'riding of Parliament' and could be summoned at shorter notice than the forty days required to summon Parliament.
[106] BL Add. MSS. 11,252, f. 8, 'Privat instructions To our intirelie beloved Brother, James, Duke of Albanie And York, our Commissioner in Scotland'.
[107] Mackenzie, *Memoirs*, p. 321.
[108] 'William, Duke of Hamilton to Mr. Andrew Cole, one of his Majesty's equerries', HMC *Laing*, I, 391.

challenging disputed elections and the composition of Convention sub-committees were again interpreted as intrinsically disloyal. He was duly informed by Viscount Stair, as Lord President of the Court of Session, that 'in all his Reign Scotland never refused his Matie anything or contraverted any of his comands [sic], and he hoped they wold not begin now'.[109] Although around 180 commissioners attended the Convention, representing 'the fullest appearance that ever was since the King was restored', scarcely more than thirty openly supported Hamilton, despite the latter's efforts to 'use more then Pharisaical diligence to proselyte the members from their duty'.[110] Consequently, little opposition was made to approval of a further fiscal contribution of £1.8m to be collected over four years specifically to defray domestic military commitments.

In England, alarmed members of the House of Commons continued to pass motions petitioning Charles II to remove Lauderdale permanently from the royal presence. According to Sir John Hotham, since 'in Scotland, if any man looks but discontented, then kill him, shoot him, eat him up!' he wondered if his parliamentary colleagues were content to 'have him do the same thing here?'[111] Such motions were nevertheless ignored or dismissed by a monarch committed to defending his political servant. Scottish sensitivities notwithstanding, Charles remained convinced that 'all other kings in the world governed their kingdomes & territories where they could not be themselves by one man'.[112] In Scotland, Lauder of Fountainhall reported widespread disquiet provoked by the 'extraordinar favors' conferred by Charles II on Lauderdale, that included 'refusing to hear all his ennemies, cloathing him in purple royall robes, making him a Duke, and partaker of his dominions, and his chieff friend'.[113] Although Lauderdale found himself obliged to remain in Edinburgh for the duration of the Convention of 1678, Mackenzie reassured him from London that a 'cheerfull countenance & a joviall humour is great policie' since 'yow were never so fixt in your masters affection'.[114] Observing the manner by which Hamilton and his colleagues had been rebuffed, Mackenzie consoled Lauderdale that there was 'no greater bafl for so many men of quality then to be admitted as criminalls & get no kisse of the Kings hand'.[115] From another source, Lauderdale likewise received confirmation from the earl of Arran that Charles took 'more painse to

[109] Airy ed., *Lauderdale Papers*, III, 156.
[110] 'Dr. George Hickes to Dr. [Simon] Patrick, 31 [sic] June 1678', in HMC, *Thirteenth Report, Appendix, Part II, The Manuscripts of His Grace, the Duke of Portland preserved at Welbeck Abbey*, Volume II (London, 1893), p. 50.
[111] Grey ed., *Debates of the House of Commons*, V, 359.
[112] Airy ed., *Lauderdale Papers*, III, 19.
[113] Lauder of Fountainhall, *Historical Observes*, p. 254. As Lauder continued, 'some think it a parallel case of what Alexander did to Jonathan the Hy Preiest, in the 1 Book of the Maccabees, 10 chapter, verse 61, et sequentibus' (*Ibid.*).
[114] BL Add. MSS. 32,095, 'Sir George Mackenzie of Rosehaugh to the earl of Lauderdale, April or May 1678', f. 94.
[115] BL Add. MSS. 32,095, 'Sir George Mackenzie of Rosehaugh to the earl of Lauderdale, [received 25 May 1678]', f. 102.

justify the Councell and you then your Grace wold doe your self', observing how 'he loves to talk of it to evry body'.[116]

When the Convention of 1678 closed, Lauderdale evidently 'conceived he had recovered any thing he lost in the Parliament of 1673'. According to Lauder of Fountainhall, Lauderdale 'triumphed mightilie with his successe, and Whythall was made to resound with it', thereby 'casting England a copie, and in showing the malecontents their how impotent their faction was in Scotland'.[117] Mackenzie had also perceived the multiple monarchy advantage of Lauderdale's success, predicting that if Lauderdale managed to convince English politicians that control had been asserted in Scotland 'they will blesse yow for they are at present in great dreadour [sic] of a Scottish rebellion'.[118] In London, James, duke of York, also confessed his relief to Lauderdale that the Convention had enjoyed 'so calme and good an ending', observing that 'the ill people here had great hopes of sturs [sic] where you are, and I belive some of our neighbours did build upon it also'.[119]

Secondly, in addition to Lauderdale's skilful political management, the opposition was unable to command widespread popular support throughout Scotland for their constitutional attacks upon parliamentary abuses and the system of the Lords of the Articles and its monopoly of legislative initiative. Despite Hamilton's assertion that 'never people wer more unite in any thing then I am sure this kingdom will be in this', his party were insufficiently radical to appeal to what Matthew Mackaile had termed the 'interest of religion and presbytery'.[120] This contrasted with Shaftesbury's political opposition in England which seized on the emotive and popular issue of anti-Catholicism. As the presbyterian, James Kirkton, remarked, at this critical juncture, 'neither of the sides mentioned the notion of religion, either for distress or danger'. Since the activities of the duke Hamilton's party merely focused upon specific administrative and fiscal abuses of power by the duke of Lauderdale and his colleagues, 'this made the lovers of religion to be lesse concerned for either' since both avoided 'the most noble interest, which was in great hazard.'[121]

Ironically, but perhaps inevitably, the interest of religion was nonetheless invoked to discredit the political concerns of both sides. Stated concern for constitutional proprieties was deemed by Lauderdale and members of the episcopalian establishment to be disingenuous cover for the promotion of presbyterian interests by members of Hamilton's opposition. During one of Hamilton's visits to London in 1676, for instance, it was reported that he had privately suggested that a second prerogative Indulgence for moderate nonconformist

116 Airy ed., *Lauderdale Papers*, III, 102.
117 Lauder of Fountainhall, *Historical Observes*, p. 279.
118 BL Add. MSS. 32,095, 'Sir George Mackenzie of Rosehaugh to the earl of Lauderdale, April or May 1678', f. 94.
119 Airy ed., *Lauderdale Papers*, III, 160.
120 'Duke of Hamilton to Cole', HMC *Laing*, I, 391.
121 Kirkton, *History*, p. 201. See the contemporary lampoon entitled 'A Dialogue betwixt Hamiltoune and Lauderdaill', in David Laing ed., *Various Pieces of Fugitive Scottish Poetry: Principally of the Seventeenth Century* (2nd series, Edinburgh, 1853).

ministers to return would serve to promote civil peace. On receiving this information, Archbishop Sharp of St. Andrews immediately reported to Lauderdale that 'the party have taken off their masque', thus revealing 'whence the phanaticks have taken there encouragement'.[122] For his part, Lauderdale acquiesced in any construction that further eroded the opposition's assertions of unswerving loyalty to Charles II's authority. As Matthew Mackaile explained in a letter intercepted by the authorities, Lauderdale was obliged to represent the various factions in Scotland as 'only divided in appearance, but really ready to rise in actual rebellion and shake off all government'. For his part, Lauderdale responded by devising such an intricate series of oaths 'that would have obliged those that pretend for liberty and privileges to persecute those that pretend for religion and presbytery'.[123] But amidst such chicanery, Lauderdale inevitably also found himself subject to misrepresentation. As his chaplain, George Hickes, acknowledged in 1677, members of the Scottish political opposition were so intent on undermining his patron's repute among members of the Anglican establishment that a 'thousand such tricks and reports' had been 'contrived to make the world at London believe that my Lord is a favourer of the fanatics, and that he is not capable to govern this country'.[124]

In the absence of regular parliamentary sittings, the government of Scotland was increasingly conducted by royal proclamations which were manifestly unpopular as an instrument of rule. In 1674, Hamilton had specifically complained to Charles II about the use of a proclamation discharging all cess dues owed since 1660, arguing that 'it was hard to see that ther wold be no end' to such orders that were 'contrare to the fundamentall laues of this & all other nations'. While Hamilton did not dispute the legality of the practice of government by proclamation, he sought to impress upon Charles its unpopularity in Scotland and the potential extent to which 'his Maties authority is abused in such inderect wayes'.[125] The use of proclamations was likewise singled out for attack by the Covenanters' *Apologetick Declaration* of 1681 which protested that Scots laws were 'no more made the rule', but only that of the monarch's will, rendering Scotland a focus of 'reproach to other Nations who say that wee have only the Law of Letters instead of the Letter of the Law'.[126]

The practical potential for opponents of Lauderdale's administration to

---

[122]   NLS MS. 2512, 'Archbishop James Sharp to the duke of Lauderdale, 12 February 1676', f. 195.

[123]   'Mackaile to Frederick, 19 June 1678', in Blackburne Daniell ed., *Calendar of State Papers Domestic Series, March 1st, 1678, to December 31st, 1678*, p. 232. In a different confessional context, however, interest in the domestic politics of Restoration Scotland evidently extended overseas. In November 1674, Arran learned of reports circulating in Edinburgh about 'ane letter come from Rome' which alleged that there was 'great talking there of the two grand dukes of Scotland'. According to the Italian construction of events, 'La[uderdale] is said to favour the Catholick partie and yet to be more Loyall, and Ha[milton] is said to be head of the puritan partie' (NAS GD 406/1/5924, [?James Johnston] to the earl of Arran, 20 November 1674').

[124]   'Hickes to Patrick, 20 November 1677', in HMC, *Thirteenth Report, Appendix, Part II . . . [Manuscripts of] the Duke of Portland preserved at Welbeck Abbey, Volume II*, p. 39.

[125]   Airy ed., *Lauderdale Papers*, III, 38.

[126]   NAS GD 157/1861, 'The Act and Apologetick Declaration of the presbyterians of the Church of Scotland [1681]'.

register their disquiet was directly hampered by a further proclamation issued in 1678 forbidding subjects to leave Scotland without permission, thus preventing the presentation of unauthorised personal addresses to the monarch. According to Sir James Turner, this injunction placed Hamilton in a precarious position, having 'the wolfe by the eares; he dare neither bite nor let goe'. For, as Turner recognised, although Hamilton wished to leave for London immediately the Convention ended, he elected to stay in Scotland, aware that since an English Parliament was due to convene, Lauderdale would inevitably 'represent to the King groundlesse fears, needles jealousies and apprehensions, well masked with seeming reasons of state'.[127] Proclaiming that he could never be 'understood a contemner of His Maj[ties] authority', Hamilton wrote to Charles II entreating him to allow him to travel to London 'with the same freedom, as if he had still his residence in Scotland'.[128] Once in London, however, Hamilton allegedly proclaimed 'uithe an oathe' to the English House of Commons that he 'uold never returne to Scotland to live in sutch slaevery as they were under', but 'uould rather go to Turky'.[129]

Claiming that there was 'nothing more his Maj[ties] interest than that the last resort and application of his subjects should be made to him', anonymous writers continued to warn Charles that restrictions governing subjects' freedom of movement were 'only made use of by usurpers who have no confidence in the affects and hearts of their subjects, but never by His Maj[ty] or his Royal predecessors'. Since the liberty to dispose of one's person appropriately was considered 'the highest degree of right or property', imposing such restraints without sufficient reason was 'more or less a degree and tendency to servitude'.[130] Another pamphleteer agreed, declaring this edict to be no less contrary to Charles II's interest as 'the refuge of the People' as to the natural rights of his subjects.[131] A similar language of natural rights was deployed when another proclamation of 1678 required the nobility in the western shires to surrender their horses and arms. Complaints were then lodged on the grounds that such legislation cast aspersions on the otherwise unimpeachable loyalty of such individuals, but also

---

127   Thomson ed., *Memoirs . . . by Sir James Turner*, pp. 273–4.
128   NAS GD 406/2/642/3, 'The Case of the Duke of Hamilton, April, 1678'. The following month, Hamilton submitted another address, pointing out that since those who wanted to articulate their concerns were 'not being admitted to his Maj[ties] presence', they had delegated lawyers to act on their behalf whom Hamilton was anxious should 'incur no hazard or censure thereby' (NAS GD 406/2/635/5, 'Copy of a paper given to the King Charles II by the Duke of Hamilton, May 1678'). In 1679, Hamilton presented another memorandum, advising Charles to 'make use of others of untainted loyaltie and in whom the Nation may have some reasonable confidence'. By such means, Hamilton was confident that it would be possible 'not onlie to settle and compose the present disorders without the assistance of England but [also to] secure the Kingdome for the future from the hasard of the like or greater insurrections' (NAS GD 406/2/635/10, 'Copy of a paper presented to the King Charles II by the Duke of Hamilton, June 1679').
129   Airy ed., *Lauderdale Papers*, III, 132–3.
130   NAS GD 406/2/637/4, 'That freequarter is against the fundamental laws of the Kingdom [1678]'.
131   Anon., *Some Particular matters of Fact, relating to the Administration of Affairs in Scotland under the Duke of Lauderdale, Humbly offered to his Majesties Consideration, in Obedience to his Royal Commands* ([London], ?1680), p. 2.

that 'self-defence and the use of arms against private injuries or force is juris naturalis'.[132]

In conclusion, notions of 'fundamental law' thus became intertwined with an older religious rhetoric of natural rights in providing the gravamen of domestic opposition to Stuart rule in Scotland, as articulated in the various private remonstrances and public utterances directed at the Restoration administration. In 1674, for instance, an anonymous address to Charles II vigorously defended the loyalty of the nobility, gentry and majority of the Scottish commons and denied that any wished to behave 'contrare to the established laws of the Kingdom' which they allegedly 'now profess mor then any religion even the sacred scripture it self'. If the most urgent political grievances were not speedily addressed, however, the same author warned that 'they may cloak themselves w^t the old professions of religion to revege y^r restraint & vindicat their Liberties'.[133] It was, however, far from clear what contemporaries substantively understood by the term 'fundamental law'. In May 1678, Hamilton petitioned Charles II in May 1678, to confirm 'what is the fundamental law of the Kingdom in such cases', adding that 'if any do question it', Charles might formally 'say the same in parliament'.[134] Ostensibly, such a demand assumed that fundamental law operated to circumscribe the monarch's conduct within a set of *leges regni* separate from the traditional constraints of the laws of God and of nature. Such an interpretation was thereby liable to undermine claims that the absolute monarch was *legibus solutus*. Addressing both houses of the English Parliament in 1607, James VI & I had attempted to confine fundamental law to those principles that established and regulated succession to the crown. As he contended, by the notion of fundamental laws, the Scots 'intend therby only those Lawes wherby confusion is avoyded' with reference to hereditary succession. Hence the Scots did not interpret fundamental law 'as you doe', denoting 'their Common Law, for they have none'. James was, however, unwilling to jettison entirely the reciprocal aspect of his duty to his subjects within the framework of fundamental law. As he explained in 1610, a king was effectively 'Lex loquens, after a sort, binding himselfe by a double oath to the obseruation of the fundamentall Lawes of his kingdome' as indicated by the commitment to rule according to law sworn in the coronation oath.[135]

---

[132] NAS GD 406/2/637/4, 'That freequarter is against the fundamental laws of the Kingdom [1678]'.

[133] NAS GD 331/18/1–2, 'Paper addressed to the King on current political affairs, 1674'. As the author insinuates, this claim was entirely different from the presbyterian defences of the fundamental status of engagements such as the National Covenant of 1638. In their tract entitled *Naphtali* of 1668, for instance, James Steuart and John Stirling had claimed that the Covenant which 'from the beginning was and is the most firm and indispensable Oath of God became at last the very fundamental law of the Kingdom' ([Steuart and Stirling], *Napthali*, p. 72).

[134] NAS GD 406/2/635/5, 'Copy of a paper given to King Charles II'.

[135] James VI & I, 'A Speech to Both the Hovses of Parliament, Delivered in the Great Chamber at White-hall, the Last Day of March 1607', in Sommerville ed., *Political Writings*, p. 172; 'A Speech to the Lords and Commons of the Parliament at White-Hall, on Wednesday the XXI. Of March, Anno. 1610', in Sommerville ed., *Political Writings*, p. 183. For earlier uses of the term in Scotland, see Burns, *The True Law of Kingship*, pp. 286–8. See also J. W. Gough, *Fundamental Law in English Constitutional History* (Oxford, 1961) and Martyn P. Thompson, 'The History of Fundamental Law in Political

In similar vein, Mackenzie of Rosehaugh declared in 1691 that a 'fundamentall Law is properly that Law, upon which the Acts of Parliament depend and which was it self prior to acts of Parliament, and was the cause of them', rendering it immune from subsequent repeal or amendment. Echoing James' arguments, Mackenzie thus regarded the hereditary succession of the monarchy to be one such instance of a fundamental law 'without which the nature of that thing would be alter'd'. Within this context, Mackenzie had earlier discussed the problem of accommodating Scottish fundamental laws within any proposed legislative union that incorporated Scotland and England. As he argued, a future British Parliament was not entitled to alter the rules governing Scottish parliamentary representation on the grounds that since 'the true Difference betwixt Fundamental and other Laws' was that 'Parliaments cannot overturn Fundamentals'.[136]

In his *Leviathan* of 1651, the English philosopher, Thomas Hobbes, had directly addressed the potential legal ambiguity that appeared to surround the relationship between fundamental law and absolute monarchy. Although Hobbes acknowledged a distinction between fundamental and non-fundamental laws, he confessed that he 'could never see in any Author, what a Fundamentall Law signifieth'. Hence he saw little reason to adhere to Bodinian-style constructions inferring that fundamental laws necessarily denoted certain popular rights and liberties unalterable by the sovereign. Instead, Hobbes controversially proposed that 'a Fundamentall Law is that, by which Subjects are bound to uphold whatever power is given to the Soveraign', whether monarch or popular assembly, 'without which the Common-wealth cannot stand'.[137] The implications of such an alternative and diametrically-opposite understanding were to assume increasing practical importance in Scotland during the second half of the Restoration. For although Mackenzie continued to recognise liberty and property as 'indeed the fundamentall Rights of the People', without which neither individuals nor society could subsist, in the aftermath of the 'Killing Times' of the late-1670s and early-1680s, he observed that 'factions and restless Spiritts have made every thing by very remote and ill deduc'd consequences to be a Violation of these fundamentall Rights'. Hence Mackenzie was forced to concede that 'what these fundamentall Laws are, I cannot determine', rendering it 'hard to make that a Crime in innocent co[u]ntry men, which the best Lawyers understand not'.[138] Given the increasing requirement to secure the Scottish nation from civil unrest during the Restoration, Hobbes' definition of a fundamental law as 'what power is given to the Soveraign . . . without which the Common-wealth cannot stand' acquired particular resonance. For contained

---

Thought from the French Wars of Religion to the American Revolution', *American Historical Review*, 91 (1986), pp. 1103–28.
[136] BL Add. MS. 18,236, 'Discourse on the 4 First Chapters of the Digest', ff. 44v, 47r; 'Discourse concerning The three Unions', in *Works*, II, 668.
[137] Hobbes, *Leviathan*, p. 199.
[138] BL Add. MSS. 18,236, 'Discourse on the 4 First Chapters of the Digest', f. 47v.

within the Hobbesian sovereign's authority was also 'the Supreme Power in all causes, as well Ecclesiastically, as Civill'.[139] To understand the degree to which ecclesiastical issues determined the character of late-seventeenth century debate, the politics of religion in Restoration Scotland now require investigation.

---

[139] Hobbes, *Leviathan*, p. 378.

5

The Politics of Religion

Orthodox historiography has largely tended to attribute blame for most of the political instability and civil strife experienced throughout Scotland between 1660 and 1689 to the unpopularity of the Restoration religious settlement which re-imposed an episcopalian system of church government on a predominantly presbyterian population. Correspondingly little attempt has hitherto been made, however, to examine the relationship between ecclesiastical divisions and political sympathies. The previous chapter demonstrated that differing degrees of practical political opposition did not necessarily preclude theoretical attachment to the Stuart monarchy. It is likewise far from clear that religious nonconformity instantly denoted political disloyalty. Opponents of prelacy were thus not invariably part of a truculent, outlawed and rebellious underground, for whom allegiance to 'King Jesus' forestalled loyalty to Charles II. Despite the claims of some episcopalian apologists in the aftermath of the Williamite Revolution which re-imposed presbyterianism, it was not necessarily the case during the Restoration that 'he who hates a Bishop, can never love a King' while 'he who treads on a Mitre, will quickly pull off the Crown'.[1] Nor did religious conformity always equate with committed support for the established church. Consequently, it is far from evident that active support for either the re-establishment of, or the maintenance of, episcopacy was a prerequisite for orderly government under Charles II.

This chapter considers the wider relationship between political allegiance and religious sympathies in Restoration Scotland. It begins by examining the various motives surrounding the decision to restore episcopacy that occurred amidst widespread anticlericalism in the aftermath of the civil wars. It then considers the ideological support for episcopacy articulated during the Restoration, arguing that the absence of any tradition of *iure divino* support for episcopacy in Scotland meant that the episcopalian establishment instead adopted a predominantly pragmatic, indifferentist and erastian attitude which ultimately undermined its own chances of survival. The third section investigates the increasing extent of state control over the church as the absence of *iure divino* defences of

---

[1]   [Thomas Morer], *The Prelatical Church-Man, against the Phanatical Kirk-Man, or a Vindication of the Author of the Sufferings of the Church of Scotland* (London, 1690), p. 6.

church government allowed the government to address more immediate problems of enforcing ecclesiastical discipline by embarking on a series of attempted indulgence schemes and accommodation projects. The fourth section explores the ways in which the vagaries of Restoration ecclesiastical policy prompted a number of internal episcopalian critiques from within the established church. The chapter concludes with a consideration of the increasingly serious divisions provoked among presbyterians over the extent to which religious conformity should be compromised for political obedience.

I

Underpinning the political and religious history of the Restoration in Scotland was the character of the religious settlement resolved upon at the end of the civil wars. At his original coronation as King of Scotland, England, Wales and Ireland in Scone Palace on 1 January 1651, Charles II had been solemnly informed by the preacher, Robert Douglas, that not only was he 'the onely Covenanted king with God and his People in the world', but he was consequently 'obliged to maintaine Presbyteriall Government, as well against Erastians as Sectaries'. Should he subsequently attempt to overthrow this ecclesiastical arrangement which formed 'the very Fundamentals of this Contract and Covenant', Charles was further apprised that 'the Estates of a Land, may and ought to resist by arms'.[2] Despite the strikingly unambiguous nature of these commitments, it was, however, far from clear whether Charles would abide by them when he was unconditionally invited to return to the throne nine years later. By 1660, the presbyterian kirk was itself internally divided between 'Protestor' and 'Resolutioner' factions over the degrees of secular involvement suitable for a godly state. While the former adhered to strict theocratic models, the latter was prepared to grant the monarch a much greater role in church government.

Before returning to England, representations had been made to Charles in the Netherlands by various Scots, including the earl of Lauderdale and the Resolutioner minister, James Sharp, but little conclusive indication was forthcoming regarding the future civil or ecclesiastical government of Scotland.[3] Following the Restoration, Charles wrote to the presbytery of Edinburgh in June 1660, committing himself 'to uphold the government of the church as it was established by law', which was generally construed 'to infer from the King an homolgation of the presbyterian government', together with the laws supporting its establishment.[4] Deeming the royal interest to be best served by having

[2]   Robert Douglas, *The Form and Order of the Coronation of Charles the II. King of Scotland, together with the Sermon then Preached, by Mr. Robert Douglas, &c.* (Aberdeen, 1660), pp. 38, 25, 15.
[3]   See Julia Buckroyd, 'The Resolutioners and the Scottish Nobility in the early months of 1660', *Studies in Church History*, 12 (1975), pp. 245–52.
[4]   Mackenzie, *Memoirs*, p. 16.

Scotland 'united in an intire obedience to his royall authority', Sharp was dispatched to London to negotiate the religious settlement on behalf of the Resolutioner faction. From the English capital, Sharp reassured his brethren in December 1660 that maintenance of presbyterianism was guaranteed, since the violence which had accompanied previous attempts to alter Scottish ecclesiastical policy provided 'a shrewd document for this time'. Sharp was, however, perturbed by intemperate demands being made by the rival Protestor delegation that, in the ecclesiastical sphere, not only Charles II and his court, but also all three kingdoms in the Stuart monarchy should 'be wholly conformed to ther fancied modell and absurd dictats'. If their wishes were to be frustrated, Sharp reported their intention to 'abominat' Charles personally, and 'doe what they can to weaken his interest and reputation with the people'. Despite such fears, Sharp dismissed rumours doubting the future security of presbyterianism, remaining confident that when 'the matter is putt to the push', it would become clear that 'the setting up of Bishops is not at the Bottom'.[5] To this end, Sharp preached a number of sermons before the English Parliament at the beginning of 1661 which repeatedly enjoined that just as Charles was 'not to encroach upon the property & liberty of the subject', so neither could subjects infringe the king's royal prerogative. By corollary, just as magistrates were not entitled 'to medle with what is competent to the minister', Sharp insisted that ministers were not entitled to involve themselves in civil affairs. Moreover, within the context of the Stuart multiple monarchy, Sharp further reiterated that one kingdom was not at liberty to influence the civil or ecclesiastical government of another, unless expressly invited to do so by both the king and the inhabitants of that kingdom.[6]

What subsequently jeopardised this apparent understanding, however, were the political measures duly adopted to reassert the royal prerogative. As the initiative appeared to pass from clerical advisors to government ministers, even Sharp himself acknowledged that 'ministers now are as great strangers to state transactions as befor they were medlers in them'.[7] By early 1661, the parliamentary High Commissioner, Middleton, had begun to make known his controversial intention to pass the Act Rescissory, rescinding all legislation enacted since the late-1630s. As the presbyterian, James Kirkton, later recalled, the Protestor faction 'smiled, and said to their brethren, they were bade grammarians in taking the infinitive mode for the indicative', since Charles II's letter the preceding June had only committed him to maintain the form of ecclesiastical government as defined by the laws currently in force.[8]

As seen in the previous chapter, however, Middleton was by no means unanimously supported in this initiative. Whilst in London, Lauderdale recognised immediately that this proposal would 'wholly take away the Church government

---

5   Airy ed., *Lauderdale Papers*, I, 44, 57, 49.
6   *Ibid.*, I, 68.
7   *Ibid.*, I, 66.
8   Kirkton, *History*, p. 41.

& settle Episcopacie', thus removing the established status of presbyterianism which Charles II had previously declared his resolution to preserve. Anticipating that 'great prejudice may come by breaking the unanimity of Scotland', Lauderdale advised further deliberation before proceeding with 'so sudden a change at this time'.[9] Even more unequivocal dissuasion came from Charles II's Lord Chancellor, the earl of Clarendon. Discussing the eventual restoration of episcopacy in Scotland, Clarendon conceded privately to Middleton that Charles 'could not choose, but wish the thing done, and would be glade if it were done, and hoped it would at some time be done', but insisted that he was not prepared to use his prerogative power to impose it. For although Charles recognised that the Scots Parliament was 'so devoted to his Maties service, that if hee shall require it to be done', legislation restoring episcopacy would be assured, Clarendon confirmed that this did not render the change 'acceptable to the Kingdome'. Evidently more concerned to preserve domestic harmony in Scotland than to achieve British congruity in church government, Clarendon thus relayed Charles' firm opinion that 'it will not be safe' if a consequence of the Act Rescissory was to suppress presbyterianism and impose episcopalianism. Hoping to restrain Middleton's zeal, Clarendon advised that Middleton should instead content himself only with rescinding 'particular ill Acts, the supporting whereof must prejudice the Kings Lawfull authority', thus deferring the possibility of restoring episcopacy until 'a more generall consent' could be obtained.[10]

Undeterred, Middleton persevered, securing a passage for the Act Rescissory in March 1661, which nullified the civil sanction of the Covenant and enabled the subsequent reintroduction of episcopacy. As Clarendon had predicted, not only were most Scots undeceived by Middleton's manoeuvre, but they were also alarmed about its practical prudence. In a letter to Lauderdale in April 1661, the presbyterian Principal of Glasgow University, Robert Baillie, doubted the wisdom of bringing 'bak upon us the Canterburian tyms, the same designs, the same practises', forecasting that such policy would 'bring on at last the same horribill effects'. For failing to avert such an eventuality, Baillie judged Lauderdale 'a prime transgressor and liable among the first to answer to God for that grit sin & opening a doer which in hast will no be closit'.[11] As for reaction across Scotland, reports received in London indicated that although magistrates in Ayrshire had received news of the reimposition of episcopacy with resignation, copies of the official proclamation had been torn down 'by rude hands' who 'all pretend zeal to the King, but not in a way consistent to his authority'.[12]

Not all observers were, however, hostile. William Cunningham, earl of Glencairn, for instance, was reported as having claimed that presbyterianism

[9] Bodl. Clarendon MSS. 75, 'Ld Lauderdale to the Earl of Glencairn', f. 400v. See also Davies and Hardacre, 'The Restoration of the Scottish Episcopacy'.
[10] Bodl. Clarendon MSS. 74, '[Earl of Clarendon] to [Earl of Middleton], ff. 291r–292v.
[11] Airy ed., *Lauderdale Papers*, I, 95.
[12] 'Colonel William Daniel to the Duke of Albemarle, 4 November 1661', HMC, *Report on the Manuscripts of F. W. Leyborne-Popham Esq.* (London, 1899), p. 190.

had never survived 'in any country without blood and rebellion'. Newly-appointed as Chancellor, Glencairn believed that presbyterian insolence and arrogance had so alienated 'all loyal subjects and wise men, that six for one in Scotland long'd for Episcopacy' as a means of avoiding future unrest.[13] Middleton's design was also enthusiastically supported by the former bishop of Galloway, Thomas Sydserf, who became the only member of the Caroline episcopate to regain episcopal office under Charles II. Towards the end of 1660, Sydserf had composed a memorial for Charles, arguing that the most appropriate way to restore bishops was by parliamentary legislation to ensure that 'the same hand may take them in orderly, which disorderly did thrust them out'. Sydserf had also emphasised the imperative need to restore episcopacy as soon as possible to support royal authority against presbyterian insistence that 'Kings may be deposed from their throne.' In doing so, he had also alluded to the potential personnel of a re-established episcopate by ingenuously counselling Charles to 'tak speciall notice' of those who had remained faithful to his interests. Furthermore, Sydserf had advised that not only should all subjects be compelled to swear oaths of allegiance and ecclesiastical supremacy, but also that specific legislation be passed condemning the sermon preached by Robert Douglas at Charles II's coronation in 1651 'as most treasonfull, appointing the same to be burnt with the hand of the hang-man'.[14]

Members of the first Scottish Parliament of the Restoration were also exposed to sermons articulating similar sentiments by other potential members of the Scottish episcopate. In February 1661, for example, John Paterson preached an address based on the somewhat unconciliatory text from Ezekiel 7:23: 'Make a chain, for the land is full of bloody crimes and the city is full of violence.' Maintaining the propriety of civil magistrates seeking 'to medle with Things that are Ecclesiastick', Paterson exhorted the Parliament to enact speedily 'a chain of new Laws' to thwart 'the like Treachery, Disloyalty and Usurpation in time coming'. Hence Paterson envisaged legislation which not only prevented the church from prescribing limits on monarchical authority, but also precluded clerics from 'starting or venting Questions, Principles, or Tenets, destructive to the Supream Civil Authority'.[15] A month later, the minister of Stirling, Matthias Symson, preached before the same assembly, reiterating

---

[13] Mackenzie, *Memoirs*, p. 53.

[14] Bodl. Clarendon MSS. 75, '[Thomas Sydserf], Information for his sacred Matie', ff. 427–8.

[15] John Paterson, *Tandem Bona Causa Triumphat, Or Scotlands Late Misery bewailed, and the Honour and Loyalty of this Ancient Kingdom, asserted in a Sermon Preached before His Majesties High Commissioner, and the Honourable Parliament of the Kingdom of Scotland. At Edinburgh, the 17 day of February 1661* (Edinburgh, 1661), pp. 17–18, 20. In later years, the uncompromising position adopted by clerics like Paterson was not forgotten by presbyterian opponents. Justifying the refusal of nonconformist ministers to accept the prerogative Indulgence offered by the government in 1671, for instance, the Covenanting preacher, Robert MacWard, charged members of the ecclesiastical establishment with hypocrisy. Albeit now 'their wish is for charity', MacWard denied that their motives were sincerely intended or likely 'to produce a desireable Accommodation . . . [since] at first it was *make a chaine, the land is full of bloodie crimes, and the city is full of violence*' (Robert MacWard, *The True Non-Conformist in Answere to the Modest and free Conference Betwixt a Conformist and a Non-Conformist About the present Distempers of Scotland* (n.p., 1671), pp. 497–8).

Paterson's call for Parliament to 'Make a chain' ensuring that the laws preserving the royal prerogative were 'as sharp pricks against which it shall be hard for a man to kick'. Regarding the standing of the established church, Symson also petitioned the politicians not only to safeguard 'our Maintenance that it be not diminished', but also to have 'a care of our credit and reputation' by acting as 'our noble Guardians to shield us from that contempt, which we have been but too active to draw down upon our selves'.[16] Elsewhere, the former Cromwellian principal of Edinburgh University, Robert Leighton, contended that Charles II's administration should not regard religion as 'an enemy to their dignity and authority'. On the contrary, religion offered the most effective way of enhancing royal authority, for although 'Civil Laws may tie the hands and tongue to their obedience . . . religion binds all due subjection to them upon the very consciences of the people.'[17]

Such a 'chain of new laws' to secure religious conformity, as envisaged by Paterson and Symson, were indeed forthcoming in the aftermath of the passage of the Act Rescissory when Leighton, together with three other ministers, Andrew Fairfoul, James Hamilton and James Sharp, travelled to London to receive consecration in Westminster Abbey. Together with the other members of the reconstituted Scottish episcopate, bishops were thereafter not only read-mitted to parliamentary sittings, but also restored to all their former privileges and jurisdictions. Across Scotland, 270 ministers, representing one quarter of all parish incumbents were, however, deprived when the Act for Presentation and Collation enacted in 1662 forced ministers to demit their cures unless they received formal episcopal presentation and collation. Moreover, as the number of ministerial ejections increased, lay nonconformity also escalated, particularly in south-west Scotland, as growing numbers refused to attend the established church, preferring instead to frequent illegal conventicles and to incur heavy fines for their absenteeism.

Despite such initial dislocation, it was repeatedly claimed, by outside observers and conformist clergy alike, that little practical difference thereafter subsisted between the two ecclesiastical systems. Travelling in Scotland in the late-1670s, for instance, the Anglican minister of St. Ann's in Aldersgate, London, Thomas Morer, remarked of the Scottish church that although it was termed episcopalian 'in Name and Jurisdiction', he believed that 'the way of its Administration is so wide from Episcopacy elsewhere, that any Stranger would take it for little else than Presbyterian'. In Morer's opinion, 'an indifferent Eye' that witnessed the similarity between episcopalian and presbyterian worship and discipline 'cannot but think it a Dispute about words, which Temporal Interest and Prejudice decides to the shame of better Reason and Christianity'.[18] Subse-quently concerned that episcopalian government might prove a casualty of the

---

[16] Symson, *Yehoveh ve melek, or God and the King*, pp. 16, 19–20.

[17] Leighton, 'Sermon on Romans XIII 5–8', in Jerment ed., *Works*, III, 213. Leighton pressed home his point by adding that even 'that master of irreligious policy, Machiavel confesses that the profession of religion is a friend to authority (*Ibid.*).

[18] Thomas Morer, *A Short Account of Scotland* (London, 1702), p. 47.

Revolution in 1689, Sir George Mackenzie of Rosehaugh and his cousin, Sir George Mackenzie, Viscount Tarbat, jointly composed a memorial for William of Orange, advising him that 'Episcopacy is necessary for the support of Monarchy'. They explained that their opposition to presbyterianism was not predicated on its intrinsic structure, but on its 'having incorporated into it many horrid Principles, inconsistent with humane Society in which the Monarchy is more concerned than we'. Moreover, Mackenzie and Tarbat conceded that, of episcopalianism and presbyterianism in practice, there had been 'in a word not one Ace of difference between the two'.[19] As Mackenzie of Rosehaugh confirmed elsewhere in 1691, episcopalian worship during the Restoration differed from presbyterian practice only in the use of the Doxology, the Lord's Prayer, baptism and the Nicene Creed. There had, however, been 'no Ceremonies, Surplices, Altars, Cross in Baptisms, nor the meanest of those things' which Mackenzie contended would have been 'allowed in England by the Dissenters, in way of Accommodation'.[20]

II

From Charles II's perspective, it appeared that the decision to restore episcopacy was to be sanctioned on the twofold grounds that not only was presbyterianism intrinsically incompatible with monarchical government, but also that neither he nor his father could be bound in conscience by either of the former undertakings to maintain presbyterianism conceded in 1638 and 1651 respectively. Such reasoning was seemingly shared by members of the re-established church who signally failed to produce a convincing *iure divino* case for episcopacy, evidently preferring instead to concur in the opinion that the civil magistrate might adopt whatever form of ecclesiastical government seemed most conducive to the preservation of civil order.

Such views were articulated in the pamphlet literature generated by discussion of the Restoration religious settlement. In 1661, the anonymous author of *A Letter containing an Humble and Serious Advice* recalled Scotland's recent history, pointing out 'how many thousands' had died 'by a misguided zeal, or implicit adherence to a Party'. Those who survived were merely 'a remnant left', fortunate enough to have 'outlived a long age of War'. Hence the author urged the Scottish people to submit peaceably to whatever form of church government Charles II's administration thought fit to establish. If episcopacy was to be the preferred option, the author advised his readers to 'remember you lived happily under it' and its abolition had been 'as the opening of that Box of Pandora', spawning the subsequent miseries 'you have labour'd under for more

[19] [Sir George Mackenzie and Sir George Mackenzie], *A Memorial for His Highness the Prince of Orange in Relation to the Affairs of Scotland* (London, 1689), p. 5.
[20] Sir George Mackenzie, *A Vindication of the Government in Scotland. During the Reign of King Charles II. Against Mis-representations made in several Scandalous Pamphlets* (London, 1691), p. 9.

than half of the time the People of Israel wandered in the Wilderness'. If nothing else, episcopacy could be supported on the grounds that it was admirably suited for a country with such a long and historic tradition of monarchical government, rendering episcopacy's support for 'Order and Peace, in extrinsick things' particularly appropriate. Since monarchical government was 'natural to you', the author concluded that since episcopacy reinforced monarchical authority and there was 'no Divine prohibition to the country', the Scots people should honour its restitution 'as bearing a Divine impression, and the will of your Prince'.[21]

As well as preaching before the Scottish Parliament, the future archbishop of Glasgow, John Paterson, published an anonymous treatise in 1661, declaring that Charles II's former consent to the National Covenant and Solemn League and Covenant had been 'forc'd and coacted' at a time when he had been 'most undutifully, and disloyally kept, as a Noble Prisoner, rather then as a free King'. Among the Scots people, Paterson was aware that both engagements were currently being used 'as the Master engines of some Poly-pragmatick Malecontents' to divert honest and dutiful subjects from loyal obedience. Their binding nature was, however, discredited on the grounds that both bonds were entirely illegal, being 'in their very essence, combinations among factious Subjects, without and against the known will and consent of the Supreme Authority'. Hence submission was required even for those who judged episcopacy to be intrinsically sinful and unlawful. Irrespective of their inherent merits and demerits, the very attempt either to establish new laws or rescind former laws, Paterson accounted 'heinously sinful and rebellious' and 'plainly Anarchical and eversive of all Government whatsoever'.[22]

In similar vein, the newly-consecrated archbishop of St. Andrews, James Sharp, attempted to rehabilitate what he himself acknowledged to be 'the severity of a censure of a crackt credit & prostituted conscience', following his apparent apostasy from Resolutioner spokesman to Restoration archbishop.[23] Preaching his first sermon as archbishop in the town church of St. Andrews in 1662, Sharp exhorted his listeners to 'look on themselves as men such as I am, not infallible bot lyable to mistake in the poynt'. More specifically, Sharp averred that he had not himself counselled Charles to restore episcopacy, but had only concurred in parliamentary deliberations. Hence he directed the congregation thereafter to ground their religious duty on obedience to the monarch's directions rather than regarding 'ther opinion as ane Inspiration from god, or as a fundamentall poynt of religion . . . ffor its twentie to one if that opinion be absolute and certain'.[24] That same year, the newly-consecrated bishop of Orkney, Andrew Honyman, published *The seasonable Case of*

---

[21] Anon., *A Letter containing An Humble and Serious Advice to some in Scotland. In Reference to their Late Troubles and Calamities. By a Person of that Nation* (Edinburgh, 1661), pp. 7, 12, 14.
[22] [Paterson], *Brief Resolution*, pp. 18, 4, 11, 14.
[23] Airy ed., *Lauderdale Papers*, I, 86–7.
[24] NLS MS. 597, 'The Apologie of M[r] J[ames] S[harp]', f. 75. The text of the sermon was from 1 Corinthians 2.2: 'I resolved to know nothing amongst you, but Christ, and him crucified.'

Submission to the Church-government arguing that 'difference in Religion, or in these inferior and lower points about Church-government' in no way released subjects from their primary duty of loyalty to the monarch. By contrast, Honyman insisted that it was 'high time' for the Scottish people to pursue the course that appeared most conducive to peace, thereby avoiding the traditional Scottish tendency to embrace 'tempestuous Agitations and diverse winds of Doctrine, Engagements and professions'. The authority of Scripture, natural law and reason indicated 'as with a Sun-beam' that public security required subjects to acquiesce in the present establishment 'not only for wrath but for conscience sake'. Elsewhere, Honyman characterised Charles I's consent to the abolition of episcopacy in 1638 as analogous to the consent 'Merchants or Mariners give for casting their Goods over-board for avoiding a ship-wrack'. Arguing that many who had originally sworn the National Covenant and the Solemn League and Covenant had merely 'went on as they were led', Honyman insisted that the Scottish people recognise that such matters were subject to the magistrate's direction, even 'when his determination proves contrary to our Oath'.[25]

Such reasoning went unheeded, however, as members of the ecclesiastical establishment found themselves confronted by the recrudesence of Covenanting violence in the years following the Restoration settlement. Episcopalian apologists responded by continuing to defend the established church more in terms of its ability to safeguard civil order than from any wider theological or Scriptural justification. Amidst escalating civil unrest among nonconformists in 1669, Gilbert Burnet published a pamphlet dialogue in which it was pointed out to a presbyterian straw-man that 'however bigly you talked of *jus divinum*' there was no greater Scriptural authority for presbyterianism than for episcopalianism. For Burnet, 'in matters of Government, the Church is at liberty'.[26] Four years later, Burnet published another tract in which he refused to regard the office of presbyter as different from that of a bishop, regarding each as 'a different degree in the same Office', the preference of which was to be determined by considerations of public order.[27] From his readings of patristic authors, the minister of Banchory, James Gordon, likewise claimed in 1679 that all ecclesiastical controversy in Scotland stemmed from a simple logomachy, since at the inception of the Christian Church 'there was an Identity of Names; and that Episcopus and Presbyter signified one and the same thing'.[28] No member of the established church was thus prepared to construct a theological case for episcopacy by

---

[25] [Andrew Honyman], *The seasonable Case of Submission to the Church-government, As now re-established by Law, briefly stated and determined* (Edinburgh, 1662), pp. 42, 45; *Survey of Naphtali. Part II*, pp. 150, 161, 142. Such claims were, of course, repeatedly refuted by many presbyterians. Alexander Brodie of Brodie, for instance, denied the right of 'a thousand Parliaments, and Emperors, and Pops, To absolv from it, or dispenc with a lawful oath made to God. It's not man we have to doe with, or can requir the breach, but God' (Brodie, *Diary*, p. lviii).

[26] Gilbert Burnet, *A Modest and Free Conference betwixt a Conformist and a Nonconformist about the present distempers of Scotland* (second edition, [?Edinburgh], 1669), pp. 34, 44.

[27] Burnet, *Vindication of the Authority, Constitution and Laws*, pp. 334, 310–11.

[28] [James Gordon], *The Reformed Bishop or XIX Articles Tendered by . . . A Well-wisher of the present Government of the Church of Scotland (As it is settled by Law)* ([London], 1679), p. 142.

upholding the existence of bishops as a distinctive order in the primitive church. Preaching before the Privy Council in 1684, the future archbishop of St. Andrews, Alexander Rose, instead argued that he should not be expected to show that episcopacy, as a form of church government 'hath any immediat influence upon the special things of our Religion'. The merits of episcopacy were instead to be judged 'from its aptitude, to keep out the dangerous Fox, and the destroying Boar of Schism, so destructive to the vineyard'.[29]

Specifically addressing ecclesiastical issues, Andrew Honyman defended conjoint supervision within the established Church on the grounds that when a church and state were 'materially one body' it was logical that the supreme governor retained overall supervision. Since Honyman conceived it to be essential that in every church one individual should be invested with the supreme gubernative power over religious matters, he accepted that 'an infidel Magistrate hath as much Magistratical power to be Supreme' in directing religious affairs 'as a Christian Magistrate hath, only the Christian hath grace to use his power aright, which the other wants'. Writing before the passage of the Act of Supremacy in 1669, he nevertheless insisted that a clear demarcation existed between civil and religious spheres that should not be abrogated or compromised. As Honyman made clear, he did 'neither with the Erastian and Arminian make the supreme Magistrate the fountain of Church-power, as if it were wholly derived from him'.[30] In the aftermath of the Supremacy Act, however, the minister of Balquhidder, Robert Kirk, privately conceded that since men were men before they were Christians, the civil power over the outward man was 'more ancient and natural' than an ecclesiastical direction over men's inner consciences. Hence although the monarchs of Scotland were now indisputably Christian, Kirk conceded that if the king retained a similar power over the Church 'as before when pagan', the church was no more entitled to resist his authority than before 'when he was alien'. Like Honyman, however, Kirk distanced himself from defending an entirely erastian stance by denying the King to be 'a mixt person so as to comprehend mystical power of the Church as well as political'.[31] Despite such attempts to renounce overt erastianism, however, the failure of the established church to construct a convincing defence of its own *raison d'être* ensured that it was to be the political establishment, rather than the ecclesiastical, which promptly appropriated the ideological initiative.

---

[29] Alexander Rose, *A Sermon Preached Before the Right Honourable The Lords Commissioners of his Majesties most Honourable Privy Council at Glasgow* (Glasgow, 1684), p. 34.
[30] [Honyman], *Survey of Naphtali. Part II*, pp. 64, 59.
[31] NLS MS. 3932, '[Robert Kirk], Miscellany of thoughts occurring . . . 1678', ff. 88v–89r. In Chapter Two, Kirk was referred to as the minister of Aberfoyle, since he served as minister of Balquhidder from 1664–85 and as minister of Aberfoyle from 1685–92.

III

To a large extent, the more practical and political arguments articulated in favour of restoring episcopacy in the early 1660s reflected a wider intellectual climate of secular anticlericalism shared by a large proportion of Restoration magnates. Eclipsed politically by church leaders during the civil wars, many nobles were determined to retain the political initiative under Charles II. Observing noble conduct during this period, James Kirkton announced bitterly that, amidst all the vociferous support for the restoration of the monarchy, many held religion 'in the same esteem a chamber-maid has a spider in a window, wishing heartily to be rid of it', to the extent that 'if they could not destroy the thing, they resolved at least to suppresse the name'.[32]

For his part, Lauderdale confessed privately to Sir Robert Moray in 1669 that he was certain that the authority of a bishop or a minister in any '[d]iocese or parish was not Jure Divino, but depended solely on the supreme Magistrat'.[33] As Clarendon had suspected, Lauderdale's concern to secure civil peace remained more influential than any anxiety about the purity of church government. Writing to his wife in 1663, Lauderdale had confirmed his resolution 'to prefer the Kings interests [over] all others on earth', rendering him 'an ingrate rogue' unless he strove to ensure that 'whatever the King com[ma]nds shall be punctually obeyd'.[34] Since Charles II had effectively rescued Scotland from slavish subservience to English military occupation, Lauderdale thus conceived that the minimum duty the monarch could exact was obedience in church affairs. Such sentiments remained seemingly consonant with the personal predilections of the Stuart monarchs themselves. Around 1688, for example, the fourth duke of Hamilton transcribed extracts from the private reflections of both Charles II and James VII. Defending the notion of one universal Catholic church on earth, Hamilton observed that James had counselled against 'entring into that ocean of particular disputes'. For his part, Charles II had evidently wondered whether there was any other foundation of the Protestant church but that 'if the Civill Magistrate pleases he may call such Clergy as he thinkes fitt for his turn at that tyme' and thus 'turn the Church e[i]ther to presbytery, indepedency, or indeede what he pleases'.[35]

In the years after 1660, however, the failure of the established church to develop a convincing *raison d'etre* rendered it increasingly vulnerable when reassurances were sought regarding support from Charles II's administration. As

[32] Kirkton, *History*, p. 42. See also Julia Buckroyd, 'Anticlericalism in Scotland during the Restoration', in Norman Macdougall ed., *Church, Politics and Society: Scotland 1408–1929* (Edinburgh, 1983), pp. 167–85.
[33] Airy ed., *Lauderdale Papers*, II, 172.
[34] NLS MS. 2617, 'Earl of Lauderdale to the Countess of Lauderdale, 19 September 1663', f. 4.
[35] NAS GD 406/M1/337, 'Copie in the hand of the 4th duke of Hamilton of a paper by Charles II containing theological reflections . . . introductory letter by James VII' and GD406/M1/336, 'Copie . . . of a paper by Charles II containing theological reflections'.

early as 1661, Sharp had recognised that since 'our statsmen will have the world know we are not a preistridden nation', church ministers would be obliged to 'bear what we cannot mend' if not directly consulted about the direction of ecclesiastical policy.[36] Despite their re-admittance to Parliament as both members of the clerical estate and landowners, albeit very modest ones, Scottish bishops crucially lacked any of the potential jurisdictional, social and economic power which sustained the English episcopate. If not yet overtly slighted by their lay masters, the bishops became increasingly aware of their vulnerable standing and were consequently frustrated at the indifference of the civil arm in upholding their authority. Hence although Archbishop Alexander Burnet of Glasgow remained confident that 'we may live to see his Matie more absolute than any of his royall predecessors ever were', he acknowledged to Archbishop Gilbert Sheldon of Canterbury in 1664 that there were many of the Scottish political establishment 'jealous of our tottering standing'. Writing shortly before the Covenanters' Pentland Rising of 1666, Sharp complained to Sheldon that it was 'a matter of admiration how in a tym so uncertain and palpably declyning to disobedience and contempt of the laws', Charles II's administration was not being proactive in 'opposing and suppressing that spirit which hath been so fatal to monarchy and nobility' in earlier times. Seeking to reiterate their concerns in 1667, Sharp and the other Scottish bishops wrote collectively to Lauderdale admitting their impotence in curbing sedition without committed support from ministers and the judiciary. Upon reading a copy of this missive, however, Moray recounted to Lauderdale how he and the earl of Tweeddale had 'laughd till wee was weary at the letter of the Bishops . . . what a silly company of people they are'.[37]

Furthermore, categorical though the re-imposition of episcopacy seemed, it entailed no immediate commitment on the part of the laity to accept an apparatus of episcopal jurisdiction along English lines and still less any need to acknowledge *iure divino* claims about the divine authority. Accordingly, when bodies within the episcopalian establishment made tentative steps towards fortifying the church's external shell, even the most avowedly royalist commentators were dismissive in their reaction. In 1669, for instance, Archbishop Alexander Burnet ventured to issue an official remonstrance on behalf of the Glasgow synod, formally regretting that despite erecting the episcopalian edifice, there had been 'so litle done in prosecution of these laws, ffor building on these foundations'. Legislation against nonconformists had effectively 'done litle to restraine them, or strenthen the Churches Interest'. Such spirited criticism only provoked a hostile reaction from government ministers. According this to be 'the greatest ignomiy that ever Episcopall governem^t fell under since the Reformation, to go no higher', Moray insisted that episcopacy must be better managed if it were to serve as 'a support to Monarchy or a pillar to Religion'. As Moray reckoned, 'this damned paper shewes Bishops & Episcopall people are as bad on this

---

[36] Airy ed., *Lauderdale Papers*, I, 73.
[37] *Ibid.*, II, Appendix, xv, vi, xxxix, II, 70–1.

chapter as the most arrant Presbyterian or Remonstrator'.[38] Recalling the protestations issued on behalf of the extreme Covenanters during the civil wars, Mackenzie of Rosehaugh similarly denied that Archbishop Burnet of Glasgow could thereby be deemed 'more innocent' than the executed Protestor, James Guthrie, 'for both equally designed to debar the King from interposing any way in the affairs of the Church'.[39] Possibly over-reacting to the real fears of the established church, the remonstrance nevertheless provided an opportune means by which the government could eliminate one of its most captious critics and Burnet's dismissal was quickly secured.[40]

As indicated earlier in this chapter, complete monarchical control over church affairs in Scotland was ultimately enshrined in the Supremacy Act passed in 1669. Preaching to Parliament before the Act was passed, Sharp had called upon the assembly to ensure that monarchical supremacy might be 'more fully explain'd by Act of Parliament' to avoid lending credence to 'the extravagant insinuations of either the jure-divino Episcopist or Presbyterian'. Sharp had even audaciously identified what he deemed to be 'three pretenders to supremacy: the Pope, the King, and the General Assembly of the Presbyterians', but he escaped formal censure for the sermon, allegedly because the adminstration felt 'asham'd to depose two Archbishops in one year'.[41] Although Sharp did not preach this controversial sermon at the formal opening of Parliament, the practice of opening Parliaments with a sermon was discontinued in 1669 and proceedings thereafter commenced solely with prayers. As Lauderdale informed Charles II, he disliked the 'Presbiterian trick of bringing in Ministers to pray & tell God almighty news from the debates'.[42] Despite ostensibly strengthening the position of the established church, the Act of Supremacy effectively facilitated the development of Scottish ecclesiastical policy independent of church involvement. In particular, it clearly undermined legislation passed in 1662 that had confirmed episcopalianism as the established form of church government. For this reason, even Sharp himself was alleged to have 'tooke the alarum wondrous hasty' on reading a draft of the Act, appreciating that 'all King Henry the 8ths ten yeers' work was now to be done in 3 dayes' since '4 lines in this act were more comprehensive then a hundred & odd sheets' of Tudor legislation.[43] Nevertheless, as Lauder of Fountainhall observed, although the Supremacy Act 'startled all out Bischops extreimly, yet all of them ware so cunning and such tyme servers as they seimed to applaud it'.[44]

---

[38] *Ibid.*, II, Appendix, lxvi, lxv, II, 138–9.

[39] Mackenzie, *Memoirs*, pp. 157–8.

[40] See Julia Buckroyd, 'The Dismissal of Archbisop Alexander Burnet, 1669', *Records of the Scottish Church History Society*, 18 (1973), pp. 149–55. Burnet had already been obliged to demit his place as an Extraordinary Lord of Session the previous year.

[41] Mackenzie, *Memoirs*, pp. 159, 162. The text of Sharp's sermon was Matthew 5:9, 'Blessed are the peacemakers, for they shall be called the children of God'. Another account of the reception of Sharp's sermon is provided by Tweeddale in a letter to Moray dated 26 October 1669 (NLS MS. 7024, f. 185).

[42] Airy ed., *Lauderdale Papers*, II, 142.

[43] *Ibid.*, II, 152.

[44] Lauder of Fountainhall, *Journals*, p. 230.

Among lay commentators, it was widely recognised that the Supremacy Act rendered royal power 'as absolute here as could be desir'd'. As Mackenzie of Rosehaugh confirmed, Charles II's power in Scotland was 'now equal or greater' to that assumed by Henry VIII, which had subsequently been regained by Parliament 'as inconsistent with the liberties of England' under Elizabeth I.[45] As Parliamentary High Commissioner, Lauderdale quickly informed Charles that the Act 'makes you Soveraigne in the Church'. Not only could Charles appoint all bishops and ministers, but he could also 'remove & transplant them as you please', powers that Charles, as king of England, did not enjoy over the Anglican church. As Lauderdale gloried, the Act ensured that neither 'this Church, nor no meeting no Ecclesiastick Person in it, can ever trouble you more unles yow please . . . never was [a] King so absolute as yow are in poor old Scotland'.[46] The political leadership of Restoration Scotland had thus succeeded in ensuring that their wishes should never again be subjugated to those of the church. Commenting on the Supremacy Act, one of Lauderdale's correspondents confessed that he was unsure which system of church government currently prevailed in Scotland 'whither Episcopull, Presbiterean, or Erastian'. Undeterred, he cited an anecdote concerning one of the earl of Morton's relatives: 'when they told him what Erastus' tenets wer – "As I answer to God" (said He) "I have bin an Erastian all my dayes and I never knew it till now" ', from which Lauderdale's correspondent concluded, 'So be it for me'.[47]

Clerical alarm was, however, not entirely absent. As Gilbert Burnet recorded, many conformist clergy 'were highly offended at the act', construing that 'it plainly made the king our pope'.[48] Despite official assurances, the standing of the established church henceforth remained at best unsteady when predicated on such a basis. In 1684, for instance, the earl of Perth, as Chancellor, informed Archbishop William Sancroft of Canterbury that it would be 'the bishops their own faults if affaires succeed not as well as to the Church', since full support was assured from the civil magistrates. Following the flight of James VII & II to France in December 1688, however, Archbishop Alexander Rose of St. Andrews acknowledged the Scottish church's dependent position, admitting to Sancroft that 'our lawes ar so farr from protecting us in such casses' since the wording of the Supremacy Act of 1669 'leaves us so precarious as to be turned out at pleasure'. A similar point was made by his colleague, John Paterson, who also pointed out to Sancroft that since Anglican offices and benefices were secured by legal freehold, when episcopal rights were invaded in England, the nobility and gentry would be 'readie and zealous to owne and support you in them'. By contrast, in Scotland, 'if the Court chances to frowne on us, it is farr otherwise', thus apparently explaining why 'our Bishops here ly open to farr greater tentations to yeeld to the importunities of Court than yours doe'.[49]

[45] Mackenzie, *Memoirs*, p. 139.
[46] Airy ed., *Lauderdale Papers*, II, 164.
[47] 'W. Douglas to John, Earl of Lauderdale, 6 August 1669', HMC *Laing*, I, 375.
[48] Burnet, *History of My Own Times*, I, 513.
[49] Clarke ed., *Letters to Sancroft*, pp. 72, 102, 93–4.

In the years following the Supremacy Act, ecclesiastical affairs in Scotland were characterised by the adoption of a policy of prerogative indulgences aimed at attracting moderate dissenters within the framework of the established church, together with a repressive range of punitive sanctions for those who remained unreconciled. As early as 1667, Lauderdale had acquainted Sharp and others with his belief that, just as 'wilfull opposers and Contemners must be severlie punished', he wished that 'peaceable dissenters may be endeavoured to be reclaimed'.[50] To Robert Moray, Lauderdale had confirmed that, if 'the devill should againe possess our foolish fanaticks', he perceived that there was 'no way but the extremity of cruelty', for either they 'must destroy us or we them both roote & branch'.[51] Following the enactment of the Supremacy Act, an Indulgence was offered in July 1669 whereby over forty deprived ministers returned to their former parishes, although they could only receive their stipends if they accepted episcopal collation. Another ninety ministers were reinstated following the promulgation of a second Indulgence in 1672. The ingenuousness of both initiatives was, however, somewhat compromised by the simultaneous enactment of draconian legislation against obdurate nonconformists, including the notorious 'Clanking Act' of 1670 that made preaching at outdoor conventicles a capital crime. The increasingly repressive character of ecclesiastical policy during the 1670s also reflected events in England where attempts to secure political loyalty through a series of religious indulgences had similarly failed and the enactment of a Test Act in 1673 signalled the renewal of government action against religious nonconformity.

Unsurprisingly, both the Supremacy Act and the indulgence policy provoked hostile reception from committed presbyterian opponents. In exile in Rotterdam, for example, John Livingston wrote to his former parishioners in Ancram, counselling them against hearing indulged ministers, insisting that it was 'not now Episcopacy and Cermonies that is the Controversie, but whether Jesus Christ be King of his own Church'. For, as Livingston perceived, 'if the Leviathan of the Supremacy shall swallow up all', it was 'all alike whether it have Prelats or Presbyters subservient to it'.[52] His point was corroborated in another missive sent from Rotterdam by Robert MacWard, who directed people to absent themselves from services conducted by indulged ministers on the grounds that the Act of Supremacy had 'clearly everted and swallowed up all true Ecclesiastick-government'.[53]

Despite such opposition, individual members of the ecclesiastical establishment supported endeavours at reconciliation by formulating and promoting

---

[50] Dowden ed., 'Thirty Four Letters written to James Sharp', p. 263. See Buckroyd, *Church and State* and G. M. Yould, 'The Duke of Lauderdale's Religious Policy in Scotland, 1668–79. The Failure of Conciliation and the Return to Coercion', *Journal of Religious History*, 11 (1980), pp. 248–68.

[51] NLS MS. 7023, 'Earl of Lauderdale to Sir Robert Moray, 24 September 1667', f. 95.

[52] John Livingston, *A Letter written by that famous & faithfull Minister of Christ, Mr. John Livingstoun, unto his Parishioners of Ancram in Scotland, Dated Rotterdam, October 7, 1671* ([?Rotterdam, 1671]).

[53] Robert MacWard, *The Case of the Accommodation Lately proposed by the Bishop of Dunblane to Non-conforming Ministers examined* ([Rotterdam], 1671), p. 13.

schemes for accommodation that, nevertheless, ultimately proved abortive. From the late-1660s, Robert Leighton aimed to resolve the problem of widespread nonconformity by establishing a synodical church conjointly governed by bishops and their presbyters, wherein bishops would merely act as presidents, receiving guidance from presbyters in matters of jurisdiction and ordination. Insisting that his 'sole object' was to procure peace and promote religion, he accepted that his project entailed 'great diminutions of the just rights of Episcopacy'.[54] Despite the convocation of various regional synods during the restoration, as well as sundry negotiations and discussions with presbyterian representatives between 1669 and 1672, Leighton's proposals ultimately failed to obtain approval. For, as well as invoking entrenched presbyterian opposition, such overtures were regarded with alarm by fellow conformist clergy, such as James Sharp. Writing to Lauderdale, Sharp made clear his opposition to the accommodation proposals 'not having the habitude of parting by own consent with the rights of the Episcopal order'.[55] Observing the way in which Leighton had 'cut the very Nerves of Episcopal Jurisdiction' by such accommodation proposals, Lauderdale's Anglican chaplain, George Hickes, discouraged English episcopalians from adopting a similar course. According to Hickes, Leighton 'did really unbishop himself' since his accommodation scheme left 'nothing of the holy Apostolic Office, but the empty name'.[56] Formal reaction to ecclesiastical policy from the majority of the conformist clergy was lacking, since numerous petitions for the summoning of a national synod were rejected by the government, presumably unwilling to encourage public criticism of ecclesiastical affairs. Accused of having preached 'once and again [about] the Pride of prelates, and the Corruptions of the Church', John Robertson of the Greyfriars Kirk, in Edinburgh, suffered deprivation when he called publicly for a national synod in 1674.[57] As Lauderdale confessed to Leighton later that same year, his implacable opposition to all demands for the convocation of a national synod stemmed from remembering acutely 'what sad effects flowed from Petitions of Ministers in the year 1638' just as 'a burn'd Child dreads the fire'.[58]

Following the government's success in defeating an armed Covenanting uprising at Bothwell Bridge in June 1679, however, a third Indulgence was declared in Scotland, authorising house conventicles south of the River Tay, so long as they remained more than two miles away from Edinburgh and one mile away from Glasgow, St. Andrews and Stirling. Amnesties were also offered to the defeated rebels, conditional upon their acceptance of the royal supremacy. The motivation behind such conciliatory initiatives remained that of the political advantage to be obtained in fracturing religious nonconformity. As Lauder of Fountainhall observed in 1670, political Machiavellianism inculcated the

---

54 Leighton, 'A Narrative of the Treaty Anent Accommodation', in *Remains*, West ed., p. 214.
55 Airy ed., *Lauderdale Papers*, II, 215.
56 [Hickes], *Spirit of Popery speaking*, pp. 15–16.
57 [Thomas Morer], *An Account of the Present Persecution of the Church of Scotland, in Several Letters* (London, 1690), p. 41.
58 Airy ed., *Lauderdale Papers*, II, 53.

benefits 'for a prince to entertaine and foment' two factions in a state, playing one off against the other to his own advantage.[59] Referring to the nonconform- ists' reaction to the second Indulgence of 1672, Leighton confirmed that the concession 'hath divided them more amongst themselves then any thing y^t hath yet befallen them'. While some believed the measure 'girds them too straite into a corner', others were prepared to accept the Indulgence 'till better come'.[60] As indicated in the previous chapter, however, the direction of ecclesiastical policy remained constantly prey to political caricature and misrepresentation. Amidst 'all this nois against conventickles' in the late-1670s, the duke of Hamilton, for instance, endorsed reports that it was 'whisperred ther is some underhand trea- ties betuixt the phanaticks and those in pouer' to destroy presbyterian opposition through the indulgence policy.[61]

Similarly cynical interpretations were discerned by presbyterian pamphle- teers in the aftermath of the third Indulgence of 1679. In an anonymous satire entitled *The Curate's Queries*, for example, a royal courtier informed a conformist curate that the rationale behind the Indulgence was 'that Machiavel- lian principle, *Divide & impera*'. By introducing this 'Golden chance of Liberty, through our small spun Thread, and vermillian-coloured Indulgence', the courtier was confident that the majority of the people would 'suck in our Princi- ples of implicit Faith and Loyalty' to royal supremacy as opposed to that 'Lordly Prelacy, which by its bloody Face so much affrighted them'. Given that by the Indulgence, 'what we get not of their Purses, we get of their Consciences', the curate anticipated that there would not be 'much ado with our standing Forces, except to suppress and swallow up the dissenting, protesting handful'. Disregarding any sanctity of worship, the courtier directed that 'we must not be too strict, whether they go up to worship Dan your Prelacy, or Bethel your Indulgence', since it remained 'the Golden Calf of Supremacy that is bowed to, or acknowledged, or worshipped'.[62]

IV

Despite the frustrated sense of political impotence shared by members of the established church, its leaders remained ironically vulnerable to charges of prelatical pomposity and sycophantic courtliness from lesser members of the conformist clergy. As early as 1666, for instance, Gilbert Burnet composed a trenchant attack on the Scottish bishops for having been seduced into

---

[59] Lauder of Fountainhall, 'Observations on Public Affairs, 1669–1670', in *Journals*, p. 233.
[60] Quoted by R. Douglas in 'An Account of the Foundation of the Leightonian Library', in *The Bannatyne Miscellany: Containing Original Papers and Tracts, chiefly Relating to the History and Literature of Scotland. Volume III* (Edinburgh, 1855), pp. 212–13.
[61] 'William Douglas, third Duke of Hamilton to William Douglas . . . first Duke of Queensberry, 30 August [c. 1677]', HMC *Buccleuch & Queensberry*, I, 223.
[62] Anon., *The Curate's Queries, and the Malignant or Courtier's Answer thereto, according to their known Principles of Policy, their Methods, and Ends obtained thereby* ([?Edinburgh], 1679), pp. 2, 3, 4–5.

relinquishing their basic pastoral duties in favour of seeking political influence. Aged only twenty-three, Burnet dispatched individual copies of his manuscript critique directly to each of the bishops from his parish of Saltoun in East Lothian. Enquiring which 'moral virtue or Christian grace is raised to any greater height by yor coming in?', Burnet doubted 'if some of yow have visited one Church', let alone their own diocese, since their consecration. Although Burnet accepted the bishops' right to offer political advice, he regretted that they had instead engaged themselves 'wholly in the affairs of State', wishing that 'the Church touched yor hearts as much as the Court and State does'. Furthermore, Burnet found it difficult to promote humility among the Scottish people, given the ostentatious amount of 'pomp and parad[e] in which some of yow live'.[63] According to a later Jacobite commentator, although the bishops were highly offended 'that a Stripling should be so insolent', they were initially inclined 'to drop it, as an Act of novitious Fervour'. Fearing that his attack might be suppressed and ignored, however, Burnet allegedly then distributed copies 'to his Presbyterian Friends and others, which were handed secretly about the Town' while copies could also 'be purchased for a little Money, before those sent to some of the Bishops could reach them'.[64] Duly summoned before his ecclesiastical superiors, Burnet was, however, later obliged to make a formal apology.

As ecclesiastical divisions continued during the 1670s, a similar confrontation was launched more publicly by the Banchory minister, James Gordon, in *The Reform'd Bishop*, which appeared in 1679. Attacking the mediocrity of those occupying the highest offices within the established church, Gordon contended that, were Charles II aware of their insufficiencies, he would have chosen rather to have 'sent down some English Doctors' rather than allow 'any of those Willy-wisps to jump into these empty Chairs'. While 'the Primitive Bishops used not Coaches', Gordon ventured that the Restoration bishops were 'expending more on their Horses yearly, than some poor Ministers have to maintain their Families'. Such abuses could only encourage the prevailing opinion that 'Bishops are only the Creatures of Courtiers', rendering the episcopal office 'nothing but a Politick Design, contrived rather to serve Secular ends, than the Evangelical and Ecclesiastical Interests'. As Gordon warned, 'one haughty expression of a proud Priest' was more likely to encourage new defections to fanaticism 'than twenty uttered by the humblest of them, can bring over to Conformity'. To support his contentions, Gordon claimed that he had heard 'many well-meaning Persons, who pass under the Notion of Fanaticks' acknowledge that if they observed bishops sincerely performing the religious duties incumbent on their office, they would 'be as forward as any to hugg them

---

[63] Gilbert Burnet, 'A Memorial of diverse grievances and abuses in this Church', in H. C. Foxcroft ed., *Miscellany of the Scottish History Society. Volume II* (Edinburgh, 1904), pp. 342, 343–4, 348.
[64] John Cockburn, *A Specimen of Some Free and Impartial Remarks on Publick Affairs and Particular Persons, Especially relating to Scotland; Occasion'd by Dr. Burnet's History of his own Times* (London, [1724]), pp. 39–40.

in their Arms' and submit to episcopal jurisdiction.[65] Incensed by Gordon's unrestrained attack, emanating as it did from within the conformist clergy, Bishop John Paterson of Edinburgh claimed that 'ye church is more wounded by it . . . then by anie or all of the lying and malicious pamphlets sent by Brown, Macquair [*i.e.* MacWard] etc. from Holland'.[66] Following the Williamite Revolution in 1689, Gordon subsequently pursued an unsuccessful case before the Privy Council claiming that Paterson had illegally seized 750 copies of *The Reform'd Bishop* when they had arrived in Leith from his London publishers in 1679. According to Gordon, Paterson had falsely claimed to possess a Privy Council warrant authorising him to remove the books and thereafter 'burn them at the back or near to his own lodging'. Although Gordon insisted that the Claim of Right of 1689 entitled individuals to apply for reparation for losses unjustly suffered during the Restoration, the Council duly absolved Paterson.[67]

Moral criticism of the established church was not confined to those outside episcopal ranks. A fastidiously nervous exerciser of the duties of his see, Robert Leighton, for instance, regularly expressed disquiet about extensive prelatical involvement in the venal sphere of Restoration politics. Deeming it 'scarce lawfull to churchmen, to sit in councils and judicatories', Leighton himself avoided attending Parliament unless ecclesiastical affairs were under direct discussion, preferring instead to incur a daily fine of £12 for his non-attendance.[68] Moreover, since bishops still retained the right to select all personnel connected with commissary courts, Leighton was also concerned about potentially dangerous allegations of patronage. Concerning a recent appointment to a vacant and unlucrative commissary post in 1673, for example, he alleged that 'more was offerd mee by some of the competitors then I think one much better worth, if sett to sale in ye market-place'.[69]

It could also be argued that the weak standing of the established church further derived from its lack of enforced and strict canons. In seeking to avoid a repetition of the Laudian disasters, the Restoration religious settlement had not attempted to reform church courts or modes of discipline or to impose set liturgies. Consequently, as Gilbert Burnet pointed out in 1666, the established church remained 'the only one in the world which hath no rule for worship', as the prayers of the church depended solely on 'the extemporary gift of the minister'.[70] That same year, the earl of Argyll wrote to Lauderdale, recommending that the worship and discipline of the church be subject to the same legislation as its government, in order to prove more clearly the illegality of unlicenced conventicles.[71] In *The Reform'd Bishop*, Gordon likewise exhorted ecclesiastical leaders

[65] [Gordon], *The Reform'd Bishop*, pp. 250, 31–2, 65–6, 136, 298.
[66] Airy ed., *Lauderdale Papers*, III, 189.
[67] 'Supplication of Mr. James Gordon', *The Register of the Privy Council of Scotland. Third Series. Volume XIV (1689)*, H. Paton ed. (Edinburgh, 1933), p. 36.
[68] Mackenzie, *Memoirs*, p. 161; Burnet, *History of My Own Time*, I, 253.
[69] Airy ed., *Lauderdale Papers*, II, 239.
[70] Burnet, 'Memorial', p. 354.
[71] 'Archibald Campbell, ninth earl of Argyll, to John, Earl of Lauderdale, August 1666', *HMC Laing*, I, 353.

to resolve upon a uniformity in worship and doctrine to redress the current situation whereby 'our National Church should resemble America, in its first Discovery'.[72] The demand for a set mode of worship was reflected in the frequent use made privately of the Anglican liturgy. Whilst in Edinburgh in 1681, for instance, the duke of York's chaplain, Francis Turner, reported that 'our Common Prayer Bookes do sell (the booksellers tell me) in great numbers in Edinburgh'.[73]

Lastly, episcopalians also condemned the reluctance of the established church to address the problem of nonconformity with its own powers of excommunication, rather than relying unduly on civil sanctions. As Mackenzie of Rosehaugh pointed out, severity on the part of the state was only liable to increase the 'number and Zeal of Bigots', since it was instinctively assumed that 'the Magistrates are still in League with the National Church, and its Hierarchy', rendering them apt to 'consider Churchmen but as Pensioners, and so Partizans to the Civil Magistrate.'[74] Gordon likewise accounted it 'a most invidious thing' for church governors to petition criminal judges to 'Fine and Confine those Delinquents, whom they have scarce ever noted as such in their Ecclesiastical Courts'. While prepared to countenance a secular role for the church should 'a very grand Case of Conscience' arise, Gordon nevertheless reiterated the ancient maxim that 'Church-men never made good Politicians', citing the violent ends awaiting sundry prominent clerics throughout history.[75]

V

While episcopalian conformists found themselves under constant pressure and criticism, the fluctuating course of Restoration ecclesiastical policy also inevitably generated divisions among presbyterian brethren regarding appropriate levels of political compliance. In the 1660s, religious dissent generally sustained a fairly unified appearance, as presbyterians directed their opposition at the re-establishment of bishops, but retained their commitment to defend royal power and authority in temporal matters, as originally indicated in the National Covenant of 1638. Condemned to death in 1661 for his allegedly treasonable co-operation with the Cromwellian regime, the marquis of Argyll, for instance, composed a memorial for his son in which he acknowledged 'a long and strong imputation' that the presbyterian Kirk sought to 'teach sedition against, or at least the diminution of the Authority of their Princes'. Rejecting such inferences, however, Argyll enjoined his son always to 'make your duty to your Soveraign one of the chief points of your Religion, so far as it may consist with your obedience to God'.[76] On the scaffold, Argyll publicly repeated his rejection of those who taught 'that Religion and Loyalty are inconsistent', insisting that if

---

[72] [Gordon], *Reform'd Bishop*, p. 161.
[73] Clarke ed., *Letters to Sancroft*, p. 29.
[74] Sir George Mackenzie, *Reason. An Essay* (London, 1690), pp. 136–7.
[75] [Gordon], *Reform'd Bishop*, pp. 117, 190.
[76] Argyll, *Instructions to a Son*, p. 33.

'any man think otherwise, Religion is not to be blamed, but they'.[77] Even when armed resistance broke out during the Pentland Rising of 1666, the former Protestor, Robert Law, insisted that the rebels 'declared for the King and the Covenant', maintaining only that 'their quarrell was at the bishops newly sett up in the land'.[78]

From the late-1660s, however, irreconcilable divisions emerged among nonconformists between those who were prepared to retain their primary allegiance to the monarch and those members of more radical sects who resisted all compromise with temporal authority. The latter included, for example, those followers of Richard Cameron who subsequently became known as 'Cameronians' after Cameron himself was killed at a skirmish with government forces at Aird's Moss in 1680. Among moderate presbyterians, however, several ministers sought to address directly the issue of nonconformist co-operation with temporal authorities. Attempting to promote mutual forbearance among disaffected presbyterians, the Paisley minister, John Baird, recognised that in times of extreme instability, 'Necessity has no Law.' As Baird argued in a manuscript tract written in 1674, the policy of prerogative indulgences could be seen as falling within the civil magistrate's sphere of competence, since indulgences served only 'to dispense with the Legal Inhibition' excluding nonconformist ministers, without seeking 'to invest them with new spiritual power to officiate, as some invidiously alledge'.[79] By the time Baird's conciliatory tract was published in 1681, however, even Robert Law had become increasingly fearful of 'these men of the new mode against monarchie', who subscribed to precepts articulated in documents such as the *Sanquhar* and *Queensferry Declarations*. Law considered the contents of such assertions to be entirely subversive of civil society encouraging children to 'rebell [*sic*] against their parents, servants against their masters, tennants against their landlords, upon any supposed injurie done to them', whilst 'any privat person may kill his prince upon any supposed mal-administration, though it be not true'.[80] Equally incisive criticism came from the indulged minister of Cambusnethan, William Violant, who recognised that the National Covenant of 1638 had obliged its subscribers to uphold parliamentary privileges, established liberties and the monarch's person and authority. By contrast, recent Covenanting manifestos expressed an alarming, and quite contrary, commitment to 'alter the very form of Government' wherein 'there would be no King, nor Parliament, nor Kingdom in the Nation'. Moderate dissenters therefore faced a dilemma in seeking to maintain opposition to the established state church while simultaneously professing

---

[77] *My Lord Marquis of Argyle His Speech upon the Scaffold, the 27 of May 1661* (Edinburgh, 1661), p. 2. An illuminating account of 'presbyterian moderation' is provided in Colin Kidd, 'Religious realignment between the Restoration and Union', in Robertson ed., *A Union for Empire*, pp. 145–68. For further information, see also Cowan, *Scottish Covenanters* and Elizabeth H. Hyman, 'A Church Militant: Scotland, 1661–1690', *Sixteenth Century Journal*, 26 (1995), pp. 49–74.

[78] Law, *Memorialls*, p. 16.

[79] [John Baird], *Balm from Gilead: or, the Differences about the Indulgence, Stated and Impleaded: In a serious letter to Ministers and Christians in Scotland. By a Healing Hand* (London, 1681), p. 39.

[80] Law, *Memorialls*, pp. 185, 206–7.

peaceful support for the Stuart administration. As Violant perceived, while most presbyterians ultimately sought to remove episcopalianism and erastianism, they did not consider 'it their Duty to overturn Civil Government to erect Presbyterial Government; to destroy Civil Order in the Kingdom, to erect Ecclesiastical Order in the Kirk'.[81]

Such predicaments confronted presbyterian ministers and parishioners alike. Among those frequently suspected of latent disloyalty on account of his refusal to attend established church services was, for example, the Highland laird, Alexander Brodie of Brodie. Summoned to account for his non-attendance before a commissary court in Elgin in 1676, Brodie remained convinced that episcopacy was inconsistent with Scriptural precepts. Notwithstanding, he protested that there was no-one among Charles II's subjects who 'detests and abhors disloyalti mor, and that shal mor willingly pour out his blood and lyf at his fiat than I'. For his part, Brodie wished that Charles and his ministers would realise that the security of monarchical government was 'more surlie bottomd on the true affections of his peopl then on the civil places of Kirkmen, to the wounding of the consciences of his faithful subjects'.[82]

Specific incidents inevitably served to polarise dissent further. On 11 July 1668, a veteran of the Pentland Rising, James Mitchell, launched an unsuccessful assassination attempt against Archbishop James Sharp of St. Andrews, which seriously wounded Bishop Andrew Honyman of Orkney. Writing to Lauderdale shortly afterwards, Sharp acknowledged that his escape had been 'indeed marveilous and extraordinary', but remained concerned 'the design was against me', having been 'layed and contryved by a combination of those, who influenced and acted in the late rebellion, which being defeated, they resolved upon another more ugly, yet more expeditious and effectual method for destroying the government'.[83] Over a decade later, on 3 May 1679, Sharp was brutally murdered by a group of Covenanting extremists, who allegedly sang psalms as they thrust their swords into the primate's body, convinced that their actions were divinely-inspired, for '[t]hey had Judas kill'd'.[84] Upon hearing the news, Brodie himself recorded privately that he 'did disclaim that act which was laid against the Bischop' and would 'hav rescud him if it had bein in my power'. Moreover, Brodie predicted that his murder 'would do mor harm to religion than ever his life had done or could hav done'.[85] Aware that 'monarchomach'

---

[81] [William Violant], *A Review and Examination of A Book bearing the Title of the History of the Indulgence* (London, 1681), pp. 555–6, 206–7.

[82] Brodie, *Diary*, pp. lvii–lviii.

[83] NLS MS. 2512, 'Archbishop Sharp to the earl of Lauderdale, 23 July 1668', f. 118.

[84] Anon., *A Narrative of the Horrid Murther Committed on the Body of the Late Right Reverend James, Lord Arch-Bishop of St. Andrews, Primate of all Scotland* (London, 1679), p. 3. Other contemporary reports included *A True Account of the Horrid Murther Committed upon His Grace, The Late Lord Archbishop of St. Andrews, Primate and Metropolitan of all Scotland &c.* (London, 1679) and the anonymous verse account in *The Manner of the Barbarous Murder of James, Late Lord Arch-Bishop of St. Andrews, Primate and Metropolitan of all Scotland* (London, 1679).

[85] Brodie, *Diary*, p. 412.

Plate 5 A contemporary depiction of Sharp's murder in a broadside entitled *The Manner of the Barbarous Murther of James, Late Lord Arch-Bishop of St Andrews, Primate and Metropolitan of all Scotland &c.* (London, 1679). By permission of the Trustees of

resistance theories were frequently deemed to be popish in origin, moderate presbyterians thus became increasingly concerned to avoid all imputations of Romish sympathies. Hearing of Sharp's murder, Lauder of Fountainhall recorded rumours that 'the remonstrant Presbyterians ware his murderers; others laid the blame on the Jesuits'.[86] Had not secure proof been discovered against the presbyterian malefactors, another anonymous pamphleteer confirmed in 1681 that blame would certainly have been placed 'at the Papists door'.[87]

Anxious to avoid allegations of popish disloyalty, moderate presbyterians consequently became alarmed at numerous other episodes including the public pope-burnings staged during the duke of York's residence in the city between 1679 and 1682 by students of Edinburgh University. Referring to allegations surrounding the 'Popish Plot' in England, the students defended their right to register 'Publick Testimony of our Abhorrence of the Romish superstition' whilst denying 'that the Plot is altogether disbelieved in Scotland'. Proclaiming themselves satisfied that there was no dependence subsisting between either the established state or church in Scotland and their counterparts in Rome, the students provocatively challenged their opponents to prove 'that an affront to the latter must needs redound upon the former'. Complaining, moreover, that 'our Childish divertisements' had been represented to the city's magistrates 'as formidable Combinations against the State' and 'a Mountain hath been made of our Molehill', the students emphasised the alarming possibility that their future monarch might be 'resolved to look upon peoples professing their detestation of Popery to be a Crime equal to Rebellion'.[88] Observing events in Edinburgh, Fountainhall observed how many students had started wearing blue ribbons in their hats, while members of 'the Episcopall and Court party have in opposition got rid [red] ribbans'. Suggesting that the blue colour had been adopted from the verse in Numbers when God appointed a monarch for the Israelites enjoining them to sew a blue fringe into their garments, Fountainhall added that 'the watermen and apprentices of London, in this far have imitat us' by wearing blue ribbons to denote their partisan affiliations during parliamentary attempts to exclude James, duke of York, from succession to the English throne.[89]

As unconvinced by the students' audacity as by Cameronian militancy, moderate presbyterians could only reiterate their fears about the detrimental constructions liable to be placed upon all acts of political disloyalty. Writing a month after Sharp's murder, Alexander Skene exhorted his disaffected brethren to 'forsake that principle and practice of Fighting' and to adopt more peaceable

[86] Lauder of Fountainhall, *Historical Notices*, II, 225.

[87] [N.M.], *A Modest Apology For The Students of Edenburgh Burning a Pope December 25. 1680, Humbly Rescuing the Actors from the Imputation of Disloyalty and Rebellion, with which they were charged in a Letter* (London, 1681), p. 4.

[88] *Ibid.*, pp. 7, 8, 18. Regarding similar occurrences in England, see Sheila Williams, 'The Pope-Burning Processions of 1679, 1680 and 1681', *Journal of the Warburg and Courtauld Institutes*, 21 (1958), pp. 104–18.

[89] Lauder of Fountainhall, *Historical Observes*, p. 19; for more on London party politics, see David Allen, 'Political Clubs in Restoration London', *Historical Journal*, 19 (1976), pp. 561–80.

means in imitation of Christ. Not only had their violent activities incurred considerable misery upon themselves, but Skene also contended that they had provoked 'greater severities to be enacted' against dissenters 'then probably would otherwise have been'.[90] Observing the prevalent bloodshed and civil strife, Violant rued how such unrest 'gratifies the Papists exceedingly' in their continued attempts to foment divisions between magistrates and subjects. Moreover, by ordering brethren not to attend services conducted by indulged ministers, Violant charged that extreme Covenanters were consciously imitating popish policies of excommunication.[91]

Any suspicions of convergence between radical Covenanting and radical Catholic 'king-killing' doctrines thus provoked immediate alarm. For his part, the former presbyterian Protestor, Robert Law, made explicit that the 'strain and matter' of the *Sanquhar Declaration* and other papers were 'the same with the principles of the Papists, and do wholly agree with their confessions'. As proof of his claims, Law asserted that several scaffold speeches recently issued in the name of radical Covenanters from Edinburgh 'have been penned by papists, and put out in their names to make the protestant religion odious to the world'.[92] Similar claims were made by an indulged minister in a memorial written in July 1680, contained among the Scott of Harden muniments. The minister acknowledged his initial inclination to regard such incitements to violence as 'a forgerie of some adversary', but reluctantly found himself obliged to recognise their presbyterian provenance. The minister insisted, however, that he spoke for the majority of presbyterians when he whole-heartedly sought to 'abominat ye Anti-Scripturall, anti-magistraticall tenets & the seditious & rebellious designes of these papers' as 'most diametricall[y] opposite to ye principalls & hearts' of all loyal Protestants, whether presbyterian or episcopalian. While detecting 'no Parallel so proper as ye Anabaptistic furies of Tom of Munster & John of Leyden', the indulged minister simultaneously emphasised 'how popish & jesuiticall like [are] those king-disposeing, king-killing, state-disturbing & confounding principles & practises'.[93]

Catholic perceptions of events also served to confirm such fears. In 1685, for instance, an Irish Catholic priest wrote anonymously to James VII & II, supporting various initiatives to allow dissenters to worship privately, on the grounds that 'the more privat an enemie the more dangerous'. Contending that of all private enemies 'an indiscreet hot-headed zealot is the worst and most irreclaimable', the priest cited as an example 'the Covenanting Whiggs in Scotland' whom he perceived to be 'soe obstinat & resolut even at deaths door . . . that they could not be induced to save their lives at soe dear a rate as to pray in four

---

[90] Alexander Skene, *Plain and Peaceable Advice to Those called Presbyterians in Scotland* (London, 1681), 'To the Reader'. Although not published until 1681, the tract is dated 5 June 1679.
[91] [Violant], *Review and Examination*, p. 125.
[92] Law, *Memorialls*, pp. 200, 185–6.
[93] NAS GD 30/1723, 'Letter, unaddressed and unsigned, describing the religious situation in Scotland in detail, 5 July 1680', ff. 1r–2r.

words for the Kings safety'.[94] As Covenanting violence in Scotland intensified, Scots presbyterian ministers resident in Ulster also found themselves under increasing pressure to denounce the actions of their more extremist brethren. Summoned to appear in Armagh before the local landowner, Viscount Granard, in July 1680, for instance, four ministers protested that 'these distracted courses of late' adopted in Scotland were 'lamented and abhorred' by all clerics and parishioners 'in this country both as rebellious against our lawful sovereign and highly sinful against God' who commanded subjection to lawful authority.[95]

Among those moderate presbyterians who remained in Scotland and suffered under the penal laws, resentment was also increasingly directed towards those of their brethren who had fled to Holland 'treacherouslie deserting the interest of the Lord and Leaving their charges and the poor persecute flocks'.[96] Particularly objectionable was the continuous arrival in Scotland of radical works by those associated with the Scots church in Rotterdam, Robert MacWard, or his colleague, John Brown of Wamphray. In his detailed refutation of Brown's *History of the Indulgence* (1678), Violant attacked Brown's injunctions to presbyterians in Scotland to remain 'aloof from all listnings to proposals made to us, and from making any proposals to them' as well as to abstain from hearing indulged ministers. In response, Violant contended that even had the Indulgences been 'free of clogs', the inflexibility of the exiled presbyterians would 'still have called the people to leave the Kirks, and come to the fields and mountains'. Furthermore, even if ecclesiastical policy in Scotland were to be reversed in the future, Violant denied that those who had 'so easily shaken themselves loose of subjection' to lawful authority would be unlikely to be any more 'tender of the Consciences of others' and avoid persecuting those from whom they differed.[97] This point was endorsed by the exiled minister, John Livingston, who wrote to his former parishioners from the Netherlands acknowledging 'that if we had been at home, we might not have done worse than any others'.[98]

Confronted by such a social reality, growing numbers of nonconformist and conformist clergy alike concurred with Leighton's view that there was no greater enemy to religion 'then the wranglings and bitter contentions that are caused about the external formes of it'.[99] On one occasion, even Leighton himself dismissed the ecclesiastical troubles of Restoration Scotland as 'a

[94] William Fraser ed., 'A Series of Eight Anonymous and Confidential Letters to James II about the State of Ireland', *Notes & Queries*, 6th series, V (1882), 484. The four words in question were, of course, 'God save the King'.
[95] 'A letter of four Scottish ministers against taking up arms against his Majesty, delivered by Viscount Granard to his Majesty', in F. H. Blackburne Daniell ed., *Calendar of State Papers Domestic Series, January 1st 1679, to August 31st, 1680* (London, 1915), p. 576.
[96] Anon., *The Protestatione of the Antipopish, Antiprelatick, Antierastian, True Presbyterian But poor and persecuted, Church of Scotland. Against the Scottish Congregation at Rotterdam in Holland* ([Glasgow], 1684), sig. A2v.
[97] [Violant], *Review and Examination*, pp. 57, 124–5, 553.
[98] Livingston, *Letter written by that famous & faithfull Minister of Christ*, p. 13.
[99] Robert Leighton, 'The Copy of two Letters, Commonly reputed to have been written by the Bishop of Dumblane [sic], at least by him communicat to several Friends', in MacWard, *Case of the Accommodation*, p. 102.

drunken scuffle in the dark'.[100] The following chapter considers the ways in which escalating domestic instability, thus characterised as a 'drunken scuffle', provoked claims that the defence of fundamental laws and liberties could only be safeguarded by first ensuring the preservation of order.

---

[100] Airy ed., *Lauderdale Papers*, III, 76.

6

The Preservation of Order

Amidst the religious and political turmoil unleashed by the European wars of religion, post-Reformation political theorists increasingly distinguished between a normal state of affairs where the rule of law strictly prevailed and a state of emergency which allowed civil authorities unrestricted powers to ensure civil order. Despite a prevailing consensus that absolute monarchical government in Scotland should conform to the rule of law, this precept was increasingly undermined as popular unrest escalated across the country during the late-1670s and 1680s. Acknowledging 'a distinction of ordinary and extraordinary times' in a commonplace-book from around 1682, one episcopalian minister nevertheless stressed the need to be 'cautelous and dextrous' in devising appropriate policies for such uncertain times.[1] Recognising 'some kind of undefineable Power' vested in a sovereign, the Selkirk minister, James Canaries, insisted that such power defied legal expression since 'only certain extraordinary Emergencies in the State can bring [it] out'. Although Canaries generally grounded obedience on conscience, he warned that no government could rest secure without placing 'Shackles upon the very minds of Mankind, as well as upon their hands' and retaining 'Locks no less to the Doors of their Retirements, than to those of their Prisons'.[2] Responsible for preserving civil order during the later years of the Restoration, the Lord Advocate, Mackenzie of Rosehaugh, thus identified 'Necessity of State' as 'that Supereminent Law to which upon occasion all particular Acts must bow'.[3] Originally developed to counter arguments for resistance *in extremis*, the application of this 'supereminent law' increasingly came to assume theoretical and practical prominence.

It has been argued that historians of late-seventeenth century England are

---

[1] Lambeth Palace Library, London, MS. 1520 (Eccles Collection), 'Collection of Extracts from printed books, sermons and other documents made in about 1682 by a Scottish clergyman', f. 54.

[2] James Canaries, *A Sermon Preached at Edinburgh, In the East-Church of St. Giles, upon the 30th of January, 1689. Being the Anniversary of the Martyrdome of King Charles the First* (Edinburgh, 1689), pp. 23–4.

[3] Mackenzie, *Vindication of the Government in Scotland. During the Reign of King Charles II*, p. 25. For a general survey of the language of 'reason of state', see Peter Burke, 'Tacitism, scepticism and reason of state', in J.H. Burns and Mark Goldie eds., *The Cambridge History of Political Thought, 1450–1700* (Cambridge, 1991), pp. 479–98 and Friedrich Meinecke, *Machiavellism. The Doctrine of Raison d'Etat and Its Place in Modern History*, Douglas Scott trans. (London, 1984).

belatedly beginning to appreciate that Restoration political culture was 'more violent, more sharply divided, more absolutist, and at the same time more radical, than is usually thought'.[4] Paradoxically, however, the increasing pressure to adopt extra-legal measures simultaneously focused intellectual attention on the theoretical scope of the law, reflected in William Blackstone's eighteenth-century claim that 1679 denoted the year in which 'the theoretical perfection' of English law was achieved, most noticeably by the abolition of feudal tenures and the enactment of *habeas corpus*.[5] In Scotland, by contrast, although Stair and Mackenzie also produced the first codifications of Scots law in the 1680s, there was no writ of *habeas corpus*, judicial torture was still regularly practised in state trials and the authority of hereditary jurisdictions remained. Accordingly, the period became immortalised as 'the Killing Times' for the bloody and brutal manner in which the civil authorities secured political loyalty and religious conformity by persecutory means.

Focusing chiefly on the latter half of the Restoration, this chapter examines the manner in which political debate increasingly revolved around the extent to which government policies could be justified by the stated ends to which they were directed, rather than by the practical means employed. It first considers the greater priority accorded to the preservation of social and political order by a generation still recovering from the disruptive aftermath of the mid-century civil wars. It then explores the theoretical defences constructed by Restoration Scots to justify dispensing with traditional constitutional praxis to secure civil peace. Encapsulated within such reasoning were debates about reason of state and 'king-craft', as well as the perceived need to introduce legislation that undermined traditional beliefs in the sanctity of private property. The chapter then examines the effects of the widespread imposition of state oaths by the Restoration authorities, reflecting a prevalent concern that political rebellion was being dishonestly cloaked in languages of religious and spiritual freedom. It concludes by considering the reconfiguration of political loyalties provoked by the accession to power of James VII & II, focusing on the emergence of a campaign of civil disobedience initiated by those members of the political establishment formerly regarded as natural allies of the Stuart monarchy.

I

Modern political theory has posthumously accorded an exalted worth to radical revolution that was not shared by contemporaries. Post-Reformation Scottish royalist writing was not predominantly characterised by an aggressive agenda for Protestant apocalypticism: it frequently espoused a desire for domestic peace

[4] Lois Green Schwoerer, 'The Shape of Restoration England: A Response', in Howard Nenner ed., *Politics and the Political Imagination in Later Stuart England* (Rochester, NY, 1997), p. 198.
[5] See Robert Willmann, 'Blackstone and the "Theoretical Perfection" of English Law in the Reign of Charles II', *Historical Journal*, 26 (1983), pp. 39–70.

and political order, as reflected in an extensive literature of retreat and disengagement from politics.[6] The violent setting of late-sixteenth century Scottish politics explained James VI's rejection of the notion that individuals should take action to relieve a disturbed commonwealth, arguing that such initiatives would merely 'heape double distresse and desolation vpon it; and so their rebellion shall procure the contrary effects'.[7] In 1643, the royalist, Lord Napier, had judged that the 'meaner people of Scotland' were 'not capable of a Republic', warning that if the Scots chose to hazard 'a race of kings who have governed you two thousand years with peace and justice', they would receive 'vultures and tigers' in exchange. As Napier predicted with remarkable perspicuity, given the later Cromwellian experience, Scotland would then 'fall again into the hands of One, who of necessity must, and for reason of state, will tyrannize over you'.[8] Hence the widespread rejoicing that greeted Charles II's restoration in 1660 was accompanied by a recognition of the legacy of the preceding decades when 'all the Fundamental Laws were shaken, and all honest Men ruin'd'.[9] The Scots people were therefore exhorted to 'forget not, forget not, the blood [that] lyeth under your table'.[10] Preaching before the Scottish Parliament in March 1661, Hugh Blair reminded its members that merely having 'a King as god from God, surely any King' was better than 'none at all'. For 'Tyranny its self is better' that anarchy and '[a]ny one to be King is better . . . [than] every one. Tyranny is better . . . [than] Ataxie.'[11]

Restoration Scots were determined that the preservation of order should become the chief priority to avoid a repetition of the misery and confusion of the civil war years. Confronted by escalating violence and unequivocal challenges to the government's authority, the defence of strong monarchy and the maintenance of order became issues of foremost importance. As indicated in the previous chapter, the brutal murder of Archbishop James Sharp of St. Andrews by a band of armed Covenanters in May 1679 represented an unprecedented act of political violence. The military defeat inflicted by government forces on the Covenanters at Bothwell Bridge the following month provoked various forms of published reaction between 1680 and 1685, including the radical *Rutherglen Declaration*, *Queensferry Paper*, *Sanquhar Declaration* and *Apologetical Declaration*. The contents of the *Sanquhar Declaration*, for example, publicly articulated the Covenanters' decision to 'disown' Charles II who had been

---

[6] For a broader analysis of this literature, see David Allan, *Philosophy and Politics in Later Stuart Scotland: Neostoicism, Culture and Ideology in an Age of Crisis 1540–1690* (East Linton, 2000).

[7] James VI & I, 'The Trew Law', in *Political Writings*, p. 79.

[8] Napier, 'Letter to a Friend', in *Memoirs . . . of Montrose*, I, 288.

[9] Mackenzie, *Vindication of the Government. During the Reign of King Charles II*, p. 4.

[10] Anon., 'The true Copy of a Letter directed to the Provost and Preachers of the city of Edinburgh, delivered by an unknown Hand at the Cross on June 19th, 1660 in the time of the solemnizing the proclaiming of his sacred Majesty, Charles II., fully discovering the horrid Treacheries of the Lord Marquis of Argyll and his Accomplices', in Scott ed., *Collection of Scarce and Valuable Tracts*, VII, 490.

[11] Hugh Blair, *Gods Soveraignity [sic], His Sacred Majesties Supremacy, The Subjects Duty. Asserted in a Sermon Preached before His Majesties High Commissioner, and the Honourable Parliament of the Kingdom of Scotland, At Edinburgh the 31st of March, 1661* (Glasgow, 1661), p. 10.

'reigning (or rather tyrannising, as we might say) on the throne of Britain' from henceforth 'having any right, title to, or interest in, the said crown of Scotland'. Charles II had allegedly forfeited his right not only by his 'perjury and breach of covenant both to God and his kirk', but also by having unlawfully usurped the ecclesiastical supremacy and by 'his tyranny and breach of the very *leges regnandi* in matters civil'. Proclaiming themselves to be solely 'under the standard of our Lord Jesus Christ, Captain of Salvation', the Covenanters further declared war on this 'tyrant and usurper', together with all those crown servants who 'have strengthened him in his tyranny, civil or ecclesiastic'.[12]

Such pronouncements were not intended to be of purely rhetorical effect. Visiting Galloway in 1683, John Grahame of Claverhouse reported to a Privy Council committee that the shire had long been regarded 'as almost in a state of war', rendering it 'unsaife for any thing less than an army to ventur into it'.[13] Evaluating the failure of the government's policy in discouraging nonconformity the previous December, Claverhouse complained that there remained 'as many Elephants and Crocodiles in Galloway as loyal or regular persons'.[14] Confronted by alarming provocations and apprehensive of universal civil disobedience, the Restoration political establishment was obliged to unite. According to Lauder of Fountainhall, despite initial scepticism that the *Sanquhar Declaration* contained claims so extreme that the document might in fact be 'a State invention, set on foot by the souldiers, to make that party odious, and themselfes necessar', when two of the king's guards were murdered shortly afterwards, everyone became convinced 'of the reality of this declared war'.[15] Although not eclipsed entirely, moderate royalist critics of Charles II's administration inevitably became less vociferous amidst the increasingly polarised character of political debate.

Justifying their official reaction to printed documents such as the *Rutherglen Declaration*, *Queensferry Paper*, *Sanquhar Declaration* and *Apologetical Declaration*, government officials consciously imitated Covenanting theories of the rights of resistance *in extremis*, declaring that 'by their own Principle of *Salus Populi*, better some few of the Society should perish than that the whole should go to ruin'.[16] In Edinburgh, Privy Council members read the *Queensferry Paper* with 'horror and amazement', claiming that it 'exceeded our beleiffe and all the wickednesse practised by these murtherers formerly'.[17] Mackenzie of Rosehaugh confirmed to the earl of Queensberry that he regarded the *Apologetical Declaration* as solemnly 'declareing warre with the Government and promiseing to kill us all'.[18] Informal political violence became a feature of

---

[12] 'Sanquhar Declaration, 1680', in Wodrow, *Sufferings*, III, 213.
[13] Dunn ed., *Letters Illustrative of Public Affairs*, p. 107.
[14] Lauder of Fountainhall, *Decisions*, p. 201.
[15] Lauder of Fountainhall, *Historical Observes*, p. 141.
[16] Mackenzie, *Vindication of the Government. During the Reign of King Charles II*, p. 9.
[17] 'Letter to the Duke of Lauderdale . . . 30 June 1680', in Hume Brown ed., *Register of the Privy Council of Scotland. Volume VI (1678–80)*, p. 481.
[18] Quoted by Steele, 'Covenanting Political Propaganda', pp. 370–1.

the political landscape. In 1677 Mackenzie had himself been assaulted by a gang of angry political adversaries and suffered a broken leg, the effects of which caused him to limp permanently thereafter, earning him the nickname 'Vulcan' in popular pasquils. As he protested to Archbishop Sharp, however, apart from bodily harm, he doubted his enemies' ability to break his resolve, given his own 'secret pleasur in serving the King'.[19] In responding to such threats, members of the Restoration political establishment thus concurred with the precepts of mid-seventeenth century Covenanters, such as Samuel Rutherford, that there was indeed 'a Court of necessity, no lesse than a Court of Justice'.[20] Demonstrating that the language of necessity was not an exclusively presbyterian preserve, Archbishop Robert Leighton thus sought to dissuade nonconformists from attending illegal conventicles in the early-1670s, by contending that the 'Law of Necessity sometimes doth sufficiently warrant our actions before God'. Hence 'Necessity, though it hath no law, yet it is a law unto itself' which could remove the obligation of positive laws to the contrary, though both remained of divine institution.[21]

Hence although James VI & I had acknowledged it to be 'a sure Axiome in Theologie, that euill should not be done, that good may come of it', if the danger of anarchy was perceived to be greater than that of tyranny, the necessity of the state justified any measure which might be requisite to avert this danger.[22] In late-1674, an anonymous manuscript addressed to Charles II advised him to preserve the common good, by heeding 'yor grandfathers maxime' and always seeking to 'mack a royall vertue of down right necessitie'.[23] In 1679, Mackenzie of Rosehaugh composed a private memorial for Charles II wherein he conceded that, at worst, 'two or three only can suffer by the Latitude allowd to yow, wheras many thousands may suffer by restricting yow'. For, as he reminded Charles, if due legal process came into conflict with civil order 'the public saftie and the subsistance of the government doth still preponderat'.[24] In a commonplace-book of 1681, the Balquhidder minister, Robert Kirk, likewise remarked that the 'Balance of justice needs a strong arm to hold it.' As Kirk discerned, this argument had been used by Cromwell during the 1650s to prevent justice from being left 'naked to all wants, under the notion of an imaginary, ancient and notional liberty under an effeminate native sovereign'.[25] A similar point was made by the university authorities at St. Andrews in a public address attempting to bolster support for James VII & II in 1689. Defending the absolute monarch's freedom of action, the authorities claimed that although 'some Severities actually happen which are generally lookt upon as excesses of Government',

---

[19] BL Add. MSS. 23,138, 'Sir George Mackenzie to Archbishop James Sharp, April 1677', f. 53v.
[20] [Rutherford], *Lex Rex*, p. 213.
[21] Leighton, 'The Rule of Conscience', in *Remains*, p. 257.
[22] James VI & I, 'The Trew Law', in *Political Writings*, p. 78.
[23] NAS GD 331/18/1–2, 'Paper addressed to the King on current political affairs, 1674'.
[24] BL Add. MSS. 23,244, ff. 20–8, 'My Lord Advocats arguments in law against the paper of the partie lords, Windsor Castle, 1679', f. 23v.
[25] EUL MSS. La.III.529, 'Robert Kirk, Ane account Of some occasional mediationes, Resolutiones, & practices; Which concern a public & private statione [1681]', ff. 180, 182.

they were 'never so heavy in Nature, nor so Universal in their Extent and Duration, as the dreadful Calamities of Civil War'.[26]

Different methods of government increasingly reflected changing political priorities. Arguments that government should be allowed to operate in secret for the benefit of national security gained credence at the expense of the forms of constitutional parliamentary opposition witnessed during the mid-1670s. Preaching at the opening of the first Restoration Parliament as early as 1661, Robert Douglas had informed Commissioners that 'as there are Mysteries in Divinity, so there are also Mysteries of State', including the royal prerogative, parliamentary privileges and popular liberties. Douglas hoped that, henceforth, 'State Mysteries may be lockt up in a Cabinet of State fit for them, as things sacred, and not easily to be brought unto debate, much lesse of the Vulgar.'[27] A few months later, Hugh Blair counselled the same assembly that civil order was undermined when politicians 'begin to dispute the prerogatives of a Prince, or search them unto the bottom, here is *abyssus magna*, there is some *arcanæ imperii*, not curiously to be searched into'.[28] Within the episcopalian establishment, Archbishop Robert Leighton also conceded that specific government actions might indeed 'seem quite wrong and unreasonable', but maintained that 'if we knew the secrets of State, the reasons and motives inducing them, we would be another mind'.[29] Preaching a sermon about what he termed 'Magistrate-Craft' in 1674, Leighton's friend and colleague, the Dean of Edinburgh, William Annand, likewise recalled that James VI & I had followed 'somewhat he now and then called King-Craft, and this none was to learn but himself and his Son'.[30]

Reason of state also formed the theoretical animus behind the justification of prerogative taxation articulated by the former St. Andrews lecturer, Robert Hamilton, when he defended his doctoral dissertation in law at the University of Leiden in 1671. Dedicating his thesis to Charles II, Hamilton regarded the king's power to tax without consent as a fundamental mark of sovereignty, insisting thereby that 'any true Monarch, who reigns alone and to whom others are subject' was entitled to an 'absolute, full and independent power of imposing taxes'. To succeed in the competitive sphere of international power politics, parliamentary consultation was an unaffordable luxury, for 'while the people take advice, while elections are called, which is a business of some months, the right moment to declare war slips away amongst delays'. By contrast, a limited monarch who was required to justify all his expenditure 'and explain his plans, bringing the secrets of his mind into the public domain' would be obliged to 'have scattered his intentions on the breeze for all to hear'. Subjects' liberties were, moreover, paradoxically rendered more secure under a pecunious absolute

---

[26] *Addres [sic] of the University of St. Andrews*, p. 15.

[27] Douglas, *Master Dowglasse, His Sermon*, p. 20.

[28] Blair, *Gods Soveraignity [sic]*, p. 8.

[29] Leighton, 'The Rule of Conscience', in *Remains*, p. 270.

[30] William Annand, *Dualitas: Or A Two-fold Subject Displayed and Opened conducible to Godliness, and Peace* (Edinburgh, 1674), p. 20.

monarch who enjoyed sufficient resources to preserve civil order. According to Hamilton, both 'the happy and unhappy resolutions of civil wars' could be attributed to money's 'great ability to reconcile people'.[31]

Such reasoning gained increased currency when civil disorder became so extensive that the very social and political fabric of the nation appeared under threat. Although Lauderdale had privately acknowledged to Charles II in 1669 that 'all yo[r] comands are to me above all human lawes', his attempted impeachment by Whig members of the English House of Commons in the mid-1670s had, however, been predicated upon precisely the illegality of such an allegation.[32] In private memoranda penned during the late-1670s, Mackenzie of Rosehaugh nevertheless continued to argue that, as an absolute monarch, Charles could ignore 'the new way of reasoning in matters of your power obliedging your servants and ministers to produce a statut as a warrand for every thing they doe in your name'. As Mackenzie perceived, Charles was not required 'to shew a Law for what yow doe els yow behoovd to deryve your power from the parliament and people and not from God'. In support of his reasoning, Mackenzie cited the Roman law maxim '*quod principi placuit legis habet vigorem*' which effectively implied that the only source of law was the legislator's will. Equally applicable in early modern aristocracies and democracies, this maxim explained why republican governments also exercised the right to imprison, banish and execute 'without any citation or processe but upon the proofs probably taken by themselves', avoiding the need 'to divulge the Ragione di Stato wherupon they proceed'. As far as Mackenzie was concerned, secrecy remained essential, since political affairs 'proceed upon informations, intelligence and reasons of state which are not fitt to be divulged to those who ar without doors'.[33]

Widespread aversion to notions of legislative tyranny generated further support for the occasional adoption of prerogative powers. Bishop Honyman of Orkney invoked Ciceronian precepts to argue that in judicial matters 'sometimes *æquum* is to be preferred to *justum*'. Prerogative latitude was to be deployed to achieve 'an equitable interpretation of the Law' since 'precile cleaving to the rigidity of the letter thereof, might make *summa jus, summa iniuria*'.[34] Preaching before the magistrates of Edinburgh in 1674, Dean Annand lamented that the civil governors were guilty of 'a sin which they had not been subject to

---

[31] Hamilton, *Disputatio Politico-Juridica Inauguralis*, pp. 10–11, 5. Such a line of reasoning must have been appreciated keenly by Charles II during the summer of 1671 when his attempts to extract sufficient revenue from the English Cavalier Parliament were approaching crisis point, as Charles attempted to stave off bankruptcy while funding an impending war against the Dutch. It appears that Charles may well have been familiar with Hamilton's arguments, since royal letters secured Hamilton's entrance to the King's Inns in Dublin in January 1672, after which Hamilton became Secretary to the Commission of Accounts and the Council of Trade in Ireland.

[32] Airy ed., *Lauderdale Papers*, II, 141.

[33] BL Add. MSS. 23,244, 'My Lord Advocats Arguments in law', ff. 20v–21r, 23v, 25v.

[34] [Honyman], *Survey of Naphtali, Part II*, p. 35; [Honyman], *Survey of the Insolent and Infamous Libel entituled Naphtali*, p. 76. *Summa jus summa iniuria* translates as 'law pushed to extremes be extreme injustice'.

of a long time', the transgression being 'the sin of secrecy in keiping all ther affairs very closse'. He recognised, however, that a city was rendered more 'prosperous by a good Prince, then by good Laws', since the latter were 'but as paper Bullets, creating a noise, but doing no execution; the former being a speaking, moving Law'.[35] Similarly Ciceronian arguments had earlier been articulated by James VI & I when he had reminded both Houses of the English Parliament of the essentially duplex nature of his kingship in 1607. As 'a speaking law', a king was entitled to alter and suspend laws 'upon causes onely knowen to him' when extraordinary circumstances required.[36] Defending their continued allegiance to his grandson, James VII & II, the university authorities in St. Andrews likewise upheld absolute monarchy on the grounds that 'Strict, Riged, and Litteral Laws, is the Severest and Bloodiest Master in the World.'[37]

Furthermore, since Scotland lacked a formal court of chancery on the English model, it could further be argued that it was in the subjects' interests that monarchs retained extra-legal prerogative powers. Hence strict interpretations of the law would not permit what Mackenzie of Rosehaugh termed 'that useful, tho' illegal Justice which is requisit in some cases'. Believing that 'strict and rigid Law is a greater Tyrant than absolute Monarchy', Mackenzie perceived how the royal prerogative 'doth like the blood circle through the whole Body of our Law and animates it as the Blood doth the Body', while acknowledging it to be 'very dangerous when it goes out of its due course, as blood doth'.[38] It was, however, precisely the existence of this potential danger that moved the Covenanting lawyer, Steuart of Goodtrees, to argue against unlimited monarchical prerogative. As Steuart perceived, it was 'brutish ignorance' to cite the letter of the law against those seeking 'to preserve the Commonwealth from ruine, and destruction, against which no law is, or can be, of any force or value . . . for here it holdeth true, that *summa jus* is *summa injuria* [sic]'.[39]

II

Contemporary political contingencies thus prompted renewed theoretical interest in discussions of natural law that suggested standards on which government should be founded and that transcended the vagaries of individual monarchs and statesmen alike. Across early modern Europe, the language of natural law was continually subjected to conflicting constructions that could alternatively endorse or preclude resistance to political authority across a range

[35] Annand, *Dualitas*, p. 17.
[36] James VI & I, 'A Speech to Both the Hovses of Parliament, Delivered . . . the Last Day of March 1607', in *Political Writings*, p. 161 and 'Trew Law', in *Ibid.*, p. 75.
[37] *Addres* [sic] *of the University of St. Andrews*, p. 9.
[38] Mackenzie, *Jus Regium*, p. 47; BL Add. MSS. 18,236, 'Discourse on the 4 First Chapters of the Digest', f. 53v.
[39] [Steuart], *Jus Populi Vindicatum*, pp. 158–9. In the eighteenth century, the radical Whig historian, Gilbert Stuart, agreed with such arguments, deeming the Scottish practice of *nobile officium* to be 'a Turkish jurisdiction in a country of liberty' (*Observations concerning the Public Law*, p. 275).

of different constitutional and confessional contexts. Hence despite Charles II's confident belief that the Scots possessed 'the best laws off [*sic*] any peaple in the world', the methods employed by members of his Scottish administration to secure civil peace were subjected to unprecedented degrees of scrutiny.[40]

Renewed theoretical interest in the juridical content of natural law was conspicuously apparent in the divergent characterisations produced by Viscount Stair and Mackenzie of Rosehaugh whilst serving as President of the Court of Session and as Lord Advocate respectively. For his part, Stair recognised natural law as a universal standard to which legislators aspired, declaring in his *Institutions of the Law of Scotland* in 1681 that, since 'equity and the law of nature and reason is perfect and perpetual', the purpose of positive municipal law was 'only to declare equity, or make it effectual'. As Stair conceived, if 'man had not fallen, there had been no distinction betwixt *bonum* and *æquum*' and likewise nothing would have been more 'profitable, than the full following of the natural law'. Given human depravity, however, Stair conceded that it was better for man to 'quit something of that which by equity is his due, for peace and quietness sake', rather than using 'compulsion and quarrelling in all things'. Hence he acknowledged the practical necessity of observing positive laws, but avoided drawing too sharp a distinction between legal and moral rights, regarding the former as a specialised and distinct case of the latter.[41] Stair's reasoning further denied justification for an equity jurisdiction comparable to the English common law court of Chancery, since this interpretation of equity primarily arose from natural law.

A very different construction of *ius naturae* was, however, articulated by Mackenzie of Rosehaugh in his *Institutions of the Law of Scotland*, published three years later, in 1684, since Mackenzie's instinctive attachment to legislation as a source of legal authority rendered him less likely to defend notions of an independent natural morality. Adopting the Justinianic division of law into the law of nature, the law of nations and the civil, or municipal, law of each country, Mackenzie defined natural law as being 'those common principles which are common to Man and beasts . . . rather innate instinct, than positive Law'. Denuding *ius naturae* of any effective moral quality, he followed contemporary Continental practice by differentiating further between a 'primary' natural law representing the shared legal principles upon which mankind rationally ordered its world and a 'secondary' law of nature governing specific legal arrangements between sovereign states in an embryonic form of international law. Intent on 'inserting nothing that is controverted' in his *Institutions*,

---

[40] Airy ed., *Lauderdale Papers*, III, 104.
[41] Sir James Dalrymple, Viscount Stair, *The Institutions of the Law of Scotland*, D. Walker ed. (Edinburgh, 1981), pp. 82 (I.15), 90 (I.17–18), 91 (I.18). For more on this subject, see Clare Jackson, 'Natural Law and the Construction of Political Sovereignty in Scotland 1660–1690', in Ian Hunter and David Saunders eds., *Natural Law and Civil Sovereignty: Moral Right and State Authority in Early Modern Political Thought* (Basingstoke, 2002), pp. 155–69.

Mackenzie thus had difficulty accommodating more uncertain Grotian notions of natural law since they lacked clear evidence of a legislator's will.[42]

Mackenzie was later to address the potential conflict that arose between his own instinctive attachment to regard all law as derived from the sovereign's will and his recognition of each individual's capacity to use correctly his own *recta ratio* to obtain knowledge of the natural law. In an essay, *On Reason*, published in 1690, he defended notions of universal justice, but distanced himself from notions of an independent morality along the lines of the Grotian *etiamsi daremus* clause, by emphasising that 'all the Principles of Justice and Government, without which, the World could not subsist', depended upon belief in an infinite and immortal deity.[43] The absence of this religious foundation also explained why Justinian's definition of natural law as instincts common to all living creatures lacked effective meaning. In a commentary on Justinian's *Digest* left unfinished at his death, Mackenzie likewise reiterated that the laws of nature were 'dictates written in our harts' by God, rather than deductions inferred by men. Since humans themselves had, however, been created by a morally perfect deity, he recognised that this definition necessarily entailed degrees of circularity in attempting to define morality in terms of God's will. Nevertheless Mackenzie remained confident that had he the 'time to make a Scheme of Law and vertues', he would proceed 'from my principle of ye Preservation of the Universe, and the Order that God hath established in it'.[44]

In his professional capacity as Lord Advocate from 1677 to 1686, and again from 1687 to 1688, Mackenzie was well placed to translate his theoretical convictions regarding the pre-eminent requirement to preserve order into praxis. In doing so, he became involved in a series of controversial state trials that raised questions regarding the extent to which extra-judicial procedures were justifiable in terms of reason of state. Immediately after his appointment in 1677, for example, Mackenzie was instructed to prosecute the Covenanter, James Mitchell, for the attempted murder of Archbishop Sharp in 1668 described in the previous chapter. The case was, however, somewhat ambiguous for although Mitchell had confessed his guilt to a Privy Council committee when arrested in 1674, apparently upon a promise of pardon, he had later refused to reaffirm that confession before the Justiciary Court, fearing that the Council's sentence of forfeiture and loss of his right hand might be commuted to the death penalty. When Mackenzie proceeded to prosecute Mitchell in 1678, under an obsolete statute rendering it a capital offence to assault a Privy Councillor, the only proof remained the retracted confession which was now

---

[42] Sir George Mackenzie, 'The Institutions of the Law of Scotland', in *The Works of that Noble and Eminent Lawyer*, II, 277–8. For more on the Continental context, see John W. Cairns, 'The Civil Law Tradition in Scottish Legal Thought', in David L. Carey Miller and Reinhard Zimmermann eds., *The Civilian Tradition and Scots Law* (Berlin, 1997), pp. 191–223 and Alan Watson, 'Some Notes on Mackenzie's *Institutions* and the European Legal Tradition', *Ius Commune: Zeitschrift für Europäische Rechtesgeschichte*, 16 (1989), pp. 303–13.

[43] Mackenzie, *Reason. An Essay*, p. 25.

[44] BL Add. MSS. 18,236, 'Discourse on the 4 First Chapters of the Digest', ff. 8r–8v, 6r.

permitted as evidence. Although several Privy Council members including Lauderdale, Hatton, Rothes and Sharp himself swore on oath that no mercy had been promised, when the relevant excerpt from the Council Registers was read aloud in court, proof of the Privy Councillors' perjury became apparent. Attending the trial, Lauderdale's Anglican chaplain, George Hickes, found the courtroom 'full of disaffected villans' who spat on his clerical habit and 'pelted me now & then, wth such things as bits of apple, & crusts of bread'.[45] Although Hickes regarded Mackenzie as 'almost the only great man of this country' who pursued Mitchell 'like a gallant man and a good Christian', the trial was clearly mismanaged.[46] While Mitchell was duly convicted and executed, a subsequent attempt to charge Hatton with perjury in relation to the trial failed in 1681.

Suspicions of sharp practice continued during the 1680s. Opening his political memoirs for the year 1683, John Lauder of Fountainhall observed 'no change in the arbitrary government', despite the duke of Lauderdale's death the previous year.[47] Later in 1683, William Lawrie of Blackwood, estate factor to James, second marquis of Douglas, was prosecuted for 'resetting', or harbouring rebels, in the aftermath of the Covenanters' defeat at Bothwell Bridge. According to Fountainhall, the crime of resetting rebels had 'been little noticed in Scotland as treason', and from '1540 till now, the rigorous purshueing of this cryme of reset hes sleiped'. Recognising that Lawrie's conviction would be rendered unsound should the alleged rebels subsequently be found to have been innocent, Fountainhall nevertheless concluded that 'reason of State may prevaill over all this', since 'the Chancelor and Statsmen have over-ruled the Judges to this decision . . . upon a very politicall designe.'[48] In prosecuting Lawrie, Mackenzie insisted that former 'laxness has been the occasion of rebellions in which we have exceeded all the nations of the world, to that hight that wee have even lost the notion of treasons'.[49] Despite a series of legal consultations deeming the charge to be unsubstantiated, Lawrie was convicted and sentenced to death. Although the sentence was not carried out, Lawrie remained in prison until 1688 and Douglas' estate suffered financial ruin. Recording the verdict as 'a strange sentence', Gilbert Burnet concluded that such procedures demonstrated 'the impudence of a sort of men' who had long condemned the 'parliamentary attainder for a constructive treason in the case of the earl of Strafford' in 1641, but 'did now in a common court of justice condemn a man upon a train of so many inferences that it was not possible to make it look like a constructive treason'.[50]

In addition to concerns about the irregular administration of civil and criminal

[45] BL Lansdowne MSS. 988, 'George Hickes to Dr. Patrick or Dr. Oughram, 10 January 1678', f. 155r.
[46] Henry Ellis ed., *Original Letters Illustrative of English History*, Second Series, 4 vols. (London, 1877), IV, 49.
[47] Lauder of Fountainhall, *Historical Observes*, p. 87.
[48] Lauder of Fountainhall, *Historical Notices*, I, 413–14, 411.
[49] 'Trial of Lowrie or Weir of Blackwood', in Howell ed., *Complete Collection of State Trials*, IX, 1034.
[50] Burnet, *History of My Own Time*, II, 331.

justice within the courtrooms of Restoration Scotland, considerable disquiet also arose over issues concerning the defence of private property. Bodinian-style absolutism sought to protect subjects' rights by according property rights a basis in natural law which the sovereign was precluded from violating. Civil law similarly granted considerable importance to the division of law into persons, things or actions, rendering alien Hobbesian notions that the disposal of all private property lay in the hands of the absolute sovereign. The sanctity of private property was thus acknowledged as an integral component of constitutional monarchy. As Mackenzie himself emphasised, it was 'a Rule in the Law of all Nations that that which is mine cannot be taken from me without my consent'. Regarding the royal prerogative, he explained that since 'Government is the Kings, and Property is the Subjects Birth-right', monarchy was 'a Government, and so can include no more, than what is necessary for Government'. In no sense therefore could absolute monarchy threaten individual rights and liberties. Mackenzie thus deemed it 'absurd to think that Mens Property should be taken away without their speciall Consent or Crime; for it is all one to me if I be oppressed, whether I am soe by an Absolute & Dispotick Monarch or an unlimited Parliament'. Ingenuously, he further conceded that 'even the most flattering Lawyers under absolute Monarchy's [sic] confess that Monarchs cannot invert property'.[51]

Notwithstanding such theoretical commitments, increasing concern emerged that private property was being endangered. In the 1660s, considerable opposition arose to suggested alterations in Scottish land law that would make it easier for the government to appropriate landed assets in lieu of debt repayments. As one anonymous writer informed Charles II, such proposals were regarded 'by Lawyers and the most eminent of yor Judges, as great Innovationes', subverting 'what was formerlie believed and acquiesced to, as undoubted Law'.[52] Within the reason of state tradition, there were, however, influential theoretical justifications at the government's disposal which could be invoked during times of national crisis. For his part, Mackenzie accepted that when normal and peaceful conditions prevailed, subjects enjoyed inviolable property rights, although they were obliged to assist with defraying requisite maintenance costs through taxation and other obligations to the king or whomsoever possessed the *'dominium directum'* or right of superiority. Citing Grotius, however, Mackenzie acknowledged that when such peaceful conditions were threatened, it could be claimed that the sovereign possessed a *'dominium eminens'*, understood as 'a Paramount and transcendent Right over even private Estates, in case of necessity, when the common Interest cannot be otherwise maintained'. This *dominium eminens* could, however, only be sustained in cases where there was 'a necessity for the State to make use of this extraordinary power' and where 'Reparation be given for what is soe inverted by virtue of this power'.[53]

[51] BL Add. MSS. 18,236, 'Discourse on the 4 First Chapters of the Digest', f. 20v; *Jus Regium*, p. 50; BL Add. MSS, 18,236, 'Discourse on the 4 First Chapters of the Digest', ff. 22r–v.
[52] NAS 406/2/640/5, 'Address to his Majesty giving a repn of the state and interest of Scotland'.
[53] Mackenzie, *Jus Regium*, pp. 54–5; BL Add. MSS. 18,236, 'Discourse on the 4 First Chapters of the Digest', ff. 25v–26r.

The issue of the unlawful invasion of private property crystallised prominently in the late-1670s when the government sanctioned the partial free quartering of members of the so-called 'Highland Host' who had been dispatched in an attempt to suppress recalcitrant Covenanters in south-west Scotland. Throughout the Restoration, the government's simultaneous use of the armed forces to collect fiscal dues and to repress religious dissent proved seriously destabilising. The use of free quarter has been regarded as especially oppressive and, accordingly, it has been argued that 'military intervention was often no more than a cloak for fiscal extortion' in contrast to the situation in Restoration England where there was no systematic use of the military to exact fiscal dues or to collect fines from dissenters.[54] In Scotland, one anonymous private address to Charles II claimed, for instance, that it was a 'fundamental of government above any positive law' that subjects should remain free from additional burdens on their own land. Although the author willingly accepted that absolute government was consistent with private property rights, he believed that the very notion of free quarter served only to 'subvert and overturn all property', since 'mens estates are so secured by law, as His Maj[ty] can have no interest therein, except by forfeiture or delinquence'. As fiscal impositions were only lawful if sanctioned by parliamentary consent, free quarter not only contradicted this precept, but could also be construed as even more unlawful, since it took the form of a military invasion. Using free quarter also negated prevailing arguments supporting the establishment of a state militia on the grounds that such a militia would be separately financed without any liability placed on the people. Furthermore, the anonymous writer addressed the provocative manner in which free quarter was deployed to deter treasonable intentions as inferred from popular attendance at presbyterian conventicles. Since such conventicles were clearly 'defined, considered and punished with pecuniary mulcts' by acts of Parliament, they were 'not in law lookt on as public rebellion, importing treason or lese Majesty' and should not be treated as such by the government.[55]

For their part, members of Charles II's administration repeatedly protested that, with regard to the imposition of free quarter, they had 'done what possiblie we can' in order to 'satisfie all manner of scruples and objections . . . moved against the legalitie of this new modell'. Convinced that 'nothing appears against Law in it', the Privy Councillors denied their opponents' right either to promote domestic disaffection or to travel to Whitehall to complain about free

[54] Allan Macinnes, *Clanship, Commerce and the House of Stuart, 1603–1788* (East Linton, 1996), p. 124.
[55] NAS GD 406/2/637/4, 'That freequarter is against the fundamental laws of the Kingdom'. For more on the militia issue, see Bruce P. Lenman, 'Militia, Fencible Men, and Home Defence, 1660–1797', in Norman Macdougall ed., *Scotland and War A.D. 79–1918* (Edinburgh, 1991), pp. 170–92. From an operational viewpoint, the former royalist commander, Sir James Turner, also questioned the efficacy of the free quarter policy. Recalling how around 2,000 soldiers and a thousand horses had been earlier quartered on around three or four hundred households during the Pentland Rising of 1666, he recalled how 'even where strict limits are placed on soldiers' requirements, the grievance continues heavy and great' (Turner, *Pallas Armata*, p. 202).

quarter to Charles II 'to creat him unjust trouble, and to raise unnecessarie noise in England'.[56] Contemplating whether or not to prosecute a nephew of the duke of Hamilton, Lord Bargeny, for refusing to take a bond of peaceable behaviour in February 1680, Lord Advocate Mackenzie warned Lauderdale that attempts to expedite matters by bringing such cases directly before the Privy Council would be 'unsafe for your interest, for it is a stretch against Law & would leav the odium upon your friends'. Adding that the duke of York, as parliamentary high Commissioner, also considered it 'unsafe', since it 'wold be imputed to his arbitrary inclinations', Mackenzie acknowledged that the government owed 'really much to his being heer . . . & if were imagine wee can stand upon our oun leggs wee are fools'.[57]

Published attempts to exonerate the government's actions were also produced. Commenting on the bond passed requiring landlords to guarantee their tenants' peaceable behaviour, Lauderdale's Anglican chaplain, George Hickes, acknowledged the seemingly controversial character of such legislation to an English audience in 1678. As he maintained, however, enforcement was feasible, since Scottish 'Heritors have such a despotic power over their Tenants, as you cannot imagine, unless you had lived here'.[58] A printed defence of the government's actions was also presented in a pamphlet purporting to offer *A True Narrative of the Proceedings of his Majesties Privy Council in Scotland, For Securing the Peace of the Kingdom in 1678* which only generated vitriolic denunciation from critics who attributed its authorship to Lord Advocate Mackenzie. So apparently specious were the grounds on which the government's actions were ostensibly justified, that one anonymous author desired that the pamphlet be renamed 'ye second particular of Aretina', referring to a prolix Greek romance penned by Mackenzie in 1660 when he was still in his early twenties.[59] Elsewhere, in a letter intercepted by the authorities, the political observer, Matthew Mackaile, ironically averred to a London correspondent in 1678 that all government actions were now regarded as 'higher than Acts of Parliament and entrusted with the execution of the law by immediate divine authority'. As a means of explaining current disorders, Mackaile sarcastically concluded that the people of Scotland observed a new 'first principle of equity, that sovereign authority is absolutely to be obeyed and that no pretence of religion or liberty ought to bound that obedience, but obedience ought to bound them'.[60]

---

[56] Airy ed., *Lauderdale Papers*, II, 208.

[57] *Ibid.*, III, 191–2.

[58] [Hickes], *Ravillac Redivivus*, p. 50.

[59] NLS Adv. MS. 31.6.16, 'Ane Answer be way of a letter to Sr George McKeinzie Ks Advocate his printed narrative of the Councells proceedings in 1678; anent the bond and the Kings forces sent to the Western shires [c.1678]', f. 169r. For more on the political content of Mackenzie's *Aretina*, see Clare Jackson, 'The Paradoxical Virtue of the Historical Romance: Sir George Mackenzie's *Aretina* (1660) and the Civil Wars', in John R. Young ed., *Celtic Dimensions of the British Civil Wars* (Edinburgh, 1997), pp. 205–25.

[60] 'Matthew Mackaile to John Adams, merchant, Lisbon [i.e. Sir John Frederick], 16 July 1678', in Blackburne Daniell ed., *Calendar of State Papers Domestic Series, March 1st, 1678 to December 31st, 1678*, p. 292.

III

Underpinning the government's repression of religious nonconformity and popular unrest was a persistent belief that the claims of conscience were being fraudulently used as a pretext to justify political rebellion. From the outset of the Restoration, concerns had been expressed that the ecclesiastical issue of church government could be appropriated for nefarious political ends. The defence of religion might be pretended, but the enterprise of rebellion was thereby intended. Preaching before the first Restoration Parliament in 1661, for instance, the Stirling minister, Matthias Symson, exhorted his audience to ensure that nobody 'under pretence of upholding the Government of the Church be permitted to undermine the Government of the State'. Declaring himself 'confident there is room enough in Scotland for them both', Symson thus cautioned the assembly to 'take care, that no man upon pretence of erecting a Throne for Christ, do shake the Throne of the King'.[61] Preaching before the same Parliament, John Paterson voiced similar fears that 'the design of some Zelots against Episcopacy' might contain 'worse at the bottom', effectively tending instead 'to lead Subjects into misconstructions of His Majesties Gracious Intentions'.[62]

Following the unpopular re-imposition of episcopacy, however, popular discontent soon emerged and erupted into armed violence during the Pentland Rising of November 1666. Anticipating an imminent uprising, the earl of Rothes had predicted shortly beforehand that ecclesiastical policy 'will be maid the pretext' although specific grievances against episcopacy 'are not much considerable'.[63] In the aftermath of the Rising itself, Bishop Andrew Honyman ruefully declared that the rebels had not acted 'really for Religion', but instead had aimed to 'pull down all Authorities in the Land'. From the rebels' written manifestoes, Honyman perceived that 'Prerogative is the mark that is shot at as well as Prelacy', the one being 'as great an eye-sore as the other'. Were 'Episcopacy out of the Nation and out of the World', Honyman contended that the continuous spread of their subversive principles would leave 'no security for the most just and justly acting Authority', rendering constant vigilance essential.[64] At the trial of several Covenanters accused of participating in the Pentland Rising, the Lord Advocate, Sir John Nisbet of Dirleton, defended the treason charges levied against the rebels as deserved. Judging the defence claim that the Rising was 'founded upon a pretended *bellum justum*, is most irrelevant', Nisbet

---

[61] Symson, *Yehoveh ve melek, or God and the King*, p. 19.
[62] [John Paterson] (pseudonym 'Phil-alethio'), *A Brief resolution of the Present Case of the Subjects of Scotland, In Order to Episcopal Government, by Sacred Authority re-established in this Kingdom. Or Episcopus Scotus Redivivus* ([London], 1661), p. 17.
[63] Airy ed., *Lauderdale Papers*, I, 209, 215.
[64] [Honyman], *Survey of Naphtali. Part II*, p. 263; *Survey of the Insolent and Infamous Libel entituled Naphtali*, pp. 11–12.

restricted the definition of *bellum justum* as applying only to conflicts between sovereign monarchs or sovereign states.[65]

Persistent antagonism thus arose as supporters of the Stuart government continually sought to reconcile the claims of individual conscience with the essential preservation of order. For Archbishop Robert Leighton, conscience was 'either the best friend, or the worst enemy a man hath'. For as he was aware, hypocrisy could be 'sheltered under the cloak of conscience' by some individuals, while others genuinely regarded the current civil government as unacceptable. Since discontented elements were deterred by clear civil penalties from expressing their political grievances openly, however, Leighton observed how 'Religion and Conscience must be pretended, when under hand they are undoing the interest both of God and Caesar'.[66] In 1679, Mackenzie of Rosehaugh also counselled Charles II privately to 'Remember, Remember that such pretexts borrowed from Libertie and conscience grew up in the last age to a rebellion', when 'Archbishop Laud, Montrose and Strafford were rebells and Monarchie it self was declared at last to be tirrany.' If contemporary political divisions could be found to be 'Material and did proceed from Conscience', Mackenzie accepted that this might lessen, but not justify, the guilt of civil disobedience, 'for Conscience should neither be a Crime, nor a defence for Crimes'.[67]

Similar allegations persisted as the 'Killing Times' escalated. Describing events in Scotland for an English audience in 1680, George Hickes reported encountering a military officer in south-west Scotland who had recently searched a 'Countrey-Fellow, going to a Conventicle', and 'in one of his Pockets found *Naphtali*, and in the other a Pocket-Pistol charged with two Bullets'. As the officer had commented, the items represented 'the Doctrine . . . in one Pocket, and the use in other', before confirming that many more copies of 'that Cursed Book' were discovered among Covenanting rebels captured at Bothwell Bridge.[68] As public executions of convicted traitors became an increasingly regular occurrence, popular disquiet increased. In 1684, for instance, the Selkirk minister, James Canaries, attacked that 'desperate Crew of brain-sick and giddy People' that were possessed with 'strangely delusive & odd Chymæara's & fancies' and armed with 'barbarous Weapons of Cruelty, Syths, Pitch-forks, Spades, [and] Flails'. Perceiving how extreme presbyterian Covenanters would evidently rather be hanged than say 'God save the King', Canaries concluded that 'all that they die for, is but the meer figment and opinion of their own distempered and raving Brain, the product of some fermented Enthusiastick temper'.[69] The judge, Lauder of Fountainhall, shared Canaries' suspicions, reporting a growing belief that instead of executing

[65] 'Process against Captain Andrew Arnot &c., December 4th, 1666', in Wodrow, *Sufferings*, II, 42.
[66] Leighton, 'The Rule of Conscience', in *Remains*, p. 258.
[67] Mackenzie, BL Add. MSS. 23,244, 'My Lord Advocats Arguments in law', f. 27v; *A Vindication of His Majesties Government & Judicatures*, p. 8.
[68] Hickes, *Spirit of Popery speaking*, p. 67.
[69] James Canaries, *A Discourse Representing the Sufficient Manifestation of the Will of God to his Church in all its several Periods and Dispensations* (Edinburgh, 1684), pp. 184–5, 189.

individuals for their allegedly unorthodox political principles, the authorities could perhaps have 'employed physitians to use ther skill upon them as on hypocondriack persones.' For as Fountainhall regretfully observed, 'the putting to death for opinions, is a popish maxime not yet receaved among protestants'.[70]

As public executions continued, however, members of the political and eccle-siastical establishment maintained that removing such diseased parts of the body politic was essential to preserve the health of the whole commonwealth. Preaching a thanksgiving sermon to commemorate Charles II's restoration on 29 May 1685, Canaries concluded that if 'Religion is still to be the Plea' with everyone allegedly entitled to decide matters for themselves, this was 'all one with Hobbs's fancied State of Nature, only putting in the word Religion, for that of Right' from which 'the same Mischiefs and Confusions' could be expected.[71] Two years later, in a thanksgiving sermon preached in St. Giles' Cathedral in Edinburgh, on James VII & II's birthday in 1687, John MackQueen likewise contended that all 'Grand Conspiracies against the Government' were defended by 'a Sham- zeal for Religion, a Counterfit Affection to the Publick, a Crocodile Piety for oppressed Liberty', all of which were managed by 'Shaftsburian Harangues, and Cromwellian Devotions'. Surrounded by such destabilising disorder, MackQueen warned that 'too much caution is needless, where neces-sity requires speed; dilatory Methods against Traytors has diminish'd the Authority of Monarchy' with potentially fatal consequences for the survival of the body politic.[72]

The extent to which Charles II's administration became increasingly concerned to ascertain the loyal disposition of all of its subjects was reflected in the growing number and extent of state oaths imposed on the population. Given the steady proliferation of state oaths devised throughout Britain during the civil wars, reconfiguring and extending such tests of loyalty might not have been thought conducive to stability following the restoration of the monarchy. Charles II had himself only been crowned as a 'covenanted' king at Scone after swearing both the National Covenant and the Solemn League and Covenant in the Hague in 1650. In retrospect, however, one of the Scots commissioners who had tendered the oaths to the then Prince of Wales, Alexander Jaffray, regretted

---

[70] Lauder of Fountainhall, *Historical Observes*, pp. 30, 11. For an account of how 'the public execution remained one of the principal methods by which the power of the state was demonstrated' in an English context, see J. A. Sharpe, ' "Last Dying Speeches": Religion, Ideology and Public Execution in Seventeenth-Century England', *Past and Present*, 107 (1985), pp. 144–67 at p. 161.

[71] James Canaries, *A Sermon Preacht at Selkirk Upon the 29th of May, 1685. Being the Anniversary of the Restoration of the Royal Family to the Throne of these Kingdoms* (Edinburgh, 1685), p. 20.

[72] MackQueen, *God's Interest in the King*, pp. 21, 16. Nor did such suspicions abate after the Williamite Revolution. In an official report on Scottish affairs prepared by an English civil servant in 1691, for example, it was contended that so significant was ecclesiastical policy in determining civil affairs 'that it is impossible to touch one without moving the other'. Nevertheless, the author warned that 'one must not be mistaken, religion serves here sometimes as a pretext' while 'gold and silver, or the hope of obtaining some, is always the principal motive which moves them' ('Memorial concerning affairs in Scotland', in W. Hardy ed., *Calendar of State Papers Domestic Series, of the Reign of William and Mary, 1st November 1691–End of 1692* (London, 1900), p. 63).

how '[w]e did sinfully both entangle the nation and ourselves, and that poor young prince', by 'making him sign and swear a covenant which we knew he hated in his heart'.[73] Celebrating Charles II's restoration in 1660, the Eccles minister, John Jameson, specifically attacked the extensive imposition of oaths on the Scottish people during the mid-century civil wars and denounced those who had dishonestly used oaths 'like a sleep pillow they put under peoples heads to lull them fast asleep, that they may neither see their projects, nor fear their power'.[74] Such sentiments were widely endorsed during the Restoration. In 1669 Bishop Andrew Honyman observed that just as Scots were 'noted by Forraigners to be too much given to suddain and rash swearing in ordinary discourse', they also tended 'beyond other people, to multiple oaths and seditious combinations'. This was not a national characteristic of which the Scots should be proud, for 'they that swear often, manifest that they think themselves not worthy to be believed otherwise'. Hence Honyman suspected that 'multitudes of oaths debaseth the dignity of them', encouraging people freely to disregard former commitments. Hence he detected 'a sign of too much distemper in a State, where oaths are multiplied to form Parties and Factions', observing that it would have been 'good for Scotland that there had been amongst us fewer oaths, but better qualified and more stedfastly kept'.[75]

Despite such concerns, the very first enactment of the first Restoration Parliament that convened in Edinburgh in January 1661 enforced on its members an oath of allegiance that emphasised the king's authority and superiority in both secular and ecclesiastical affairs. A proposal mooted by Lord Dumfries in 1663 that the oath taken by parliamentary commissioners be extended to all heritors and ministers, in conscious imitation of the success enjoyed by the mid-century Covenants, was not adopted, despite Dumfries' confident prediction that such a requirement would discourage the government's enemies and 'at on[e] stroak disapoint ther hoops, prevent ther Endeavours, and give a publick testimonie of the kings securitie'.[76] Between 1661 and 1663, however, a further series of oaths declaring the illegality of the National Covenant and the Solemn League and Covenant were devised. Such oaths were to be sworn by all who held offices of public trust, thereby including Lords of Session, members of the College of Justice, exchequer commissioners, sheriffs, stewards, their deputies and clerks, burgh magistrates and councillors as well as Justices of the Peace and their clerks. Scots criminal law procedure did not, however, require the process of empanelling sworn juries as in Restoration England.

Dilemmas nevertheless soon arose for those Scots who desired to hold public

---

[73] 'Report on the Records of the Burgh of Aberdeen', in HMC, *First Report of the Royal Commission on Historical Manuscripts* (London, 1874), p. 122.

[74] Jameson, *Rebellio Debellata*, p. 11.

[75] [Honyman], *Survey of Naphtali. Part II*, p. 180.

[76] NLS MS. 597, f. 95, 'Ane humble overture concerning the takeing of the declaratione allreadie taken and subscryved by the members of parliament, 19 August 1663'. For more information on oath-taking in England during this period, see David Martin Jones, *Conscience and Allegiance in Seventeenth Century England. The Political Significance of Oaths and Engagements* (Rochester, NY, 1999).

office but remained unwilling to endorse the lawfulness of erastian episco-palianism. In 1662, for instance, Sir Mungo Stirling of Glorat was advised by his son, George Stirling, to relinquish his office as a Justice of the Peace in Stirlingshire, rather than renounce the authority of the National Covenant and Solemn League and Covenant. His son offered this advice, not from a desire to see his father lose public office, but as a 'casuist resolving the grand case of conscience of this tyme'. As he acknowledged to his father, these were 'searching tymes for Christianes who ar of tender conscience' and he therefore implored his father to quit his public employments and 'seek after the durable riches which lasts to eternitie'.[77] Substantial fines were also imposed on more prominent office-holders who remained recalcitrant, even after they had surren-dered parliamentary office. Confronted with a fine of £6,000 for refusing to swear the oath of abjuration, William Kerr, third earl of Lothian, wrote to Sir Robert Moray in 1666, disputing the rationale behind such punitive measures and denying that there was any individual 'in the thrie kyngdomes [who] loves the Royalty more, nor his Majestie's person', nor any 'who would more readily lay doune his lyfe for the maintenance of both'. Rejecting the notion that his refusal to swear the oath rendered him in any way politically untrustworthy, Lothian argued that if every member of Parliament who ever objected to a proposal was deemed 'disloyall and disafected to the Kyng's service' with 'designes to overturn the government, – what a consequence is this!' If matters continued thus, Lothian warned Moray that any 'remedy would be many tymes worse then the dissease, present or future'.[78] Such reasoning was unheeded, however, by those who sought to associate religious nonconformity with trea-sonable intention and the need for military coercion. As the earl of Tweeddale duly informed Moray, the earl of Lothian 'shall be quartered on if he pays not as others are'.[79] Lothian's sensitivities contrasted starkly with the apparent cavalierish venality of other former Covenanters. When it was suggested to the earl of Lauderdale, for instance, that he might scruple at swearing the new oaths, he allegedly 'laugh'd at this contrivance, and told them he would sign a cartfull of such oaths before he would lose his place'.[80]

Continual conflicts therefore regularly arose whenever individuals sought to reconcile the dictates of their own consciences with the outward expressions of political and religious conformity required by the government. Such tensions were most conspicuously encapsulated in the issues that arose from the passing of the 1681 Test Act designed to safeguard the Protestant religion from possible attack by a non-Protestant monarch. Imposed on all public office-holders, the Act required a profession of the Protestant religion and an affirmation of royal supremacy in all temporal and spiritual matters. Concern had been expressed during the parliamentary debates that accompanied its enactment, by members

---

[77] Sir William Fraser, *The Stirlings of Keir and their Family Papers* (Edinburgh, 1858), p. 499.
[78] David Laing ed., *Correspondence of Sir Robert Kerr, first Earl of Ancram and his son, William, third earl of Lothian*, 2 vols. (Edinburgh, 1875), II, 476.
[79] NLS MS. 7024, 'Earl of Tweeddale to Sir Robert Moray, 20 March 1666', f. 11.
[80] Mackenzie, *Memoirs*, pp. 64–5.

such as the laird of Gordonstoun who publicly declared himself 'against all pænall and sanguinary laws in matters of religion', since 'the conscience could not be forced' and such 'severe sanctions and penalties operated nothing, save to render men hypocrites'.[81] At Viscount Stair's suggestion, the specific definition of 'Protestantism' was taken as that supplied by the Confession of Faith formulated in 1567. Since the Confession of Faith acknowledged lawful resistance, the insertion of this definition immediately rendered the oath internally inconsistent. As Gilbert Burnet later recalled, the Confession was 'a book so worn out of use, that scarce any one in the whole parliament had ever read it: None of the bishops had, as appeared afterwards'. According to Burnet, Stair had assumed that the passage of the Test Act would be immediately obstructed since it employed a definition wherein 'the repressing of tyranny is reckoned a duty incumbent on good subjects'.[82] Moreover, the Confession of Faith also contradicted the 1669 Act of Supremacy that the Test Act had been ostensibly designed to confirm. Hence another parliamentary commissioner, Lord Belhaven, presciently acknowledged it to be 'a very good Act for secureing our religion' from invasion by an individual subject, but he did not regard it as serving 'to secure our Protestant religion against a Popish or phanaticall successor to the Croun.'[83]

Confusion ensued immediately. In Balquhidder, the minister, Robert Kirk, recorded privately that by the Test, many 'see such alterations in poynts of policy's, Government, & other indifferencies that they ar now required to falsifie their Solemn Word' or be deprived of their public office and paid employment. Given the 'spiritual & secular Hazard', Kirk decided the most prudent course was to 'hold out so long as beseemingly we can without offending of any other, or wronging our own Soul or Credit', whilst also seeking to 'sift and search the judgement of others . . . to do, or not do, accordingly'.[84] More notoriously, however, when Archibald Campbell, ninth earl of Argyll, subsequently attempted to swear the oath 'in so far as it was consistent with itself', he was placed on trial for treason. In his prosecution, Mackenzie of Rosehaugh argued that Argyll's interpretation undermined not only the Test Act, but all security of government, since it 'makes every man's conscience, under which there goes ordinarily in this age humor and interest, to be the rule of the taker's obedience'. As he warned, those responsible for deciding Argyll's fate should consider the scandalous light in which 'this new way may look in an age wherein we are too much tracing the steps of our rebellious progenitors in the last'.[85] When the guilty sentence was pronounced and Argyll was sentenced to death, vociferous opposition arose immediately. As one spectator at the trial allegedly concluded, he

---

[81] Lauder of Fountainhall, *Historical Notices*, I, 316.
[82] Burnet, *History of My Own Time*, II, 314.
[83] Lauder of Fountainhall, *Historical Notices*, I, 307.
[84] EUL MSS. La.III.529, 'Robert Kirk, Ane account Of some occasional meditationes', ff. 10–11. A few years earlier, Kirk had hoped that the 'world should becom so wise after long Experience . . . as to require no oaths, but deal with every man according to his Behaviour, For it is the sword that Commands all however, & not Oaths' (NLS MS. 3932 'Miscellany of occurring thoughts on various occasions . . . Balquhidder, 1678', f. 155r).
[85] 'Trial of the Earl of Argyll', in Howell ed., *Complete collection of State Trials*, VIII, 924–5.

believed that Argyll's words must have been 'by popish magic transubstantiate, for he saw them the same as before'. Elsewhere, Lauder of Fountainhall recorded how children in Heriot's Hospital in Edinburgh discovered that the Hospital dog occupied a public office and thus required him to swear the Test. When the dog apparently refused to eat the paper, 'they rubbed it over with butter (which they called an Explication of the Test in imitation of Argile,) and he licked of [sic] the butter, but did spite out the paper'. Thereafter the children held a jury to consider the case whereupon 'in derision of the sentence against Argile, they found the dog guilty of treason, and actually hanged him'.[86] In this context, Fountainhall also mentioned reports circulating from London, that the earl of Halifax had confessed to Charles II that 'he knew not the Scots law, but by the law of England that Explanation could not hang a dog'.[87]

Certainly Halifax had a point. For, as Argyll had himself maintained during his trial, he was not being prosecuted for any actions of political disloyalty, but only for 'the sense of words misconstrued to the greatest height, and stretched to imaginary inclinations, quite contrary to my scope and design'. Hence Argyll personally entreated Mackenzie to acknowledge that 'he hath gone too far in this Process, and say plainly what he knows to be true by his acquaintance with me . . . that I am neither Papist nor Phanatick'.[88] In England, Argyll's case was eagerly discussed by polemical pamphleteers, who criticised the government's accusation on the grounds that 'Letters, Syllables, Words, without meaning can be no Law to the Subject, nor more then Scotch-men can dance to their own Bag-pipes when they give an indistinct and uncertain Sound'. Wishing to prevent Englishmen being similarly 'wet to the skin' by the 'Scotch-Mist' that surrounded the conviction, pamphleteers defended Argyll's right to supply his own understanding of an oath of which 'the sense and meaning be obscure'.[89] Moreover, Argyll was also aware that were he to be found guilty, a large proportion of the episcopalian establishment would, ironically, come under immediate suspicion for having submitted reflections on the Test Act that contained 'expressions that may be stretched to a worse sense than I am charged for'.[90] The bishop and synod of Aberdeen had, for instance, explicitly indicated that, by taking the Test, they were not electing to 'swear to all the particular assertions and expressions of the Confession of Faith', acknowledging 'the ambiguity and

---

[86] Lauder of Fountainhall, *Historical Observes*, pp. 55–6. This anecdote prompted another pamphleteer to depict Argyll as a dog who apparently swallowed the Test Act whole, but subsequently retched up certain parts, upon which the assembled child-advocates decreed that 'all his irksome champing and chowing of it, was only . . . to separat the concomitant nutrient, and that was mikel worse than a flat refusal of it, and gif [sic] it were rightly examined, would upon Tryal, be found no less than Leising-making' ('M.D.', *An Account of the Arraignment, Tryal, Escape and Condemnation of the Dog of Heriot's Hospital in Scotland, that was supposed to have been Hang'd, but did at last slip the Halter* (London, 1682), p. 1).

[87] Lauder of Fountainhall, *Historical Observes*, p. 56.

[88] *The Speech of the Earl of Argyle at his Trial on the 12th of December, 1681* (London, 1682), p. 2.

[89] Anon., *The Scotch-Mist Cleared Up. To prevent Englishmen being wet to the skin. Being a true Account of the Proceedings against Archibald Earl of Argyle, for High-Treason* ([?London], 1681), p. 34.

[90] *Speech of the Earl of Argyle*, p. 2.

obscure expressions thereof'. A similar opinion was collectively voiced by, among others, the ministers of Aberdeen, together with the bishop of Dunkeld and the clergy of Perth.[91] Other members of the Scottish episcopate were not, however, so easily perturbed. Writing to Archbishop William Sancroft of Canterbury in December 1682, for example, Archbishop Alexander Burnet of St. Andrews acknowledged that there were indeed probably 'many deceitfull and dangerous dissemblers among our new converts', but judged it to be 'well that they who doe not obey for conscience sake, are brought at last to submitt for feare'.[92]

Despite the death sentence being pronounced, Argyll temporarily avoided execution by escaping prison and fleeing to join an increasingly large exile community in the Netherlands. Soon afterwards, Argyll's legal counsel, Viscount Stair, also fled to the Netherlands, deeming himself unable to swear the Act. In the courtrooms of Restoration Scotland, however, the claims of conscience continued to be pitted against perceived threats to the state. In 1684, for example, Gilbert Burnet's cousin, Robert Baillie of Jerviswood, was prose-cuted for allegedly participating in an unsuccessful project hatched the previous year by English Whigs to murder Charles II and his brother, known as the 'Rye House Plot'. When the validity of incriminating adminicular evidence supplied by absent witnesses was questioned, Mackenzie, as Lord Advocate, informed the jury that although, strictly, Scots law did not admit such testimony, 'our juries whom the law allows to be arbitrarie and to be confyned by no rule but their conscience' were allowed to consider 'the deposition of witnesses though not taken befor themselves'. In concluding his prosecution of Baillie, Mackenzie exhorted the jury to 'Remember the danger lykewayes of embold-ening conspiracies against the Kings sacred life and of encouraging a civill warre wherein your selves and your posteritie may bleed by making the least difficulty' to convict a traitor for so serious a crime.[93] Having been convicted and sentenced to death, Jerviswood declared himself 'very apprehensive' that 'popish idolatry will be the plague of Scotland'. For, as he perceived, 'the gener-ation is fitted for it', since 'all the engines of hell have been made use of to debauch the consciences of people' as individuals were 'compelled to take contradictory oaths, that they may believe things that have a contradiction in them'.[94]

---

[91] 'Bishop and synod of Aberdeen, their sense of the Test', in Wodrow, *Sufferings*, III, 308. See also 'The ministers of Aberdeen their objections against the Test' and 'Bishop of Dunkeld and clergy of Perth, their sense of the Test', in Wodrow, *Sufferings*, III, 304–6, 308.

[92] William Clarke ed., *A Collection of Letters, addressed by Prelates and Individuals of High Rank in Scotland and By Two Bishops of Sodor and Man to Sancroft, Archbishop of Canterbury in the Reigns of King Charles II and James VII* (Edinburgh, 1848), p. 49.

[93] NAS JC 39/44/7, 'His Maties Advocats Speech to the Inquest'.

[94] 'The trial of Robert Baillie of Jerviswood', in Howell ed., *Complete Collection of State Trials*, X, 720. According to Wodrow, Jerviswood also challenged Mackenzie's own integrity, by informing him publicly that 'when you came to see me in prison, you told me such things were laid to my charge, but that you did not believe them . . . are you now convinced in your conscience, that I am more guilty than before?' At this, Mackenzie then 'appeared in no small confusion, and said, "Jerviswood, I own what you say, my thoughts were then as a private man; but what I say here is by special direction of the privy

152

Mackenzie's concern to regulate individual conscience for the sake of the perceived public good was even more evident in his interrogation before the Privy Council of another Covenanter, Alexander Shields, in 1685. According to Shields' own private account of proceedings, when ordered to reject various political precepts, he responded by declaring that 'I had been in several places of ye world but had never heard of such impositions and that I perceived it was a Misery to be a Scotchman', to which Mackenzie 'replied that it was Misery to have to do with such rascalls as I am'. The Privy Council then ordained that if Shields did not disown a Covenanting manifesto, he would be sentenced to death on the grounds that 'by ye Law of all Nations when war is declared against a king, they have a right to know the allegiance of every citizen'. In response, Shields protested that not only was he uninvolved in domestic politics, being frequently absent from Scotland, but also that 'thought is free and diverse of men have diverse sentiments about government' which remained private, to which Mackenzie had objected that 'such a freedome would destroy humane societies'. When the Council reiterated that 'the Lawes and Acts of Parl^t did reach mens thoughts' and demanded a formal declaration, Shields demanded proof, but observed that the clerk 'could not find the act'. Although the Claim of Right of 1689 subsequently declared it illegal for judges to penalise individuals for refusing to disclose their private thoughts, Shields ultimately elected to preserve his own life in 1685 by owning the king's lawful authority. But he later found himself unable to 'express what a hell of horror I have been in since' which he hoped would deter fellow brethren from capitulation.[95] Mackenzie's suggestion that an individual's private thoughts could form a legitimate object of state scrutiny echoed controversial claims made during the notorious trial of the Whig republican, Algernon Sidney, in England two years previously. Prosecuting Sidney for treason, the English Lord Chief Justice, George Jeffreys, had warned Sidney to 'Curse not the King, not in thy thoughts, nor in thy bedchamber, the birds of the air will carry it.' Although Jeffreys had subsequently accepted that 'the imagination of a man's heart is not to be discerned', he insisted that if such thoughts were articulated by an 'overt-act' suggesting opposition to the monarch, guilt of treason was provided.[96]

For their part, members of Charles II's administration defended their actions as chiefly necessary to isolate those who were determined to undermine civil society and magistracy, rather than as an attempt to deny individual liberties. If particular individuals genuinely deemed the current government in Scotland anathema to their conscience, then Mackenzie, for one, advised that they should 'remove from places where they cannot obey', for 'they will always find some place where the Government will please them'. But if such individuals elected to stay and oppose the government, he maintained that 'it must be excus'd, to

council" to which Jerviswood had replied, "if your lordship have one conscience for yourself, and another for the council, I pray God forgive you, I do" ' (Wodrow, *Sufferings*, IV, 112).
[95] NAS JC 39/73/1, 'Letter from [Alexander] Shields in the Tolbooth of Edinburgh [to John Forbes, Rotterdam], 9 April 1685'.
[96] 'Trial of Algernon Sidney', in Howell ed., *Complete Collection of State Trials*, IX, 369, 889.

execute those who would destroy it'.[97] In 1681, Argyll had escaped sentence of death by fleeing to the Netherlands and increasing numbers were eventually obliged to follow suit. In 1685, for instance, the earl of Craufurd confessed privately that 'the more I have thought on this thing I am the more in the mist', venturing that 'the wisest of men, Solomon himself, if alive and in my case, if the guidance by the spirit of God were but for a time suspended, might be difficulted what resolution to take'.[98]

Voluntary emigration coexisted alongside enforced banishment. For as early as 1667, Lauderdale had ordered Sir Robert Moray 'for the Lords sake be vigilant over that pervers incorrigible fanatick partie . . . Let them rather goe to America Than plott the trouble of Scotland.'[99] Such views became increasingly apposite as Scottish colonies were being founded by Quaker settlers in New Jersey and by discontented presbyterian colonists in South Carolina in the early-1680s. Submitting a proposal before the Privy Council to found a Scottish colony 'in any part of America' in 1681, for example, the provost of Linlithgow emphasised the potential for such a settlement to 'be a great ease to the c[o]untrey and void it of very maney both idle and dissenting persones'.[100] Responsible for prosecuting obdurate nonconformists, Mackenzie of Rosehaugh likewise remarked to the Scottish Chancellor, the earl of Aberdeen, in 1682, that 'the Carolina project encourages much our fanaticks, thinking they ar now secur of a retreat'.[101] On the colonists' part, freedom of conscience was indeed widely

---

[97] Mackenzie, *Jus Regium*, p. 134. The government's message was quite clearly intended to travel beyond Scotland. In an anonymous satirical pamphlet of 1682, for instance, the episcopalian 'Anonymus' declared that all 'who are not pleased with our Laws, let them go and search for better elsewhere, or stand to their hazard at home'. 'Anonymus' then pressed his presbyterian antagonist 'Antiprælatus' to deny that 'it was a principle of Conscience made you Phanatick', urging him instead to be 'ingenuous, confess all to be Cheat, you have an indulgent Prince'. To this charge, 'Antiprælatus' countered that although 'the propogation of religion is the end I aim at; but I use not alwayes the same means: In Scotland I am Preacher, in England Pedlar, in Holland I deal in Books' (Anon., *A Letter from Scotland, with Observations upon the Anti-Erastian, Anti-Prælatical, and Phanatical Presbyterian Party there: By way of a Dialogue between Anonymus and Antiprælatus* (London, 1682), p. 2). The image of Scots preachers evangelising in England whilst disguised as pedlars recurs in other anonymous pamphlets. For example, in *Scots Memoirs*, the presbyterian character boasted that, having observed a prevalent nervousness in England, he warned that 'Armies to introduce Popery and Government have over-run Scotland, and are on their March to you'. As he continued, however, all his endeavours to apprise English nonconformists of this danger, 'I ow'd to this form of Pedlar, which got me admittance without suspicion' (Anon., *Scots Memoirs. Number 1* (London, 1683), p. 2).
[98] 'Letter from the Earl of Craufurd on his proposal to leave the kingdom, with the reasons for and against it', in Wodrow, *Sufferings*, IV, Appendix, 513.
[99] NLS MS. 7023, 'The earl of Lauderdale to Sir Robert Moray, 8 October 1667', f. 100.
[100] 'Memorial to be submitted to the Committee of Trade in Scotland', RPCS, 3rd series, VII, 671.
[101] Dunn ed., *Letters Illustrative of Public Affairs*, p. 69. In July 1684, the committed presbyterian, Sir John Erskine of Carnock, bid farewell to his brother, whom he claimed had decided to emigrate to Carolina 'because of the cruelty and illegall proceedings . . . and the corruptions and antichristian latitude of bishops and their dependents, the now pretended officers of the church, and because of the tyranny and usurpation of both which was daily growing' at a time when the 'number, presumption, and interest of pa-sts [sic] was now growing fast in Scotland, notwithstanding of all the standing laws against it' (W. MacLeod, ed., *Journal of the Hon. John Erskine of Carnock 1683–7* (Edinburgh, 1893), p. 72). For an account of Scottish colonial projects during this period, see Ian Adams and Meredyth Sommerville, *Cargoes of Hope and Despair: Scottish Emigration to North America 1603–1805* (Edinburgh, 1993); David Dobson, *Scottish Emigration to Colonial America 1607–1785* (Athens, Ga., 1994);

promoted as an inducement to emigration. Publishing a prospectus in the hope of attracting settlers, the presbyterian, George Scott of Pitlochie, regretted that 'the distractions of this Kingdom' provoked by ecclesiastical policy had 'come to that hight that the sad and fatal consequences thereof, are astonishing to all sober persons'. Since a harmonious reconciliation seemed 'improbable in the highest degree', Scott concluded that individuals were obliged to concur with the government in whatever civil or religious obligations were imposed. Alternatively, however, they could find a retreat 'where by Law a Toleration is by His Majestie allowed' which 'doth at present offer it self in America; and is no where else to be found in His Majesties Dominions'.[102]

IV

During the short reign of James VII & II, the consciences of Restoration Scots were, however, to be tested even more severely than under his older brother. According to Lauder of Fountainhall, the official news of Charles II's unexpected apoplectic fit and subsequent death in February 1685 'put our Statsmen in a hurley-burley' and provoked scenes of public mourning throughout the country. In Aberdeen, for example, a black pall was immediately draped over the Mercat Cross. The following day, however, commensurate degrees of popular revelry hailed his brother's accession and civic revelries included a series of loyal toasts, ceremonial music, cannon salutes, bell-ringing and the decoration of all the ships in the town harbour with lanterns.[103] At the Mercat Cross in Edinburgh, the Chancellor, James Drummond, earl of Perth, immediately declared James, former duke of Albany, as 'the only undoubted and lawfull King of this realme', to be known as James VII & II. As Fountainhall observed, this gesture was a deliberate confirmation of James' sovereign authority and 'not a proclamation of him as King, leist that should seime to import the peeple had any hand in giving him his power'.[104] Perth's announcement was greeted by 'an Universal Acclamation from more than 30000 of all Ranks of people present, who with uplifted hands swore Allegiance to his Majesty' while the city was once again 'full of Bonefires' and 'the Canons from the Castle fired all the while'.[105]

Appropriate legislative measures to uphold the new monarch's authority were

---

P. Gouldesborough, 'An Attempted Scottish Voyage to New York in 1669', *Scottish Historical Review*, 40 (1961), pp. 56–62; George Pratt Insh, *Scottish Colonial Schemes 1620–1686* (Glasgow, 1922) and Ned Landsman, *Scotland and its first American Colony 1683–1785* (Princeton, 1985) and 'Nation, Migration and the Province in the First British Empire: Scotland and the Americas 1600–1800', *American Historical Review*, 104 (1999), pp. 463–75.

[102] [George Scott], *The Model Of the Government Of the Province of East-New-Jersey in America; And Encouragements for such as Design to be concerned there* (Edinburgh, 1685), pp. 47, 49–50.

[103] Alexander Keith, *A Thousand Years of Aberdeen* (Aberdeen, 1972), pp. 271–2.

[104] Lauder of Fountainhall, *Historical Notices*, II, 615.

[105] *The Privy Council of Scotland's Letter to the King, together with the Arch-bishops and Bishops: As also several English Addresses to His Majesty* (Edinburgh, 1685), p. 1.

also duly taken when Parliament convened the following April under the direc- tion of William Douglas, first duke of Queensberry, as parliamentary High Commissioner. Addressing the Parliament as Chancellor, Perth appealed to the assembled commissioners to suppress permanently those rebellious Cove- nanting 'Monsters [who] bring a publike reproach upon the Nations in the Eyes of all our Neigbours abroad', while in foreign 'Gazets we are mentioned as Acting the vilest Assassinations and the horridest Villainies'.[106] Royal authority was accordingly enhanced when even attending a conventicle was made a capital offence, the fiscal excise was granted in perpetuity and all men aged between sixteen and sixty were henceforth committed to military service if required. Expressing their fulsome support for hereditary, absolute monarchy, the commissioners apprised James VII & II that Scotland had enjoyed royal government for over two thousand years 'under the uninterrupted line of one hundred and eleven Kings'. Generations of Scots had thus been free from conquest, property had remained secure, the rule of law in force and their lives and liberties preserved, enjoying 'those Securitys and tranquillities which the Greater and more flourishing Kingdoms have frequently wanted'. Such bless- ings were directly attributable to divine providence as well as to 'the solid, abso- lute authority wherwith they were invested by the first and fundamentall Law of our Monarchy'.[107] With such ardent professions of devoted loyalty, James was likely to concur in Perth's confident assertion that 'Scotland is not as England.' After converting to Catholicism himself a few months later, Perth re-assured James that 'Measures need not be too nicely kept with this people', since it was inconceivable that Scots could 'imagine that your Majesty is not so far above your laws as that you cannot dispense with them'.[108]

A potentially critical challenge to James' authority was also overcome when an armed rebellion, launched by the earl of Argyll in western Scotland in the early summer of 1685, proved abortive. Planned to coincide with the rising simultaneously launched by Charles II's natural son, the duke of Monmouth, in the west of England, both Argyll and Monmouth issued declarations explaining their objectives. Drafted by James Steuart of Goodtrees, Argyll's *Declaration*

---

[106] *The Manner of Procession to the Parliament-House of Scotland with His Majesties Letter to the Parliament; the Lord High Commissioner's Speech, the Lord High Chancellor's Speech, and the Parlia- ment's Answer* (Dublin, 1685), p. 7.

[107] Thomson and Innes eds., *Acts of the Parliament of Scotland*, VIII, 459. Although little controversial legislation was proposed during the Parliament of 1685, an indication of latent tension appears from an anonymous poem published by the royalist author, Francis Sempill, entitled *A Discourse between Law and Conscience, When they were both Banished from Parliament*. According to Sempill's poem, the character 'Law' attacks 'Conscience' for his seeming pusillanimity, whereupon 'Conscience' declares he will no longer attend Parliament, since the day before 'They swore that Conscience was a whigg, / For him they have no veneration, / Cause banish him out of the Nation'. 'Conscience' then laments that he has been unwelcome in Scotland since 1662, at which 'Law' is most perturbed, claiming that 'If Conscience turns like the weather-cock, / Then they will cut the Nazaren lock / My strength lies in the Penal Law / Cut off these, well lose the cause . . . If Noble Conscience leave the Land, / Who then will Popery withstand?' ([Francis Sempill], *A Discourse between Law and Conscience, When they were both Banished from Parliament. In the first Parliament of K. James the Seventh* ([Edinburgh, 1685]), p. 1.)

[108] 'James, Earl of Perth, Lord Chancellor of Scotland, to the King, 29 December 1685', HMC *Laing*, I, 443.

insisted that the participants in the rising were obliged to take up arms 'by extreme necessity, and for common safety (the supreme laws)'. In addition to petitioning that the nation's grievances should be heard before 'a free, full, just, and sovereign Representative', the *Declaration* also called for the restoration of Scots' former rights and liberties as Argyll himself sought restitution for his extensive estates that had been forfeited during his trial in 1681.[109] A printed account of the rebellion, issued on the government's behalf, described how the insurgents had flown blue flags bearing the motto '*Pro Deo et Patria*', thus 'pretending for God and their Country, like the Rebels in the late times . . . when their Design was to destroy both'. Although the author perceived them to be 'infatuated with the Fanatick Notion of the Fifth Monarchy men in England', the paltry size of the 2,500-strong army compared unfavourably with the force of 8,000 Covenanters that had fought at Bothwell Bridge in 1679.[110] Regretting that Argyll's *Declaration* 'was not concerted according to the ancient plea of the Scotch Covenanters', recalcitrant presbyterians remained suspicious of the enterprise, fearing that it was primarily intended to advance Argyll's personal interests and might open 'a door for a sinful confederacy' with disaffected rebels elsewhere.[111] Woefully outnumbered by his enemies, Argyll's rising was no more successful than that of Monmouth and Argyll himself was eventually captured and executed on 30 June.

While Argyll's rebellion only attracted limited support within Scotland, enthusiastic endorsement of James VII & II's authority was, however, neither universal nor unconditional. For although it had conventionally been accepted by most royalists that the greatest threat to orderly government was likely to come from extreme nonconformists before James' accession, it subsequently seemed that the largest risk to civil liberties and the established religion might come from the crown itself. Popular disquiet had been provoked by the opening of a Catholic Chapel in Edinburgh by the earl of Perth in December 1685. Even more categorical opposition emerged, however, when the second session of James' Parliament convened the following April and another Catholic-convert, Alexander Stewart, fifth earl of Moray, was appointed to replace Queensberry as parliamentary High Commissioner. Although Lauderdale had tried to discontinue the practice of opening Parliaments with a sermon, the English Whig, Roger Morrice, recorded reports that the bishop of Edinburgh had inaugurated proceedings by preaching 'against resisting in any Case whatsoever' with 'an exhortation to Comply in what was desired for the Repealing of the Lawes

---

[109] 'Declaration of the Earl of Argyle &c.' in 'Proceedings against James, Earl of Loudon, George Lord Melville, Sir John Cochrane of Ochiltree, and John Cochrane, his Son, for Treason', in Howell ed., *Complete Collection of State Trials*, X, 1038–9.

[110] Anon., *A True and Perfect Account of the Earl of Argile's Landing in the North of Scotland: With the Particulars of that whole Transaction* (London, 1685), p. 2.

[111] Michael Shields, *Faithful Contendings Displayed: being An historical relation of the State and Actings of the Suffering Remnant in the Church of Scotland, who subsisted in Select Societies, and were united in general correspondencies during the hottest time of the late Persecution, viz. From the year 1681 to 1691* (Glasgow, 1780), p. 166.

against the Papists' since 'it was their duty to do so as subjects'.[112] For, in his letter to Parliament, James had indeed ventured to make specific his request that the restrictions of the penal laws be removed from his Catholic co-religionists. As an incentive, James had also proclaimed his intention to pursue 'the Opening of a Free Trade with England', to which end his ministers were working 'with all Imaginable Application'. Despite this attractive offer, the official reply of the parliamentary commissioners merely indicated their intention to consider the legislative proposals with 'serious and dutiful Consideration, and go as great Lengths therein, as our Conscience will allow'.[113] Although the numbers of practising Catholics who lived between the River Solway and the Moray Firth was estimated to be less than 2,000 in 1677, it was argued that the toleration of Catholics could not be comprehended within the framework of national security.[114] In opposing James, the Restoration Scottish political establishment thus demonstrated that there were indeed limits to the extent of the royal prerogative beyond which active co-operation would not be automatically forthcoming. While remaining firmly committed to the authority of the Stuart monarchy and resolutely opposed to arguments for active political resistance, a growing proportion of the Restoration political and religious establishment found themselves obliged to embrace passive resistance.

Incensed by the Parliament's equivocal response, James directed Moray to undertake a purge of recalcitrant officials to serve as 'warning shots' to 'terrify and divert other Members of Parliament from their opposition'.[115] A number of formerly loyal supporters were thus summarily dismissed from their posts, including Mackenzie of Rosehaugh as Lord Advocate, Alexander Seton of Pitmedden from the Session and Sir William Bruce from the Privy Council. When such intimidation failed to alter the disposition of the assembly and the likelihood of assent to his toleration proposals remained remote, James adjourned Parliament. Hearing news of such events in London, Roger Morrice deemed it 'most certaine that this surprizing and conspicuous Miscarriage . . . has clogged all theire affaires elsewhere'.[116] Although Mackenzie of Rosehaugh then travelled to London, he returned 'without seeing the king'. Obliged to 'put on his gown as ane ordinary Advocat' when the Session resumed that autumn, Mackenzie thereafter proved ironically successful at defending accused Covenanters against his successor, Sir John Dalrymple, before being re-appointed as Lord Advocate in January 1688.[117]

Within Scotland, individual parliamentary commissioners, such as Lauder of Fountainhall, heralded such events as unprecedented, remarking that ordinary

112 Morrice Ent'ring Book, 'P', f. 536.
113 *His Majesties Most Gracious Letter to the Parliament of Scotland* (Edinburgh, 1686), pp. 2, 4.
114 See D. Maclean, 'Roman Catholicism in Scotland during the Reign of Charles II', *Records of the Scottish Church History Society*, 3 (1929), pp. 43–54.
115 Lauder of Fountainhall, *Decisions*, I, 414.
116 Morrice Ent'ring Book, 'P', f. 600.
117 Sir John Lauder of Fountainhall, *Chronological Notes of Scottish Affairs, From 1680 till 1701; Being Chiefly taken from the Diary of Lord Fountainhall*, [Walter Scott ed.] (Edinburgh, 1822), pp. 189, 201.

commissioners had never been 'so unanimous in any Parliament as in this . . . therfor some called this ane Independent Parliament.' As Fountainhall opined, 'the finger of God was much seen in the steadfastnes of this Parliament', since commissioners 'had not one great man in publict place to oune them'. Consequently, it was 'from some hyer principle' that nobles, gentry and bishops 'cheerfully laid doune their places, rather than violat their consciences.' Acknowledging that if a monarch requested a particular act in a letter to Parliament, it was 'æquivalent to a command', Fountainhall accounted it 'a great misfortune' that subjects were obliged to dissent from royal orders, enjoining that if so, 'they are to refuse him with all the discretion, humility, sorrow and regrate imaginable.'[118] Another member of the same Parliament, Colin Lindsay, earl of Balcarres, later apprised the exiled James VII & II that the events during the Parliament provided the 'first Symptoms of Discontent' that appeared in Scotland after Charles II's restoration. Balcarres justified this allegation by judging neither 'the two Tumultuous Risings in the Western Fanatick Countries, nor the Jarring of Duke Hamilton's Party, as being nothing Rational'. Hence the Scots Parliament provided a crucial channel for the expression of secular, or, as Balcarres implied, 'rational' discontent, in contrast to England where no Parliament sat from the autumn of 1685 until January 1689.

Increasingly outspoken opposition to James' catholicising policies also emerged outside Parliament. Long accustomed to censuring intractable presbyterian ministers for the incendiary content of their sermons, growing numbers of established clergy also started appearing before the archbishop of St. Andrews and the bishop of Edinburgh who had been accorded royal authority to suspend or deprive any 'who preached sedition, tho' they should be Bischops'. Summoned before his ecclesiastical superiors for having reportedly preached an anti-Catholic sermon in the Abbey Church in Edinburgh, one George Shiell, for instance, remained unrepentant, declaring that 'a ridiculous religion might be treated in ridicule'. Accordingly, he confirmed he would rather 'beleive the moon to be made of green-cheese, and swallow Arthurseat, as soon as beleive Transubstantiation.'[119]

As James' commission indicated, formal reprimands were by no means confined to the lesser clergy. In 1687, Alexander Cairncross was deprived of his archbishopric in Glasgow for failing to censure several anti-Catholic sermons being preached within his diocese, most notably those of the Selkirk minister, James Canaries. Evidently regretting his own brief and infelicitous conversion to Catholicism during the 1670s, in 1686 Canaries had exhorted a congregation to remain constant in their Protestantism and 'be not entangled again in the Yoke of Bondage, of a superstitious, and unreasonable, and disloyal Religion.' The sermon was later published in London, prefaced with a disclaimer by

---

[118] Lauder of Fountainhall, *Historical Notices*, II, 734, 737, 738. As he added, although some members declared 'that by staying in that party and giving them moderat counsells, they could doe the Protestant Religion better service then to cast themselves out of employment', others responded by quoting 'from [St.] Paul, "We must not doe ill, that good may come thereof" ' (*Ibid.*, II, 737).
[119] *Ibid.*, II, 717.

Canaries indicating that 'the Sermon is as bitter against the Fanatical Principles and Methods, as against Popery it self', thus upholding Protestantism 'as much for its Loyalty, as for its Truth'. With all the conviction of an ex-renegade, Canaries nevertheless denied that there was anything more likely to promote disaffection amongst James' subjects than for 'the Papists thus to scrue up the quarrel about Religion, till it become one of the Crown, and to muzzle up our Mouths from uttering one syllable against Popery'.[120] As far as Canaries' ecclesiastical superiors were concerned, it was further alleged, at a conference held to discuss the matter, that not only had Cairncross failed to censure Canaries adequately, but he had also secretly connived in the project by procuring assistance in publishing the sermon from the bishop of Ely, Francis Turner. Canaries' words had thus been used 'to amuse his Lᵒ & the English court & clergie', suggesting that no minister was able to preach in support of Protestantism and against Catholicism, even 'discreetlie without being censured for it or persecuted for it by the Government of Scotland'. Cairncross' duplicitous conduct was accounted even more inexcusable since he had apparently also promised James VII & II that he would 'shew greater indulgence & favour to papists then any other Bᵖ in Scotland', making 'his dioces a sanctuarie for papists & so to form the mind of his presbyters, as that they might become favourers of that interest'.[121] The apparent pusillanimity of the episcopalian establishment provoked Lauder of Fountainhall to liken the reception of the sixteenth-century Protestant Reformation, when 'the English bishops carried it on, so the Scottish bischops opposed it', with the situation 'now, when we are struggling against Popery, our bischops comply to let it in, and the English bischops keep ther ground firme to hold it out.'[122]

Frustrated in his attempts to procure legislative assent to his proposals for religious toleration in Scotland, James VII & II proceeded to impose toleration by edict. A Declaration of Indulgence was duly promulgated in February 1687, two months before a similar declaration was issued in England. Reflecting on the Scottish Declaration of Indulgence from his political exile in Holland, Gilbert Burnet detected a tocsin of 'such an Extraordinary Nature' that it implied 'a new Designation of his Majesty's Authority here set forth of his Absolute Power'.[123] As early as the 1670s, Burnet had warned James that the political doctrine of non-resistance embraced a 'number of distinctions and reserves'.[124] But as he now perceived, the implications of James' decrees,

---

[120] James Canaries, *Rome's Additions to Christianity Shewn to be Inconsistent with the True Design of so Spiritual a Religion in a Sermon Preached at Edinburgh, in the East-Church of St. Giles, Feb. 14. 1686. To which is prefixt, A Letter, Vindicating it from the Misrepresentations of the Romish Church* (London, 1686), pp. 20, sig. A3r, A4v.

[121] NAS CH 12/12/1754, 'Memorial concerning Cairncross and Canaries, December 1686'.

[122] Lauder of Fountainhall, *Historical Observes*, p. 243.

[123] Gilbert Burnet, 'Some Reflections on his Majesty's Proclamation Of the Twelfth of February 1686/₇ for a Toleration in Scotland', in *A Collection of Eighteen Papers Relating to Church and State* (London, 1689), p. 10.

[124] Quoted by Mark Goldie, 'The Political Thought of the Anglican Revolution', in Robert Beddard ed., *The Revolutions of 1688* (Oxford, 1991), pp. 102–36 at p. 113.

enjoining unqualified obedience, ensured that 'those poor Pretensions of Conscience, Religion, Honour, and Reason' would now be accounted obstacles to obedience. Burnet particularly criticised James' violation of those 'Maxims that unhinge all the Securities of Humane Society, and all that is sacred in Government', warning that subjects would 'lose the Respect that is due to everything that carries a Royal Stamp upon it'. In defining James' conception of absolute power as 'the short Execution by the Bow-strings of Turkey', Burnet's sentiments corresponded with those of extremist Covenanters, such as Alexander Shields, who denounced the proclamation as announcing 'by sound of Trumpet a Power Paramount to all Law; Reason & Religion, and outvying the hight of Ottoman Tyranny'.[125] As far as Shields was concerned, James was presiding over an administration whose abuse of 'that Monster of Prerogative' far surmounted 'all the lust, impudence & insolence of the Roman, Sicilian, Turkish, Tartarian, or Indian Tyrants, that ever trampled upon the Liberties of Mankind'.[126]

One unforeseen consequence of James's prerogative action was the forging of several unorthodox political alliances between episcopalian laymen and radical presbyterians in the defence of a common Protestantism. Although the majority of presbyterian ministers who convened in Edinburgh in October 1687 had enthusiastically resolved to thank James for establishing toleration, such gratitude was not unanimous. For instance, one Dr. John Hardy allegedly declared in a sermon preached before the gathering that such freedom was welcome, but if James 'behooved to take away the laws against Popery, it ware better to want it'. With regard to any ministers who consented to such toleration, 'the curse mentioned [by] Zachery would enter their houses like a flying roll, and eat the stones and timber.'[127] At the Court's insistence, the Privy Council summoned Hardy before them and dismissed him with a reprimand, but James subsequently demanded that Hardy be tried for treason. Maintaining that the penal laws were 'just, lawful and necessary', Hardy shrewdly responded by desiring that Mackenzie of Rosehaugh be appointed to prosecute him 'for he foresaw some hazard to pannel a man for owning the standing laws'.[128] Aware that Mackenzie had been forced to demit office for denying the legality of religious toleration, Mackenzie's successor as Lord Advocate, Sir John Dalrymple, pursued the case by lamely observing that 'the law has been so jealous of ministers meddling in sermons'. Defending Hardy, Sir Patrick Hume rejected the view that discussing policies of religious toleration could be deemed treasonous, given the many volumes printed on the subject in countries such as England and Holland where different degrees of religious toleration prevailed. As Hume concluded, the question of religious toleration remained 'ane opinion

---

[125] Burnet, 'Some Reflections on his Majesty's Proclamation', pp. 11, 13, 16; [Shields], *A Hind let loose*, p. 162.
[126] [Shields], *A Hind let loose*, p. 152.
[127] Lauder of Fountainhall, *Historical Notices*, II, 819.
[128] Lauder of Fountainhall, *Decisions*, I, 474.

problematick' that continued to form a legitimate subject of enquiry for divines and scholars.[129]

Unsurprisingly, it was therefore hailed as a major victory for Protestantism when the predominantly episcopalian judges of the Session ultimately ruled that the sentiments expressed in Hardy's sermon were insufficient to sustain the charge of treason. During the case, another defence lawyer, David Thoirs, had objected to the prosecution's assumption that 'a single sentence or expression in a sermon, or any long continued discourse can be pickt out *separatim et per se*'.[130] As the next chapter illustrates, the subject of religion remained indeed 'ane opinion problematick' in the late seventeenth century. The high degrees of civil dislocation experienced during the Restoration prompted considerable numbers of episcopalians and presbyterians alike to eschew engagement in the politics of religion in Restoration Scotland and to embrace instead a defence of 'true religion'.

[129] 'The Trial of Dr. John Hardy', in Howell ed., *Complete Collection of State Trials*, XI, 591, 589.
[130] *Ibid.*, XI, 593.

7

The Defence of True Religion

In depicting the Restoration period as 'the Killing Times', a vivid and venerable historiographical tradition characterised late-seventeenth century religious culture as bitterly divided between episcopalians and presbyterians. Yet, for all the moments of fanatic violence and extremism and government oppression and brutality, a substantial middle ground always existed that deplored denominational division. For while the majority of the political establishment was prepared to support the re-establishment of episcopalian church government as part of the Restoration settlement, few were convinced that enforcing strict ecclesiastical discipline necessarily served to enhance the spiritual welfare of the Scottish people. As Gilbert Burnet lamented in 1673, it was not 'by Political Arts, nor by the execution of Penal Laws, that the power of Religion can be recovered from these decays'.[1] Perceiving that a 'new sort of negative Religion is like to come in fashion in this Generation', moderate presbyterians, such as William Violant, also worried about the effects of rigorous compulsion on the part of the secular state.[2] In this context, the various government initiatives adopted to promote reconciliation, such as accommodation schemes and prerogative indulgences, were underpinned by a pervasive ideology that has subsequently been termed 'latitudinarian' in content.[3] As this chapter reveals, numerous Restoration commentators insisted that religion was as much, if not more, concerned with humane ethics as with adherence to abstruse doctrine. Distinguishing between a few 'fundamental' articles of religion and a much larger number of non-fundamental *adiaphora*,[4] moderate writers were even

---

[1] Burnet, *Vindication of the Authority, Constitution and Laws*, 'To the Reader'.
[2] [Violant], *Review and Examination*, p. 113.
[3] The term 'latitudinarian' is used *faute de mieux* to denote those moderate members of the Restoration episcopalian church who promoted theological moderation, the importance of Christian ethics, mutual forbearance and obedience to lawful authority. As John Spurr and other historians of Restoration England have pointed out, however, among contemporaries, the term was more frequently used in a polemical and derogatory manner to insinuate the dubious readiness to enlarge one's conscience as changing political and religious circumstances required (see John Spurr, 'Latitudinarianism and the Restoration Church', *Historical Journal*, 31 (1988), pp. 61–82).
[4] Deriving from the Greek *'adiaphoros'*, meaning 'not different', the term *'adiaphora'* was conventionally attributed to those church rites and matters that were neither commanded nor forbidden by Scripture and were also known as 'things indifferent' or 'non-essential matters'.

prepared to envisage a greater toleration of private heterodox opinion if civil harmony could be ensured. In reaction to the violent resistance theories of the more extreme theocratic Covenanting sects, moderate members of the Restoration establishment increasingly espoused a syncretic and eirenic attitude to religious controversy. As with the debates over political resistance *in extremis*, former divisions between episcopalians and presbyterians were, to some extent, redefined along lines whereby the preservation of civil order was ultimately accorded a higher priority than religious orthodoxy.

Seeking to delineate more clearly the contours of intellectual debate during this period, the chapter begins with a brief examination of the ways in which moderate episcopalians and presbyterians alike feared that the greatest casualty of ecclesiastical division within Restoration Scotland would be religion itself. For not only was mutual forbearance and Christian charity undermined, but the bloody manner in which debates over the external forms of church government had been used to legitimate violence was liable to foster increasingly sceptical and irreligious attitudes among members of the lay political elite. As Bishop Andrew Honyman of Orkney put it, it was the fate of the Restoration established church to be 'grinded betwixt the two mill-stones of a professedly profane and atheistical world, and of a party pretending highly for Truth and Piety'.[5] The chapter then shows how this predominantly latitudinarian ideology underpinned the practical endeavours of moderate episcopalians to promote those schemes for accommodation and comprehension considered in Chapter Five. In this context, it also examines how members of the conformist clergy defended their insistence that mens' consciences be subjected to formal ecclesiastical organisation from charges of excessive erastianism and Hobbesian voluntarism. In their attempts to steer a perilous course between the Scylla of religious enthusiasm and the Charybidis of rationalist scepticism, defending the magistratical imposition of religious externals from charges of Hobbism presented a substantial intellectual challenge. Nevertheless, in the virtual absence of any theocratic high church defences of episcopacy being articulated in Scotland, such accusations originated almost exclusively from presbyterian nonconformists. The third section considers the epistemological implications of such charges, by assessing the ways in which moderate episcopalians were also obliged to defend universal notions of justice in an attempt to refute broader allegations of moral relativism. The chapter concludes with a section outlining the various ways in which contemporary developments in natural philosophy were also promoted by those episcopalians seeking to defend a *via media* between excessive scepticism and puritan inspiration.

[5]   [Honyman], *A Survey of the Insolent and Infamous Libel entituled Naphtali*, Preface, p. 3.

I

The recrudescence of violent internecine division during the Restoration inevitably provoked a pervasive fear among moderate conformist and nonconformist clergy alike that religion itself was liable to become fatally imperilled. Preaching before the Privy Council in 1684, Alexander Rose lamented the legacy of 'full twenty years sad hurries and confusions intermixed with blood and gore, Tragical Battels, unnaturall rebellions, bloody assassinations, and daily tumults'. As Rose observed, the consequence of this bitter and bloody legacy was the triumph of intolerance as violent contests erupted, invoking not only 'words of Poyson and bitterness', but also 'Instruments of cruelty, to kill and murder'. In the name of religious purity therefore, sectarianism had spawned 'a murthering Principle . . . not only destructive of Christian charity, but humanity it self'.[6] The Principal of Edinburgh University, Alexander Monro, deemed it 'a wild fancy and Enthusiastick madness' that men should promote God's glory by becoming 'sanguinary Rebels, and barbarous Murderers' as if the divine purpose could be fulfilled by violating divine ordinances and 'reversing the boundaries between Good and Evil'.[7] Similar sentiments were expressed by nonconformists such as the minister of the Scots Church in Rotterdam, Robert Fleming, who counselled moderation and reconciliation, despite refusing to accept the government's offers of indulgence. In 1681, for instance, Fleming exhorted his divided brethren to eschew overt militancy, wondering who could observe contemporary ruptures among ministers and parishioners without being 'in hazard to take prejudice at the whole of Religion'? Denying that 'much reall exercise of soul in the serious and internall work of Religion' was evident in the internecine debates, Fleming predicted that Scottish religious history would 'be yet further write in letters of blood?' With the Scottish kirk riven by internal dissension, Fleming unequivocally warned that such discord 'threatens no less than utterly quenching the light of the Gospel' throughout Scotland, 'to be overwhelmed with Popery, Atheism and all ungodliness'.[8]

For as Fleming and other commentators were only too aware, as suspicions regarding the truth and integrity of all organised religion intensified, anticlerical members of the lay elite were tempted into adopting ironic, witty, sceptical and rationalist poses which offered alarming models to the populace. In 1665,

6 Rose, *Sermon Preached before the . . . Privy Council*, pp. 18, 25.
7 Alexander Monro, *Sermons Preached upon Several Occasions: (Most of them) Before the Magistrates and Judges in the North-East Auditory of S. Giles's Church Edinburgh* (London, 1693), p. 266. Presumably alluding to Archbishop Sharp's assassins, Monro was here employing the term 'enthusiasm' in its newly-coined perjorative sense of excessive, bigoted zeal.
8 [Robert Fleming], *The Church wounded and rent. By a Spirit of Division Held forth in a short account of some sad differences* [which] *hath been of late in the Church of Scotland, with the occasion, grounds, and too evident product thereof, whose wounds are bleeding to this day* (n.p., 1681), pp. 5, 8, 9–10.

Gilbert Burnet had observed of the Scottish people that 'their very minds are become mean and sordid', drawing attention to 'the Great footing that French contagion of Atheism' had established.[9] In a manuscript memorandum of 1674, 'Jock a Bread Scotland' advised Charles II to declare clearly 'your Royall inclinations either for Church or Kirk', warning that each 'poor Churchman from the Bishop to the pettie Curate' had become 'the contemptiblist people in the world despysed even by my ladys grooms and foot boyes'.[10] Elsewhere, the Banchory minister, James Gordon, contended that there was 'no Civil Nation under Heaven which conferrs so little Respect on their Church-men' as Scotland in recent years. In Gordon's opinion, the 'ancient Pagan Druides were (almost infinitely) more Honoured in this Land, than the present Ministers of the Gospel'.[11] Another moderate episcopalian, Laurence Charteris, worried about the ways in which religious faith was being 'much shaken and weakened by the boldness and confidence of scoffers and mockers', who exploited ecclesiastical debates to render 'all revealed religion to be the subject of their scorn and raillery'.[12] As James Canaries observed in 1684, there was 'hardly any more à-la-mode entertainment than to droll and baffle Religion', as if it were 'the only thing which deserv'd most to be hiss't at, and houted out of all rational and virtuoso Company'.[13] Among lay episcopalians, Sir George Mackenzie of Rosehaugh confessed himself 'astonish'd to hear Ballads against Moses and David so much admir'd by such as confess there is a God'. Explaining that the reason why classical writers had 'term'd Wit a Salt' was because it was 'not Fit for Food, but for Seasoning', Mackenzie inferred that it was thus to be 'us'd plentifully in Conversation, moderately in Business, but never in Religion'.[14]

In addition, therefore, to distancing themselves from the bloody outcome of sectarian zeal in the fields, moderate episcopalians and presbyterians alike attacked the intellectual framework of theological disputation, or *odium theologicum*, recognised as encouraging both perennial dogmatising and irreligious scepticism. Charteris, for instance, attacked those lay and clerical individuals who 'presume they know divine things much better than indeed they do', styling themselves learned 'if they can talk more copiously' on religious matters than their peers and 'can jangle and debate thereanent on all occasions'.[15] The Balquhidder minister, Robert Kirk, recorded his disapproval of those preachers seemingly intent on 'carving on the phrase, & crumbling a verse in to words, to treat on every word, as preaching on a dictionary', only serving to ensure that there was 'not an intire Truth & sentence yᵗ had a drift & scope & meaning'.[16]

---

[9]   [Gilbert Burnet], *A Discourse on the Memory of that Rare and Truly Virtuous Person Sir Robert Fletcher of Saltoun: Who died the 13. of January last, In the thirty-ninth year of his Age* (Edinburgh, 1665), p. 121.
[10]   NAS GD 30/1716, 'Jock a Bread Scotland'.
[11]   [Gordon], *Reform'd Bishop*, p. 50.
[12]   Laurence Charteris, *The Corruptions of this Age and the remedy thereof* (Edinburgh, 1704), p. 13.
[13]   Canaries, *Discourse representing the Sufficient Manifestations of the Will of God*, Preface.
[14]   Mackenzie, *Reason. An Essay*, pp. 150, 155–6.
[15]   Charteris, *The Corruptions of this Age*, p. 125.
[16]   EUL MSS. La.III.549, 'Robert Kirk, Occasional thoughts and meditationes, August 5, 1669', f. 60v.

Among oppressed presbyterians, John Baird counselled similar forbearance, dissuading them from seeking to 'censure, nor rigidly strain or wrest one anothers words or deeds, commenting and putting glosses upon them, or wringing consequences from them . . . which they never dreamed of'.[17] Mackenzie of Rosehaugh warned that religious debates in general 'by the curiosity of School-men and the bigotrie of Tub-preachers, as now formed into a Body of Divinity' was not only unnecessary, but highly dangerous. As he conceived, 'dogmaticless and paralitick scepticisme, are but the Apocrypha of true Religion'. Referring to sermons in particular, Mackenzie also abhorred seeing the pulpit 'made either a Bar, whereat secular quarrels, are with passion pleaded, or a Stage whereon revenge is, by Satyres satisfied; or a School-chair, from which unintelligible questions are mysteriously debated'.[18]

Reacting to the alienating effects of incessant theological controversialism, moderate episcopalians sought to advocate both a credal and rhetorical minimalism on the part of those seeking to promote religion among the people. As bishop of Dunblane, Robert Leighton addressed the Scottish Parliament in 1669, averring that certain religious truths were of so little consequence that, if a man remained ignorant or mistaken about them 'charitably, meekly and calmly', he was probably 'both a wiser Man, and a better Christian, than he who is furiously, stormily, and uncharitably Orthodox'.[19] As Professor of Divinity at King's College, Aberdeen, Henry Scougal likewise denied that it was necessary for civil magistrates to acquire detailed knowledge of 'Metaphysicks, of Philosophie, of all Tongues' in which Scripture had been originally written, but only that Scripture was read diligently to discern, as far as possible, true religion from false.[20] Preaching before the bishop and synod of Edinburgh in April 1687, Alexander Monro similarly blamed Aristotelian scholasticism for the manner in which Christian scholarship had become miserably 'mangled and broken into airy Questions, uncertain Conclusions and idle Problems' which 'eat out the Life of true Learning and Devotion'. By contrast, Monro insisted that 'the Credenda of our Religion are but very few', for since Christ had intended his religion for mankind, rather than any particular party or sect, he was unlikely to have intended it should be 'spun out into Nice Decisions, Metaphysical Distinctions, odd and Barbarous Words'.[21] Not only did such acrimonious disputation encourage facetious and satirical scepticism, but it also stimulated the evangelising spirit espoused by religious sects, such as the Quakers, who took to meeting together in silence to await God's direct guidance, having lost

---

[17] [Baird], *Balm from Gilead*, p. 7.

[18] George Mackenzie, *Religio Stoici* (Edinburgh, 1663), pp. 20, 156–7, 69. According to Robert Kirk, the ideal balance was to be struck when 'the pulpit guyds the court by counsel on Sunday [and] Court commands the Pulpit all the week so it makes not a Faction in the house of Unity' (NLS MS. 3932, 'Miscellany of thoughts occurring . . . 1678', f. 66v).

[19] Robert Leighton, *Three Posthumous Tracts of the Famous Dr. Rob. Leighton, late Archbishop of Glasgow* (second edition, London, 1711), pp. 5–6.

[20] AUL MS. 2612, 'Descriptive list of a collection of sermons c.1675' (A short discourse concerning the civill [*sic*] Magistrate), f. 191.

[21] Monro, *Sermons*, p. 213.

confidence in the clergy's leadership. Speaking for his Quaker brethren, Robert Barclay thus advocated exclusive reliance on 'that simple Naked Truth, which Man by his Wisdom hath rendred so obscure and mysterious' that voluminous devotional treatises abounded. In Barclay's opinion, all such 'vain jangling and Commentaries' only served to render Scripture 'a hundred fold more dark and intricate than of it self it is'.[22]

Concomitant with the rigid enforcement of ecclesiastical discipline were fears that individual conscience was being continually compromised to varying degrees. As Barclay himself had warned, not only was the secular magistrate treating 'men as if they were brutes, void of understanding' by imposing civil penalties, but he was also sanctioning that course whereby 'men may be made Hypocrites, but can never be made Christians'.[23] Sympathy for Barclay's position could be found at the highest levels of the established church. As archbishop of Glasgow, for instance, Leighton confessed in a letter to Burnet in 1672 'what pitifull things are wee if in our higher station in ye world and particularly in ye church, wee project to no higher end, then to drive poor people about vs into a forc't compliance with our little wretched interests and humours . . . ye french persecution is another mad frisk upon the stage'.[24] As Leighton pointed out the following year, the large proportion of those attending services within the established church were driven 'by the power of civil and church laws, or carried to it only with the stream of company and custom'.[25] In Balquhidder, Kirk recorded privately in 1678 how many of his parishioners displayed 'as much Religion as will save their Estates, but care not what will save their Souls', perceiving that many attended church 'the minimum 7 yearly requird by Council, but not a jote beyond'. As Kirk concluded, if people deemed attendance at the established church against divine law and their own conscience 'they should not come for Life or Estate; if not, they may com oftner'.[26] With spiritual well-being thus being overtly prostituted for material benefit, increasing disquiet arose over the rigid enforcement of penal laws against nonconformity.

II

Lacking a convincing *iure divino* case for episcopacy, surrounded by popular and political anticlericalism, embarrassed by various notorious excesses and abuses of some of their prelatical brethren, disillusioned by the extremist stance of the Restoration Covenanters and fearing the disintegration of public order

---

[22] Barclay, *Apology for the True Christian Divinity*, sig. B2v.
[23] *Ibid.*, p. 339.
[24] H. C. Foxcroft ed., 'Certain Papers of Robert Burnet, afterwards Lord Crimond, Gilbert Burnet, afterwards Bishop of Salisbury and Robert Leighton, sometime Archbishop of Glasgow', *Miscellany of the Scottish History Society. Volume II* (Edinburgh, 1904), p. 362.
[25] Leighton, 'Sermon on Romans XIII 5–8', in Jerment ed., *Works*, III, 210.
[26] NLS MS. 3932, 'Miscellany of occurring thoughts . . . 168', f. 2v.

throughout the country, moderate episcopalian writers during the Restoration adopted a combination of ecclesiastical erastianism, latitudinarian theology and ethical naturalism. With neither episcopalianism nor presbyterianism deemed able to demonstrate a convincing *iure divino* Scriptural basis, increasing support was voiced for the right of the secular magistrate to determine outward forms of public worship, grounded on the belief that certain religious practices were indifferent to salvation. In no sense, however, did such *politique* views of positive institutions and specific rituals endorse wider moves to achieve full toleration which would have entirely precluded the magistrate's right to determine such questions. Although episcopalian latitude could encompass a greater tolerance of private heterodox opinion, it was always crucially predicated on secular involvement to ensure civil order.

To a large extent, the origins of the mid-century civil wars and the sectarian sensitivities subsequently spawned by those wars had arisen from hostile reaction to the imposition of the Five Articles of Perth of 1618. Devised by James VI & I to promote congruity between the Scottish and English churches, the Articles enjoined kneeling before the altar, private Communion, regular baptism, episcopal participation in confirmation and the observance of certain holy days. In the pamphlet debate that ensued regarding the propriety of their observance, considerable importance was attached to the essentially moderate and submissive teaching of John Calvin with regard to the external constraints of human laws. As the Covenanters urged resistance, episcopalian defenders, such as John Forbes of Corse, upheld the lawfulness of the Articles in his *Irenicum* of 1629. In any case, Forbes had argued that even when church authorities 'decree something which it were expedient rather should not be decreed', disobedience was not sanctioned if the duty could be observed without incurring sin. Regarding secular powers in general, Forbes had thus been adamant that their responsibility was 'to make laws, and yours to obey, and error on their part will not excuse arrogance on yours'.[27] Although observance of the Articles themselves was not enforced during the Restoration, opinion continued to diverge over the extent to which individual Christians should either exert their freedom in conscience by acquiescing in human laws, or, alternatively, believe themselves to be freed in conscience from their observance. Unsurprisingly, one of the texts most frequently selected by ministers for their sermons on this subject was Romans 13:5–8 which contained the essentially ambiguous Pauline injunction that Christians should submit to their rulers not only for wrath, but also for the sake of conscience.

Seeking to promote reconciliation and mutual forbearance therefore, the Principal of Edinburgh University, William Colvill, was among those who pleaded

---

[27] E. Selwyn ed., *The First Book of the Irenicum of John Forbes of Corse* (Cambridge, 1923), pp. 98–9. For more on the debate, see Ian Cowan, 'The Five Articles of Perth', in D. Shaw ed., *Reformation and Revolution* (Edinburgh, 1967), pp. 160–77; John Ford, 'Conformity in Conscience: The Structure of the Perth Articles Debate in Scotland 1618–38', *Journal of Ecclesiastical History*, 46 (1995), pp. 256–77; D. Stewart, 'The Aberdeen Doctors and the Covenanters', *Records of the Scottish Church History Society*, 22 (1984), pp. 35–44.

for Christian charity on the grounds that, since episcopalians and presbyterians were 'all members of one mystical body', such contentious division was 'like two sandy-stones grateing one upon the other, till they be crumbled into nothing'. Although Colvill defended the right of the established church to order conformity in worship, with regard to dissenters he maintained that rapprochement was desirable 'especially if the errours in judgement be of smaller moment, and no ways do concern the foundation of Faith'. Hence Colvill instructed that minor differences of opinion in religious matters were to be accommodated 'as we tolerat some distempers in the body, but delight not in them . . . we tolerat them as Ulcers to be cured' as opposed to debarring a nonconformist from communion 'as a member affected with a Gangren'.[28] Similar sentiments were articulated in the early writings of Gilbert Burnet, who in 1669 alleged that, since 'to lay too great a weight upon any thing, is superstition', anyone who judged an indifferent rite to be either indispensable or unlawful was superstitious. Consequently, Burnet deplored the current situation wherein he perceived clerics 'agreeing in all the essential parts' of Protestant doctrine, but 'differing only in some less material and more disputable things'. While clerics remained intent on sustaining such minor differences 'with a Zeal so disproportioned to the value of them', Burnet rued that such belligerency could only 'astonish every Impartial beholder' and foment prejudice against clerics 'as made up of Contradictions; professing love, but breaking out in all the acts of hatred'. Preaching a funeral sermon in 1665 for his patron, Sir Robert Fletcher of Saltoun, Burnet celebrated Fletcher as one who had instead 'judged none of our Debates, to be about matters essential to Religion', but had lived peaceably and happily amongst all pious brethren 'however they might disagree about the Outside and model of Church-Polity'. As one whose 'Spirit was too large to shrink into the narrow Orb of a Party of Interest', Fletcher had evidently accepted the relative claims of episcopalianism over presbyterianism as the established religion, 'yet he judged Forms to be but Forms', which were 'neither so Good as to make Men Good, nor so Evil, as to make men Evil'. As Burnet himself put it elsewhere, in 'contending for the shell, we are like to lose the kernell of Religion'.[29]

Preaching before Parliament in 1669, Burnet's mentor and friend, Leighton, sought to foster this conciliatory temper by speculating publicly that contentions about aspects of religion did not render the 'Whole an Invention'. Translated to the archbishopric of Glasgow the following year, Leighton privately acknowledged to the earl of Lauderdale that he deeply regretted seeing 'a poor church

[28] William Colvill, *The Righteous Branch Growing out of the Root of Jesse, and healing the Nations. Held forth in several Sermons upon Isai. Chap. 11 from vers. 1 to 10. Together with some few sermons relating to all who live under the shadow of the Branch* (Edinburgh, 1673), pp. 187, 177.
[29] Burnet, *Modest and Free Conference*, p. 13; Henry Scougal, *The Life of God in the Soul of Man: Or, The Nature and Excellency of the Christian Religion. With the Methods of attaining the Happiness which it proposes. Also An Account of the Beginnings and Advances of a Spiritual Life. With a Preface by Gilbert Burnet, now Lord Bishop of Sarum* (London, 1707), sig. A6v; Burnet, *Discourse On the Memory of . . . Sir Robert Fletcher*, pp. 130–1, 129, 132; Burnet, *Modest and Free Conference*, sig. A4r–A4v.

doing its utmost to destroy both itself & religion in furious zeals & endlesse debates about ye empty name & shadow of a difference in government', while simultaneously failing to provide 'so much as a shadow' of orderly public worship.[30] In his commonplace-book, Kirk also pondered in 1669 that, since all 'sydes and parties are faulty in many things', he concluded it was best to 'love all who agree with yow in Fundamentals', but abstain from debating excessively about 'the pinnacles, [for] none agree in them all'. Admiring the devotional works of Hugo Grotius and James Ussher, Kirk regretted that such writers who had previously promoted Christian reconciliation 'ar snarled at as neutralls by those who keep open the differences meerly for want of understanding' to the detriment of religion. Several years later, Kirk likewise alleged that when factionalism emerged among Protestants 'down goes Liberty, and oaths and covenants must be invented'. By such measures, moreover, was 'Toleration deny'd, unity and Government cry'd up, no more free use of indifferent things' while 'the Crocodile weeps and devours'.[31] In the aftermath of the Covenanters' unsuccessful Pentland Rising of 1666, Honyman had also pondered 'that an intelligent people' should credit that the interests of Christ and their own salvation would 'lye with so much stresse upon this point'. Over this sole issue of exterior church government, he observed how 'this World is endeavoured to be turned upside-down, Kingdoms shaken, Thrones overturned, the blood of the people of God lavishly poured out'. Amidst such extremism, Honyman counselled latitude, admiring those persons 'of a better, more excellent and noble spirit', who remained steadfast in their religious beliefs, but were 'not so wedded to their opinions' about ecclesiastical policy that they refused to 'lend a patient ear to such as are otherwise minded'.[32]

Once latitude was granted to the magistrate with respect to the forms of worship, however, the requirement of obedience was unconditional. As Honyman himself pointed out, since God had consistently enjoined subjection to lawful authority, although a ceremony or rite might be in itself indifferent, it became a divine requirement if commanded by lawful authority. The individual could not, however, deduce very much regarding the rectitude of ceremony itself, since '[e]xpediencies and inexpediencies in the use of things indifferent, may vary according to circumstances and occasions', ensuring that a particular obligation which 'may be this year expedient, may another year be inexpedient'.[33] In no sense, however, was it to be construed that the abdication of such

---

[30] Leighton, *Three Posthumous Tracts*, p. 7; Airy ed., *Lauderdale Papers*, III, 76.
[31] EUL MSS. La.III.549, 'Robert Kirk, Occasional thoughts and meditationes. August 5 1669', ff. 55v–56r, 67v; NLS MS. 3932, 'Miscellany of occuring thoughts . . . 1678', f. 131r. Grotius' tract, *De Veritate Religionis* was translated into English for the first time by Simon Patrick in 1680. Referring to the work, James Gordon had declared 'without any Hyperbole' that it was 'worth it's [*sic*] weight in the purest Gold', exhorting divinity regents to ensure that university students had it 'so inculcated into their Memories, that they may, not only have it all by heart, but also throughly [*sic*] understand it' (*Reform'd Bishop*, p. 260).
[32] [Honyman], *A Survey of the Insolent and Infamous Libel entituled Naphtali*, Preface, p. 6; *Survey of Naphtali. Part II*, p. 197 and 'To the Reader'.
[33] [Honyman], *Survey of Naphtali. Part II*, p. 139.

powers to the civil magistrate in any way compromised individual conscience. As Colvill explained in 1673, the magistrate's ordaining particular requirements did not affect the liberty of individual judgement, but only 'the liberty of our outward practice; which restraint, is thought expedient for the good of the Church by the Christian Magistrat'. Seeking at all costs to 'curb the inconsiderat zeal of too many, who would have this Kingdom to be propagat by force of armes', Colvill thus reminded his readers that God had consistently inculcated subjection to all lawful commands issued by authority.[34] That same year, Burnet deemed it 'intolerable peevishness' to deem an indifferent rite unlawful, solely because it was commanded, since Christian liberty consisted 'in the exemption of our Consciences from all humane yoak, but not of our actions' which remained under the direction of superior powers.[35]

In this sense, episcopalian latitude safeguarded the freedom of individual conscience while preserving the magistrate's role in regularising worship. In 1661, an anonymous edition appeared of a speech on the subject of religious toleration by the early-seventeenth century royalist, William Drummond of Hawthornden, which offered a pregnant critique of the dangers involved in adopting a course of ecclesiastical coercion. Putatively set in 1539, Drummond's speech rejected the 'false and erroneous Opinion, that a Kingdome cannot subsist, which tolerateth two Religions', providing those religions 'enterprize or practice nothing against politike Laws of the Kingdome'. Defending the right of individual conscience, Drummond had insisted that no monarch could 'lay upon a man a necessity to believe what he will not' or to condemn 'what he will believe or doth believe', since he did not possess 'such power over the souls, and thoughts of men, as he hath over their bodies'.[36] Although Drummond's speech ostensibly discussed relations between Catholics and Protestants in the early years of the European Reformation, his arguments for the promotion of the liberty of conscience remained resonant, however much the majority of Restoration Scots were reluctant to accord full civil rights to Catholics. Moreover, when James VII & II began to petition for the religious toleration of Catholics in 1686, immediate foreign parallels could be drawn. For instance, one anonymous author of a manuscript memorial penned that year pondered that it was indeed somewhat difficult to 'condemn the persecutione in ffrance of the ffrench kings methods in forcing mens consciences & obliedging them to pairt with their religione by dragonnes and all manner of cruelties whereby he reduced peaceable subjects to the greatest miseries and hardships',

---

[34] Colvill, *Righteous Branch*, pp. 174, 47.
[35] Burnet, *Vindication of the Authority, Constitution and Laws*, p. 169.
[36] [William Drummond of Hawthornden], *Seasonable Advice concerning Ecclesiasticall Affairs: or, The Prudent Speech of a Learned Privy Councillor to King James the 5th of Scotland in the Year, 1539 occasioned by the diversity of Opinions in matters of Religion then in that Kingdome. Presented to the Publick View by a Cordial Wel-wisher to the Peace and Tranquillity of this Kingdome* (London, 1661), pp. 4, 3.

solely because the monarch's religion differed from that of some of his subjects.[37]

If civil peace could thus be ensured, the toleration of private heterodox opinion could be envisaged. As already discussed in the previous chapter, this was an argument widely articulated by those seeking to promote emigration to the newly-established American colonies during the 1680s. Advertising the opportunities available in East New Jersey in 1685, for example, George Scott of Pitlochie acknowledged that if men found themselves 'straitned in point of their opinion' they should consider emigrating to a place where such freedom abounded. For those interested in joining the colonial ventures, no more precise commitment was required beyond an acknowledgement of God's existence. To hold public office, only a 'simple profession of faith of Jesus Christ' was like-wise demanded, without descending into further theological or ecclesiastical differences among Christians. Moreover, to ensure that religion did not become 'a cloak for disturbance', Scott explained that anyone intending to become a colonial magistrate was obliged to declare that they did not consider themselves 'in conscience obliged, for Religions sake, to make an alteration, or endeavour to turn out their partners in Government, because they differ in Opinion from them'. Scott defended this form of credal minimalism on the grounds that this was 'no more then to follow that great Rule, To do as they would be done by'.[38] One persecuted nonconformist who subsequently became the Governor of East New Jersey was the Quaker, Robert Barclay, who had long held that 'forcing of mens consciences is contrary to sound Reason, and to the very law of Nature'. For, as Barclay expanded, since human understanding could not be forced by any degree of bodily suffering, corporal punishment 'may well destroy the Body, but can never inform the Soul, which is a free agent'.[39] Interestingly, a characteristically similar form of credal minimalism was required for member-ship of the early Scottish masonic lodges during the Restoration. As David Stevenson has shown, one of the most distinctive features of late-seventeenth century Scottish freemasonry was 'the exclusion of overt religious elements from lodge activities', while 'clearly accepting the existence of God and the truth of Christianity'.[40]

Ironically, similar lines of reasoning were also being articulated by those responsible for applying the letter of the law to religious nonconformity. Over a decade before he became Lord Advocate, for instance, Mackenzie of Rosehaugh

---

[37] NAS GD 406/M1/229/15, 'Reasons for consenting to some moderate ease [1686]', f. 7. According to Gilbert Burnet, in an attempt to ingratiate himself with James VII, Archbishop John Paterson of Glasgow had allegedly confessed that 'the two religions, popish and protestant, were so equally stated in his mind, that a few grains of loyalty in which the protestants had the better of the papists turned the balance with him' (Burnet, *History of My Own Time*, II, 314).

[38] Scott, *Model of the Government*, pp. 37, 103–4.

[39] Barclay, *Apology for the True Christian Divinity*, p. 339. For more on Barclay, see Linda G. Fryer, 'Robert Barclay of Ury and East New Jersey', *Northern Scotland*, 15 (1995), pp. 1–17.

[40] David Stevenson, *The Origins of Freemasonry. Scotland's Century, 1590–1710* (Cambridge, 1988), p. 123.

published a tract entitled *Religio Stoici* in which he defended the notion that 'Opinion, kept within it's proper bounds, is a pure act of the mind', meaning that to punish 'the body for that which is a guilt of the soul' was as unjust as penalising one family member for the crime of a relative. Reprinted eight times during the Restoration, Mackenzie's tract was probably modelled on Sir Thomas Browne's *Religio Medici* (1643) and was directed against those 'mad-cap Zealots of this bigot Age, intending to mount heaven, Elias-like in Zeals fiery Chariot'. For his part, Mackenzie deemed it incomprehensible that Christians were more concerned with refuting each others' arguments than endeavouring 'to convince Gentiles', while 'Episcopists and Presbyterians [stood] at greater distance, than either do with Turks and Pagans.'[41] Disregarding the bitter disputes over specific rituals appropriate for ceremonies such as Communion, Mackenzie concluded that 'most of all Religions are made up of the same elements', albeit that some 'symbolic qualities predomine in some more than in others'.[42] For this reason, Mackenzie made explicit that 'in all Articles not absolutely necessary for being saved', he made 'the Laws of my country to be my Creed'. Nevertheless, although Mackenzie defended liberty of conscience, he insisted that each individual should be compelled to observe 'that exteriour uniformity of worship, which the Laws of his Countrey injoins'. For as he explained, when nonconformists not only receded from the established church, but also sought to undermine the civil government, they became 'the most dangerous' who 'should be most severely punished'.[43] Throughout his life, from being a young and ambitious author to a notorious Lord Advocate, Mackenzie

---

[41] Mackenzie, *Religio Stoici*, Introduction, pp. 10–11, 1, 15. Numerous parallels can be drawn between Mackenzie's text and that of Browne. To take one example, according to the *OED*, Browne was the first author to suggest that there was 'a Geography of Religions, as well as of Land' (Thomas Browne, *Religio Medici* (London, 1643), p. 2). In the preface to *Religio Stoici*, Mackenzie declares he believes that 'there is a Church-militant, which, like the Ark, must lodge in it's [*sic*] bowels all such as are to be saved from the flood of condemnation: but to chalk out its bordering lines, is beyond the geography of my Religion' (*Religio Stoici*, p. 4). For more detail, see Daniela Havenstein, '*Religio* Writing in Seventeenth-Century England and Scotland: Sir Thomas Browne's *Religio Medici* (1643) and Sir George Mackenzie's *Religio Stoici* (1663)', *Scottish Literary Journal*, 25 (1998), pp. 17–33. It has also been suggested that Mackenzie's *Religio Stoici* formed the inspiration behind John Dryden's *Religio Laici* of 1682 since Dryden and Mackenzie enjoyed a long mutual acquaintance (David Nichol Smith, *Dryden* (Cambridge, 1950), p. 62), but for a more conventional interpretation, see D. Benson, '*Who bred Religio Laici?*', *Journal of English and Germanic Philology*, 65 (1966), pp. 238–51. Certainly Mackenzie was himself the victim of substantial plagiarism by the authors of another tract published in 1691 allegedly in imitation of Browne's *Religio Medici*. As Daniela Havenstein has shown, entire paragraphs of *Religio Stoici* were reprinted *verbatim* by Benjamin Bridgewater and John Dunton in their *Religio Bibliopolæ* of 1691 (see Daniela Havenstein, ' "In Imitation of Dr. Browns *Religio Medici?*": *Religio Bibliopolæ* and the New Practice of Piety', *Notes & Queries* (March 1995), pp. 52–4). In a somewhat different vein, in 1694, another Scots royalist, Archibald Pitcairne, confided privately that he had 'a vast propensitie to writ the Relligio [*sic*] Mathematici' which would provide 'ane immortal confusion of poperie & every thing that smels of poperie' (W. T. Johnston ed., *The Best of our Owne: Letters of Archibald Pitcairne, 1652–1713* (Edinburgh, 1979), pp. 18–19).
[42] Mackenzie, 'The Religious Stoic', in *Works*, I, 54. This sentence does not appear in the first edition of 1663.
[43] Mackenzie, *Religio Stoici*, pp. 19–20, 10.

thus evinced what Mark Goldie has termed 'the Erastian paradox', in being 'liberal and anticlerical, yet capable of intense dislike for sectarianism'.[44]

Such latitudinarian sentiments unsurprisingly encountered deeply hostile opposition from those nonconformists who denied that the obligation of individual conscience could be transcended by the impositions of civil powers. Concerned about the potential for episcopalian latitude to be transmuted into erastian licence, the presbyterian minister, Gilbert Rule, acknowledged that 'a Municipal Religion, many would fain promote, following Reasons of State more than Rules of Conscience'.[45] Later promoted to become Monro's successor as Principal of Edinburgh University after the Williamite Revolution, Rule had issued a tract in 1680 which contained a series of animadversions on the *Irenicum*, originally published in 1659 by Edward Stillingfleet, later the Anglican bishop of Worcester. In his treatise, Stillingfleet had argued for the necessity of mutual forbearance in indifferent things on the grounds that the potential for complete licence emerged if all things judged unlawful were to be disobeyed. The year before Rule produced his response, Stillingfleet had been forced to retract the most avowedly erastian parts of his *Irenicum*, reiterating instead the established church's traditional claims to constitute a separate society.[46]

From a Scottish perspective, although Rule proclaimed himself desirous to foster peace among dissenting brethren by mutual forbearance, he denied that this was to be achieved by deeming the content of controversial issues to be indifferent and jettisoning debate regarding their propriety or otherwise. Were this policy to be adopted, Rule inferred that 'those Churches are in the best way to peace, who cast away the Bible, and will not look there what God has commanded'. According to Rule, subjecting such questions to the vagaries of secular determination could only prove 'a fine device to cast loose all, to bring in Scepticism instead of faith' and to allow 'a false Sophister to nullifie all truth, by disputing speciously against it'. Hinting that mercenary motives might have encouraged such latitude, Rule further contended that episcopalianism was being defended by 'some who have spoken of their fat benefices'. Arguing that presbyterian nonconformists, by contrast, 'have no Worldly baits to allure us at this time, to plead for the Divine Right of Presbyterian Government', Rule alleged that presbyterian ecclesiology avoided all such disputed areas by entirely forbidding the clergy to interfere in the workings of the state and *vice versa*. Moreover, Rule did not envisage any necessary conflict of interest, arguing that the two distinct 'Powers need not clash', since they concerned

---

[44] Mark Goldie, 'Sir Peter Pett, Sceptical Toryism and the Science of Toleration in the 1680s', in W. J. Shiels ed., *Persecution and Toleration* (Oxford, 1984), p. 264.

[45] [Gilbert Rule], *An Answer to Dr. Stillingfleet's Irenicum: By a Learned Pen* (London, 1680), sig. A4r.

[46] See John Marshall, 'The Ecclesiology of the Latitude-Men 1660–1689: Stillingfleet, Tenison and "Hobbism" ', *Journal of Ecclesiastical History*, 36 (1985), pp. 407–27.

'things so different as are this world and that which is to come, the Soul and the Body'.[47]

Even more overt attacks came from members of the exiled Covenanting community in the Netherlands, such as Robert MacWard. In 1671, MacWard responded to Burnet's *Modest and Free Conference* by succinctly informing its author that 'rectitude and not latitude is the measure and character of the wayes of God'. Considering the likely source of ideological inspiration for the claims of the Scottish episcopate, MacWard deemed the arguments of English clerics, such as Jeremy Taylor and Henry More, to be as equally erroneous and nefarious as those of Thomas Hobbes and Samuel Parker. As MacWard put it, while Taylor and More set about 'dissolute relaxing', Hobbes and Parker embraced 'a wretched blindfolding and enslaving', both schools of thought seeking to denude the conscience of any force in arbitrating between lawful and unlawful commands. Pervading all such discussions of *adiaphora* and things indifferent, MacWard thus perceived a consistent disposition to 'weigh things Religious and Profane in the same ballance of vain conjecture'. Denying that notions of usurpation in the state and usurpation in the church could ever be equiparated, MacWard rejected claims of passive submission, reiterating that, in the case of 'our present Church-usurpation', acknowledging the supremacy of secular authority 'to which neither the events of providence, nor immemoriable possession, can give the least shadow of title, is altogether unlawfull'.[48]

Similar sentiments were expressed by a former episcopalian minister, Thomas Forrester, who had converted to presbyterianism after reading John Brown of Wamphray's *Apologetical Relation* of 1665. In his own *Rectius Instruendum* of 1684, Forrester attacked what he termed a 'new plagiary divinity' which remained dependent on 'the camelion-rule of worldly wisdom', in 'steering to its course by the versatil rule of human lawes'. In addition to evincing a careless disregard for the *magnalia Dei* 'as if they were meer trifles and indifferencies', Forrester accused the episcopalian establishment of charging presbyterians with 'aspersions of supercilius [*sic*] scrupulositie upon true zeal for God, [and] of rebellion, upon true loyalti and faithfulness to the King of saints'. Moreover, Forrester contended their episcopalian charity 'extended to the dimensions of a Metropolitans pallace', evidently envisaging 'entertaining rooms for Papists, Quakers, Arminians &c.', while presbyterians remained excluded.[49]

---

47 [Rule], *Answer*, pp. 6, 10, 97, 31.
48 [MacWard], *The true Non-Conformist*, pp. 40, 517, 143, 186. The influence of latitudinarian English writers was also evident in Robert Leighton's manuscript tract entitled 'The Rule of Conscience considered according to the Four Causes of Things' which was probably modelled on Jeremy Taylor's *Doctor Dubitantium, or Rule of Conscience* (London, 1660), a copy of the first edition of which was in Leighton's library (see Leighton, *Remains*, West ed., p. 221).
49 [Thomas Forrester], *Rectius Instruendum, Or A Review and Examination Of the doctrine presented by one assuming the Name of ane Informer, in three dialogues with a certain Doubter, upon the controverted points of Episcopacy, the Covenants against Episcopacy, and Separation* (London, 1684), 'The Preface to the Reader'.

III

Confronted by such sharp challenges, it became essential for members of the conformist clergy to repudiate all associations whatsoever with what was perceived to be 'that extreme Atheistical flattery of Thomas Hobbs and his followers' whose writings had been taken as affirming that subjects were bound to obey the commands of the magistrate even when they contradicted divine injunctions.[50] Unconvinced that religious latitude recognised good and evil as anything other than the arbitrary proclivities of the civil magistrate, nonconformists were quick to charge that episcopalian relativism towards positive institutions often belied a wider moral relativism. According to the nonconformist Whig activist, Robert Ferguson, for instance, some conformist clergy appeared to doubt that there were 'as well indubitable maximes of Reason, relating to Moral Practice, as there are relating to Science'. Convincing responses were therefore required to repudiate affinity with the alarming challenges laid down by 'Hobbs and some other wild, Atheistically disposed persons of late' who espoused an 'opposition to all natural Law', contending that all entities were intrinsically indifferent and that there were 'no laws of Right and Wrong previous to the laws of the Commonwealth'.[51] In the late-1680s, radical Covenanters, such as Alexander Shields, continued to exhort excluded presbyterians to avoid availing themselves of government incentives and indulgences. As Shields insisted in *A Hind Let Loose*, those presbyterians who were willing to acquiesce in a state-sponsored religious toleration out of a sense of allegiance to the monarch were only abetting the 'Principle of Atheistical Hobbes'.[52]

The need to withstand such charges prompted reaction from both clerical and lay episcopalians alike. Even devoted servants of the state, such as Lauderdale, were careful to avoid incurring charges of heterodoxy by appearing to countenance notions that obligation in religious matters derived solely from the capricious command of the civil magistrate. Although an early twentieth-century biographer declared the duke of Lauderdale's 'political standpoint was unadulterated Hobbesianism', when his former chaplain, John Gaskarth, preached at Ham House after Lauderdale's death, he denied hearing 'any speak against Hobbes's Doctrines with more concern and Spirit' than Lauderdale, and not just 'at Randome, but in proper Argument, as one that had well perused his pernicious Writings'.[53] The early-eighteenth century Professor of Divinity at St. Andrews, Thomas Halyburton, likewise recalled that, during the Restoration, Hobbesian ideas, together with those of Benedict Spinoza 'and some others of

---

[50] Colvill, *Righteous Branch*, p. 173.

[51] Robert Ferguson, *A Sober Enquiry into the Nature, Measure, and Principle of Moral Virtue. Its distinction from Gospel-Holiness* (London, 1673), pp. 59, 51.

[52] Shields, *Hind Let Loose*, p. 193.

[53] W. C. Mackenzie, *The Life and Times of John Maitland, Duke of Lauderdale (1616–1682)* (London, 1923), p. 216; Gaskarth, *Sermon preached upon the first occasion*, p. 34.

the same Kidney', enjoyed 'a great Vogue among our young Gentry and Students'.[54] As nonconformist violence escalated, Hobbesian injunctions regarding the magistrate's primary injunction to secure lives and liberties were not only increasingly resonant, but proved conducive to the adoption of pragmatic and indifferentist attitudes that encouraged magistrates to approve whatever form of ecclesiastical government appeared most conducive to preserve civil order. The need for members of the political and religious establishment to defend a *via media* between Hobbesian moral relativism and radical calls for Covenanting resistance was emphasised in graduation theses published in June 1679 by an Edinburgh University regent, William Paterson, a month after the assassination of Archbishop James Sharp. Denouncing Sharp's murder, Paterson unequivocally sought to 'condemn the Atheists of this age' whose precepts taught that 'nothing is Honourable or Dishonourable, Just or Unjust, Good or Bad'. But, as Paterson conceded, in propagating such doctrines, 'Rutherford and Hobbes run neck and neck', rendering it impossible to determine whether Samuel Rutherford's *Lex Rex* or Hobbes' *Leviathan* 'has had the more pernicious influence on our affairs'.[55]

Simultaneous attacks were also, however, launched by those who perceived the reduction of Christian evangelical teaching to a Christian Stoic or Socinian belief in natural virtue that adhered to those moral truths deducible by reason alone. As Robert Ferguson perceived, it could be deduced from some contemporary constructions that 'vertue & grace are not only made co-incident', but also that 'morality and Religion in its utmost latitude made convertible terms'.[56] In this context, the Highland laird, Alexander Brodie of Brodie, recorded in his diary his fears that the world was thus becoming one wherein 'Socinianism is growing ryf; Justification by Christ questiond and denied: Supernatural assistanc [*sic*] of grace or influences of the Spirit not needful'. As Brodie perceived, 'Moraliti is al that is requird in religion: Plato and Seneca of [as] much authoriti as Peter or Paul.'[57] Hence in attempting to defend a set of religious beliefs that were founded on reason, defenders of the established episcopalian church were obliged to counter not only Hobbesian relativism, but also the challenges posed by extreme Covenanting sects who championed the roles of illumination, grace and private revelation over reason. As in Restoration England, the effects of the mid-century civil wars thus generated an epistemological shift away from irrational illuminism as those divines who were hostile to religious enthusiasm stressed the compatibility of reason with religion and revelation. Such compatibility could be further grounded in a Platonist conception of reason as a divine faculty, or a fragmented emanation of the divine mind and a faculty equipped with a sense of eternal law since God

---

[54] Thomas Halyburton, *Natural Religion Insufficient: and Reveal'd Necessary to Man's Happiness in its Present State* (Edinburgh, 1714), p. 31.

[55] Quoted by C. P. Finlayson, 'Edinburgh University and the Darien Scheme', *Scottish Historical Review*, 34 (1955), p. 99.

[56] Ferguson, *Sober Enquiry*, p. 4.

[57] Brodie, *Diary*, p. 404.

inscribed eternal laws upon the mind. In this context, the right use of conscience was regarded as the heuristic means by which good was to be discerned from evil and moral obligation was deemed to be more than merely consensual.

In 1669, for instance, Burnet argued that since God had created man as a rational creature, religion must be consonant with this supreme faculty, rendering it possible to determine the legality of civil injunctions. Although he conceded that reason could become corrupted, he declared this to be 'man's own fault', for 'if his rational faculties were duly applied, and well purified, they should provide unerring touchstones of truth'. Having left Scotland for London a few months previously, Burnet preached a sermon in Covent Garden in December 1674 on Romans 13:5–8 where this notion of conscience as a law-giver was extended metonymically into a fount of moral judgement. For Burnet, conscience was thus 'a Tribunal set up by God for the Magistrate in all our Breasts, which will pass Sentence severely, and not be put off by the tricks of law, the boldness of Denials, the cunning of Excuses, or any other Arts'. Obedience to the civil magistrate was thus to be rendered wherever his commands did not contravene those of God. Moreover, Burnet categorically rejected any suggestion that the magistrate retained authority to command what-ever religious duty he wished 'according to the pestiferous spawn of that Infernal *Leviathan*'.[58] Similar ideas were articulated within Scotland by those such as Burnet's close friend, Henry Scougal, of whom it was alleged that in controversial matters 'he studied rather to lessen than multiply' on the grounds that 'men were apter to be reasoned out of their erroneous persuasions by a good life, than many arguments'. Hence in his attempts to demonstrate that philos-ophy and religion were not inimical to one another, Scougal had been primarily concerned to provide his students at King's College, Aberdeen, with lessons in moral philosophy that would 'guard them against the debauched sentiments of *Leviathan*'.[59]

Disdaining disputatious belligerence, moderate episcopalians preached the virtues of personal religion and credal minimalism. Addressing the Privy Council in 1684, for instance, Alexander Rose maintained that God had not intended Christianity to consist of 'a Baggage of ceremoniall and positive rits [*sic*], hard to learn and impossible to be kept'. According to Rose, the recogni-tion of godliness could instead be described as 'a rational Law, written in mens' hearts and 'engraven with the finger of God, upon the mind of man'. As he insisted, God did not intend to enslave men with a multitude of active require-ments, but 'Christianity's speciality' was instead a pattern of 'eminent Morals,

---

58 Burnet, *Modest and Free Conference*, p. 85; *Vindication of the Authority, Constitution and Laws*, p. 214; Gilbert Burnet, *Subjection for Conscience-sake Asserted; In a Sermon Preached at Covent-Garden-Church, the Sixth of December, 1674* (London, 1675), p. 17. For an account of similar debates in Restoration England, see John Spurr, ' "Rational Religion" in Restoration England', *Journal of the History of Ideas*, 49 (1988), pp. 563–85.
59 'A Sermon preached at the funeral of the Revd. Henry Scougal, A.M., By George Gairden, D.D.', in *The Works of the Reverend Mr. Henry Scougal, Professor of Divinity in the King's-College, Aberdeen* (Aberdeen, 1761), pp. 275, 267.

with lovely impressions of Heaven'.[60] In similar vein, Alexander Monro preached before a congregation in the Abbey at Holyroodhouse in May 1686, informing his listeners that they should always 'prefer the moral of Religion to its lesser Appendages, and Ceremonies', remembering that the latter were always subordinate to the former. As Monro explained elsewhere, reason and religion operated in symbiosis, the strength of one depending on that of the other. Since religion depended on a rational nature, God had specifically endowed men with 'such intellectual furniture' without which they would only 'move above the surface of the ground for some few Months or Years, and then lye down in eternal silence, in the cold embraces of the Grave'. As Monro conceived, this 'Religious Reason is the Characteristick difference' of human nature, deeming it imperative that men regarded their ability to reason as the crucial distinction 'between choice and blind fate; between Men and Beasts; between Reason and Mechanism; between Intellect and Matter'.[61] Ironically, however, theories of divine inscription could also produce a piety of aspiration to mystic union that could incur charges of enthusiasm. These tendencies appeared most prominently in the writings of Robert Leighton who defended universal notions of an innate knowledge of God, however imperfect or weak, despite recent reports of heathenish tribes 'in that part of the new world called Brazil' among whom were 'no symptoms that they have the least sense of a Deity'.[62] Leighton thus concluded that it were better to attach more importance to 'this universal harmony and consent of mankind in a few of the great and universal principles' than to those 'innumerable disputes that still subsist with regard to the other points'.[63]

As reliance on natural and rational religion assumed increasing prominence, moderate episcopalian religious discourse also became inextricably involved in contemporary interest in universal notions of justice. Gilbert Burnet, for example, later attributed his ability to form 'just notions of humane society and of government' to his earlier studies of civil and feudal law in France, and imputed 'the wrong notions that many Divines have of government to their being unacquainted with the principles of law'.[64] In a manuscript tract left unfinished at his death in 1691, the former Lord Advocate, Mackenzie of Rosehaugh, opened his discussion of the law of nature by insisting that 'all the Principles of

[60] Rose, *Sermon Preached before the . . . Privy Counsel*, pp. 5–6.
[61] Monro, *Sermons*, pp. 361, 57–8, 270, 160.
[62] Leighton, 'Theological Lectures', in *Works*, Jerment ed., IV, 228–9. As Leighton expanded, even heathenish classical philosophers had conceded that all moral philosophy was predicated on 'some law or rule, either revealed from Heaven, or stamped upon the hearts of men, to be the measure and test of good and evil, that is, virtue and vice' (*Ibid.*, IV, 241). Referring to those 'profane scoffers of religion', Leighton thus pointed out that 'nothing is more commonly to be heard from them, than that the whole doctrine of religion was invented by some wise men, to encourage the practice of justice and virtue throughout the world' (*Ibid.*, IV, 243–4). For more on Leighton, see Roger Emerson, 'The religious, the secular and the worldly: Scotland 1680–1800', in James E. Crimmins ed., *Religion, Secularization and Political Thought* (London, 1989), pp. 68–89.
[63] Leighton, 'Theological Lectures', in *Works*, Jerment ed., IV, 237.
[64] H. C. Foxcroft ed., *A Supplement from Unpublished MSS. to Burnet's History of My Own Time* (Oxford, 1902), p. 454.

Justice and Government, without which the world could not subsist' depended upon belief in an infinite deity. Attacking the ideas of Hobbes who had 'of all others erred most in this Inquiry' from 'Principles of ill Nature and Singularity', Mackenzie contended that Hobbes had fatally inverted God's design by regarding self-preservation as the criterion on which human nature was to be grounded. In this context, he also denounced as Hobbesian notions that universal justice could be derived from universal consent. Reacting to John Locke's recent rejection of innatism in his *Essay Concerning Human Under-standing* of 1689, Mackenzie maintained that innate ideas were necessary to supply men with 'some comon Ground wherein they were obliged to agree'. He did, however, sufficiently accept Lockean arguments regarding moral diversity to justify his own doubts about 'how farr Right Reason may be looked on as the fountaine of the Law of Nature'.[65] More concerned to refute the *Essay*'s alleged moral relativism than to denounce Locke's apparent Socinian tendencies, Mackenzie's criticisms typified early reaction to the *Essay*. In a letter to Locke in June 1690, for instance, James Tyrrell reported 'discourseing with some thinking men at Oxford', finding them 'dissatisfyed with what you have sayed concerning the Law of nature, (or reason,) whereby wee distinguish moral good, from evil and vertue, from vice'. Having left Scotland during the Revolution of 1689, Mackenzie had settled in Oxford and thus may well have been one of those critics who, according to Tyrrell, considered that Locke's account 'seems to come very near what is so cryed out in Mr. Hobs' who had asserted that good and evil did not exist independently of the commonwealth.[66] Finally, Mackenzie also rejected as insufficiently binding the claims of universal benevolence artic-ulated by the Anglican bishop of Peterborough, Richard Cumberland. As a lawyer, Mackenzie had conceived that benevolence 'relates rather to Religious and Morall vertues then to Law' which he suspected 'inclines to great Lenity in punishing Crimes' despite Cumberland's attempts to ground his notions of benevolence on the common good. Defending instead 'my principle of ye preservation of ye Universe, and the order God hath established in it', Mackenzie concluded by arguing that the sanctity of government was to be preferred over each individual and that severity in government 'seems to be only an excess of Benevolence and Love'.[67]

In order to rehabilitate the role of human reason, another way in which revealed religion could be exonerated from the twin charges of both credulous fideism and rationalistic scepticism was by acceptance of the Stoic distinction between those phenomena within our power to comprehend and those beyond.

---

[65] Mackenzie, *Reason. An Essay*, p. 25; BL Add. MSS. 18,236, 'Discourse on the 4 First Chapters', ff. 6r, 7r, 8r. As Mackenzie elaborated, he perceived a congruity between different ways of reasoning in different kingdoms, generating 'a different Geography in the Reason which they adore', together with different traditions of reasoning across different historical ages (Mackenzie, *Reason, An Essay*, p. 4).

[66] E. S. de Beer ed., *The Correspondence of John Locke*, 8 vols. (Oxford, 1976–89), IV, 101–2; for more on the early reception of the *Two Treatises*, see Mark Goldie, 'The Earliest Attack on Locke's *Two Treatises of Government*', *Locke Newsletter*, 1999, pp. 73–84.

[67] BL Add. MSS. 18,236, 'Discourse on the 4 First Chapters', ff. 5r–v.

In seeking to frame their ideas of natural virtue in terms of the legacy of Stoic moralism, the classical text most commonly used by Scottish writers was the discourses of Epictetus. A former slave who had lived from 55 to 135 AD, Epictetus had taught that although a body might be enslaved, a man could be master of his own thoughts and make his own judgements. As recorded by his pupil, Flavius Arrianus, his lectures thus emphasised submissiveness, humility and charity, but also stressed the ability and duty of each individual to use their own character to achieve self-government, independent of external circumstances. Quoting Epictetus to this end, for example, Alexander Monro argued that by ordering prudently that which came within the human sphere of competence, while suffering cheerfully that which was unavoidable, 'the Light of Nature could not possibly prescribe a more excellent method to attain true tranquillity of Spirit'. Nevertheless, Monro argued that only Christianity emancipated the individual from Stoic imperturbability since the passions of grief, joy, fear and anger were best used when directed by reason. Hence they were 'not to be extirpated as the Stoicks vainly pretended, but they are to be kept in awe and within their bounds'.[68] In similar vein, Mackenzie of Rosehaugh argued against developing 'an itch to understand' God's art of governing the world, but instead advocated the adoption of as practical a form of Christianity as possible which he conceived 'corresponds best likewayes with Stoicisme, because it pulls the hands of a sluggard from his bosome and setts them awork to prepare for himself'. By thus incurring responsibility for his actions, each individual was not only prevented from being able to 'repose his unreasonable hopes upon divine Providence', but also from being tempted to 'lay over his vitiousness upon Providence'.[69] In this manner, practical Christianity often provided a more satisfying alternative to complete withdrawal when pervasive civil strife threatened to render true religion impotent.

Couched in such terms, advocates of personal religion sought to deflect presbyterian accusations of ideological defeatism and practical incapacity. Latitudinarian sentiments nevertheless inevitably tended to foster certain degrees of asceticism if one believed that temporal government derived initially from self-government. Although presbyterian opponents, such as Robert MacWard, disparagingly attacked Leighton for his 'weak monastic spirit, long habituat to an affected abstraction & stoicisme', practical aspects of Stoicism proved attractive for those aiming to eschew involvement in current disputations.[70] Leighton himself recommended to Parliament in 1669 that it was 'an excellent Posture of the Soul, so to be fixed, that although the Frame of the Creation should crack, yet to be unmoved'. Elsewhere Leighton quoted Epictetus' observation that the Greeks frequently visited Olympia to see the works of Phidias, but apparently displayed no inclination to see 'those works which may be seen without

---

[68] Monro, *Sermons*, pp. 153, 138. For more on Epictetus, see Andrew Erskine, *The Hellenistic Stoa: Political Thought and Action* (London, 1990).

[69] Mackenzie, *Religio Stoici*, pp. 31, 36.

[70] MacWard, *Case of the Accommodation*, p. 69.

travelling at all' within their own minds. Hence Epictetus had insisted that men would never understand themselves or their purpose in the world without seeking to discover that 'which you have now an opportunity to view and contemplate'.[71]

Epictetus' writings evidently inspired a generation of Restoration Scottish episcopalians obliged to contemplate a country riven by continued civil unrest. In 1668, for instance, Gilbert Burnet was commissioned to compose a tract on the appropriate education for a young nobleman. According to Burnet, in seeking to impress upon his pupil 'the vanity of the world', a responsible tutor would not only explain the history of Stoic philosophy but would ensure that the works of Epictetus were 'carefully read to him'.[72] A similarly practical philosophy was articulated by Burnet's friend and colleague, Laurence Charteris, who recommended that Christians embrace personal retirement and contemplation. Charteris recognised, however, that such a course was not only averse to men's natural inclination but also that many were dissuaded from doing so by teachers and ministers who feared 'lest they should seem to countenance and approve the monastic life'.[73] In Aberdeen, Scougal similarly exhorted Christians to adopt 'such a measure of indefference [sic] towards outwards things', though 'kingdoms should quake, and the earth totter, and heavens fall about his ears', a man's spirit should remain constant.[74] Meanwhile in his *Reform'd Bishop* of 1679, James Gordon also advised members of the established clergy to avoid appearing as 'Bellows of Sedition, and Whirlwinds, agitating the contrary Tides of Faction'. By contrast, they should 'study such an abstractedness from the World', that observers should judge them 'Persons who use the World . . . as if they used it not'.[75]

Among lay episcopalians, the first President of the Royal Society, Sir Robert Moray, frequently alluded to his constant concern 'to understand and regulate my passions' by focusing on divine matters to the exclusion of temporal concerns.[76] Deeming him 'in practice the only stoic I ever knew', Burnet later related how Moray had 'studied Epictetus much and had wrought upon his mind to all his maxims', ensuring that external affairs 'seemed to make no impression

[71] Leighton, *Three Posthumous Tracts*, p. 10; 'Theological Lectures', in *Works*, Jerment ed., IV, 269. To the parliamentary commissioners, Leighton also cited approvingly the Stoic maxim 'that the Necessities of Nature, such as Food and Rayment, ought to be look'd after', but not those 'vain things, [such] as rich Coaches, gorgeous Apparel, stately Buildings, sumptuous Feasts' (*Three Posthumous Tracts*, p. 9). For more on Leighton's Stoicism, see David Allan, 'Reconciliation and Retirement in the Restoration Scottish Church: The Neostoicism of Robert Leighton', *Journal of Ecclesiastical History*, 50 (1999), pp. 251–78. Elsewhere, the physician, Sir Robert Sibbald, recorded in his autobiography how, in his youth, he had 'read Seneca, and Epictetus, and some other of the stoicks, and affected y^m, because of y^r contempt of riches and honours' (Hett ed., *Memoirs of Sir Robert Sibbald*, p. 61).
[72] John Clarke ed., *Bishop Gilbert Burnet as Educationist being His Thoughts on Education, with Notes and Life of the Author* (Aberdeen, 1914), pp. 58–9.
[73] Charteris, *Corruptions of this Age*, pp. 19–20.
[74] Scougal, 'Private Reflections and Occasional Meditations', in *Works*, pp. 327–8.
[75] [Gordon], *Reform'd Bishop*, pp. 119, 121.
[76] Quoted by Alexander Robertson, *The Life of Sir Robert Moray. Soldier, Statesman and Man of Science (1608–1673)* (London, 1922), p. 173.

on him, and he was ever the same'.[77] At a time when the Royal Society was being accused of propagating excessively materialistic, irreligious and amoral views, Moray admitted that his own eirenic and heterodox religious outlook had generated reports that he was variously 'writing against Scriptur, an Atheist, a Magician or Necromancer, and a Malignant, for ought I know by half a kingdom'.[78] During the 1660s, Moray corresponded on religious and ethical issues with the English essayist and erstwhile Epicurean defender, John Evelyn, who was also simultaneously engaged in discussions of moral philosophy with Mackenzie of Rosehaugh. Pondering the competing claims of action over contemplation, Mackenzie had somewhat disingenuously attempted to advocate retirement from civil affairs in his *Moral Essay Preferring Solitude to Publick Employment* of 1666, regarding the world as 'a Comedy, where every man acts that part which Providence hath assigned to him'. Although Mackenzie had allegedly deemed there to be 'no securer box, from which to behold it, than from a safe solitude', his reasoning was comprehensively assailed the following year when Evelyn produced a polite, but devastatingly skilful, rejoinder rejecting Mackenzie's epideictic elevation of *otium* over *negotium*.[79]

IV

Moving from defences against the Scylla of religious enthusiasm to the Charybdis of anticlerical scepticism, another way in which the defence of religious orthodoxy could be fostered was by embracing intellectual developments in the sphere of natural philosophy. While the influence of Cartesian ideas was being gradually absorbed into Scottish university curricula during the Restoration, proposals were also sporadically mooted to establish a similar association to that of the Royal Society in England by groups of Scots *virtuosi* who regularly gathered to debate intellectual issues and correspond with luminaries abroad. In 1684, the Dublin Philosophical Society learned of 'great hopes of a society in Scotland' whereby 'learning may be advanc't by a joynt force'. In Aberdeen, George Garden informed the Principal of King's College that there

---

[77] Burnet, *History of My Own Time*, I, 105; H. C. Foxcroft ed., *A Supplement to Burnet's History of My Own Time* (Oxford, 1902), p. 43.

[78] Quoted by David Stevenson, 'Masonry, symbolism and ethics in the life of Sir Robert Moray, FRS', *Proceedings of the Society of Antiquaries in Scotland*, 114 (1984), p. 426. Stoically, Moray declared he dealt with such allegations by not allowing 'my self but one passionate word but suppress all under the Ashes of Christian virtue' (*Ibid.*).

[79] Mackenzie, *Essay preferring Solitude*, pp. 89–90; see Brian Vickers ed., *Public and Private Life in the Seventeenth Century: The Mackenzie-Evelyn Debate* (New York, 1986). Dining with 'the famous Lawyer' Mackenzie and Bishop Edward Lloyd in London in 1689, Evelyn recalled how all three authors had variously opposed one another in print, but were 'now most friendly reconciled' (De Beer ed., *Diary of John Evelyn*, p. 921). In similar vein, Leighton had previously informed his students before their graduation in Edinburgh University that the world was 'a kind of stage, and its inhabitants mere actors' who should observe how 'the scenes are shifted, the actors also disappear; and in the same manner, the greatest shews of this vain world will likewise pass away' ('Exhortation to the Candidates for Master of Arts in the University of Edinburgh', in Jerment ed., *Works*, IV, 366, 362).

was nothing that could promote scholarship and knowledge more than establishing 'many such societies throughout the learned world, and their maintaining of a mutuall correspondence'. Support for setting up a scientific society was also expressed in St. Andrews, albeit with the caveat that such activity be conducted 'without disparaging Aristotle' to whom 'the world ow[e]s very much'.[80] In England, the Royal Society's efforts were underpinned by the acquisition and analysis of empirical information and members of the Society actively welcomed information about all aspects of the natural history, topography and geology of remoter parts of Scotland. Having attended the foundation meeting of the Society on 28 November 1660, Alexander Bruce, second earl of Kincardine, was subsequently encouraged by the Society's first President, the Scot, Sir Robert Moray, to 'behave your self lyke a true member of the Royall Society' by communicating detailed accounts of subterranean mining experiments conducted in his home estate at Culross in Fife.[81] It was also deemed imperative that all observations presented to the Society were 'as well attested as may be' to ensure that no information was amassed 'in our philosophical storehouse but what is supported by truth' as the Society's secretary, Henry Oldenburg reminded Sir George Mackenzie, Viscount Tarbat, in 1675.[82]

Considerable support was therefore expressed for the potential of natural philosophy to emancipate religious belief from obscure dogmatism and superstition. During the 1650s, for instance, Sir Thomas Urquhart of Cromarty had attacked those presbyterian ministers who not only wore 'gowns and beards longer than ever did Aristotle and Æsculapius', but also, on witnessing comets or lunar and solar eclipses, would 'delude the commons with an opinion that those things are immediately from God; for the sins of the people', entirely forsaking any physical explanations. In this manner, Cromarty argued that since clerics deemed all natural phenomena 'to be rancke Witch-craft', they sought to 'ruine the best part of Learning, and make their owne unskilfulnes Supream Judge, to passe an Irrevocable sentence upon the Condemnation of Knowledge'.[83] In 1665, Gilbert Burnet preached the funeral sermon of his patron, Sir Robert Fletcher of Saltoun, who had died after catching a fatal cold while watching comets at night with Burnet. According to Burnet, however, Fletcher had welcomed the establishment of the Royal Society for its potential to vindicate traditional religious beliefs, accounting it 'the strongest Attempt the World had seen' to rescue religion from ignorance and scepticism. Although Fletcher

[80] Quoted by K. Theodore Hoppen, *The Common Scientist in the Seventeenth Century: A Study of the Dublin Philosophical Society 1683–1708* (London, 1970), pp. 210–11.

[81] NLS MSS. 5049–50, 'Correspondence of Sir Robert Moray to Alexander Bruce, second earl of Kincardine 1658–65', 5049, f. 104. In May 1665, Moray informed Kincardine that he had intended sending him copies of the Society's *Monthly Transactions* 'were it not that they are to be had at Edinburgh, whither the printers send numbers of them' (MS. 5050, f. 143).

[82] Sir William Fraser ed., *The Earls of Cromartie, Their Kindred, Country and Correspondence*, 2 vols. (Edinburgh, 1876), pp. 22–3. See also H. Turnbull, 'Early Scottish Relations with the Royal Society', *Royal Society Notes and Records*, 3 (1940–1), pp. 27–38.

[83] Sir Thomas Urquhart, *Logopandecteision, Or An Introduction to the Universal Language* (London, 1653), pp. 8–9.

had evidently become increasingly dissatisfied with 'that empty Scelet of Aristotles Philosophy', he had also been 'incensed against some Pretenders to the Mathematicks, who ranked themselves under Leviathans Banner'.[84]

In this way, scientific experimentation was regarded as the most conducive means by which human understanding of God's overall design and purpose was to be enhanced. As the physician, Sir Robert Sibbald, explained, understanding natural philosophy was essential to comprehending 'that Art by which God made preserves and Governeth all the Beings in this world'.[85] In sermons preached while he was Principal of Edinburgh University, Alexander Monro also defended Baconian empiricism as the avenue via which it could be demonstrated that although 'a superficial Insight into Nature inclin'd men to Atheism', a sustained attempt to understand 'its regular Methods, and the causes of things, did necessarily lead us to the acknowledgement of the Deity'. As Monro perceived, it was impossible to imagine that such an infinitely complex entity as Creation 'should be destitute of some supreme and infinitely wise Contriver; to regulate its Motions and order all its Revolutions'.[86] In 1690 Mackenzie of Rosehaugh published an essay entitled *Reason*, contending that if microscopes were now able to reveal 'new and strange things in Objects that have been daily seen, without being considered', it was impossible to predict 'what wonderful discoveries may serious thinking men make' through comprehensive investigation of the deity. Moreover, Mackenzie dedicated his treatise to the 'Christian Virtuoso', Robert Boyle, whose theological works had consistently advocated the compatibility and integration of natural philosophy as a means of illuminating revelation.[87] By embracing increasingly rationalist impulses, moderate episcopalian discourse in Scotland thus contrasted with the polarised and intolerant character of High Church Anglicanism in England which, according to John Spurr, was 'edging ever closer to a dangerous anti-intellectualism' in defensively denouncing all challenges to established religious orthodoxy.[88]

Notwithstanding, disquiet arose over the extent to which natural philosophy could be expected to provide the type of undeniable confirmation of divine matters required by determined sceptics. Deeply wedded to traditional notions of innate ideas, for example, Archbishop Leighton urged caution, contending that there were very few incontrovertible scientific demonstrations, since even various mathematical formulae, if 'examined by the strict rules and ideas of Aristotle', remained uncertain. Hence, although religious belief should 'be outwardly guarded and defended by reason', Leighton warned that if anyone 'promises demonstration; his undertaking is certainly too much; if he desires or expects it from another, he requires too much'. Leighton was particularly alarmed by the materialist tendencies of neo-Epicurean and Lucretian theories that sought to govern 'that beautiful fabric which we behold . . . merely by a

[84] Burnet, *Discourse on the Memory of . . . Sir Robert Fletcher*, pp. 65, 67, 128.
[85] Quoted by Emerson, 'Sir Robert Sibbald', p. 44.
[86] Monro, *Sermons*, p. 2.
[87] Mackenzie, *Reason. An Essay*, p. 12.
[88] John Spurr, *The Restoration Church of England, 1646–1689* (New Haven, 1991), p. 236.

lucky hit, or fortunate throw of the dice'. Denouncing such ideas, Leighton insisted that 'the unerring course of the stars is not the effect of blind fortune', since the velocity of all physical phenomena was regulated 'by the influence of a fixed, eternal law'.[89] In denying that God could be unequivocally identified with nature, Leighton thus remained highly sensitive to the possibility that a fatal combination of Epicurean materialism, Stoic fatalism and Hobbesian egoism might eventually conspire to remove all divine and moral motives for virtuous behaviour.

The vehement reactions provoked by the impact of Cartesian ideas on Scottish natural philosophy was encapsulated most vividly in the published reaction to the works of a presbyterian regent of Glasgow University, George Sinclair, who was deprived of his teaching post in 1666 on account of his nonconformity. Having read Sinclair's *Hydrostaticks* (1672) as well as his *Ars Nova et Magna* (1673), the episcopalian mathematician, James Gregory, denounced Sinclair as 'a pitiful, ignorant fellow, who hath lately written horrid nonsense'. Resolving nonetheless to 'make excellent sport with him', Gregory published his own *Great and New Art of Weighing Vanity* in which he warned Sinclair not to 'call experiments new inventions, otherwise we are all making new inventions every day'.[90] For his part, Sinclair remained undeterred, maintaining not only that the 'Proteus of Nature, must be bound with stronger chains, then the Fantastick Nugae of Des-Cartes', but also that Gregory's Cartesianism had lured him into studying natural philosophy 'as hereticks do the Scripture . . . to be a Fanatick Philosopher'.[91] Referring to subsequent reports that 'Mr. Sinclair is printing again', Gregory anticipated that Sinclair might 'turn out our Hobbes'.[92] Whilst in exile in Holland in the early 1680s, James Dalrymple, Viscount Stair, likewise composed his *Physiologia Nova Experimentalis*, originally conceiving it as one of a tetralogy of works on human knowledge, natural theology, ethics and physiology. In addition to voicing support for the Royal Society's activities, Stair's tract also denounced the 'Horrendus Hobbesius' as an atheist who had 'subverted all moral and political principles, and substituted in their place natural form and humane agreement' as the first principles of morality, society and government.[93] Reviewing the *Physiologia*, Pierre Bayle interpreted Stair as one who refused to endorse fully Descartes' radical bifurcation of the spiritual

---

[89] Leighton, 'Theological Lectures', in Jerment ed., *Works*, IV, 215, 249, 234.

[90] 'James Gregory to John Collins, 2 July 1672', in Stephen Rigaud ed., *Correspondence of Scientific Men of the Seventeenth Century. Including Letters of Barrow, Flamsteed, Wallis, and Newton, Printed from the Originals*, 2 vols. (Oxford, 1841), II, 241–2; [James Gregory], *The Great and New Art of Weighing Vanity, Or, A Discovery of the Ignorance and Arrogance of the great and new Artist, in his Pseudo-Philosophical Writings* (Glasgow, 1672), sig. A5v.

[91] George Sinclair, *Hydrostaticks; Or, The Weights, Force, and Pressure of Fluid Bodies. Made evident by Physical and Sensible Experiments* (Edinburgh, 1672), p. 316.

[92] 'Gregory to Collins, 7 March 1673', in Rigaud ed., *Correspondence*, II, 249.

[93] James Dalrymple, Viscount Stair, *Physiologia Nova Experimentalis, in Qua Generales Notiones Aristotelis, Epicuri, & Cartesii supplentur: Errors deteguntur & emendatur &c.* (Leiden, 1686), p. 17. Stair's intended treatise on natural theology appears to have been *The Vindication of the Divine Perfections* (Glasgow, 1695) which adhered to innatism.

from the material world, evidently preferring 'le milieu entre Epicure & M. Descartes'.[94]

The animus behind suspicions about adherence to purely mechanical interpretations of the natural world derived largely from fears that they reduced the likelihood of its operation depending upon an immaterial presence or spirit. Not only did such theories potentially circumscribe the power of the deity, but they also served to undermine belief in supernatural phenomena such as the devil and witches. For this reason, in 1685 Sinclair published *Satan's Invisible World* in which he sought empirically to prove the existence of spirits, devils, witches and all other types of ghostly apparitions by appealing to popular sensory experience rather than 'thousands of subtle Metaphysical Arguments'. Individually enumerating the detrimental and erroneous foundations of over fifty Cartesian propositions, Sinclair deemed Cartesianism's influence to be 'a Gangrea' which sought to 'eat up the most part of the whole body of Theology' with fatal effects upon Christian faith. Moreover, Sinclair attacked 'a monstrous rable of men' who adopted Hobbesian and Spinozistic materialism to doubt God's existence.[95] In similar vein, Robert Kirk composed his *Secret Commonwealth* in 1691, alerting readers to what he perceived as 'courteous endeavours of our fellow creatures in the invisible world' to draw attention to the possibility of correspondence between this world and the next in defiance of atheistic and Socinian arguments. Like Sinclair, Kirk sought to integrate his understanding of 'this entercourse betwixt the two kinds of Rational Inhabitants of the sam[e] Earth' within the context of recent scientific discoveries.[96]

Finally, to a greater extent than hydrostatics, pneumatics, physiology, astronomy, barometry or other enquiries, discussions of witchcraft and supernatural phenomena permeated all levels of late-seventeenth century Scottish culture. As Stuart Clark has recently demonstrated, demonology was 'capable of enunciating theocratic political ideals with unusual, even unique, force'. Living under a monarch whose authority was widely regarded as being of divine ordination, witches represented 'the perfect antagonists' in terms of their perceived

---

[94] Pierre Bayle, *Nouvelles de la République des Lettres. Mois de Décembre 1685* (Amsterdam, 1685), p. 1337. Within Scotland, Cartesian ideas were usually admired more for their methodological approach than for their epistemological implications; see John L. Russell, 'Cosmological teaching in the seventeenth century Scottish universities', *Journal of the History of Astronomy*, 5 (1974), pp. 122–32 and 145–54, and Shepherd, 'Philosophy and Science in the Arts Curriculum of the Scottish Universities of the 17th century' (University of Edinburgh, Ph.D. dissertation, 1974). For further discussion of this subject, see Roger L. Emerson, 'Natural philosophy and the problem of the Scottish Enlightenment', *Studies on Voltaire and the Eighteenth Century*, 242 (1986), pp. 243–91 and 'Science and Moral Philosophy in the Scottish Enlightenment', in M. A. Stewart ed., *Oxford Studies in the History of Philosophy. Volume 1* (Oxford, 1990), pp. 11–36.

[95] Sinclair, *Satan's Invisible World Discovered, Or, A choice collection of Modern Relations; proving evidently against the Saducees and Atheists of this present Age, that there are Devils, Spirits, Witches, and Apparitions from Authentick Records, Attestations of Famous Witnesses, and undoubted Veracity* (Edinburgh, 1685), 'The Preface to the Reader', sig. A2r, B3r, A4r.

[96] Robert Kirk, 'The Secret Common-Wealth Or A Treatise Displaying the Chief Curiosities Among the People of Scotland as they are in Use to this Day', in Michael Hunter, *The Occult Laboratory. Magic, Science and Second Sight in Late Seventeenth-Century Scotland* (Woodbridge, 2001), pp. 96, 100.

ability to exert supernatural powers to the detriment of the commonwealth.[97] Defending 'true religion' therefore also entailed a commitment to destroy those pretenders to false religion, such as witches and sorcerers. In a royalist pageant held in Linlithgow on 29 May 1661 to celebrate the first anniversary of Charles II's restoration, crowds saw a 'picture of Rebellion in religious habit', holding a copy of Samuel Rutherford's *Lex Rex* in one hand and a copy of *The Causes of God's Wrath* by James Guthrie and Archibald Johnston in the other. Prominently placed above the tableau was a banner reading 'Rebellion is the Mother of Witchcraft'.[98] As agents of Charles II's divinely-endowed authority, those responsible for preserving civil order in Restoration Scotland were thus entrusted with eliminating such demonic threats. Between 1661 and 1662, around 660 people in Scotland were publicly accused of diabolic activity within sixteen months.[99]

From a radical presbyterian perspective, however, the language of late seventeenth century witchcraft also supplied a powerful rhetorical tool, since it was constructed around 'the Scottish idiom of covenant-making and covenant-breaking'. As Ian Bostridge has shown, Scottish political theory coincided neatly with political theology to ensure that committed presbyterians thereby regarded the toleration of erastian prelacy as a 'diabolical form of covenant-breaking'. To this end, the murderers of Archbishop James Sharp of St. Andrews in May 1679 held their victim to be guilty of 'sorceries', as well as perfidious apostasy.[100] Despite the frenzied levels of witch-hunting activity witnessed in Scotland during the early years of the Restoration, however, it was the emergence of increasingly sceptical attitudes to mystical phenomena that had impelled George Sinclair to begin collating material for *Satan's Invisible World*. For while empirical investigation and the rise of Spinozistic materialism were undermining beliefs in supernatural phenomena, increasing interest in ideas about substance, causality and agency also began to alter attitudes towards evidential certainty.

The changing approach to concepts of demonology were articulated most prominently in Restoration Scotland by Mackenzie of Rosehaugh who served as a Justice-Depute in the witchcraft trials of the 1660s, before becoming Lord Advocate in the late-1670s. Mackenzie refused to deny witchcraft's existence, recognising that the appropriation of demonic power, if proven, represented the essence of false religion. Nevertheless, he insisted that it was the 'very horridness of this Crime' that demanded 'the clearest relevancy and most convincing probation'. Suspecting that excessive superstition regularly produced miscarriages of justice, he suggested that while 'many true Mathemeticians and

---

[97]   Stuart Clark, *Thinking with Demons. The Idea of Witchcraft in Early Modern Europe* (Oxford, 1997), p. 552.
[98]   Kirkton, *Secret History*, p. 68.
[99]   See Christina Larner, *Enemies of God: The Witch-hunt in Scotland* (Oxford, 1981) and Brian P. Levack, 'The Great Scottish Witch-hunt of 1661–1662', *Journal of British Studies*, 20 (1980), pp. 90–108.
[100] Ian Bostridge, *Witchcraft and its Transformations c.1650–c.1750* (Oxford, 1997), pp. 22–3.

Physicians have past for Magicians in duller ages of the World', advances in scientific understanding had rendered such prejudices obsolete. Notwithstanding, Mackenzie perceived that current opinion dictated when anyone became suddenly afflicted by a strange disease, 'it is instantly said to come by Witch-craft, and then the next old, deform'd, or envyed woman is presently charged'. Conceiving it to be 'dangerous that these who are of all others the most simple' should instantly be 'tryed for a Crime, which of all others is most mysterious', Mackenzie ordained that priority be given to the proper evaluation of testimonies. Denouncing the manner in which 'poor Innocents die in multitudes by an unworthy Martyrdom, and Burning comes in fashion', Mackenzie attributed blame directly on 'those cruel and too forward Judges, who burn persons by thousands'. Particularly suspicious of the virtually assured convictions produced in trials conducted on Privy Council commission by local authorities, Mackenzie argued that it was only through rigorous and impartial judicial investigation into each case at the highest levels that ignorance could be overcome. The alternative of resorting 'to kill one another, because we cannot comprehend the reason of what each other do', he deplored as 'the effect of a terrible distraction'. Moreover, as he pointed out, if the authorities strictly adhered to the principle of only trusting that to which identifiable cause could be attributed, 'we may come to doubt, whether the curing of the Kings Evil by the touch of a Monarch, may not likewise be called Charming'.[101]

In juxtaposing the ways in which Charles II's practice of 'touching for the King's Evil' enjoyed unprecedented levels of popularity among contemporaries with his own sceptical treatment of contemporary witchcraft persecutions, Mackenzie exemplified the Janus-faced complexion of much of the religious and philosophical writing examined in this chapter. Aiming to transcend ecclesiastical controversy through abstract moral rationalism, moderate episcopalians and presbyterians alike sought to defend the core of a religious truth once it had been freed from traditionally controversial accretions. Seeking to reinforce and conserve the religious consciousness of the age, Restoration Scots thus increasingly espoused an essentially non-doctrinal religiosity to escape the constraints of credal warfare. But just as 'the Killing Times' began to subside and extremist Covenanting opposition began to be neutralised, the Williamite Revolution of 1688–90 presented a new source of political and ecclesiastical destabilisation. The following chapter examines how Restoration Scots were obliged to return once more to Samuel 15:23 to contemplate whether opposition to the monarch really was 'indeed Rebellion, and as the sin of witchcraft'.

---

[101] Mackenzie, *Laws and Customes*, p. 85; *Pleadings, In some remarkable Cases*, p. 196; *Laws and Customes*, p. 86, *Pleadings, In some remarkable Cases*, p. 196; *Laws and Customes*, p. 85; *Pleadings, In some remarkable Cases*, p. 186. This theme is explored further in a case study by Richard L. Harris, 'Janet Douglas and the Witches of Pollock: The Background of Scepticism in Scotland in the 1670s', in S. R. McKenna ed., *Selected Essays on Scottish Language and Literature* (Lampeter, 1992), pp. 97–124.

8

The Revolution of 1688–1689

Historiographical orthodoxy has long maintained that in 1688 the Scots were the 'Reluctant Revolutionaries'. Having devoted the majority of their intellectual energies since 1660 to refuting extreme presbyterian fanaticism, by 1688 many politicians and writers apparently found that they lacked the mental resources to confront an arbitrary and papistical monarch. Hence the reported birth of the Prince of Wales in June 1688 evidently 'occasioned little interest north of the border', despite heralding the prospect of a perennial Catholic succession. William of Orange's proclamation addressed to the Scots in October of that year also 'fell on equally deaf ears'. Nor were any formal political discussions about the revolution conducted until the Convention of Estates met in Edinburgh on 14 March 1689, three months after James' flight to France in December 1688.[1]

Assertions of initial political apathy have in turn generated a historiographical tendency to denigrate 'the poverty of political theory in the Scottish Revolution of 1688–90'. Contrary to such interpretations, however, this chapter demonstrates that although the narrative political history of the Revolution still awaits detailed reconstruction, a clearly articulated body of political literature did exist, offering active ideological justifications of, as well as objections to, the sequence of revolutionary events in Scotland. Such works inevitably varied in quality and purpose: one writer condemned, for instance, 'the number of these Scribblers, who now a dayes fill the Press, with every little Product of their Empty Brains'.[2] Another observed how 'these things are so much talk't of by every Body' that 'the Itch of Writing is so Universal'.[3] If nothing else, the

---

[1] The phrase 'Reluctant Revolutionaries' was coined by Ian B. Cowan in 'The Reluctant Revolutionaries: Scotland in 1688', in Eveline Cruikshanks ed., *By Force or by Default? The Revolution of 1688–89* (Edinburgh, 1989), pp. 65–81; the above quotes appear on p. 65. For more on the Revolution, see the same author's 'Church and state reformed? The Revolution of 1688–89 in Scotland', in Jonathan I. Israel ed., *The Anglo-Dutch Moment: Essays on the Glorious Revolution and its World Impact* (Cambridge, 1991), pp. 163–83 and Tim Harris, ' "Reluctant Revolutionaries": The Scots and the Revolution of 1688–89', in Howard Nenner ed., *Politics and the Political Imagination in Later Stuart Britain* (Rochester, New York, 1997), pp. 97–117.
[2] [William Sherlock], *A Letter to a Member of the Convention of States in Scotland. By a Lover of His Religion and Country* ([Edinburgh], 1689), p. 3.
[3] Anon., *Allegiance and Prerogative Considered In a Letter from a Gentleman In the Country to his Friend Upon His being Chosen a Member of the Meeting of States in Scotland* (?Edinburgh, 1689), p. 3.

events of 1688–90 unquestionably provided the opportunity to apply the elements of monarchical political theory discussed in previous chapters to rapidly changing political circumstances. Hence Scottish reaction to the collapse of James VII & II's authority spawned a wide spectrum of different political theories, ranging from defences of individual rights of resistance against a vicious king to unequivocal Jacobite opposition to events, based on James' divine right to rule and the duty of his subjects to obey his authority without reserve. Hence this chapter establishes, for the first time, the extensive nature of a Scottish allegiance debate. Although historians such as Mark Goldie, John Kenyon and Gerald Straka have previously examined the allegiance debate generated by the Williamite Revolution in England, the extent of political debate that occurred north of the border has never hitherto been fully explored.[4]

Hence while the Scots can, to some extent, perhaps be deemed 'reluctant revolutionaries' in practice, such reticence by no means translated to the sphere of political argument. This chapter begins by examining the practical manner in which the Convention of Estates justified the Revolution on account of James' having forfeited his right to the Scottish throne by his allegedly illegal actions as king. The second section shows how this decision related to ideological accounts of the contractarian nature of the Scottish monarchy, drawing attention to the tendency for defenders of the Revolution to abstain from proposing overtly contractarian justifications of James' forfeiture, preferring to argue a case of resistance *in extremis*. The chapter also considers the use of *de facto* arguments, whereby the very possession of power by William and Mary was perceived as sufficient for allegiance to be paid to them, together with the ways in which such *de facto* arguments could be accommodated within a providentialist rhetoric of godly rule and the divine sanction of the Protestant William. The third section examines alternative arguments that allegiance to William was legitimated by his status as a just conqueror of both the English and Scottish thrones in an international war. Within this context, it also considers the ways in which the Revolution in Scotland not only affected debates regarding the possibility of Anglo-Scottish union being incorporated into the Revolution settlement, but also those concerning the wider European balance of power and the threat of universal monarchy. The chapter concludes by exploring the ideological content of Jacobite opposition to the Revolution by laymen and clerics alike, who vociferously reiterated the doctrines of passive obedience and non-resistance, together with accounts of their philosophical and moral objections to the accession to power of William and Mary.

---

[4] See Mark Goldie, 'The Revolution of 1689 and the Structure of Political Argument', *Bulletin of Research in the Humanities*, 83 (1980), pp. 473–564; J. P. Kenyon, *Revolution Principles: The Politics of Party, 1689–1720* (second edition, Cambridge, 1990) and Gerald Straka, *Anglican Reaction to the Revolution of 1688* (Madison, 1962).

I

Despite initial claims of political procrastination, once the Convention of Estates assembled in March 1689, the pace of political events rapidly accelerated. Within two days of its opening, the Convention had assessed the rival claims to the Scottish throne of both James VII & II and his son-in-law, William of Orange, as outlined in the separate letters submitted by each. Aware that '[s]itting, speaking, and voting in that assembly were men outlawed and virtually condemned, who were now rulers', the Convention began by resolving that it was a free and lawful meeting which would not be dissolved until both the nation's laws and liberties and the Protestant religion had been secured, notwithstanding the potential contents of either communication.[5] The contrast between the two missives themselves could not have been more pronounced. Although James VII & II's letter warned that the Convention's proceedings were being held on the 'Usurped Authority' of the Prince of Orange, he remained confident that he could rely on 'the faithfullness and affection of you our Antient People' to vindicate his right 'against Our Ennamys who hav depressed the same by blackest of usurpations'. Unspecific assurances were also given with regard to securing the nation's religion, laws and property 'as soon as it is possible'. By contrast, William's letter presented a more impersonal and detached observation that 'it lyes upon you' to hold 'such Consultations as are most probable to setle you on sure and Lasting foundations' with regard to the public good and the popular will.[6]

Responsibility for constitutional arrangements thereafter passed to a committee for 'Settling the Government', composed of twenty-four individuals whose meetings were open to all Convention members. From the committee's proceedings, the Convention passed a resolution on 4 April declaring that James VII & II had forfeited his right to the Scottish throne on account of his illegal actions as king. Only twelve members of the Convention, comprising seven bishops and five peers, voted against the list enumerating these various contraventions. On 11 April, an 'Instrument', or Claim, of Right was issued, establishing a number of fundamental constitutional principles on which any future government of Scotland would be based, followed two days later by a list of grievances which such a future administration would be expected to redress. On 18 April, the Convention approved a Coronation Oath to be tendered to William and Mary, as joint sovereigns of Scotland, together with the Claim of Right and the list of grievances.

Within a month, therefore, it appeared that the most ancient monarchy in the

---

5 John Hill Burton, *The History of Scotland from Agricola's Invasion to the Extinction of the last Jacobite Insurrection*, 8 vols. (Edinburgh, 1873), VII, 287. For an account of events in the Convention, see E. Balfour-Melville, *An Account of the Proceedings of the Estates in Scotland 1689–1690*, 2 vols. (Edinburgh, 1954–5).
6 Thomson and Innes eds., *Acts of the Parliament of Scotland*, IX, 10, 9.

world had effected a change of government directly contradictory to those principles of monarchical succession hitherto considered so pivotal to the Scottish constitution. Only the ultimately unsuccessful military rising led by John Graham of Claverhouse, Viscount Dundee, delayed the final ecclesiastical settlement establishing presbyterianism until 1690. The ostensibly conditional premises on which the Scottish crown was offered to William and Mary nevertheless differed significantly from events in England. Writing to William on 16 April, the future Scottish Secretary, George Melville, first earl of Melville, acknowledged that 'our actions may justly seem to be incomprehensible to those who live at a distance'. As Melville recognised, it might appear 'strange' that the Scots had proclaimed William and Mary as king and queen and annexed an Instrument of Government to that affirmation 'without ever acquainting your Majesties to know whether you were satisfied'. Although anxious 'not to lay open the nakedness of my country', Melville also regretted that the Scots proclamation had 'been printed and published so soon, so that the Court of Vien may have an account of our procedure before your Majesty have it'.[7]

Outside Scotland, however, widespread admiration was expressed for the speed with which the Convention had concluded their deliberations. In London at the end of March 1689, for instance, Lord Yester wrote to his father, the earl of Tweeddale, describing English perceptions of events north of the border. According to Yester, English politicians appeared to be 'approving of them more then they doe theire owne', complaining that proceedings in London 'have been so slow . . . and the hazard Irland is in of being utterly lost ascrivd to it'.[8] The conceptual clarity of the Scottish position also attracted admiration. In 1693, for instance, the Whig commentator, Samuel Johnson, denounced 'those wretched inventions of usurpation, conquest and desertion' current in English political thought, later renewing his attack on all such 'disguising terms and blinds' and lamenting the use of 'desertion and abdication, instead of plain English forfeiture, which the Scots parliament honestly called forefaulting'.[9] As the eighteenth-century historian, Sir John Dalrymple, later confirmed, the Convention had 'struck their blow without ceremony' in deciding that James had forfeited his right to the throne, thus averting the difficulties inherent in 'amusing themselves with school-disputes about words' that had so embarrassed their political counterparts in England.[10]

Within Scotland too, few challenged the Convention's authority to enact such resolutions. As one anonymous writer observed, laws that restricted subjects from meeting and consulting without express royal authority 'suppose that

---

[7] '[Lord] Melvill to King [William]', HMC, *Report on the Manuscripts of the Duke of Buccleuch & Queensberry . . . at Montagu House, Whitehall*, 2 vols. (London, 1903), I, 43.
[8] CUL, Add. MSS. 9362/51, 'Lord Yester to the earl of Tweeddale, 30 March 1689'.
[9] Quoted by Kenyon, *Revolution Principles*, p. 39.
[10] Sir John Dalrymple, *Memoirs of Great Britain and Ireland. From the Dissolution of the last Parliament of King Charles II until the Sea Battle of La Hague*, 2 vols. (fourth edition, Dublin, 1773), I, 324.

Subjects have a King to order and appoint such meetings'.[11] A young advocate, Francis Grant, deemed proceedings consistent with divine and natural law, presuming that 'the God of Order, Peace and Government' would not obstruct this only chance of avoiding 'Confusion, War and Anarchy'.[12] Grant thus accorded the Convention a declarative power to regulate the office of the Scottish throne, while denying it authority to try the former king privately for his allegedly illegal actions as king. More casuistically, it was unlikely that James himself would have dared to challenge the Convention's gathering had it proceeded to invite him to return to Scotland as king, given the absence of any other forum in which loyal subjects could have been expected to advance his interest. At the end of March, James wrote to the earl of Balcarres from Dublin, conveying his confidence in the Convention's proceedings and observing that 'Presbyterians are not good masters in any government'. Accordingly, James instructed Balcarres to 'assure yourselves we will stand by you' and to 'let the ancient Cavalier party know that they are the only true basis that Monarchy can rest upon in Scotland'.[13]

Unsurprisingly, James' opponents were, however, just as concerned that the Convention should settle the future government of Scotland as speedily as possible. As the anonymous author of one manuscript memorial pointed out, if James were suddenly to return to Edinburgh and undertake to redress all grievances 'being in the Kingdome he cannot be said to have deserted or abdicated the government'. But as matters stood, the author argued that the Convention effectively had little choice but to settle for William, since they would only incur a repetition of former miseries if they declared for James, whilst 'they cannot erect themselves into a commonwealth ffor that is contrare to the fundamentall constitutione of the government qᶜʰ is monarchie'.[14] Other supporters of the Revolution, such as Lord Melville, directly sought to reassure William by clarifying the Convention's unique, but limited, role at this juncture. Counselling that William 'need not be much stumbled at our Instrument of Government and grievances', Melville explained that it had been necessary for the Convention to declare publicly that James had forefaulted his right to the throne in order to render it vacant, but denied that the Convention had assumed the power to forefault James on its own authority. Although Melville conceded that there were 'some pragmatical persons who have strange schemes of government' which they intended to discuss, he remained confident that 'these things may quickly evanish'.[15]

According to the Convention's proceedings, the most conspicuous grounds

---

[11] Anon., *Vindication of the Proceedings of the Convention of Estates*, p. 3.

[12] Grant, *Loyalists Reasons*, p. 8.

[13] 'King James II to Colin, Earl of Balcarres', in HMC *Buccleuch & Queensberry (Montagu House)*, I, 39.

[14] NAS GD 406/M9/200/1, 'A resolutione of tuo questiones. The one concerneing the meaning of that clause in the act of parliaᵗ in the year 1685 By which the parliaᵗ declairs the Kings absolute power and that they are firmly resolved to give ther enteir obedience without reserve and the other concerneing the settleing of the government presently'.

[15] '[Lord] Melvill to King [William]', in HMC *Buccleuch & Queensberry (Montagu House)*, I, 44–5.

on which James could be deemed to have forfeited his right to the throne derived from the claim that, since James had never sworn the Coronation Oath, his regal power had been illegally assumed. If government was perceived as a trust, then James had been civilly incapacitated from occupying that office. Hence the first reason expounded by the Convention in their reasons for declaring the Scottish throne vacant was that James had assumed regal power 'and acted as King without ever takeing ye oath required by law' whereby monarchs undertook to maintain Protestantism and to govern by the rule of law.[16] As the Claim of Right made clear, all future monarchs of Scotland would therefore be obliged to swear the Coronation Oath before commencing their administration. Virtually absent from English allegiance debates, the implications of this theoretical claim were potentially crucial, since it implied that James had never been king of Scotland and had effectively ruled as both a usurper and a tyrant. Having been condemned to death himself for a 'treasonable' interpretation of the Test Act in 1681, Archibald Campbell, ninth earl of Argyll, had later insisted on the binding sanctity of the Coronation Oath on Scottish monarchs. According to Argyll, before swearing the Oath, a monarch was 'espoused but not betrothed to the commonwealth'. Accordingly, 'ther is respect but no full subjection due' and it remained possible to deprive an unsuitable successor of the throne before the Coronation ceremony since the 'commonwealth starkly owes not aleadgance nor subjection to him till he be crouned or admited'.[17]

There were, however, problems with depending on this argument, since the precise status and binding nature of the Coronation Oath in Scotland remained ambiguous. Although James VI & I had regarded the Oath as 'the clearest, ciuill, and fundamentall Law, whereby the Kings office is properly defined', he had also maintained that God remained the ultimate arbiter in this contract between king and people. In cases of ostensible monarchical misrule, James had thus asserted that 'God must first giue sentence' on an errant monarch 'before the people can thinke themselues freed of their oath'.[18] During the Revolution of 1688–89, it was also pointed out by Archbishop John Paterson of Glasgow that although it had been 'nottour' that James VII & II's father, Charles I, had exercised royal power in Scotland for eight years between his accession to the throne in 1625 and his Scottish coronation in 1633, even 'his most implacable & sanguinary enimys never Charg'd that upon him as a Crime'.[19] Moreover, although the 1681 Succession Act had been passed in his favour, as a Roman Catholic, James would never have been able to have sworn the Scottish Coronation Oath as it stood. Less significance was therefore conventionally attached to the Coronation Oath by Stuart apologists than by their opponents. Shortly before James VII & II's accession, for instance, Mackenzie of Rosehaugh had denied that the laws protecting Protestantism were in any way undermined by a lawful

---

[16] Thomson and Innes eds., *Acts of the Parliament of Scotland*, IX, 33.
[17] Inverary Castle MSS. Inventory NRA(S), p. 29, Bundle 56, ff. 9, 32.
[18] James VI and I, 'The Trew Law', in Sommerville ed., *Political Writings*, pp. 65, 81.
[19] NAS GD 12/12/1785, 'Copy of a draft account of the Scottish bishops at the Revolution, written by ABP. Paterson, n.d. [c.1695]', f. 6.

successor declining to swear the Oath, since all parliamentary acts remained in force until repealed by a subsequent Parliament 'and the King cannot repeal an Act without the consent of Parliament'.[20] By 1688, however, it had become abundantly clear that James VII & II had not been prepared to abide by such constitutional niceties and, like many erstwhile supporters of the Stuarts, Mackenzie reluctantly recognised that the problem with the divine right of kings occurred when the king himself began to subvert the divine right of the church.

In the absence of a definitive understanding of the legal basis on which James' authority had been established, the decision to declare the Scottish throne vacant was therefore more conspicuously predicated on James' actions as king. According to the Convention's formal resolution, following his accession, James had proceeded to subvert 'the fundamentall constitution of this Kingdome', changing it from 'a legall limited Monarchie to ane Arbitrary Despotick Power'.[21] The majority of contemporary pamphleteers concurred in the Convention's decision that James had been guilty of 'un-kinging' himself by exposing the Scottish nation to the threats of foreign Catholic powers, as well as endangering the domestic lives and liberties of the people if they refused to comply with popery and arbitrary government. As Francis Grant opined, James had effectively transformed 'the constitution it self (by Word, Write, and Deed) from Legal according to, to Despotical above and against, all these Laws'.[22] In addition to emphasising the iniquity of James' reign, attention was also focused on the servility and culpability of those who had assisted his misgovernment. Referring to the parliamentary act passed in 1685 that confirmed the absolute nature of James' power, for instance, one anonymous author dismissed it as 'the most unaccountable piece of Law that was ever published', since 'giving such power to the King was more than any Parliament could do'. Since such legislation could be regarded as being no more valid than that which ordered a man to surrender 'what belongs to another, of which he has no power nor right to dispose', the writer concluded that the Parliament 'might as well have resigned the whole Parliamentary power, and all the peoples Rights and Properties'.[23] Another manuscript defence of the Revolution likewise declared that the 1685 Act should only be understood in strict juridical terms as referring to the executive aspect of government within which the monarch was obliged to govern by the rule of law, as opposed to any more arbitrary and despotic construction. For, as the author explained, 'if obedience without reserve were understood in that Latitude', such reasoning would undermine 'the very essence of government which is ffor the preservatione of the Subjects and not ffor destroying them'.[24]

---

[20] Mackenzie, *Lawful Successor*, p. 186.
[21] Thomson and Innes eds., *Acts of the Parliament of Scotland*, IX, 33.
[22] Grant, *Loyalists Reasons*, p. 3. Similar sentiments also appeared in verse. In *Britain's Jubilee*, for instance, the presbyterian minister of the Scots Church in Rotterdam, Robert Fleming, enquired of William, '. . . who else can that Country claim? / 'Tis thou, that from oppressions rage, / Whereof it was of late the dismal stage, / Hast rescu'd all its Laws, Religion, Liberty, / Which shackl'd were before and ready to expire and die' (Robert Fleming, *Britain's Jubilee* (London, 1689), sig. A4r).
[23] Anon., *Vindication of the Proceedings of the Convention of Estates*, pp. 10–11.
[24] NAS GD 406/M9/200/1, 'A resolutione of tuo questiones'.

II

Although agreement could be reached regarding James' forfeiture of his regal power, this consensus did not, however, immediately confer a right of resistance against that particular king. As seen in earlier chapters, injunctions enjoining passive obedience had been reiterated frequently and forcefully under both James and his elder brother. Launching his unsuccessful uprising against James' authority in 1685, for example, the earl of Argyll regretted 'my former too much complying with, and conniving at the Methods that have been taken to bring us to the sad condition we are now in'.[25] By 1689, increasing numbers of the Scottish population were likewise ready to construe passive obedience as supine enslavement. As Francis Grant pointed out, 'Passive Obedience hath never got (*de facto* at least) a larger Field than we have given it', but following James VII & II's flight to France, events had now reached a critical situation beyond which lay higher 'Prerogatives than ever (*de jure*) it could pretend to'.[26] In a pamphlet attributed to William Sherlock, it was also argued that, in Scotland, the 'Speculative Doctrine of passive Obedience, has done too much Mischief among us', as James' misfortunes were attributable to his 'believing that without Opposition he might do what he pleased'.[27] Another writer likewise condemned the manner in which the Scots had been formerly 'poysoned with false notions about Government', nothing having 'more contributed to enslave the Nation, and debauch Mens Consciences, than the Preaching up the Doctrine of Absolute Power and Non-resistance'.[28]

As seen in the third chapter of this book, theories regarding popular rights of resistance in the event of manifest monarchical misrule enjoyed a long pedigree in Scotland, despite their vehement condemnation by succeeding generations of Stuart monarchs. While George Buchanan's *De Jure Regni apud Scotos* had been translated into English for the first time in 1680, another edition appeared in 1689 and contemporary pamphleteers followed Buchanan in expounding the popular origins of the Scottish monarchy, together with its necessarily limited nature. The records of Scottish history were thus ransacked to provide evidence confirming that whenever a king 'broke the original Contract with the People', the Estates of Parliament had always thought it 'fit to lay aside any of their Kings, or did alter the Succession'.[29] As an anonymous author pointed out, Buchanan's account of Scottish history demonstrated that monarchs had always

---

[25] Archibald Campbell (Earl of Argyll), *The Declaration and Apology of the Protestant People, that is, Of the Noblemen, Burgesses and Commons of all sorts now in Arms within the Kingdom of Scotland, with the Concurrence of the most Faithful Pastors, and of several Gentlemen of the English Nation joyned with them in the same cause, &c.* (Edinburgh, 1685), p. 3.

[26] Grant, *Loyalists Reasons*, p. 16.

[27] [Sherlock], *Letter to a Member of the Convention of States*, p. 5.

[28] Anon., *Vindication of the Proceedings of the Convention of Estates*, p. 12.

[29] Anon., *A Short Historical Account, Concerning the Succession to the Crown of Scotland: And the Estates disposing of it upon Occasion as they thought fit* ([?Edinburgh, 1689]), p. 4.

sworn to uphold the nation's religion and to rule in the national interest with parliamentary counsel. If certain kings thereafter began to tyrannise and over-turn the fundamental constitution, such kings were usually 'Censured, and upon promise of amendment, continued on the Throne', while more obstinate monarchs were 'put from the Government'.[30] The anonymous author of another pamphlet entitled *Salus Populi Suprema Lex* confirmed that the Scottish people had for too long been seduced 'by Men of Corrupt Designs, and practices, to a certain false Cant, that the King holds his Crown immediatly from God Almighty alone'. Since James VII & II was, by contrast, actually a 'King by Contract', if his actions contravened those contractual terms, then the author concluded that such an errant king 'wholly breaks his part, dissolves the Contract and looses us, from our part'.[31]

Precisely because of their associations with notions of popular sovereignty and Buchanan's radical rights of individual resistance, overt defences of the contractarian nature of the Scottish monarchy were generally eschewed by most defenders of the Revolution. It was instead possible to adhere to older 'double contract' theories which legitimised James' forfeiture of the government, but minimised the extent of popular resistance that had actually occurred. According to this formulation, while the people of Scotland remained bound together for the purposes of government by a primary *pactum unionis*, their allegiance to the monarch, as expressed in a secondary *pactum subjectionis*, thus came under scrutiny. If James could be judged to have broken his part of the secondary contract, his actions thereby freed the people from their obligation of obedience. As the anonymous author of the *Vindication of the Proceedings of the Conven-tion of Estates* insisted, since 'Allegiance is a relative duty', if the relation is dissolved, 'the Allegiance is extinguished', in an analogous manner to the grounds on which divorce could be granted in the event of adultery. As the author pointed out, allegiance could also never be surrendered irrevocably, since transfers of individual allegiance occurred daily 'without being Condemned by Lawyers or Casuists' whenever the subject of one sovereign moved elsewhere to be the naturalised subject of another sovereign.[32]

Significantly, however, in no sense could the subjects have 'un-kinged' James on their own initiative by re-arranging the secondary *pactum subjectionis*. For, as Francis Grant explained, 'our engagements being Correlats (tho unequal) stand and fall together', the inequality denoting that if a king broke the contract, it was dissolved, but if a subject broke the contract, it remained intact. Nor were the people freed from allegiance to the ruler's lineal successor, as shown by the vote taken to declare the throne vacant, since this decision automatically assumed the prior existence of such a throne. With regard to present circum-stances, however, Grant discounted the possibility of transferring the sovereign

---

[30] Anon., *Vindication of the Proceedings of the Convention of Estates*, p. 24.

[31] Anon., *Salus Populi Suprema Lex, or, The Free Thoughts of a Well-Wisher, for a good Settlement, in a Letter to a Friend* ([?Edinburgh], 1689), p. 4.

[32] Anon., *Vindication of the Proceedings of the Convention of Estates*, p. 31.

power to the Prince of Wales, since James VII & II's violation of the rectoral contract had occurred between 1685 and 1688, thus precluding 'all born after (but not before) that amission'.[33] Nor could the Convention attach any authority to subsequent commands from James, since they were solely obliged to obey James' civil person in his public and judicial capacity as king.

From an alternative viewpoint, lawyers such as Sir James Dalrymple of Stair sought to restrict the Convention's role at this juncture. As he remarked in April 1689, the decision to forefault 'the king's right seems harsh, implying that the Conventione had a superiority of jurisdictione'. Since James had violated the political and religious integrity of the nation, the Convention needed only to 'declair, that seeing he had violat his pairt of the mutuall engagements, they wer frie of ther pairt'.[34] Just such a theoretical possibility had ironically been anticipated by generations of royalist political theorists. As John Locke pointed out in his *Two Treatises of Government,* published in 1689, even the early-seventeenth century writings of 'that great Assertor of the Power and Sacredness of Kings', William Barclay, had identified certain conditions 'whereby a King *ipso facto,* becomes no King; and loses all Power and Regal Authority over his People'.[35] During the 1680s, Mackenzie of Rosehaugh had also incorporated a potential rupture of the *pactum subjectionis* into his account of absolute monarchy. As Mackenzie conceived, however, if a king alienated his kingdom through misgovernment, his former subjects were free 'not by their power to reassume their first Liberty; but because the King will not continue King'. Hence they were liberated 'by His Deed, but not by their own Right'.[36]

From this position it was relatively straightforward to retain conventional languages of attachment to notions of fundamental law and the iniquity of resistance to lawful monarchy while advancing a case for resistance *in extremis* which sanctioned an exception to prevailing injunctions regarding passive obedience and non-resistance on the grounds of extreme necessity. This was the strategy adopted, for example, by James Canaries, in a sermon preached in St. Giles' Cathedral on 30 January 1689 that commemorated the fortieth anniversary of Charles I's regicide. As seen earlier, after a brief and unhappy conversion to Catholicism, Canaries had suffered deprivation under James for the virulently anti-Catholic nature of his preaching. Although subsequently dubbed a 'Vicar of Bray' for the alacrity with which he seemingly adapted his principles to suit current political circumstances, Canaries constructed a comprehensive defence of Lockean rights of individual resistance when the subjects' right in general was invaded.[37] Taking as his text Romans 13:5, regarding the need to remain subject 'not only for wrath, but also for conscience sake', Canaries

---

[33] Grant, *Loyalists Reasons*, pp. 6, 9.
[34] William Melville ed., *Letters and State Papers chiefly addressed to George, Earl of Melville, Secretary of State for Scotland 1689–91* (Edinburgh, 1843), p. 9.
[35] Locke, *Two Treatises*, pp. 419, 423.
[36] Mackenzie, *Jus Regium*, p. 66.
[37] The appellation appears in a character sketch of Canaries by A. Philp, 'Dr. Canaries: A Vicar of Bray', in *The Evangel in Gowrie* (Edinburgh, 1911), pp. 151–63.

maintained that there was 'something included in the Liberty of the Subject that fully corresponds to that Prerogative Power in the Soveraign', since it would be otherwise impossible to differentiate 'between a subject and a slave'. As Canaries made clear, subjects enjoyed 'a true and real and practical Right in the Law' as opposed to 'an Imaginary and Speculative, and Ineffectual one'. Hence he rejected the claims of those 'flattering Parasites' who had sought 'to infuse the biggest, the most swoln thoughts' of royal authority into the imaginations of the Stuart kings. But Canaries also remained unequivocally opposed to all notions of individual resistance, insisting that each subject was obliged to suffer passively rather than undertake any action that might 'set his whole Fellow-Subjects and the Soveraign by the Ears together'. If the subject's right in general was invaded and the public interest directly undermined, however, then Canaries directed that 'every particular Subject not only may, but . . . ought to do whatever he can' to relieve that right 'from that Tyranny and Oppression it is falling, or fallen under'.[38]

Despite its conservative caveats, this last proposition remained extremely radical and accorded with Lockean arguments regarding individual rights of resistance amidst conditions of general tyranny. Like Canaries, Locke denied particular individuals the right to seek redress for private injuries sustained at the sovereign's hands, deeming it 'safer for the Body, that some few private Men should be sometimes in danger to suffer, than the head of the Republick should be easily, and upon slight occasions exposed'. Locke did, however, enumerate several conditions under which sovereignty was voided, including a situation within which a monarch acted arbitrarily and contrary to law, impeded the free convocation of Parliament, delivered his subjects into the hands of a foreign power, and, significantly for conditions in 1689, 'when he who has the Supream Executive Power, neglects and abandons that charge'. According to Locke, amidst such circumstances, 'when Government is dissolved, the People are at liberty to provide for themselves, by erecting a new Legislative'.[39] Although Canaries ostensibly deemed it impertinent 'to mingle the Minister and the Lawyer together', it was not difficult to misconstrue his implied conclusion that the duty of obedience placed upon the Scottish people could be mitigated in cases of unbridled tyranny and ungodliness. Furthermore, although Canaries denied that subjects were empowered to opposed the sovereign on religious grounds alone, they were entitled to 'vindicate any encroached attempts upon their Religion, when the Profession of it is embodied with their Constitution'. In this case, however, religion was to be regarded as 'a Civil Right and Property', since it denoted 'a thing wherein the Interests of the Subjects is most deeply engaged'.[40]

In the sermon which he preached on 30 January 1689, Canaries also expressed support for *de facto* claims that the very possession of power by William and Mary could be construed as sufficient for allegiance to be paid to

[38] Canaries, *Sermon Preached in Edinburgh . . . 30 January 1689*, pp. 24, 34–5, 31, 40.
[39] Locke, *Two Treatises*, pp. 402, 410, 411.
[40] Canaries, *Sermon Preached in Edinburgh . . . 30 January 1689*, pp. 28, 67.

them. Just as John Kenyon has contended that the English allegiance debate witnessed the 'triumph of *de facto* theory', the Revolution in Scotland also prompted a marked shift away from discussions of the vexed issue of hereditary titles to the throne, as depicted in the recently-completed Holyrood portraits.[41] Since there were 'no immediate Appointments from Heaven', Canaries explained that 'as the World is stated at this day, the Paternal Right for that of a Monarch, is but an empty and Chymerical Notion'. As Canaries perceived, all civil governments arose through either the free subjection of one civil society to the authority of a chosen sovereign or through forcible conquest which itself 'falls at long-run into a voluntary condescention; tho at first not absolutely so'. Hence, for Canaries, the title of conquest was 'no less good and valid, than that of Compact'.[42] In similar vein, Francis Grant reasoned that it would be 'an endless task, and require an Infallible history of the World (which is not to be made by Man) to prove clearly the just Titles' upon which all monarchs ruled. Accepting that 'Possession of the power and Force have been fixed as sufficient Charters thereof', Grant contended that if all rights of prescription were to be removed following wars between sovereign princes, there would be 'not one Lawful King, or State in all Europe'. Sustaining his position, Grant denied that he was 'serving the Times' or 'being a Trimmer, unless all Loyal Subjects since the Creation were such'.[43] Resident in London in 1689, the Aberfoyle minister, Robert Kirk, likewise pondered in his commonplace-book that the 'Titles of all Kings are doubtful whether by Birth or Conquest'. But, as Kirk judged, what remained definite was that no man should consent to 'Violating of the Laws of the Natione, oppressing the Subjects or overthrowing his Religion'.[44]

Nevertheless, although forfaulture might demonstrate the cessation of James' right as monarch, it did not specifically legitimate William's right. Insisting on the latter could evidently only be achieved by an appeal to the naked sword. In this context, the anonymous author of the *Vindication of the Proceedings of the Convention of Estates* cited Romans 13:1–2 to insist that the Scots were obliged to submit to William of Orange's authority since he was 'the Power in being, and now in possession of the Crown'. As the author pointed out, neither Christ nor the Apostles were to be found 'enjoining Christians to scan the Right and Title of the Powers then in being'.[45] Another anonymous author declared that Scotland was obliged by 'the most cogent necessity of self-preservation, to fly and betake it self to His Highness Heavens-sent Protection'.[46] Noticeably, the new oath of allegiance to William and Mary, that was framed by the Convention in 1689, contained no explicit acknowledgement of their being *de jure*

[41] Kenyon, *Revolution Principles*, p. 21.

[42] Canaries, *Sermon Preached in Edinburgh . . . 30 January 1689*, pp. 50–2.

[43] Grant, *Loyalists Reasons*, pp. 102, 102–4, 113 [72, 72–4, 83]. Since the pagination in *The Loyalists Reasons* proceeds directly from p. 64 to p. 95, the first reference given for these quotations indicates the page as printed in the text while the references in square brackets represent the actual page numbers.

[44] EUL MSS. La.III.545, 'Sermons, Conferences, Mens Opinions', f. 155r.

[45] Anon., *Vindication of the Proceedings of the Convention of Estates*, p. 21.

[46] Anon., *Salus Populi Suprema Lex*, p. 3.

monarchs. It simply read that the taker sincerely promised to 'be faithful and bear true alledgiance to their Majesties King William and Queen Mary'.[47]

The main problem with all *de facto* claims remained, however, that they immediately incurred allegations that force and success had merely been resolved, in Hobbesian manner, into right. It was, after all, only a few years since the University of Oxford had formally condemned the proposition 'that possession and strength give a right to govern' in 1683. At the restoration of Charles II in 1660, particular exception had been taken to 'this Turkish Argument built meerly upon externall passages of Providence and Successe' which had been 'most sinfully & factiously made use of, in the late Troubles and Revolutions'.[48] Faced with a renewed dissolution of authority in 1689, several writers thus attempted to accommodate arguments for *de facto* allegiance within a providentialist rhetoric of godly rule and the divine sanction of the Protestant William. Celebrating the manner in which God had moved 'the Hearts of all the People of Britain; and caused all the feared opposition to melt away, as Snow before the Sun', one pamphleteer concluded this to be 'the Lord's doing, and it marvellous in our eyes!' Together with the Princess of Orange's close hereditary relation to James VII & II, events appeared as 'nothing less then so many Lines from Gods Soveraign Power, and Wisdom, concentring to point out their Highnesses as the only Persons that ought and can possess it'.[49] In the words of another anonymous writer, 'Almighty God hath raised up the Prince of Orange' to become 'the Hereditary Hercules of the Latter World'.[50]

Comprehensive theories of the divine right of providence remained rare, however, since beliefs that subjects must recognise God's divine intervention were often associated with mid-seventeenth century suspicions of 'enthusiasm'. The author of the *Vindication* made explicit that he was not one of 'those who rashly judge the goodness or badness of an Attempt, by the Success' or deduced God's favour or disfavour 'from a frowning or favourable Providence'. Nevertheless, he conceded that, on very rare occasions, one could 'so plainly and remarkably see Almighty Power concerned' that subjects could validly infer that 'This is the doing of the Lord'.[51]

III

Turning from the question of how the ordinary subject should act when confronted by the desertion of the government to attempts to consolidate William's legitimate right, it could be argued that his title was justifiable on the grounds of military conquest in a just war. This was the strategy adopted by a

---

[47] Thomson and Innes eds., *Acts of the Parliament of Scotland*, IX, 99.
[48] Paterson, *Post nubila Phoebus*, p. 6.
[49] Anon., *Salus Populi Suprema Lex*, pp. 6–7.
[50] Anon., *Some Weighty Considerations, Humbly proposed to the Honourable Members of the Ensuing Assembly of the States of Scotland. By a Lover of his Countreys Liberty* (Edinburgh, 1689), p. 7.
[51] Anon., *Vindication of the Proceedings of the Convention of the Estates*, p. 35.

young and still unqualified advocate, Francis Grant, who published *The Loyalists Reasons For his giving Obedience, and swearing Allegiance to the Present Government* in 1689. Drawing on ideas expounded by Hugo Grotius in the early seventeenth century, Grant argued that, since the Revolution could not have succeeded without William's armed invasion, events were properly to be interpreted as a military encounter between two independent sovereigns.[52] As he put it, this 'Enterprize, as intended to be, so really was a War'. Although the extent to which William's status as Dutch stadholder conferred sovereign status was debatable, Grant argued that the conditions in 1688 fulfilled Grotius' two essential preconditions within which a just war could formally occur: that the war had been conducted by two sovereign authorities between whom there was no arbiter and that there had been a full and formal declaration of war. Regarding the circumstances whereby sovereignty had been voided, Grant charged James VII & II with 'a real and absolute present Desertion' which 'consequently gave all right desireable both to Prince and Subjects'. As he vividly recalled, James had 'thrown up the reins of Government' by 'burning the Parliament in Effigie, throwing the Great Seal in [the] Thames, and then an incontrovertible final Desertion'.[53] As another anonymous pamphleteer agreed, although Scottish monarchs had for many years lived in London, James' desertion was 'not a simple non-residence, and personal absence, but a manifest abandoning, leaving us far more negligently, then he did England, without all Cause, Care, or Concernment'.[54]

As far as the subject's duty was concerned, Grant's theory importantly preserved intact the doctrine of non-resistance. Despite his limiting conditions, Grotius had remained implacably opposed to all forms of individual resistance, arguing that there was no place for the private administration of justice within the context of the collective protection afforded by membership of a civil society. Hence Grant acknowledged that since the majority of Scottish subjects in 1688 had been 'meerly Passive till K. J. final Desertion' they were 'altogether blameless: (since all their Active concurrence sisted within their breasts without any fait ouvert)'. Arguing that although it was criminal for subjects themselves to seek redress for their grievances even in times of extreme necessity, Grant conceded that 'it remains most Lawful in a Prince not subject to do it for them'. In the same way, it was deemed criminal for a servant to punish an abusive master, but lawful for that servant to petition another master to seek recompense on his behalf. Thus Grant accepted that while individual rights of resistance potentially threatened anarchy, to deny by the laws of nations, or *ius gentium*,

---

[52] For more on Grant's writings, see Clare Jackson, 'Revolution Principles, *Ius Naturae* and *Ius Gentium* in early Enlightenment Scotland: the contribution of Sir Francis Grant, Lord Cullen (c.1660–1726)', in Tim Hochstrasser and Peter Schröder eds., *Early Modern Natural Law Theories: Contexts and Strategies in the Early Enlightenment* (forthcoming). For a discussion of a similar type of argument advanced in the English allegiance debate, see Mark Goldie, 'Edmund Bohun and *Jus Gentium* in the Revolution Debate 1689–1693', *Historical Journal*, 20 (1977), pp. 569–86.

[53] Grant, *Loyalists Reasons*, pp. 17, 48, 8.

[54] Anon., *Salus Populi Suprema Lex*, p. 4.

the potential for just wars to occur would be 'to banish Faith from all publick Negotiations, and Quiet from Mankind'.[55] In regarding the Revolution as a just war, Grant also invoked the authority of older generations of royalist authors. As Grant showed, the Restoration bishop of Orkney, Andrew Honyman, had demonstrated the iniquity of nonconformist resistance in the late-1660s by denying that illicit rebellion could be justified on the grounds of self-preservation. Nevertheless, Honyman had accepted God's readiness to sanction lawful wars involving the 'seeking of reparation or repelling of wrongs done to one Nation by another, by force of the sword'.[56] Although Grant conveniently disregarded the fact that William never set foot in Scotland during the Revolution, he nevertheless commended the Convention to treat him as 'a Foreign Prince come to rescue us by a War which was Lawful, and consequently unlawful to resist'. Since William had intended no more than the conquest of the former king, James VII & II, rather than that of his kingdoms, Grant further demonstrated how William had also surrendered the rights of conquest comprehended within his victory, ensuring that 'both by Word, Write, and Deeds' he had given the Scots 'absolute Liberty of Settleing and Disposing of the Government'.[57] Nevertheless, Grant exhorted the Convention to settle for William, perceiving any other option as only serving to assist the plans of Louis XIV of France to establish a universal monarchy against Protestantism.

Grant was not the only theorist to place revolutionary events within a wider international context, for it had become manifestly clear by the spring of 1689 that William and Mary were ruling as *de facto* monarchs, at least in England. Observers such as the English M.P., Sir John Reresby, were keenly aware that once the decision had been taken to declare the English throne vacant, the Scots Convention would eagerly 'choos for itselfe, and be noe longer a province to England, or dance attendance at the door of an English Court.'[58] Pamphleteers thus entreated members of the Scottish Convention to remember that the 'Eyes of all Europe are upon you' since it was 'in your Power to make your Selves and your Posterity either Happy or Miserable'.[59] Adopting strikingly similar phraseology, Lord Yester wrote to his father from London two days after the Convention opened in Edinburgh, warning him that 'the expectation of all Europe is upon what you doe the settlement or the confusion of thes [*sic*] Kingdoms depending much upon it'.[60] In a letter to Melville, Viscount Tarbat likewise worried that if 'attacks from Ireland will be both speedy and violent', large numbers of Scots 'who have too little religion and several who consider not the danger of the Protestant Religion' throughout Britain and Continental Europe

---

55 Grant, *Loyalists Reasons*, pp. 55, 21, 56, 43.
56 [Honyman], *Survey of that Insolent and Infamous Libel entituled Naphtali*, p. 100.
57 Grant, *Loyalists Reasons*, pp. 54, 45.
58 Andrew Browning ed., *Memoirs of Sir John Reresby. The Complete Text and a Selection from his Letters* (second edition, London, 1991), p. 550.
59 [Sherlock], *Letter to a Member of the Convention of States*, p. 3.
60 CUL Add. MSS. 9362/48, 'Lord Yester to the earl of Tweeddale, 16 March 1689'.

might readily join the Jacobite opposition.[61] In retrospect, the Convention's speedy resolution to follow the English example thus met with approval. According to one manuscript memorandum, since the 'enterest of Scotland & Ingland are now so Interwoven together being in continent & under one king . . . the one cannot be weell and the other ill'. Moreover, as the author perceived, Scotland's role should properly be seen as 'the balance of Europe', for, had the Convention joined with Ireland and declared for James VII & II instead, it was 'lyke that Scotland & Ireland with King James his pairtie in Ingland with the french assistance would have been too strong for King William and put a stope to his designes'.[62]

Historiographically, the extent to which revolutionary events re-opened debates about closer union between Scotland and England has been largely overlooked. Contemporaries, however, certainly recognised a conducive opportunity to negotiate for closer union with England, possibly thereby securing free trade in exchange for dynastic security. As many writers appreciated, it was virtually impossible for Scotland to adopt any other course than that of England 'without laying our selves open to all their dangers, with very small assurance of their assistance'.[63] The option of declaring for James VII & II was dismissed by one author on the grounds that it was 'a Dream to fancy it' as long as the 'Vatican Thunders Excommunications, against all such as do not use their utmost Endeavour to Extirpate Heresie.'[64] Another pamphleteer confirmed it to be 'a meer dream' for the Scots to imagine they could uphold James' authority as king of Scotland 'without wronging the K. of England and his Interest'. It was also highly unlikely that James would value his Scottish crown 'further then that he might thereby be enabled to recover that of England'.[65] By such a scenario, Scotland would only become the pawn of a decisive international war whose battles would inevitably bloody Scottish soil. Anxious to avert such an eventuality, a number of writers sought to conjoin directly the issue of the Scottish throne with that of union with England. As one pamphleteer conceived, Anglo-Scottish union would ensure that 'the united strength of Great Britain may be intirely laid out' for the relief of suffering Protestants throughout Europe. Hence the author counselled not only obedience to William, but active measures also taken to promote union as 'the only means to support an Impoverish'd and sinking Nation'.[66] Although later regarded as a staunch opposer of incorporating union in 1707, Andrew Fletcher of Saltoun also wrote from Rotterdam in January 1689 acknowledging that he could not conceive 'any

---

[61] '[Lord] Tarbat to Lord Melville', HMC *Buccleuch & Queensberry (Montagu House)*, I, 40. By such a scenario, Tarbat rued that 'the very embarrassing of our King in the present conjuncture will be more hurtful to the Allies abroad than Scotland is worth' (*ibid.*, I, 41).

[62] NAS GD 406/M9/2002/10, 'A Memorial discussing past relations'.

[63] Anon., *Salus Populi Suprema Lex*, p. 7.

[64] [Sherlock], *Letter to a Member of the Convention of States*, p. 6.

[65] Anon., *Allegiance and Prerogative Considered*, p. 5.

[66] Anon., *Some Weighty Considerations*, pp. 8, 7.

true settlement but by uniting with England in Parliaments', while recognising that religious and legal union remained unfeasible.[67]

In this way, debates about the future settlement of the Scottish monarchy became inextricably fused with discussions about the future status of Scotland within the Stuart multiple monarchy. As some contemporaries feared, delaying the offer of the crown to William until the union issue had been resolved could weaken the Scottish case for union. In February 1689, for example, Yester confided his belief to Tweeddale that the current situation would 'procure us a treattye upon easier and better terms than ever could have been expected', since 'a separatione is as dangerous for them as for us and ane union as much theire interest as ours'.[68] A fortnight later, however, Yester conceded that it might be more prudent to follow the English example by settling the crown on William first, since any other proposal might 'be lookt upon as but shifting proceeding from inclinations of recalling the King and returning where we were'.[69] Nevertheless, Yester regretted the idea of postponing the debate, since union remained the one issue that 'might obviat all heats and debats and would carry the most unanimous consent' within the Convention.[70] Resolving the matter of the crown first was further endorsed by another anonymous writer on the grounds that if the Convention delayed their decision, then William and the English Parliament might 'be so dissatisfed [t]hat certainly they will take occasione from this to make Scotland a province'. Continuing to insist on achieving union before settling the crown could suggest that the Scots had 'too much fondnes to have ane Unione which would make Ingland more shy to grant it'. Were the Convention to offer the crown to William and Mary first, such an action would not only 'shew that wee are [a]s indifferent as they', but might also serve as 'a mean to make them as desyreous to have ane unione with us as wee can desyre to unite with them'. If the offer of the crown was freely made to William, the author indicated that Scotland 'may justly expect to get ane unione in equall terms wheras if wee be reduced to a province', then the Scots would be obliged to 'accept of what conditiones Ingland pleases to give us as Ireland hes done'.[71] Privately, Yester considered such constructions unmerited, claiming that the only reason why union should be pressed first would be that Scotland would thereby 'be the more sure to have ane union and upon better conditions then if it were delayed'. Deferring the union question might potentially serve to render English politicians 'indifferent if not avers therto', having resolved the critical issue of dynastic security 'as we had alreadye found by experience ever sinc[e] King James the 6th came to this crowne'.[72]

Considerable confidence was initially vested in the Prince of Orange's benign

---

[67] Quoted by T. C. Smout, 'The Road to Union', in Geoffrey Holmes ed., *Britain after the Glorious Revolution* (London, 1969), pp. 183–4.
[68] CUL Add. MSS. 9362/37, 'Lord Yester to the earl of Tweeddale, 7 February 1689'.
[69] CUL Add. MSS. 9362/40, 'Lord Yester to the earl of Tweeddale, 21 February 1689'.
[70] CUL Add. MSS. 9362/44, 'Lord Yester to the earl of Tweeddale, 2 March 1689'.
[71] NAS GD 406/M9/200/1, 'A resolutione of tuo questiones'.
[72] CUL Add. MSS. 9362/40, 'Lord Yester to the earl of Tweeddale, 21 February 1689'.

intentions about the union issue. Writing to the Convention of Estates in March 1689, William confirmed that he had been pleased 'to find that so many of the Nobilitie & Gentrie when here at London, were so much inclined to ane union of both Kingdoms'. For his part, William acknowledged himself to be 'of the same opinion' as to the merits of union, since both nations occupied one island, spoke the same language and shared 'the same common interest of Religion and Liberty'. Union had also been rendered all the more desirable 'at this juncture when the Enemies of both [nations] are so restless' seeking to foment divisions and undermine British interests as a whole.[73] Despite such propitious overtures, however, William's attitude towards Anglo-Scottish union and Scots affairs in general became increasingly apathetic once he was crowned king. Questioning the decision to deploy English troops in Scotland in 1689, for instance, Sir James Dalrymple of Stair objected that 'new raised English from ther soft beds will nether be proper in Scotland, nor so fitt any wher as our hard bred people'.[74] As early as February 1689, Yester had complained about 'the almost impossibilitye [sic] there is to know his Ma[ties] sentiments he keeping his mind so much to himself'. When war against the Jacobite armies broke out in Ireland later that year, Yester shared Stair's concerns about William's approach in military matters. Observing the deployment of Swedish and Danish forces to confront the Jacobite forces in Ireland while the Scots were 'so farr neglected as not to have an troop of horse or regiment of foott levyed', Yester discerned 'even in our owne King an unwillingness to make use of us either out of distrust or disesteeme'. Hence Yester concluded that Scotland had little left to 'support its creditt and reputatione in the world' or 'its courage fidelitye and warlyk dispositione which made it in former ages considerable and its alliance sought after'.[75]

IV

Frustration at William's conduct towards the Scots was not entirely unforeseen. As Anne, countess of Erroll, had observed in a letter to the Scottish Secretary of the Chelsea Hospital in London, Dr. James Fraser, in March 1689, there were 'so many privat quarrels and every man so much endeavoring to be uppermost' in Scotland 'that they uant but a litle of a disapointment to be on fire'.[76] As William himself was aware, support for the Revolution was by no means universal. Many of the memorials and pamphlets cited above were specifically composed and circulated to counteract what one author dubbed 'the private whispers, and Coffee-house Tales of a discontented party'.[77] The events of 1688–89 undoubtedly placed all royalists in a precarious position. James VII &

---

[73] Thomson and Innes eds., *Acts of the Parliament of Scotland*, IX, 9.
[74] Melville ed., *Letters and State Papers*, p. 4.
[75] CUL Add. MSS. 9362/57, 'Lord Yester to the earl of Tweeddale, 23 September 1689'.
[76] 'Letters to Dr. James Fraser. M.DC.LXXIX–M.DC.LXXXIX', *The Miscellany of the Spalding Club. Volume Fifth*, J. Stuart ed. (Aberdeen, 1852), p. 197.
[77] Anon., *Vindication of the Proceedings of the Convention of the Estates*, p. 1.

II's success in dispensing with most constitutional safeguards on his authority had already undermined support for ideas of non-resistance and passive obedience espoused by the majority of constitutional royalists. But if William and Mary were to be recognised as lawful monarchs of Scotland, the sanctity of hereditary succession and passive obedience would be permanently ended. Addressing an audience of Scots nobles in London in January 1689, for instance, Hamilton's heir, the earl of Arran, attempted to distinguish between the 'Popery and Person' of James, acknowledging that although he might 'dislike the one', he had 'sworn obedience and do owe Allegiance to the other'.[78] Arran's subsequent proposal that James be invited to return to Scotland, conditional on his consent to summon a free parliament, was however, deemed 'bold enough and surprizd all' but generated little support.[79] Extensive theorising in defence of James' lawful right to return to the throne was not encouraged either by his previous record as monarch or by his conspicuous absence from Whitehall after his flight to France. Revolution supporters, such as Melville, therefore counted themselves fortunate, contending that if there had been 'one man of brains and courage' among James' supporters in Scotland 'as things have been managed, the kingdom in all probability had been lost'.[80]

Among those who sought to oppose revolutionary events, however, support for James could, for instance, be predicated on attachment to fundamental rights of private property and the blatant disregard for rules of inheritance were James to be deprived of his throne. As was shown in the third chapter of this study, considerable support existed for the idea that succession to the crown necessarily followed the rules of succession to private property. In Gaelic bardic poetry, one of the most powerful images presented in the aftermath of the Revolution was that of the unnatural character of William and Mary's accession, since it clearly deprived Mary's father-in-law and his progeny of their lawful inheritance. According to the bard, Duncan Macrae,

> Do thréig iad, 's cha 'n ait daibh,
> An cùigeamh fàithn' a bha casg' a shluaigh;
> Neo-nàdurr a'bheart so
> Do neach a ghabh baisteadh
> Ann an ainm nan trì perarson tha shuas.

(They broke – and it is not a nice thing for them to have done – the Fifth Commandment that had acted as a check upon his people. This is an unnatural act for one who received baptism in the name of the Trinity).[81]

---

78 James Hamilton (Earl of Arran), *A Speech made by the Right Honourable the Earl of Arran, to the Scotch Nobility and Gentry . . . about an Address to His Highness the Prince of Orange, to take upon him the Government of the Kingdom of Scotland* (London, 1689), p. 1.

79 CUL Add. MSS. 9362/36, 'Lord Yester to the earl of Tweeddale, 8 January 1689'. David Hume later explained Arran's actions in terms of the 'usual policy in Scotland, where the father and son, during civil commotions, were often observed to take opposite sides; in order to secure in all events the family from attainder' (*History of England. Volume VI*, p. 522).

80 '[Lord] Melvill to King [William]', in HMC *Buccleuch & Queensberry (Montagu House)*, I, 44.

81 Malcolm MacFarlane ed., *The Fernaig Manuscript* (Dundee, 1923), p. 187.

Ostensibly, the most vociferous criticism of the Revolution seemed likely to emanate from some of James' natural allies among the Scottish episcopalian establishment. In November 1688, the bishops had collectively affirmed their steadfast support for James 'as the darling of heaven, peaceably seated upon the throne of your royal ancestors, whose long, illustrious and unparalleled line, is the greatest glory of this your ancient kingdom'. Proclaiming themselves 'amazed' to have heard rumours of a Dutch invasion, the Scottish bishops had assured James that they would zealously promote dutiful loyalty among his subjects and would succeed in 'giving you the hearts of your subjects and the necks of your enemies'.[82] But such assistance was not immediately forthcoming in the aftermath of James' flight to France. In the event, it appeared that the legacy of James' religious policies had destroyed the practical potential of the Scottish episcopate to support him in his time of crisis. In June 1689, for example, John Grahame of Claverhouse was moved to complain about the bishops: 'I know not where they are. They are now the kirk invisible.'[83]

Notwithstanding, individual members of the ecclesiastical bench denied such accusations of political paralysis. In 1695, the former archbishop of Glasgow, John Paterson, composed a retrospective memorial justifying the bishops' adherence to the doctrines of non-resistance and passive obedience and their consistent opposition to revolutionary events. In particular, he cited a speech that he claimed to have delivered to the Convention in March 1689, opposing moves to forfeit James' right to the throne. Basing his argument largely on Scriptural authority, Paterson reiterated royalist shibboleths defending absolute and divinely-ordained monarchy by insisting that all royal power was 'deriv'd from Heaven, & flowes from God alone' irrespective of any human involvement in designating a particular royal line. Hence the Convention's actions were fundamentally illegal in presuming that there could be 'a superiour to him who is the only Supream', since in all civil societies there 'must be a Dernier resort of power & Authority unless we allow processes & Appealls to run on in Infinitum'. Although Paterson accounted himself 'as much for Governing according to Law as any man can be', he insisted that royal authority was not subject to temporal judgement, although a king's ministers could be prosecuted to protect the people. With reference to the particular circumstances prevailing in 1689, Paterson denied the judicial legality of current proceedings, arguing that 'by all fair & legall proceedings allowed even in the Case of the most plebian private Criminall', the Convention should allow James VII & II to appear before the tribunal to answer the charges being formulated in his name. He even went so far as to challenge the assumption that James had abdicated the royal power,

---

[82] 'Letter from the Scots bishops to the King, November 3rd, 1688', in Wodrow, *Sufferings*, IV, 468. For more on such sentiments, see Bruce Lenman, 'The Scottish Episcopal Clergy and the Ideology of Jacobitism', in Eveline Cruickshanks ed., *Ideology and Conspiracy: Aspects of Jacobitism, 1689–1759* (Edinburgh, 1982), pp. 36–48.
[83] 'John Grahame of Claverhouse to the earl of Melfort, 27 June 1689', in Andrew Murray Scott ed., 'Letters of John Grahame of Claverhouse', *Miscellany of the Scottish History Society XI* (Edinburgh, 1990), p. 243.

since 'he was now in Ireland exercising it, & nearer to Scotl^d, being at Dublin, then when he resided in England'. Nor did Paterson attach much credence to circulating rumours about impending military invasions from Ireland, dismissing them as 'a meer blind & amusement, Cunningly invented to distract & irritate the alreddy too much inflamed populace'.[84]

By his own account, Paterson was not alone in lodging vociferous objection to the Convention's procedures. When the presbyterian, Sir James Montgomery of Skelmorlie, cited numerous historical instances upon which lawful kings had been removed from their thrones through maladministration, he was informed by other Convention members that such instances were to be regarded as 'beacons to preserve us from running & splitting upon such dangerous rockes', rather than 'precidents & examples to follow'. Should the Convention's proposals be allowed to advance unchecked, Paterson himself prophesied all three Stuart kingdoms once more plunging themselves into a bloody civil war, on account of which future generations would 'lament & mourn for our present proceeding & curs[e] the authors & actors therin, when they shou[l]d perceive the seas of blood, the ruin, the poverty, the desolation & misery that must necessarily ensue upon it'.[85] Contained with the records of the Scottish Episcopal Church is another undated manuscript memorandum outlining several civil law arguments to demonstrate 'that meer possession cannot give right'. Drawing on Ciceronian and Justinianic maxims, the author argued that since an individual 'cannot Legally Lose any things without any Intention to lose', if James was forced to leave the kingdom and flee abroad for safety, 'by such his Relinquishing he does not Transfer any thing, to the Usurper, nor acquitt him of the guilt of Theft, and Robbery'. Rejecting the claims of 'those English Lawyers' who upheld the argument that 'meer Posession of the dominions of Depos'd Princes gives the Unjust Possessor a Right', the writer wondered how they would answer to God at the Day of Judgement for a doctrine he regarded as 'so contrary to the Naturall Principles of Justice'.[86]

Such warnings ultimately proved ineffective in the face of overwhelming support for the Convention's transactions. Only seven bishops and five peers opposed the vote taken to declare the throne forfeit on 4 April 1689. Recognising that '[m]y bigotrie for the Royall familie & Monarchie is & has been very troublesom to me', one such dissident peer, Mackenzie of Rosehaugh, lamented seeing 'our just noble & antient government pulld to peeces and sunk down to a condition wherin it will neither be able to defend itself or us'. Regretting that he had now become the target of assassination plots by former Covenanters, he

---

[84] NAS CH 12/12/1785, 'Copy of a draft account', ff. 8, 9, 8, 6. That Paterson delivered the speech seems likely, since one anonymous recorder of the Convention's proceedings alluded to an occasion upon which numerous injunctions regarding James' divine right to rule and the duty of subjects not to resist were urged 'with so much vehemency by one of that Venerable Order' (Anon., *Vindication of the Proceedings of the Convention of Estates*, p. 12).

[85] NAS CH 12/12/1785, 'Copy of a draft account', ff. 7, 9.

[86] NAS CH 12/12/311, 'An argument from the Civil Law shewing that meer possession cannot give right'.

nevertheless ventured that 'it may seem reasonable to suffer mee to live, for in conscience all the Lawyers now alyv in Scotland put together, know not how to resolve one sure rule'. Electing to leave Scotland and live in England, Mackenzie acknowledged, however, that he thereafter intended 'to live peaceably and with great satisfaction under the present new elected King, for tho' I was not clear to make a King, yet I love not civill wars nor disorders & wee owe much to him'.[87]

Nor did any of the bishops take any further part in the Convention's activities for, in their attempts to impede its proceedings, they had ultimately proved as unsuccessful as they had been in their personal representations to William before the Convention opened. Recognising that the Anglican church had always represented 'a great refuge to which wee fly', Bishop Alexander Rose of Edinburgh had been deputed by the Scottish episcopate to travel to London in December 1688 to make formal representations on the Church's behalf both at Court and to their Anglican brethren.[88] In this emergency, the Scottish bishops humbly conveyed their desire that their Anglican counterparts should 'pitie and forgive' their actions, instead of questioning 'anie yeeldings or condensions lately made by anie of our order to the King's most importunat desires'. Their apparent pusillanimity was to be excused on the grounds of 'the unequal circumstances and grounds of law' which accorded the established church in Scotland a far less favourable status than in England. Once in London, however, Rose was apprised by Archbishop William Sancroft of Canterbury that since affairs were 'very dark, & the load so thick or gross', the Anglican prelates 'knew not well what to doe for themselves, & far less what advice to give'. For his part, Bishop Henry Compton of London advised Rose that William was unlikely to be particularly well disposed towards the Scottish episcopalians. Having 'thrown himself upon the water', Compton perceived that William must 'keep himself a swimming with on[e] hand, the presbiterians having joined him clossly, & offer to support him', he 'therefor cannot cast them of[f]'. According to Rose's account, however, when subsequently presented to William, he acknowledged that he could only 'serve yow so far as law, reason, or conscience will allow me', upon which 'instantly the prince without saying any thing more turned away from me & went back to his company'.[89] Despite Rose's apparent scruples, Mackenzie of Rosehaugh accounted the Scots prelates as being 'indeed very unworthy of that Character' who 'had don much mischiefe' to the Scottish church, when dining with Sancroft in the presence of several senior Anglican bishops and the diarist, John Evelyn, in January 1689. As Mackenzie perceived, the bishops were now to be seen transferring their allegiance to William 'more to save themselves in this conjuncture, which threatned the abolishing the whole Hierarchy in that Kingdome, than for Conscience'.[90]

---

[87] BL Add. MSS. 34,516, 'Copies of Two Letters from Sir George Mackenzie addressed "For My Lord Melvill Principall Secretary of State", 1689', ff. 63, 61–2.
[88] Clarke ed., *Letters to Sancroft*, p. 90.
[89] NAS CH 12/12/1833, 'Alexander Rose to Archibald Campbell, 22 October 1713'.
[90] De Beer ed., *Diary of John Evelyn*, p. 897.

A lack of formal political theorising in James' defence need not, however, necessarily equate with popular indifference. Fighting for the Williamite army at Killiecrankie in 1689, Major-General Hugh Mackay observed that episcopalian clerics 'preached King James more than Christ as they had been accustomed to take passive obedience more than the gospel for their text'.[91] One minister, Robert Calder, issued a manifesto on behalf of the nobility and gentry of northern Scotland, acknowledging the indignation with which they were forced to 'reflect upon our own slackness and untymous appearance and that wee have not been soe active in doeing good as the presbiterians are in doeing mischief'. Deeming the present confusion to be 'a call from heaven to bestir ourselfs', Calder warned that 'the temper and complexion of presbiterian government [and] its most tragicall and tirannical methods' were 'not the accidentall but even the naturall consequences flowing from the school of politick and ecclesiastick principalls of that partie'.[92]

Plentiful evidence of committed ideological opposition also appears from the 'decreets of deprivation' served on recalcitrant episcopalians by the Privy Council during the course of 1689, usually when ministers failed to comply with official orders to read particular proclamations from their pulpits. One such proclamation, issued in April 1689, forbade any minister from acknowledging James VII & II as king or to 'presume upon ther highest perill by word, writing, In sermones' or by any other means 'Impugne or disoune the Royall authoritie of William & Mary, King and Queen of Scotland'.[93] Confronted by this injunction, some established clergy initially prevaricated. Magistrates in Edinburgh, for instance, claimed that one of the Tolbooth Church ministers, William Gairns, failed to read the proclamation on the Sunday specified, after which he 'did absent himself for severall Sabath dayes thereafter, appearing waiting for the late King James his returne'. Eventually Gairns returned but failed to read the proclamation and did not pray for William and Mary 'as our king and queen according to the proclamatione', but as one might 'doe for a theif goeing to the gibbett'.[94] Elsewhere on the appointed Sunday, the Kincardine minister, John Cameron 'did thinkingly absent himself that day and sent another to preach for him, who prayed for the late King James and his happie restauratione'.[95]

Among those ministers who elected to remain in their parishes and conduct services, evasion and equivocation often prevailed. When ordered to read another proclamation ordaining a fast as a mark of thanksgiving, it was alleged that a Dundee minister, Robert Rait, 'did not read it wholly nor altogither out as he should have done' but only 'picked out parcells and

[91] Hugh Mackay, *Memoirs of the War Carried on in Scotland and Ireland. M.DC.LXXXIX–M.DC.XCI*, J. Hog, P. Tytler and A. Urquhart eds. (Edinburgh, 1833), pp. 76–7.
[92] NAS GD 406/M9/322, 'Copy manifesto of the noblemen and gentlemen in the north of Scotland who are now in armes in their own defence against oppressiones and free quarterings and for the restauratione of the episcopall government [1689–91]'.
[93] Thomson and Innes eds., *Acts of the Parliament of Scotland*, IX, 43.
[94] 'Decreet of deprivation . . . against Doctor William Gairns, one of the ministers of the Tolbooth Church of Edinburgh', *Register of the Privy Council of Scotland. XIV (1689)*, Paton ed., p. 287.
[95] 'Decreet of deprivation . . . against Mr. John Cameron, minister of Kincardine', *ibid.*, p. 143.

paragraphes'.[96] Reports emerged that a Kilconquhar minister, Alexander Hay, offered prayers that 'ware in generall and ambigious [sic] termes for all Christian kings and princes', implying favour towards James VII & II as well as evidently commenting on the Convention of Estates' proceedings and insinuating 'usurpatione and tyranie in their present Majesties'. Moreover, Hay also often reflected in his sermons that although 'kings and princes have bein put from their right under collour of law', he remained confident that divine justice would ultimately prevail, however much 'tyrants and oppressers may gone [sic] in their oppressiones and add dominion to dominion'.[97]

Finally, there were numerous clergy who eschewed all ambiguity in explaining their reasons for failing to comply with official requirements. When warned about his failure to read the proclamation ordaining public prayers for King William and Queen Mary, the minister of Fintray, John Semple, refused, replying 'Let the Whigs pray for them, he would not pray for them, for he never gott good by them, and . . . he was five tymes sworne to King James'. For good measure, Semple added that before he could be induced to pray for Mary in particular, 'lett her gett her fathers blissing first . . . God keep him from ever having such a daughter'.[98] In Killearn, James Craig declared William was 'but a ciphered king', appearing as 'a staff stuck in the ground in comparisone to a souldier actually under command'.[99] In Comrie, John Philip continued to offer prayers for James VII & II, repeatedly suggesting to his congregation that 'our rullers [are] as Soddom and our judges as Gomorah'.[100] At Torryburn, James Aird not only prayed for James, but also supplicated God to 'send back that tirrant by the way that he came with ane hook in his jawes who hade come into invade out land'.[101] Finally, Alexander Lindsay was alleged to have observed to his congregation in Cortachie that, whereas 'it was accompted religione of old to preach up obedience to the supream magistrate', he now perceived that 'rebellione was accompted religione and to depos and dethron Kings is acompted a dutie'.[102]

Considering popular attitudes to loyalty and allegiance alongside more complex texts of political theory has revealed that discussion of the Revolution was indeed extensive within Scotland. Events were by no means viewed in a parochial context, since their pan-British, Unionist and Continental dimensions were placed at the forefront of debate. Within Scotland, however, the implacable opposition of large numbers of episcopalian clergy to the accession of William and Mary bode ill for the maintenance of the Restoration religious settlement that had re-established episcopacy. In addition to attacking James' actions as king, the majority of Revolution sympathisers argued that the Stuart

[96] 'Decreet of deprivation . . . against Mr. Robert Rait, minister at Dundee', ibid., p. 355.
[97] 'Decreet of deprivation . . . against Mr. Alexander Hay, minister at Kilconquhar', ibid., p. 264.
[98] 'Decreet of deprivation . . . against Mr. John Semple, minister at Fintray', ibid., p. 369.
[99] 'Decreet of deprivation . . . against Mr. James Craig, minister at Killearn', ibid., p. 418.
[100] 'Decreet of deprivation . . . against Mr. John Philip, minister at Comrie', ibid., p. 304.
[101] 'Decreet of deprivation . . . against Mr. James Aird, minister at Torryburn', ibid., p. 425.
[102] 'Decreet of deprivation . . . against Mr. Alexander Lindsay, minister at Cortachie', ibid., p. 445.

administration in Scotland had for too long sought to impose a form of church government on 'a devout and sincere People, to the racking of their Conscience' and 'fomenting of Broyls and Tumults'.[103] Alarmed episcopalian apologists defended the established church by arguing that projected moves to re-establish presbyterianism demonstrated that 'at last the Government it self is become a Party against them'.[104] Furthermore, if such a policy were adopted, it would ensure that the Church of Scotland and the Anglican church would henceforth 'stand on different bottoms', thus immediately gratifying Catholics who 'love extraordinarly to fish in troubled Watters, and to see Protestants divided'.[105] Notwithstanding, in 1690 presbyterianism was established as the state religion, episcopacy having been denounced by the Claim of Right as 'an intolerable grievance' and 'hostile to this nation and contrary to the inclination of the generality of the people, ever since the Reformation'.[106] Henceforth, any attempts to create a unitary British state would need to accommodate formal religious pluralism. As far as the constitutional politics of the British multiple monarchy were concerned, the Revolution of 1688–89 thus appeared to provoke more questions than it resolved.

---

[103] Anon., *Some Weighty Considerations*, p. 3.
[104] [Morer], *Account of the Present Persecution*, p. 2.
[105] Anon., *Reasons why in this Conjuncture*, p. 5.
[106] 'The Claim of Right', in William Croft Dickinson and Gordon Donaldson eds., *A Source Book of Scottish History*, 3 vols. (second edition, London, 1958–63), III, 205.

9

Conclusion

The investigation of political and religious ideas pursued in this book has constructed an evocation of shared sensibilities rather than a series of detailed expositions of individual texts. In doing so, it has drawn on an extensive range of sources, the large majority of which have not previously been used in this manner. Such sources have included anonymous political memoranda, sermon notebooks, manuscript legal depositions, private correspondence, common-place-book reflections, diary entries and bardic poetry, together with printed works encompassing a heterogeneous range of subjects from political thought and religious reflection to theoretical jurisprudence and natural and moral philosophy. While the adoption of this approach was partly dictated by the diffuse nature of the extant source material, it was also conceived with the aim of generating as comprehensive and contextualised an account of late-seventeenth century Scottish intellectual culture as possible. By closely wedding the study of political and religious ideas to the constitutional and ecclesiastical circumstances in which they were articulated, this book has therefore aimed to reconstruct the mental world of Restoration Scotland with nuance and precision.

Juxtaposing formal political theorising alongside informal political commentaries has inevitably produced some surprising insights. To take one brief example, in June 1684 the University of Oxford formally thanked Sir George Mackenzie of Rosehaugh 'for the service he had done his Majesty [Charles II] in writing and publishing *Jus Regium*'.[1] Examined in detail in the third chapter of this book, Mackenzie's tract has widely been regarded as representing the epitome of political theorising in defence of absolute Stuart kingship. A more attenuated and pragmatic impression of Mackenzie's royalism emerges, however, from consideration of his professional conduct as Charles II's Lord Advocate. The year after *Jus Regium* was published, a characteristic vignette of Mackenzie was provided by the Covenanter, Alexander Shields, who had recently been interrogated before the Privy Council by Mackenzie in an attempt to ascertain whether or not Shields endorsed ideas recently expounded in manifestoes issued by more extreme elements of the Covenanting movement.

---

[1]   Anthony à Wood, *The Life and Times of Anthony à Wood, antiquary of Oxford, described by Himself, Volume III: 1682–1685*, A. Clark ed. (Oxford, 1894), p. 96.

Describing the conduct of the Privy Councillors involved, Shields recorded that 'severalls admired' the fact that Mackenzie ingenuously acknowledged that they did not 'owne all ye administrations', while others descended from the bench to 'bid me be tender of my life & take advice', apprising Shields that 'Sr George ye K. Advocat was a man y^t could give advice. Sr George himself also offering to conference upon it when I pleased'.[2] While the above instance exiguously alters characterisations of Mackenzie himself as inflexibly authoritarian and slavishly partisan, it also serves to indicate, more widely, how much remains to be discovered about the individual activities and characters of Restoration Scots themselves. Hence although this study has been primarily concerned to establish and examine the major issues of ideological debate current among late-seventeenth century contemporaries, such arguments still perhaps need to be underset by contextualised and modern biographies of the contemporaries themselves.

As far as the ideas and arguments examined in this book are concerned, however, the combined analysis of formal political and religious theorising with more informal sensibilities and attitudes has revealed an intellectual discourse that is both eclectic and extensive. What renders it distinctive, nevertheless, is its predominant concern with ideas relating to political obedience, the extent of the *ius regni*, Scotland's historical inheritance, ecclesiastical erastianism and religious adiaphorism. Incorporated with contemporary thinking remained, for example, fundamentally divergent beliefs as to whether or not Scotland was a country wherein the monarch 'might, by his prerogative, govern much more absolutely than in England'.[3] In the ecclesiastical sphere, such claims of political omnicompetence were effectively supported by erastian assertions that church government and discipline were the prerogative of the Christian magistrate, rather than of individual church officers. In this manner, the restored episcopalian church in Scotland was underwritten by erastian pragmatism, rather than by a dogmatic commitment to Scriptural or primitive episcopacy, as was commonplace in Restoration England. Moreover, increasingly syncretic attempts were made to reconcile differing schools of thought by the adoption of adiaphorist attitudes that held theological dogmas and rites to be matters of indifference. Generated in reaction to the dislocation of the mid-century civil wars, such credal latitude rejected the spiritual elitism of older Knoxian and predestinarian Calvinist traditions. Hence the simultaneous evolution of all of these ideological tendencies produced a unique mental world which placed allegiance to the divinely-endowed, hereditary monarch, whose ancestors had ruled Scotland for two millennia, alongside Catholic and compromising desires to remove the pernicious effects of theological and philosophical doctrines deemed to induce faction, strife and civil war.

Viewed from this perspective, a number of broader conclusions can be drawn about the characteristics of Restoration intellectual culture. In the first place, the status of Scotland as an absentee monarchy had little substantive effect on the

[2] NAS JC 39/73/1, 'Letter from Shields'.
[3] Mackenzie, *Memoirs*, p. 139.

nature of political ideology. Still heavily indebted to the ideas of George Buchanan, James VI & I and Thomas Craig, late-seventeenth century theorising continued to comprise an eclectic mixture of concepts drawn from political theology, Scottish history and civil law. As was shown in the third chapter of this book, political theorists who supported individual rights of resistance in the event of monarchical misrule exploited the same historical framework of ancient Scottish constitutionalism as those who condemned such arguments wholesale. Resistance theorists, such as Shields and Sir James Steuart of Goodtrees, like-wise concentrated on defining the conditions under which resistance to that monarch was permissible, as well as alerting their readers to the dangers posed by the impositions of the secular magistrate to the spiritual autonomy of the Kirk. Conspicuous chiefly by their absence, alternative republican models of government were rarely mooted, seemingly deemed inappropriate for a country widely acclaimed as the oldest monarchy in the world. The neo-Machiavellian political ideas of Andrew Fletcher were subsequently to be articulated amidst constitutional circumstances of greater contingency, once the monarchical succession depicted so vividly in the Holyrood portraits had been irrevocably suspended by events in 1689.

Secondly, and perhaps paradoxically, it can be suggested that it was the very absence of a resident monarchy in Restoration Scotland that enabled royalist political ideas to be applied in a manner that was, however, far from monolithic. Freed from the need to define notions of monarchical government by a series of responses to the frequently capricious actions of any individual monarch, late-seventeenth century Scots instead constructed a political language predicated on the optimum manner in which monarchical government should function. As was shown in the fourth chapter of this study, attachment to monarchy by no means precluded vigorous opposition to the practicalities of kingly rule when it was feared that the absolute monarch might govern arbitrarily. As the activities of the duke of Hamilton and his followers in the mid-1670s demonstrated, regular scrutiny of the executive was deemed imperative to parry incipient corruption and abuses of power. Institutionally, constant vigilance was also regarded as necessary to maintain the integrity of the traditional organs of government, such as the Parliament and the Court of Session. As indicated by the contents of numerous memoranda penned to Charles II in the 1660s and 1670s, incisive attacks on the Restoration administration were conventionally couched as loyalist attempts to deliver the monarch and his subjects from executive mis-government, as opposed to assaults on the institution of the Stuart monarchy itself.

Thirdly, although the contours of monarchical political theory may have remained largely unchanged since the late sixteenth century, the ways in which contemporaries applied those ideas had been dramatically revised by the events of the mid-century civil wars. This was chiefly a generation whose sense of the political had been rendered highly practical. Hence their ideological responses were acutely predicated on a desire to apply the lessons of past experience, the most conspicuous of which was a prevailing concern to ensure the preservation of order. If the civil wars had arisen partly through abuses of power that had occurred under Charles I, then the members of his Scottish administration were also partly culpable for remaining impotent in the face of escalating political violence. As was demonstrated in the sixth chapter of this book, members of the Restoration political establishment were thus equally as prepared as their Covenanting opponents to invoke the Ciceronian injunction of *salus populi suprema lex* to sanction whatever legal powers the executive deemed necessary to preserve the body politic from internal division. Directed at procuring the political loyalty of the Scottish people, the actions of the Stuart administration fundamentally modified traditional conceptions of matters such as oath-taking, the sanctity of private property, the maintenance of a national militia and the legality of free quarter. Moreover, the extent to which some members of the political establishment were prepared to exploit this line of reasoning to justify their own passive obedience was conspicuously demonstrated between 1685 and 1688 when such arguments were turned against a king increasingly regarded as wayward and misguided.

Fourthly, although a nascent campaign of civil disobedience was initiated under James VII & II, it can be posited that it was the fear that political liberties and freedoms would be compromised by James' Catholicising policies, rather than any vociferous doctrinal objection to Catholicism *per se*, that proved unacceptable to disaffected members of the political establishment. The combined spectre of Jesuitical 'king-killing' resistance theories, together with Louis XIV's widely-articulated aspirations to become a universal monarch, effectively ensured that Catholicism, unlike presbyterianism, could not be made safe for civilised society. For, arguably, the extremist Covenanting threat had been confronted and neutralised by 1689. Throughout the Restoration, members of the political and ecclesiastical establishment had repeatedly vented their suspicions that, as Sir George Mackenzie, Viscount Tarbat, put it, the 'matter of Church Government hath been made a pretence for the troubles of Scotland now for 100 yeares'.[4] By repudiating notions of any immediate correlation between religious heterodoxy and political disloyalty, the more radical elements of presbyterian opposition could not only be isolated, but also largely discredited, by their refusal to countenance all forms of reconciliation with civil authority. As was seen in the fifth chapter of this study, the absence of any uncompromising 'High Church' defences of episcopalian church government along *iure divino* lines crucially enabled the political establishment to insist that forms of church government be abdicated to the magistrate's direction. In response, the most prominent and vociferous member of the Restoration episcopate, Robert Leighton, accepted that 'Episcopacy should divest itself of a great part of the authority that belonged to it.'[5] In addition to the flexibility such initiatives promoted among moderate episcopalians and presbyterians alike, the fact that little difference subsisted between the two systems in practice can also be held

---

4 Melville ed., *Letters and State Papers*, p. 125.
5 Leighton, 'A Narrative of the Treaty Anent Accommodation', in West ed., *Remains*, p. 214.

to explain the relative facility with which presbyterianism was re-established in Scotland in 1689.

Fifthly, it has been shown that the Restoration era thus witnessed a retreat from the politics of religion towards a non-doctrinal religiosity. By extending the scope of things deemed 'indifferent' to true salvation, considerable ideological convergence was forged between moderate presbyterians and episcopalians which could then be deployed against extreme nonconformist and anticlerical attacks. As was revealed in the seventh chapter of this study, increasing support for notions of 'rational religion' belied a wider concern to demonstrate that the forces of good and evil were neither consensual nor exclusively reliant on Calvinist predestinarianism. Moreover, as the writings of authors such as Leighton, Gilbert Burnet and Henry Scougal indicate, developments in both natural philosophy and natural jurisprudence could be extensively harnessed to late-seventeenth century religious apologetic. As confessional conflict receded after 1689, the persuasive nature of the case that Leighton and his colleagues had been making was confirmed: namely, that the serious intellectual challenge would henceforth not be to adjudicate between conformity and nonconformity, but between faith and incredulity.

Sixthly, taken in conjunction with one another, these ideological tendencies collectively contribute to an enhanced understanding of events in Scotland following James VII & II's flight to France in December 1688. The existence of a contemporary allegiance debate in Scotland was demonstrated for the first time in the eighth chapter of this book. Most conspicuously, the abject failure of the established church to develop a convincing ideological defence of its own position precipitated the willingness with which notions of divine-right monarchy and indefeasible hereditary succession could be quietly jettisoned. Reluctant to regard William as an instrument of divine providence, presbyterian theorists, such as Francis Grant, instead availed themselves of jurisprudential notions of *ius gentium* to account for the change in monarch, while episcopalians, such as James Canaries, expediently drew on a secularised language of interests to legitimise resistance *in extremis* to the rule of James VII & II.

Seventhly, and finally, this study has also highlighted the increasingly significant role exerted by lawyers in Restoration Scotland. With an established church that was both institutionally impotent and ideologically bankrupt, it was the members of the legal profession that gradually came to exert the greatest influence over the theory and practice of monarchy in late-seventeenth century Scotland. Although they differed significantly in conceptual perspective from one another, the institutional writings of both Mackenzie and Sir James Dalrymple, Viscount Stair evinced the same desire to establish the ultimate sources of political sovereignty in order to deduce the rights and duties mutually incumbent on monarchs and subjects alike. Nor were such projects parochially conceived. Without the constraints imposed by a sophisticated common law tradition, the civil law basis of Scottish jurisprudence was inherently more receptive to foreign influence than English law. As notions of law and legality were placed in an essentially comparative context, not only were ideas about the exercise of monarchical authority rendered more flexible, but analysis of the state could increasingly be divorced from that of civil society.

The characteristically comparative and cosmopolitan nature of Scottish legal discourse provokes one final reflection. Given the prodigious expansion of recent historiographical activity, concerns have been expressed that, as Glenn Burgess has put it, 'there is little to check the potential capacity of "British" history to distort our picture of Scottish political thought'.[6] Throughout the late seventeenth century, Scots writers on political, religious, legal and moral ideas simultaneously emulated and exploited a range of national, British and Continental perspectives. The extent to which Restoration political thought was predominantly concerned with discussions of Anglo-Scottish union and other aspects of multiple monarchy governance remained limited. Correspondingly, a greater understanding of the Continental influences on late-seventeenth century political, religious, legal and moral thought is still required in order to recognise the distinctive particularities of the Scottish intellectual heritage.

---

6   Burgess, 'Scottish or British', p. 580.

Bibliography

Manuscript Sources

Aberdeen University Library, Aberdeen
MS. 658, 'The Pourtrait [*sic*] of True Loyalty Exposed in the Family of Gordon without Interruption to this present year, 1691'.
MS. 2612, Henry Scougal, 'Descriptive list of a collection of sermons c.1675'.

Argyll Manuscripts, Inverary Castle, Argyll
Bundle 56, 'Discussion of the nature of monarchy and right to allegiance of the subjects' (n.d.).

Bodleian Library, University of Oxford
Clarendon MS. 75:
- f. 400, 'Ld Lauderdale to the Earl of Glencairn, Lord High Chancellour of Scotland, 1661'.
- ff. 427–8, '[Thomas Sydserf], Information for his sacred Matie in order to the setling [*sic*] of the Church of Scotland [1660]'.

British Library, London
Additional MSS.
- 4927, f. 13r, 'Sir George Mackenzie to Archbishop Sancroft, September 1681'.
- 11252, f. 8, 'Privat instructions To our intirelie beloved Brother, James, Duke of Albanie and York, our Commissioner in Scotland [1681]'.
- 18236, Sir George Mackenzie of Rosehaugh, 'A Discourse on the 4 First Chapters of the Digest to Shew the Excellence and usefullnesse of the Civill Law'.
- 23118, ff. 15–24, 'A Speech concerning the Act of Billeting . . . before his Majesty, 5 February 1663'.
- 23119, f. 87, 'The earl of Lauderdale to Charles II, 13 July 1663'.
- 23136, f. 80, 'The earl of Lauderdale to Charles II, 7 February 1674'.
- 23243, f. 9, 'Sir George Mackenzie to the earl of Lauderdale [1679]'.
- 23244, ff. 20–8, 'My Lord Advocats arguments in law against the paper of the partie lords, Windsor Castle, 1679'.
- 23938, ff. 12–13 'That the Duke of Lauderdale concurred in the Design for bringing in of Popery as appears by these following particulars [1679]'.
- 32095, f. 94 'Sir George Mackenzie to the earl of Lauderdale, April / May, [1678].
- f. 102, 'Sir George Mackenzie to the earl of Lauderdale, [May 1678]'.
- 34516, 'Copies of Two Letters from Sir George Mackenzie addressed "For My Lord Melvill Principall Secretary of State", 1689'.
Lansdowne MS. 988, f. 155, 'George Hickes to Dr. Patrick or Dr. Oughram, 10 January 1678'.

Cambridge University Library. Cambridge
Additional MSS.
9362/8, 'Jean, countess of Tweeddale to the earl of Tweeddale, 28 April [1670s]'.
9362/36, 'Lord Yester to earl of Tweeddale, 8 January 1689'.
9362/37, 'Lord Yester to earl of Tweeddale, 7 February 1689'.
9362/40, 'Lord Yester to earl of Tweeddale, 21 February 1689'.
9362/44, 'Lord Yester to earl of Tweeddale, 2 March 1689'.
9362/48, 'Lord Yester to earl of Tweeddale, 16 March 1689'.
9362/51, 'Lord Yester to earl of Tweeddale, 30 March 1689'.
9362/57, 'Lord Yester to earl of Tweeddale, 23 September 1689'.

Dr. Williams's Library, London
Roger Morrice, Ent'ring Books (3 volumes: 'P', 'Q' and 'R').

Edinburgh University Library, Edinburgh
MS. Dc.4.46, 'Earl of Rothes to Earl of Lauderdale, 6 April 1660'.
Dc.4.47, 'Earl of Rothes to Earl of Lauderdale, 14 March [1665], 13 May 1665'.
La.III.354, f. 70 'Sir George Mackenzie to the earl of Lauderdale, 8 April [1670s].
La.III.529, 'Robert Kirk, Ane Account Of some occasional meditationes, Resolutiones, & practices; Which concern a public & private statione [1681]'.
La.III.545, 'Robert Kirk, 'Sermons, Conferences, Mens Opinions, of the late Transactions, with a Description of London, Ann. 1689'.
La.III.549, 'Robert Kirk, Occasional thoughts and meditationes. August 5. 1669'.

Lambeth Palace Library, London
MS. 1520 (Eccles Collection), 'Collection of Extracts from printed books, sermons and other documents made in about 1682 by a Scottish clergyman'.

National Archives of Scotland, Edinburgh
NAS CH
12/12/1311, 'An argument from the Civil Law shewing that meer possession cannot give right'.
12/12/1370, 'Archbishop James Paterson to Archbishop James Sharp, 11 March 1675'.
12/12/1754, 'Memorial concerning Cairncross and Canaries, December 1686'.
12/12/1785, 'Copy of a draft account of the Scottish bishops at the Revolution, written by ABp Paterson, [c.1695]'.
12/12/1833, 'Alexander Rose to Archibald Campbell, 22 October 1713'.
GD 30/1716, 'Letter to Charles II from Jock a Bread Scotland, 29 May 1674'.
30/1723, 'Letter, unaddressed and unsigned, describing the religious situation in Scotland in detail, 5 July 1680'.
90/2/112, 'Receipt by Robert Kennedy . . . from Sir William Sharp, 30 September 1683'.
90/2/115, 'Receipt by Robert Kennedy . . . from Sir William Sharp, 1 June 1682'.
90/2/117, 'Receipt by Robert Kennedy . . . from Sir William Sharp, 22 August 1682'.
157/1861, 'The Act and Apologetick Declaration of the presbyterians of the Church of Scotland [1681]'.

157/2673/2, 'Sir James Scott to Sir William Scott of Harden, 20 January 1680'.

331/18/1–2, 'Paper addressed to the King on current political affairs, 7 December 1674'.

406/1/2691, 'Summary of sermon provided by John Paterson, November 1673'.

406/1/2690, 'John Paterson to the duke of Hamilton, 2 November 1673'.

406/1/2786, '[Earl of Arran] to James Johnston, 10 March 1674'.

406/1/5924, '[?James Johnston] to the earl of Arran, 20 November 1674'.

406/2/635/5, 'Copy of a paper given to King Charles II by the Duke of Hamilton, May 1678'.

406/2/635/10, 'Copy of a paper given to King Charles II by the Duke of Hamilton, June 1679'.

406/2/635/14, 'A short information of some few of the Grievances of the Kingdome of Scotland and their causes'.

406/2/635/16, 'A Representation of the State of Affairs in Scotland, drawn by Sir Georg [sic] Mackenzie, His Maties Advocat [1670]'.

406/2/636 (ii), 'Ane short accompt of the affaires of Scotland [1674]'.

406/2/636 (iii), 'A Representation of the present affaires of Scotland [1674]'.

406/2/637/4, 'That freequarter is against the fundamental laws of the Kingdom [1678]'.

406/2/640/3, 'Memorandum of some passages in parl: begune in October 1669 and first session'.

406/2/640/5, 'Address to his Majesty giving a rep^n of the state and interest of Scotland and listing the chief causes of complaint [c.1665]'.

406/2/642/3, 'The Case of the Duke of Hamilton, April 1678'.

406/M1/229/15, 'Reasons for consenting to some moderate ease [1686]'.

406/M1/336, 'Copie . . . of a paper by Charles II containing theological reflections'.

406/M1/337, 'Copie in the hand of the 4th duke of Hamilton of a paper by Charles II containing theological reflections . . . introductory letter by James VII'.

406/M9/148, '1661, March 28, Memorandum in the hand of the 3rd duke of Hamilton, discussing what he said in parliament about the rescinding of the acts made by the parliament in the 1640s'.

406/M9/200/1, 'A resolutione of tuo questiones. The one concerneing the meaning of that clause in the act of parlia^t in the year 1685 By which the parlia^t declairs the Kings absolute power and that they are firmly resolved to give ther enteir obedience without reserve and the other concerning the settleing of the government presently'.

406/M9/200/10, 'A memoriall discussing past relations between the Scots parliament and England and advising King William of the benefits and necessity of maintaining good relations with the Scots parliament [1689]'.

406/M9/322, 'Copy manifesto of the noblemen and gentlemen in the north of Scotland who are now in armes in their own defence against oppressiones and free quarterings and for the restauratione of the episcopall government [1689–91]'.

JC 39/44/7, 'His Maties Advocats Speech to the Inquest [1684]'.

39/73/1, 'Letter from [Alexander] Shields in the tolbooth of Edinburgh [to John Forbes, Rotterdam], 9 April 1685'.

National Library of Scotland, Edinburgh

Adv. MS. 31.6.16, f. 169, 'Ane Answer be way of a letter to Sr George McKeinzie K^s Advocate his printed narrative of the Councells proceedings in 1678; anent the bond and the Kings forces sent to the Western shires [c.1678]'.

MS. 597, f. 75, 'The apologie of M[r] J[ames] S[harp]'.

> f. 95. 'Ane humble overture concerning the takeing of the declaratione allreadie taken and subscryved by the members of parliament, 19 August 1663'.

> 2512, f. 118, 'Archbishop James Sharp to the earl of Lauderdale, 23 July 1668'.

> f. 195, 'Archbishop James Sharp to the earl of Lauderdale, 12 February 1676'.

> 3932, 'Robert Kirk, Miscellany of occurring thoughts on various occasions . . . Balquhidder, 1678'.

> 5049–5050, 'Correspondence of Sir Robert Moray to Alexander Bruce, second earl of Kincardine 1658–65'.

> 7003, f. 56, 'Earl of Lauderdale to Earl of Rothes, 19 August 1667'.

> 7004, f. 162. 'Earl of Kincardine to the marquis of Tweeddale, 24 September 1670'.

> 7023, f. 246, 'Earl of Lauderdale to the marquis of Tweeddale, 27 September 1670'.

> 7024, f. 11, 'Earl of Tweeddale to Sir Robert Moray, 20 March 1666'.

> 14407, f. 322, '[Sir George Mackenzie] to the earl of Tweeddale [n.d.]'.

Public Record Office, Kew

SP 30/24/5, 'T. Wilson to the earl of Shaftesbury, 10 September 1675'.

Tollemache Family Archives, Buckminster Estate Office, Leicestershire

MS. 1041, 'Earl of Lothian to the Earl of Lauderdale, 8 May 1660'.

> 2413, 'Earl of Lauderdale to ?, 18 November 1673'.

Printed Primary Sources

William Alexander, *Medulla Historiæ Scoticæ. Being a Comprehensive History of the Reigns of the Kings of Scotland from Fergus I to Charles II* (London, 1685).

Osmund Airy ed., *The Lauderdale Papers*, 3 vols. (London, 1884–5).

William Annand, *Dualitas: Or a Two-fold Subject Displayed and Opened conducible to Godliness, and Peace &c.* (Edinburgh, 1674).

Anon., *A Congratulation for His Sacred Majesty, Charles the third Monarch of our Great Britain* (Edinburgh, 1660).

———, *A Letter concerning the Union, with Sir George Mackenzie's Observations and Sir John Nisbet's Opinion upon the same Subject* ([Edinburgh], 1706).

———, *A Letter containing An Humble and Serious Advice to some in Scotland. In Reference to their Late Troubles and Calamities. By a Person of that Nation* (Edinburgh, 1661).

———, *A Letter from Scotland* (London, 1681).

———, *A Letter from Scotland, with Observations upon the Anti-Erastian, Anti-Prælatical, and Phanatical Presbyterian Party there: By way of a Dialogue between Anonymus and Antiprælatus* (London, 1682).

———, *A Letter sent to D. L.* (London, 1679).

————, *A Narrative of the Horrid Murther Committed on the Body of the Late Right Reverend James, Lord Arch-Bishop of St. Andrews, Primate of all Scotland* (London, 1679).

————, *A Short Historical Account, Concerning the Succession to the Crown of Scotland: And the Estates disposing of it upon Occasion as they thought fit* ([?Edinburgh, 1689]).

————, *A True Account of the Horrid Murther Committed upon His Grace, The Late Lord Archbishop of St. Andrews, Primate and Metropolitan of all Scotland &c.* (London, 1679).

————, *A True and Perfect Account of the Earl of Argile's Landing in the North of Scotland: With the Particulars of that whole Transaction* (London, 1685).

————, *A Vindication of the Proceedings of the Convention of Estates in Scotland &c* (London, 1689).

————, *Allegiance and Prerogative Considered In a Letter from a Gentleman In the Country to his Friend Upon His being Chosen a Member of the Meeting of States in Scotland* (?Edinburgh, 1689).

————, *Caledon's Gratulatory at the Happy Return of our Dread Lord and Soveraign King Charles the Second*, [Edinburgh, 1660].

————, *Five Letters from a Gentleman in Scotland To his Friend in London; Being a True Account of what Remarkable Passages have happened since the Prince's Landing; the manner of the taking of the Chancellor and his Lady in Mans Apparel, the burning of the Pope, Demolishing of the Popish Chapels &c., with the total overthrow of the Roman Catholics* (London, 1689).

————, *Grampius Congratulation, In Plain Scots Language to his Majesties thrice Happy Return of Her Sacred Soveraign Charles the Second*, [Edinburgh, 1660].

————, *Reasons why in this Conjuncture no Alteration should be made in the Government of the Church of Scotland, by a sincere Protestant and Lover of his Country* ([?Edinburgh], 1689).

————, *Salus Populi Suprema Lex, or, The Free Thoughts of a Well-Wisher, for a good Settlement, in a Letter to a Friend* ([?Edinburgh], 1689).

————, *Scots Memoirs, Number 1* (London, 1683).

————, *Some Particular matters of Fact, relating to the Administration of Affairs in Scotland under the Duke of Lauderdale, Humbly offered to his Majesties Consideration, in Obedience to his Royal Commands* ([London], ?1680).

————, *Some Weighty Considerations, Humbly proposed to the Honourable Members of the Ensuing Assembly of the States of Scotland. By a Lover of his Countreys Liberty* (Edinburgh, 1689).

————, *The Curate's Queries, and the Malignant or Courtier's Answer thereto, according to their known Principles of Policy, their Methods, and Ends obtained thereby* ([?Edinburgh], 1679).

————, *The Manner of the Barbarous Murder of James, Late Lord Arch-Bishop of St. Andrews, Primate and Metropolitan of all Scotland* (London, 1679).

————, *The Scotch-Mist Cleared Up. To prevent Englishmen being wet to the skin. Being a true Account of the Proceedings against Archibald Earl of Argyle, for High-Treason* ([?London], 1681).

————, *The Scotish [sic] Inquisition; Or A Short Account of the Proceedings of the Scotish Privy-Counsel, Judiciary Court, and those Commissionated by them, Whereby the Consciences of good Men have been tortured, and the Peace of the*

Nation these several Years past exceedingly Disturbed, and Multitudes of Innocent People cruelly oppressed, and inhumanely Murdered (London, 1689).

Robert Baillie, *The Letters and Journals of Robert Baillie A. M., Principal of the University of Glasgow, M.DC.XXXVII.–M.DC.LXII.*, David Laing ed., 3 vols. (Edinburgh, 1841–2).

[John Baird], *Balm from Gilead: or, the Differences about the Indulgence, Stated and Impleaded: In a serious letter to Ministers and Christians in Scotland. By a Healing Hand* (London, 1681).

Robert Barclay, *Apology for the True Christian Divinity, As the same is held forth, and preached by the people, Called, in Scorn, Quakers. Being a full Explanation and vindication of their Principles and Doctrines, by many Arguments deduc'd from Scripture and right Reason, and the Testimony of famous Authors, both ancient and modern, with a full answer to the strongest objections usually made against them* ([Aberdeen], 1678).

Pierre Bayle, *Nouvelles de la République des Lettres. Mois de Décembre 1685* (Amsterdam, 1685).

Hugh Blair, *God's Soveraignity [sic]. His Sacred Majesties Supremacy, the Subjects Duty. Asserted in a Sermon Preached before His Majesties High Commissioner, and the Honourable Parliament of the Kingdom of Scotland, At Edinburgh, the 31st of March, 1661* (Glasgow, 1661).

Jacques-Bénigne Bossuet, *Politics Drawn from the Very Words of Holy Scripture*, Patrick Riley ed. (Cambridge, 1990).

[John Brown], *An Apologeticall Relation. Of the particular Sufferings of the faithfull Ministers & professours of the Church of Scotland since August 1660* (n.p., 1665).

Andrew Browning ed., *Memoirs of Sir John Reresby. The Complete Text and a Selection from his Letters* (second edition, London, 1991).

Thomas Browne, *Religio Medici* (London, 1643).

Andreas Bruce, *Exercitatio Juridica de Constitutionibus Principium* (Franeker, 1683).

[George Buchanan], *De Jure Regni apud Scotos. Or, A Dialogue, concerning the Due Privilege of Government in the Kingdom of Scotland, Betwixt Buchanan And Thomas Maitland, By the said George Buchanan. And Translated out of the Original Latine into English, By Philalethes* (n.p., 1680).

Gilbert Burnet, *A Discourse on the Memory of that Rare and Truly Virtuous Person Sir Robert Fletcher of Saltoun: Who died the 13. January last, In the thirty-ninth year of his Age* (Edinburgh, 1665).

———, *A Modest and Free Conference betwixt a Conformist and a Nonconformist about the present distempers of Scotland* (second edition, [?Edinburgh], 1669).

———, *A Vindication of the Authority, Laws and Constitution of the Church and State of Scotland. In Four Conferences. Wherein the Answer to the Dialogues betwixt a Conformist and a Nonconformist, is Examined* (Glasgow, 1673).

———, *Subjection for Conscience-Sake Asserted; In a Sermon Preached at Covent-Garden-Church, the Sixth of December, 1674* (London, 1675).

———, *The Memoires of the Lives and Actions of James and William, Dukes of Hamilton and Castleherald &c.* (London, 1677).

———, *A Vindication of the Ordinations of the Church of England* (London, 1677).

———, *A Collection of Eighteen Papers Relating to Church and State* (London, 1689).

————, *The History of My Own Time*, Osmund Airy ed., 2 vols. (Oxford, 1897–1900).

————, *A Supplement to Burnet's History of My Own Time*, Helen C. Foxcroft ed. (Oxford, 1902).

————, 'A Memorial of diverse grievances and abuses in this Church', in Helen C. Foxcroft ed., *Miscellany of the Scottish History Society. Volume II* (Edinburgh, 1904).

————, *Bishop Gilbert Burnet as Educationist, being his Thoughts on Education with Notes and Life of the Author*, John Clarke ed. (Aberdeen, 1914).

Calendar of State Papers, Domestic, of the Reign of Charles II. 1661–2, M. Everett-Green ed. (London, 1861).

Calendar of State Papers, Domestic Series, March 1st to October 31st, 1673, F. H. Blackburne Daniell ed. (London, 1902).

————, *March 1st, 1677 to February 28th, 1678*, F. H. Blackburne Daniell ed. (London, 1911).

————, *March 1st 1678 to December 31st, 1678, with Addenda 1674 to 1679*, F. H. Blackburne Daniell ed. (London, 1913).

————, *January 1st 1679, to August 31st, 1680*, F. H. Blackburne Daniell ed. (London, 1915).

————, *January 1 to June 30, 1683*, F. H. Blackburne Daniell ed. (London, 1933).

————, *October 1, 1683 – April 30 1684*, F. H. Blackburne Daniell and Francis Bickley eds. (London, 1938).

Calendar of State Papers, Domestic Series of the Reign of William and Mary, 1st November 1691 – End of 1692, W. Hardy ed. (London, 1900).

Archibald Campbell (Marquis of Argyll), *Instructions to a Son* (London, 1661).

————, *My Lord Marquis of Argyle, His Speech upon the Scaffold, the 27 of May 1661* (Edinburgh, 1661).

Archibald Campbell (Earl of Argyll), *The Speech of the Earl of Argyle at his Trial on the 12th of December, 1681* (London, 1682).

————, *The Declaration and Apology of the Protestant People, that is, Of the Noblemen, Burgesses and Commons of all sorts now in Arms within the Kingdom of Scotland, with the Concurrence of the most Faithful Pastors, and of several Gentlemen of the English Nation joyned with them in the same cause, &c.* (Edinburgh, 1685).

James Canaries, *A Discourse Representing the Sufficient Manifestation of the Will of God to his Church in all its several Periods and Dispensations* (Edinburgh, 1684).

————, *A Sermon Preacht at Selkirk Upon the 29th of May, 1685. Being the Anniversary of the Restoration of the Royal Family to the Throne of these Kingdoms* (Edinburgh, 1685).

————, *Rome's Additions to Christianity Shewn to be Inconsistent with the True Design of so Spiritual a Religion in a Sermon Preached at Edinburgh, in the East-Church of St. Giles, Feb. 14, 1686. To which is prefixt, A Letter, Vindicating it from the Misrepresentations of the Romish Church* (London, 1686).

————, *A Sermon Preached at Edinburgh. In the East-Church of St. Giles, upon the 30th of January, 1689. Being the Anniversary of the Martyrdome of King Charles the First* (Edinburgh, 1689).

Charles II, *His Majesties Gracious Letter to His Parliament in Scotland, assembled October 19. 1669, Together with the Speech of his Grace the Earl of Lauderdaill,*

229

His Majesties High Commissioner; As Also The Answer of the Parliament of Scotland to His Majesties Gracious Letter (London, 1669).

————, *His Majesties Gracious Letter to His Parliament of Scotland. With the Speech of His Royal Highness the Duke, His Majesties High Commissioner, At the opening of Parliament at Edinburgh, the 28th Day of July, 1681. Together with The Parliaments most Loyal and Dutiful Answer to his Majesties Letter* (London, 1681).

Laurence Charteris, *The Corruptions of this Age and the remedy thereof* (Edinburgh, 1704).

William Clarke ed., *A Collection of Letters, addressed by Prelates and Individuals of High Rank in Scotland and By Two Bishops of Sodor and Man to Sancroft, Archbishop of Canterbury in the Reigns of King Charles II and James VII* (Edinburgh, 1848).

John Clerk of Penicuik, *Memoirs of the Life of Sir John Clerk of Penicuik. Baron of the Exchequer, Extracted by Himself from his own Journals 1676–1755*, John Gray ed. (Edinburgh, 1892).

————, *History of the Union of Scotland and England by Sir John Clerk of Penicuik*, Douglas Duncan ed. (Edinburgh, 1993).

[William Clerke], *Marciano, or The Discovery. A Tragi-Comedy. Acted with great applause, before His Majesties High Commissioner, and others of the Nobility, at the Abby of Holryud-house, on St. Johns night: By a company of gentlemen* (Edinburgh, 1663).

[James Cockburn], *Bibliotheca Universalis, or an Historical Accompt of Books and Transactions of the Learned World* (Edinburgh, 1688).

John Cockburn, *A Specimen of Some Free and Impartial Remarks on Publick Affairs and Particular Persons, Especially relating to Scotland; Occasion'd by Dr. Burnet's History of his own Times* (London, [1724]).

William Colvill, *The Righteous Branch Growing out of the Root of Jesse, and Healing the Nations. Held forth in several Sermons upon Isai. Chap. 11 from vers. 1 to 10. Together with some few sermons relating to all who live under the shadow of the Branch* (Edinburgh, 1673).

William Couper ed., *Watson's 'Preface' to the 'History of Printing', 1713* (Edinburgh, 1913).

Thomas Craig, *The Right of Succession to the Kingdom of England. In Two Books; Against the Sophisms of Parsons the Jesuite, Who assum'd the Name of Doleman, By which he endeavours to overthrow not only the Rights of Succession in Kingdoms, but also the Sacred Authority of Kings themselves*, J. Gatherer ed. (London, 1703).

————, *The Jus Feudale by Sir Thomas Craig of Riccarton with an Appendix Containing the Books of the Feus*, 2 vols., Lord Clyde ed. (Edinburgh, 1934).

[James Craufurd], *The History of the House of Esté. From the time of Forrestus until the Death of Alphonsus, the last Duke of Ferrara* (London, 1681).

————, *A Serious Expostulation with that Party in Scotland, Commonly known by the Name of Whigs. Wherein is modestly and plainly laid open the inconsistency of their Practices* (London, 1682).

'M. D.', *An Account of the Arraignment, Tryal, Escape and Condemnation of the Dog of Heriot's Hospital in Scotland, that was supposed to have been Hang'd, but did at last slip the Halter* (London, 1682).

Sir James Dalrymple, Viscount Stair, *The Institutions of the Law of Scotland,*

Deduced from the Originals and Collected with the Civil, Canon, and Feudal-Laws, and with the Customs of Neighbouring Nations (Edinburgh, 1681).

————, *The Decisions of the Lords of Council and Session . . . Observed by Sir James Dalrymple of Stair*, 2 vols. (Edinburgh, 1683, 1687).

————, *Physiologia Nova Experimentalis, in Qua Generales Notiones Aristotelis, Epicuri, & Cartesi supplentur: Errors deteguntur & emendatur &c.* (Leiden, 1686).

————, *The Vindication of the Divine Perfections* (Glasgow, 1695).

Sir John Dalrymple, *Memoirs of Great Britain and Ireland. From the Dissolution of the last Parliament of King Charles II until the Sea Battle of La Hague*, 2 vols. (fourth edition, Dublin, 1773).

Daniel Defoe, *A Tour thro' the Whole Island of Great Britain; divided into Circuits or Journies*, 3 vols. (London, 1724–7).

William Croft Dickinson and Gordon Donaldson eds., *A Source Book of Scottish History*, 3 vols. (second edition, London, 1958–63).

Gordon Donaldson ed., *Scottish Historical Documents* (Edinburgh, 1970).

Robert Douglas, *The Form and Order of the Coronation of Charles the II. King of Scotland, together with the Sermon then preached, by Mr. Robert Douglas &c.* (Aberdeen, 1660).

————, *Master Dowglasse his Sermon, Preach'd at the Down-sitting of this last Parliament of Scotland, 1661* (London, 1661).

John Dowden ed., *Thirty-four letters written to James Sharp, Archbishop of St Andrews by the Duke and Duchess of Lauderdale and by Charles Maitland, Lord Hatton 1660–1677* (Edinburgh, 1893).

[William Drummond], *Seasonable Advice concerning Ecclesiasticall Affairs: or, The Prudent Speech of a Learned Privy Councillor to King James the 5th of Scotland in the Year, 1539 occasioned by the diversity of Opinions in matters of Religion then in that Kingdome. Presented to the Publick View by a Cordial Wel-wisher to the Peace and Tranquillity of this Kingdome* (London, 1661).

John Dunn ed., *Letters Illustrative of Public Affairs in Scotland, Addressed by Contemporary Statesmen to George, earl of Aberdeen, Lord High Chancellor of Scotland, MDCLXXXI–MDCLXXXIV* (Aberdeen, 1851).

Henry Ellis ed., *Original Letters Illustrative of English History*, Second Series, 4 vols. (London, 1877).

John Erskine, *Journal of the Hon. John Erskine of Carnock 1683–7*, W. Macleod ed. (Edinburgh, 1893).

John Evelyn, *The Diary of John Evelyn*, E. S. de Beer ed. (London, 1959).

James Fall, *Memoires of My Lord Drumlanrig's and His Brother Lord William's Travells Abroad for the Space of Three Yeares beginning Septr 13th 1680*, Hew Dalrymple ed. (Edinburgh, 1931).

Robert Ferguson, *A Sober Enquiry into the Nature, Measure and Principle of Moral Virtue. Its distinction from Gospel-Holiness* (London, 1673).

Sir Robert Filmer, *Patriarcha and other Writings*, Johann P. Sommerville ed. (Cambridge, 1991).

[Robert Fleming], *The Church wounded and rent. By a Spirit of Division Held forth in a short account of some sad differences* [which] *hath been of late in the Church of Scotland, with the occasion, grounds and too evident product thereof, whose wounds are bleeding to this day* (n.p., 1681).

————, *Britain's Jubilee* (London, 1689).

Andrew Fletcher, *Political Works*, John Robertson ed. (Cambridge, 1997).

John Forbes, *The First Book of the Irenicum of John Forbes of Corse*, E. Selwyn ed. (Cambridge, 1923).

[Thomas Forrester], *Rectius Instruendum, Or A Review and Examination Of the doctrine presented by one assuming the Name of ane Informer, in three dialogues with a certain Doubter, upon the controverted points of Episcopacy, the Covenants against Episcopacy, and Separation* (London, 1684).

Helen C. Foxcroft ed., 'Certain Papers of Robert Burnet, afterwards Lord Crimond, Gilbert Burnet, afterwards Bishop of Salisbury and Robert Leighton, sometime Archbishop of Glasgow', *Miscellany of the Scottish History Society, Volume II* (Edinburgh, 1904).

James Fraser, *Memoirs of the Rev. James Fraser of Brea, A.D. 1638–1698*, Alexander Whyte ed. (Inverness, 1889).

Sir William Fraser ed., *The Stirlings of Keir and their Family Papers* (Edinburgh, 1858).

———, *The Earls of Cromartie, Their Kindred, Country and Correspondence*, 2 vols. (Edinburgh, 1876).

———, 'A Series of Eight Anonymous and Confidential Letters to James II about the State of Ireland', *Notes & Queries*, 6th series, V–VI (1882).

John Gaskarth, *A Sermon Preached upon the first occasion, After the Death of His Grace, John Duke of Lauderdale, In the Chappel at Ham* (London, 1683).

[James Gordon], *The Reformed Bishop or XIX Articles Tendered by . . . A Well-wisher of the present Government of the Church of Scotland (As it is settled by Law)* ([London], 1679).

F[rancis] G[rant], *The Loyalists Reasons. For his giving Obedience, and swearing Allegiance to the present Government* (Edinburgh, 1689).

———, *The Patriot Resolved. To an Addresser, from his Friend; of the same Sentiments with himself; concerning the Union* ([Edinburgh], 1707).

[James Gregory], *The Great and New Art of Weighing Vanity, Or, A Discovery of the Ignorance and Arrogance of the great and new Artist, in his Pseudo-Philosophical Writings* (Glasgow, 1672).

Anchitell Grey ed., *Debates of the House of Commons, from the Year 1664 to the Year 1694*, 10 vols. (London, 1768).

Nicolas de Guedeville, *Atlas Historique, ou Nouvelle Introduction à l'Histoire, à la Chronologie & à la Géographie Ancienne et Moderne*, 3 vols. (Amsterdam, 1708).

William Guthrie, *A General History of Scotland, from the Earliest Accounts to the Present Time*, 10 vols. (London, 1767–8).

Thomas Halyburton, *Natural Religion Insufficient: and Reveal'd Necessary to Man's Happiness in its Present State* (Edinburgh, 1714).

James Hamilton (Lord Arran), *A Speech made by the Right Honourable the Earl of Arran to the Scotch Nobility and Gentry . . . about an Address to His Highness the Prince of Orange, to take upon him the Government of the Kingdom of Scotland* (London, 1689).

Robert Hamilton, *Schediesmata Libero-Philosophica* (Edinburgh, 1668).

———, *Disputatio Politico-Juridica, Inauguralis, de Ærarii Publici Necessitate, ac Pleno Principum vectigalia, &c. imponendi Jure* (Leiden, 1671).

[George Hickes], *Ravillac Redivivus, being a Narrative of the late Tryal of Mr. James Mitchel a Conventicle Preacher* (London, 1678).

————, *The Spirit of Popery speaking out of the Mouths of Phanatical Protestants, or the last Speeches of Mr. John Kid and Mr. John King. Two Presbyterian Ministers, who were Executed for High-Treason and Rebellion, at Edinburgh, August the 14th, 1679* (London, 1680).

Historical Manuscripts Commission, *First Report of the Royal Commission on Historical Manuscripts* (London, 1874).

————, *Eighth Report of the Royal Commission on Historical Manuscripts, Report and Appendix (Part I)* (London, 1881).

————, *Twelfth Report, Appendix, Part VIII. The Manuscripts of the Duke of Athole Kt., and the Earl of Home* (London, 1891).

————, *Thirteenth Report, Appendix, Part II, The Manuscripts of His Grace, the Duke of Portland preserved at Welbeck Abbey, Volume II* (London, 1893).

————, *Report on the Buccleuch & Queensberry Manuscripts (Fifteenth Report, Appendix, Part VIII)*, 2 vols. (London, 1897).

————, *Report on the Manuscripts of F. W. Leyborne-Popham Esq.* (London, 1899).

————, *Report on the Laing Manuscripts (Seventh Report)*, 2 vols. (London, 1914).

Thomas Hobbes, *Leviathan*, Richard Tuck ed. (Cambridge, 1991).

[Andrew Honyman], *The seasonable Case of Submission to the Church-government, As now re-established by Law, briefly stated and determined* (Edinburgh, 1662).

————, *A Survey of the Insolent and Infamous Libel entituled Naphtali &c., Wherein several things, falling in debate in these times are considered, and some Doctrines in Lex Rex and the Apolog. Narration . . . are brought to the touch-stone, Part I* ([Edinburgh], 1668).

————, *Survey of Naphtali. Part II. Discoursing of the Heads Proposed in the Preface of the former. Together with an examination of the Doctrines of the Apolog. Narration concerning the King's Supremacy in and about Ecclesiastick Affairs, and the Obligation of the Covenants* (Edinburgh, 1669).

James Howell, *Londinopolis; an Historicall Discourse or Perlustration On the City of London, The Imperial Chamber, and chief Emporium of Great Britain* (London, 1657).

T. B. Howell ed., *A Complete Collection of State trials and Proceedings for high Treason and other Crimes and Misdemeanours from the Earliest Period to the Present Time*, 33 vols. (London, 1816–28).

David Hume, *The History of England from the Invasion of Julius Caesar to the Revolution in 1688. In Six Volumes by David Hume Esq. Volume VI. Based on the Edition of 1778 with the Author's Last Corrections and Improvements*, William B. Todd ed. (Indianapolis, 1983).

Edward Hyde, *The History of the Rebellion and Civil Wars in England*, W. Macray ed., 6 vols. (Oxford, 1888).

Christopher Irvine, *Scoticæ Historiæ Nomenclatura Latino-vernacular* (Edinburgh, 1682).

'J. I.', *A Short Treatise, Comprising a brief Survey of the beginning and continuance of Monarchical Government in Scotland* (Edinburgh, 1661).

James VI & I, *Political Writings*, Johann P. Sommerville ed. (Cambridge, 1994).

John Jameson, *Rebellio Debellata, Et Scota Rediviva* (Edinburgh, 1661).

W. T. Johnston ed., *The Best of our Owne: Letters of Archibald Pitcairne 1652–1713* (Edinburgh, 1979).

[Robert Kirk], 'The Secret Common-Wealth Or, A Treatise Displaying the Chief Curiosities Among the People of Scotland as they are in Use to this Day', in Michael Hunter, *The Occult Laboratory. Magic, Science and Second Sight in Late Seventeenth-Century Scotland* (Woodbridge, 2001).

James Kirkton, *A History of the Church of Scotland 1660–1679*, Ralph Stewart ed. (New York, 1992).

David Laing ed., *Various Pieces of Fugitive Scottish Poetry: Principally of the Seventeenth Century* (Second series, Edinburgh, 1853).

———, *The Diary of Alexander Brodie MDCLII–MDCLXXX and of his Son, James Brodie of Brodie, MDCLXXX–MDCLXXXV* (Aberdeen, 1863).

———, *Correspondence of Sir Robert Kerr, first Earl of Ancram and his son, William, third earl of Lothian*, 2 vols. (Edinburgh, 1875).

John Lamont, *The Diary of Mr. J. L. of Newton*, G. Kinloch ed. (Edinburgh, 1830).

John Lauder of Fountainhall, *Historical Observes of Memorable Occurrents in Church and State from October 1680 to April 1686 by Sir John Lauder of Fountainhall*, David Laing and A. Urquhart eds. (Edinburgh, 1840).

———, *Historical Notices of Scotish [sic] Affairs, Selected from the Manuscripts of Sir John Lauder of Fountainhall, Bart., one of the Senators of the College of Justice*, David Laing ed., 2 vols. (Edinburgh, 1848).

———, *The Decisions of the Lords of Council and Session from June 6th, 1678 to July 30th, 1712*, 2 vols. (Edinburgh, 1759).

———, *Chronological Notes of Scottish Affairs, From 1680 till 1701; Being Chiefly taken from the Diary of Lord Fountainhall*, [Walter Scott ed.] (Edinburgh, 1822).

———, *Journals of Sir John Lauder of Fountainhall with his Observations on Public Affairs and other Memoranda 1665–1676*, Donald Crawford ed. (Edinburgh, 1900).

Robert Lawrie, *God Save the King, or, The loyal and joyfull Acclamations of Subjects to their King. As it was opened in a Sermon, preached in one of the Congregations of the City of Edinburgh, upon the day of Solemn Thanksgiving for the King's Majesty his happy Return and Restauration to his Dominions; Kept, June 19, 1660* (Edinburgh, 1660).

Robert Leighton, *A Practical Commentary upon the Two first Chapters of the first Epistle General of St. Peter* (York, 1693).

———, *Three Posthumous Tracts of the Famous Dr. Rob. Leighton, late Archbishop of Glasgow* (Second edition, London, 1711).

———, *The Remains of Archbishop Leighton*, W. West ed. (London, 1875).

[William Lithgow], *A True and Experimentall Discourse upon the Beginning, Proceedings, and Victorious Event of this Last Siege of Breda* (London, 1637).

[———] *Scotland's Parænesis, To her dread Sovereign, King Charles the Second* (n.p., 1660).

John Livingston, *A Letter written by that famous & faithful Minister of Christ, Mr. John Livingstoun, unto his Parishioners of Ancram in Scotland, Dated Rotterdam, October 7, 1681* ([?Rotterdam, 1671]).

John Locke, *Two Treatises of Government*, Peter Laslett ed. (Cambridge, 1988).

———, *The Correspondence of John Locke*, E. S. de Beer ed., 8 vols. (Oxford, 1976–89).

John Gibson Lockhart, *The Life of Sir Walter Scott*, 10 vols. (London, 1902–3).

The London Gazette

'N. M.', *A Modest Apology For the Students of Edenburgh Burning a Pope*

December 25. 1680, Humbly Rescuing the Actors from the Imputation of Dis-loylty and Rebellion, with which they were charged in a Letter (London, 1681).

Archibald J. Macdonald and Angus Macdonald eds., *The Macdonald Collection of Gaelic Poetry* (Inverness, 1911).

Hugh Mackay, *Memoirs of the War Carried on in Scotland and Ireland. M.DC.LXXXIX–M.DC.XCI*, J. Hog, P. Tytler and A. Urquhart eds. (Edinburgh, 1833).

Sir George Mackenzie, *Aretina, or the Serious Romance* (London, 1660).

———, *Religio Stoici* (Edinburgh, 1663).

———, *The Laws and Customs of Scotland, in Matters Criminal. Wherein is to be seen how the Civil Law, and the Laws and Customs of other Nations, do agree with, and supply ours* (Edinburgh, 1678).

———

—, *A Vindication of His Majesties Government and Judicatures in Scotland: from some Aspersions thrown on them by Scandalous Pamphlets and News-books: and Especially with relation to the late Earl of Argyle's Process* (Edinburgh, 1683).

———, *Jus Regium: Or the Just and Solid Foundations of Monarchy In General; and more especially of the Monarchy of Scotland: Maintain'd against Buchannan [sic], Naphtali, Dolman, Milton &c.* (London, 1684).

———, *A Defence of the Antiquity of the Royal Line of Scotland. With a true Account When the Scots were Govern'd by Kings in the Isle of Britain* (London, 1685).

———, *Observations on the Acts of Parliament, Made by King James the First &c.* (Edinburgh, 1686).

———, *Reason. An Essay* (London, 1690).

———, *A Vindication of the Government in Scotland. During the Reign of King Charles II. Against the Mis-representations made in several Scandalous Pamphlets* (London, 1691).

———, *The Works of that Eminent and Learned Lawyer, Sir George Mackenzie of Rosehaugh*, Thomas Ruddiman ed., 2 vols. (Edinburgh, 1718–22).

———, *Memoirs of the Affairs of Scotland from the Restoration of King Charles II A.D.M.DC.L.X.*, Thomas Thomson ed. (Edinburgh, 1822).

———, *Oratio Inauguralis in Aperienda Jurisconsultorum Bibliotheca*, John W. Cairns and A. Cain eds. (Edinburgh, 1989).

[Sir George Mackenzie and Sir George Mackenzie (Viscount Tarbat)], *A Memorial for His Highness the Prince of Orange in Relation to the Affairs of Scotland* (London, 1689).

John MackQueen, *God's Interest in the King, set forth in a Sermon Preached in the Cathedral of Edinburgh, October the 14ᵗʰ, At the Anniversary Commemoration of his Majesties Birth* (London, 1687).

Robert MacWard, *The Case of the Accommodation lately proposed by the Bishop of Dunblane to Non-conforming Ministers examined* ([Rotterdam], 1671).

———, *The True Non-Conformist in Answere to the Modest and free Conference Betwixt a Conformist and a Non-Conformist About the present Distempers of Scotland* (n.p., 1671).

James Maidment ed., *The Spottiswoode Miscellany: A Collection of original Papers and Tracts, illustrative chiefly of the Civil and Ecclesiastical History of Scotland, Volume 1* (Edinburgh, 1844).

[John Maxwell], *Sacro-Sancta Regum Majestas; Or, The Sacred and Royall Prerogative of Christian Kings* (Oxford, 1644).

Henry W. Meikle ed., 'An Edinburgh Diary 1687–1688', *The Book of the Old Edinburgh Club*, 27 (1949), pp. 111–54.

William Melville ed., *Letters and State papers chiefly addressed to George, Earl of Melville, Secretary of State for Scotland 1689–91* (Edinburgh, 1843).

W. E. Knowles Middleton ed., *Lorenzo Magalotti at the Court of Charles II* (Waterloo, Ont., 1980).

Alexander Monro, *Sermons Preached upon Several Occasions: (Most of them) Before the Magistrates and Judges in the North-East Auditory of S. Giles's Church Edinburgh* (London, 1693).

[Thomas Morer], *An Account of the Present Persecution of the Church of Scotland, in Several Letters* (London, 1690).

————, *The Prelatical Church-Man, against the Phanatical Kirk-Man, or a Vindication of the Author of the Sufferings of the Church of Scotland* (London, 1690).

————, *A Short Account of Scotland* (London, 1702).

[Alexander Mudie], *Scotiæ Indiculum: or the Present State of Scotland. Together with divers Reflections on the Antient State thereof* (London, 1682).

Sir Thomas Murray, *The Laws and Acts of Parliament made by King James the First . . . [to] King Charles the Second Who now presently Reigns, Kings and Queens of Scotland, Collected, and Extracted, from the Publick Records of the said Kingdom, by Sir Thomas Murray of Glendook* (Edinburgh, 1681).

Mark Napier ed., *Memoirs of the Marquis of Montrose*, 2 vols. (Edinburgh, 1856).

John Nicoll, *A Diary of Publick Transactions and other Occurrences chiefly in Scotland. From January 1650 to June 1667*, David Laing ed. (Edinburgh, 1836).

Roger North, *Examen: Or, An Enquiry into the Credit and Veracity of a Pretended Complete History: Showing the Perverse and Wicked Design of it, and the Many Falsities and Abuses of Truth contained in it: Together with some Memoirs Originally inserted* (London, 1740).

James Paterson, *A Geographical Description of Scotland* (Edinburgh, 1681).

John Paterson, *Post nubila Phoebus. Or, A Sermon of Thanksgiving For the safe and happy return of our gracious Soveraign, to his Ancient Dominions, and Restauration to His just and Native Dignity, Royalties and Government* (Aberdeen, 1660).

————, *A Brief Resolution of the Present Case of the Subjects of Scotland. In Order to Episcopal Government, by Sacred Authority re-established in this Kingdom. Or Episcopus Scotus Redivius* ([London], 1661).

————, *Tandem Bona Causa Triumphat, Or Scotlands Late Misery bewailed, and the Honour and Loyalty of this Ancient Kingdom, asserted in a Sermon preached before His Majesties High Commissioner, and the Honourable Parliament of the Kingdom of Scotland. At Edinburgh, the 17 day of February, 1661* (Edinburgh, 1661).

Samuel Pepys, *The Diary of Samuel Pepys 1660–1669*, R. C. Latham and W. Matthews ed., 10 vols. (London, 1970–83).

John M. Pinkerton ed., *The Minute Book of the Faculty of Advocates, Volume 1, 1661–1712* (Edinburgh, 1976).

The Privy Council of Scotland's Letter to the King, together with the Arch-bishops and Bishops: As also several English addresses to his Majesty (Edinburgh, 1685).

Samuel Pufendorf, *An Introduction to the History of the Principal Kingdoms and States of Europe* (second edition, London, 1697).

J[ames] R[amsay], *Moses Returned from Midian: Or, God's Kindnesse to a Banished King: His Office and his Subjects Duty* (Edinburgh, 1660).

Register of the Privy Council of Scotland. Third Series. I (1661–1664), P. Hume Brown ed. (Edinburgh, 1908).

————, *Third Series. III (1669–1672)*, P. Hume Brown ed. (Edinburgh, 1910).

————, *Third Series. VI (1678–1680)*, P. Hume Brown ed. (Edinburgh, 1914).

————, *Third Series. VIII (1683–1684)*, P. Hume Brown ed. (Glasgow, 1915).

————, *Third Series. Volume XIV: 1689*, H. Paton ed. (Edinburgh, 1933).

[Robert Reid], *The Account of the Popes Procession at Aberdene, the 11ᵗʰ of January 1689 which was delivered to the new Elected Magistrates and Council thereby, by the Students of Marischal-Colledge, with the Students Letter to the said Magistrates thereanent* ([Aberdeen], 1689).

R. Renwick ed., *Extracts from the Records of the Royal Burgh of Stirling A.D. 1519–1666* (Glasgow, 1887).

Stephen Rigaud ed., *Correspondence of Scientific Men of the Seventeenth Century, Including Letters of Barrow, Flamsteed, Wallis and Newton, Printed from the Originals*, 2 vols. (Oxford, 1841).

Alexander Rose, *A Sermon Preached before the Right Honourable the Lords Commissioners of his Majesties most Honourable Privy Council at Glasgow* (Glasgow, 1684).

[Gilbert Rule], *An Answer to Dr. Stillingfleet's Irenicum: By a Learned Pen* (London, 1680).

[Samuel Rutherford], *Lex, Rex: The Law and the Prince. A Dispute for the just Prerogative of King and People &c.* (London, 1644).

['J. S.'], *Scotch Politicks, In a Letter to a Friend* (London, 1682).

William L. Sasche ed., *The Diurnal of Thomas Rugg 1659–1661* (London, 1961).

Andrew Murray Scott ed., 'Letters of John Grahame of Claverhouse', *Miscellany of the Scottish History Society XI* (Edinburgh, 1990), pp. 135–268.

[George Scott], *The Model Of the Government Of the Province of East-New-Jersey in America; And Encouragements for such as Design to be concerned there* (Edinburgh, 1685).

George Scott ed., *The Memoires of Sir James Melvil of Hal-Hill; Containing an Impartial Account of the most remarkable Affairs of State* (London, 1683).

Sir Walter Scott ed., *A Collection of Scarce and Valuable Tracts on the more interesting and entertaining Subjects, but chiefly such as relate to the History and Constitution of these Kingdoms. Selected . . . [from the library] of the late Lord Somers*, 13 vols. (London, 1809–15).

————, *The Antiquary*, David Hewitt ed. (Edinburgh, 1995).

Henry Scougal, *The Life of God in the Soul of Man: Or, the Nature and Excellency of the Christian Religion. With the Methods of attaining the Happiness which it proposes. Also An Account of the Beginnings and Advances of a Spiritual Life. With a Preface by Gilbert Burnet, now Lord Bishop of Sarum* (London, 1707).

————, *The Works of the Reverend Mr. Henry Scougal. Professor of Divinity in the King's-College, Aberdeen* (Aberdeen, 1761).

Alexander Scrougie, *Mirabilia Dei, or Britannia Gaudio Exultans. Opened in a Congratulatory Sermon for the safe Return of our Gracious Soveraign and happy*

Restitution to the full and free exercise of His Royall Authoritie Preached on the 14th June, 1660 (Edinburgh, 1660).

[Francis Sempill], *A Discourse between Law and Conscience, When they were both Banished from Parliament. In the first Parliament of K. James the Seventh* ([Edinburgh], 1685]).

Charles Sharpe ed., *Memorialls: Or, the Memorable Things that fell out within this Island of Britain from 1638 to 1684, by the Rev. Mr. Robert Law* (Edinburgh, 1818).

———, *Letters from the Lady Margaret Kennedy to John, Duke of Lauderdale* (Edinburgh, 1828).

[William Sherlock], *A Letter to a Member of the Convention of States in Scotland. By a Lover of his Religion and Country* ([Edinburgh], 1689).

[Alexander Shields], *A Hind let loose: Or, An Historical Representation of the Testimonies of the Church of Scotland for the Interest of Christ; With the true State thereof in all its Periods* ([Edinburgh], 1687).

Michael Shields, *Faithful Contendings Displayed: being An historical relation of the State and Actings of the Suffering Remnant in the Church of Scotland, who subsisted in Select Societies, and were united in general correspondencies during the hottest time of the late Persecution, viz. From the year 1681 to 1691* (Glasgow, 1780).

Sir Robert Sibbald, *An Account of the Scottish Atlas. Or the Description of Scotland Ancient and Modern* (Edinburgh, 1683).

———, *The Memoirs of Sir Robert Sibbald (1641–1722)*, Francis Hett ed. (Oxford, 1932).

George Sinclair, *Hydrostaticks: Or, The Weights, Force, and Pressure of Fluid Bodies, Made evident by Physical and Sensible Experiments* (Edinburgh, 1672).

———, *Satan's Invisible World Discovered, Or, A choice collection of Modern Relations; proving evidently against the Saducees and Atheists of this present Age, that there are Devils, Spirits, Witches, and Apparitions from Authentick Records, Attestations of Famous Witnesses, and undoubted Veracity* (Edinburgh, 1685).

Alexander Skene, *Plain and Peaceable Advice to Those called Presbyterians in Scotland* (London, 1681).

———, *Memorialls for the Government of the Royall Burghs in Scotland* (Aberdeen, 1685).

William Skene ed., *John of Fordun's Chronicle of the Scottish Nation*, 2 vols. (Lampeter, 1993).

[James Steuart], *Jus Populi Vindicatum. Or, The People's Right to Defend Themselves and their Covenanted Religion* ([Edinburgh], 1669).

———, *An Accompt of Scotlands Grievances By reason of the D. of Lauderdales Ministrie, Humbly tendred to his sacred Majesty* ([?Edinburgh], 1672).

[James Steuart and John Stirling], *Naphtali, Or the Wrestlings of the Church of Scotland for the Kingdom of Christ; Contained in A true and short Deduction thereof, from the beginning of the Reformation of Religion, until the Year 1667* ([Edinburgh], 1667).

Gilbert Stuart, *Observations concerning the Public Law, and the Constitutional History of Scotland, with Occasional Remarks concerning English Antiquity* (Edinburgh, 1779).

J. Stuart ed., 'Letters to Dr. James Fraser M.DC.LXXIX–M.DC.LXXXIX', *The Miscellany of the Spalding Club. Volume Fifth* (Aberdeen, 1852), pp. 195–290.

James Sutherland, *Hortus Medicus Edinburgensis, or a Catalogue of all the Plants in the Physic Garden at Edinburgh* (Edinburgh, 1683).

Matthias Symson, *Mephiboseth; or, the Lively Picture of a Loyal Subject* (Edinburgh, 1660).

———, *Yehoveh ve Melek, or God and the King. Being the Good Old Cause. As it was stated and discussed in a Sermon preached before his Majesties High Commissioners, and the Honourable Estates of the Parliament of the Kingdome of Scotland, at Edinburgh, on the 17th day of March 1661* (London, 1661).

Jeremy Taylor, *Doctor Dubitantium, or Rule of Conscience* (London, 1660).

C. Sandford Terry ed., *The Cromwellian Union: Papers Relating to the Negotiations for an Incorporating Union Between England and Scotland 1651–1652, with an Appendix of Papers Relating to the Negotiations in 1670* (Edinburgh, 1902).

The Addres [sic] of the University of St. Andrews to the King (London, 1689).

The Manner of Procession to the Parliament-House of Scotland with His Majesties Letter to the Parliament; the Lord High Commissioner's Speech, the Lord High Chancellor's Speech, and the Parliament's Answer (Dublin, 1685).

Thomas Thomson and Cosmo Innes eds., *The Acts of the Parliament of Scotland*, 12 vols. (Edinburgh, 1814–75).

Sir James Turner, *Pallas Armata. Military Essayes of the Ancient Grecian, Roman and Modern Art of War. Written in the Years 1670 and 1671. By Sir James Turner Knight* (London, 1683).

———, *Memoirs of his own Life and Times by Sir James Turner, M.DC.XXXII–M.DC.LXX*, Thomas Thomson ed. (Edinburgh, 1829).

Sir Thomas Urquhart, *Logopandecteision, Or an Introduction to the Universal Language* (London, 1653).

———, *The Jewel*, R. D. S. Jack and R. J. Lyall eds. (Edinburgh, 1983).

[William Violant], *A Review and Examination of a Book bearing the Title of the History of the Indulgence* (London, 1681).

Robert Wodrow, *The History of the Sufferings of the Church of Scotland, from the Restoration to the Revolution*, Robert Burns ed., 4 vols. (Glasgow, 1828–30).

Anthony à Wood, *The Life and Times of Anthony à Wood, antiquary of Oxford, described by Himself, Volume III: 1682–1685*, A. Clark ed. (Oxford, 1894), p. 96.

Printed Secondary Sources

Ian Adams and Meredyth Sommerville, *Cargoes of Hope and Despair: Scottish Emigration to North America, 1603–1805* (Edinburgh, 1993).

David Allan, 'Prudence and Patronage: The Politics of Culture in Seventeenth Century Scotland', *History of European Ideas*, 18 (1994), pp. 467–80.

———, 'Reconciliation and Retirement in the Restoration Scottish Church: The Neostoicism of Robert Leighton', *Journal of Ecclesiastical History*, 50 (1999), pp. 251–78.

————, *Philosophy and Politics in Later Stuart Scotland: Neostoicism, Culture and Ideology in an Age of Crisis 1540–1690* (East Linton, 2000).

David Allen, 'Political Clubs in Restoration London', *Historical Journal*, 19 (1976), pp. 561–80.

Ronald Asch ed., *Three Nations? – A Common History?* (Bochum, 1992).

D. Benson, 'Who bred *Religio Laici*?', *Journal of English and Germanic Philology*, 65 (1966), pp. 238–51.

Craig Beveridge and Ronnie Turnbull, *Scotland after Enlightenment. Image and Tradition in Modern Scottish Culture* (Edinburgh, 1997).

Ian Bostridge, *Witchcraft and its Transformations, c.1650–c.1750* (Oxford, 1997).

Brendan Bradshaw and John Morrill eds., *The British Problem, c.1534–1707. State Formation in the Atlantic Archipelago* (Basingstoke, 1996).

Brendan Bradshaw and Peter Roberts eds., *British consciousness and identity. The making of Britain, 1533–1707* (Cambridge, 1998).

Keith Brown, *Kingdom or Province? Scotland and the Regal Union 1603–1715* (Basingstoke, 1992).

————, 'The vanishing emperor: British kingship and its decline 1603–1707', in Mason ed., *Scots and Britons*, pp. 58–87.

Peter Hume Brown, *History of Scotland*, 3 vols. (Cambridge, 1899–1909).

S. Bruce and S. Yearley, 'The Social Construction of Tradition: The Holyrood Portraits and the Kings of Scotland', in David McCrone, Stephen Kendrick and Pat Straw eds., *The Making of Scotland: Nation, Culture and Social Change* (Edinburgh, 1989), pp. 175–87.

Henry Buckle, *History of Civilisation in England*, 2 vols. (London, 1857–61).

Julia Buckroyd, 'The Dismissal of Archbishop Alexander Burnet, 1669', *Records of the Scottish Church History Society*, 18 (1973), pp. 149–55.

————, '*Mercurius Caledonius* and its immediate successors, 1661', *Scottish Historical Review*, 54 (1975), pp. 11–21.

————, 'The Resolutioners and the Scottish Nobility in the early months of 1660', *Studies in Church History*, 12 (1975), pp. 245–52.

————, *Church and State in Scotland 1660–1681* (Edinburgh, 1980).

————, 'Anticlericalism in Scotland during the Restoration', in *Norman Macdougall ed., Church, Politics and Society: Scotland 1408–1929* (Edinburgh, 1983), pp. 167–85.

————, *The Life of Archbishop James Sharp: A Political Biography* (Edinburgh, 1987).

Glenn Burgess, *Absolute Monarchy and the Stuart Constitution* (New Haven, 1996).

————, 'Scottish or British? Politics and Political Thought in Scotland, c.1500–1707', *Historical Journal*, 41 (1998), pp. 579–90.

————, ed., *The New British History. Founding a Modern State 1603–1714* (London, 1999).

Peter Burke, 'Tacitism, scepticism and reason of state', in J. H. Burns and Mark Goldie eds., *The Cambridge History of Political Thought 1450–1700* (Cambridge, 1991), pp. 479–98.

Charles J. Burnett and Helen Bennett, *The Green Mantle: A Celebration of the Revival in 1687 of the Most Ancient and Most Noble Order of the Thistle* (Edinburgh, 1987).

J. H. Burns, 'George Buchanan and the antimonarchomachs', in Mason ed., *Scots and Britons*, pp. 138–58.

———, *The True Law of Kingship. Concepts of Monarchy in Early Modern Scotland* (Oxford, 1996).

John Hill Burton, *The History of Scotland from Agricola's Invasion to The Extinction of the last Jacobite Insurrection*, 8 vols. (Edinburgh, 1873).

John W. Cairns, 'Institutional Writings in Scotland Reconsidered', in Albert Kiralfy and Hector L. MacQueen eds., *New Perspectives in Scottish Legal History* (London, 1984), pp. 76–117.

———, 'Sir George Mackenzie, the Faculty of Advocates and the Advocates' Library', in Sir George Mackenzie, *Oratio Inauguralis in Aperienda Jurisconsultorum*, John W. Cairns and A. Cain eds. (Edinburgh, 1989), pp. 18–35.

———, 'Scottish Law, Scottish Lawyers and the Status of the Union', in Robertson ed., *A Union for Empire*, pp. 243–68.

———, 'Importing our Lawyers from Holland: Netherlands Influences on Scots Law and Lawyers in the Eighteenth Century', in Grant G. Simpson ed., *Scotland and the Low Countries 1124–1994* (East Linton, 1996), pp. 136–53.

———, 'The Civilian Tradition in Scottish Legal Thought', in David L. Carey Miller and Reinhard Zimmermann eds., *The Civilian Tradition and Scots Law* (Berlin, 1997), pp. 191–223.

———, 'Historical Introduction', in Kenneth Reid and Reinhard Zimmerman eds., *A History of Private Law in Scotland*, 2 vols. (Oxford, 2000), pp. 14–184.

———, 'The Moveable Text of Mackenzie: Bibliographical Problems for the Scottish Concept of Institutional Writing', in John W. Cairns and Olivia F. Robinson eds., *Critical Studies in Ancient Law, Comparative Law and Legal History* (Oxford, 2000), pp. 235–48.

A. Cameron, 'Theatre in Scotland 1660–1800', in Andrew Hook ed., *The History of Scottish Literature. Volume 2: 1660–1800* (Aberdeen, 1987), pp. 191–204.

James Cameron, 'A Bibliography of Slezer's *Theatrum Scotiæ*', *Papers of the Edinburgh Bibliographical Society*, 3 (1895–8), pp. 141–7.

R. H. Carnie, 'The Campbeltown Declaration and its Printer', *The Bibliotheck*, 10 (1980), pp. 59–67.

Keith Cavers, *A Vision of Scotland: The Nation observed by John Slezer 1671–1717* (Edinburgh, 1993).

J. S. Clarke, *The Life of James the Second, King of England, &c. Collected out of Memoirs writ of his own hand. Together with the King's Advice to his Son, and his Majesty's Will*, 2 vols. (London, 1816).

William Couper, *The Edinburgh Periodical Press*, 2 vols. (Stirling, 1908).

———, 'Mrs Anderson and the Royal Prerogative in Printing', *Proceedings of the Royal Philosophical Society of Glasgow*, 48 (1916–17), pp. 79–102.

E. Cowan, 'Myth and Identity in early medieval Scotland', *Scottish Historical Review*, 53 (1984), pp. 111–35.

Ian B. Cowan, 'The Five Articles of Perth', in Duncan Shaw ed., *Reformation and Revolution* (Edinburgh, 1967), pp. 160–77.

———, 'The Covenanters: A Revision Article', *Scottish Historical Review*, 47 (1968), pp. 35–52.

———, *The Scottish Covenanters 1660–1688* (London, 1976).

———, 'The Reluctant Revolutionaries: Scotland in 1688', in Eveline Cruikshanks ed., *By Force or by Default? The Revolution of 1688–89* (Edinburgh, 1989), pp. 65–81.

————, 'Church and state reformed? The Revolution of 1688–89 in Scotland', in Jonathan I. Israel ed., *The Anglo-Dutch Moment: Essays on the Glorious Revolution and its World Impact* (Cambridge, 1991), pp. 163–83.

John M. Cowan, 'The History of the Royal Botanic Garden, Edinburgh', *Notes from the Royal Botanic Garden Edinburgh*, 19 (1933–8), pp. 1–62.

William Cowan, 'The Holyrood Press, 1686–1688', *Edinburgh Bibliographic Society Transactions*, 6 (1904), pp. 83–100.

Godfrey Davies and Paul H. Hardacre, 'The Restoration of the Scottish Episcopacy, 1660–1661', *Journal of British Studies*, 1 (1960), pp. 32–51.

David Dobson, *Scottish Emigration to Colonial America 1607–1785* (Athens, Ga., 1994).

R. Douglas, 'An Account of the Foundation of the Leightonian Library', in *The Bannatyne Miscellany: Containing Original Papers and Tracts, chiefly Relating to the History and Literature of Scotland. Volume II* (Edinburgh, 1855).

Carolyn A. Edie, 'Right Rejoicing: Sermons on the Occasion of the Stuart Restoration, 1660', *Bulletin of the John Rylands University of Manchester*, 62 (1979–80), pp. 61–86.

Steven Ellis and Sarah Barber eds., *Conquest and Union: Fashioning a British State, 1485–1720* (Harlow, 1995).

Roger L. Emerson, 'The religious, the secular and the worldly: Scotland 1680–1800', in James E. Crimmins ed., *Religion, Secularization and Political Thought* (London, 1989), pp. 68–89.

————, 'Science and Moral Philosophy in the Scottish Enlightenment', in M. A. Stewart ed., *Oxford Studies in the History of Philosophy. Volume 1* (Oxford, 1990).

————, 'Scottish Cultural Change 1660–1707 and the Union of 1707', in Robertson ed., *A Union for Empire*, pp. 121–44.

George Eyre-Todd, *History of Glasgow. Volume II: From the Reformation to the Revolution* (Glasgow, 1931).

Robert Feenstra, 'Scottish-Dutch Legal relations in the 17th and 18th centuries', in Hilde de Ridder Symoens and John M. Fletcher eds., *Academic Relations between the Low Countries and the British Isles 1450–1700* (Ghent, 1989), pp. 25–45.

William Ferguson, *The Identity of the Scottish Nation. An Historic Quest* (Edinburgh, 1998).

C. P. Finlayson, 'Edinburgh University and the Darien Scheme', *Scottish Historical Review*, 34 (1955), pp. 97–102.

H. Fisher ed., *The Collected Papers of Frederic William Maitland*, 3 vols. (Cambridge, 1911).

John Ford, 'Conformity in Conscience: The Structure of the Perth Articles Debate in Scotland 1618–38', *Journal of Ecclesiastical History*, 46 (1995), pp. 256–77.

Robert von Friedeburg, 'From collective representation to the rights of individual defence: James Steuart's *Ius Populi Vindicatum* and the use of Johannes Althusius' *Politica* in Restoration Scotland', *History of European Ideas*, 24 (1998), pp. 19–42.

Linda G. Fryer, 'Robert Barclay of Ury and East New Jersey', *Northern Scotland*, 15 (1995), pp. 1–17.

Johanna Geyer-Kordesch and Fiona Macdonald, *Physicians and Surgeons in*

Glasgow. The History of the Royal College of Physicians and Surgeons in Glasgow, 2 vols. (Hambledon, 1999).

Mark Goldie, 'Edmund Bohun and *Jus Gentium* in the Revolution Debate 1689–1693', *Historical Journal*, 20 (1977), pp. 569–86.

——, 'The Revolution of 1689 and the Structure of Political Argument', *Bulletin of Research in the Humanities*, 83 (1980), pp. 473–564.

——, 'John Locke and Anglican Royalism', *Political Studies*, 31 (1983), pp. 61–85.

——, 'Sir Peter Pett, Sceptical Toryism and the Science of Toleration in the 1680s', in W. J. Shiels ed., *Persecution and Toleration* (Oxford, 1984), pp. 247–73.

——, 'The Political Thought of the Anglican Revolution', in Robert Beddard ed., *The Revolutions of 1688* (Oxford, 1991), pp. 102–36.

——, 'The Earliest Attack on John Locke's *Two Treatises of Government*', *Locke Newsletter* (1999), pp. 73–84.

Julian Goodare, 'The Estates in the Scottish Parliament, 1286–1707', *Parliamentary History*, 15 (1996), pp. 11–32.

J. W. Gough, *Fundamental Law in English Constitutional History* (Oxford, 1961).

P. Gouldesborough, 'An Attempted Scottish Voyage to New York in 1669', *Scottish Historical Review*, 40 (1961), pp. 56–62.

Alexander Grant and Keith Stringer eds., *Uniting the Kingdom: The Enigma of British History* (London, 1995).

James Grant, *Cassell's Old and New Edinburgh*, 3 vols. (London, [*c*.1890]).

John Grant, 'Archibald Hislop, Stationer, Edinburgh, 1688–1678', *Papers of the Edinburgh Bibliographical Society*, 12 (1921–5), pp. 35–51.

W. H. Greenleaf, 'Filmer's Patriarchal History', *Historical Journal*, 9 (1966), pp. 157–71.

Richard L. Harris, 'Janet Douglas and the Witches of Pollock: The Background of Scepticism in Scotland in the 1670s', in S. R. McKenna ed., *Selected Essays on Scottish Language and Literature* (Lampeter, 1992), pp. 97–124.

Tim Harris, *Politics under the Later Stuarts: Party Conflict in a Divided Society 1660–1715* (Harlow, 1993).

——, ' "Reluctant Revolutionaries": The Scots and the Revolution of 1688–89', in Howard Nenner ed., *Politics and the Political Imagination in Later Stuart Britain* (Rochester, NY, 1997), pp. 97–117.

——, 'What's New about the Restoration?', *Albion*, 29 (1997), pp. 187–222.

——, 'Critical Perspectives: The Autonomy of British History?' in Burgess ed., *The New British History*, pp. 266–86.

——, 'The People, the Law and the Constitution in Scotland and England: A Comparative Approach to the Glorious Revolution', *Journal of British Studies*, 38 (1999), pp. 25–58.

Daniela Havenstein, ' "In imitation of Dr Brown's *Religio Medici*?" *Religio Bibliopolæ* and the New Practice of Piety', *Notes & Queries* (March 1995), pp. 52–4.

——, '*Religio* Writing in Seventeenth-Century England and Scotland: Sir Thomas Browne's *Religio Medici* (1643) and Sir George Mackenzie's *Religio Stoici* (1663)', *Scottish Literary Journal*, 25 (1998), pp. 17–33.

Harro Höpfl, 'From Savage to Scotsman: Conjectural History in the Scottish Enlightenment', *Journal of British Studies*, 17 (1978), pp. 19–40.

K. Theodore Hoppen, *The Common Scientist in the Seventeenth Century: A Study of the Dublin Philosophical Society 1683–1708* (London, 1970).

David Howarth, 'Sculpture and Scotland 1540–1700', in Fiona Pearson ed., *Virtue and Vision: Sculpture and Scotland 1540–1990* (Edinburgh, 1991).

Elizabeth H. Hyman, 'A Church Militant: Scotland 1661–1690', *Sixteenth Century Journal*, 26 (1995), pp. 49–74.

George Pratt Insh, *Scottish Colonial Schemes 1620–1686* (Glasgow, 1922).

Jonathan Israel, *Radical Enlightenment. Philosophy and the Making of Modernity 1650–1750* (Oxford, 2001).

Clare Jackson, 'The Paradoxical Virtue of the Historical Romance: Sir George Mackenzie's *Aretina* (1660) and the Civil Wars', in John R. Young ed., *Celtic Dimensions of the British Civil Wars* (Edinburgh, 1997), pp. 205–25.

———, 'Restoration to Revolution', in Burgess ed., *The New British History*, pp. 92–114.

———, 'Natural Law and the Construction of Political Sovereignty in Scotland 1660–1690', in Ian Hunter and David Saunders eds., *Natural Law and Civil Sovereignty: Moral Right and State Authority in Early Modern Political Thought* (Basingstoke, 2002), pp. 155–69.

———, 'Revolution Principles, *Ius Naturae* and *Ius Gentium* in early Enlightenment Scotland: the contribution of Sir Francis Grant, Lord Cullen (*c.*1660–1726)', in Tim Hochstrasser and Peter Schröder eds., *Early Modern Natural Law Theories: Contexts and Strategies in the Early Enlightenment* (forthcoming).

David Martin Jones, *Conscience and Allegiance in Seventeenth Century England. The Political Significance of Oaths and Engagements* (Rochester, NY, 1999).

Alexander Keith, *A Thousand Years of Aberdeen* (Aberdeen, 1972).

J. P. Kenyon, *Revolution Principles: The Politics of Party 1689–1720* (second edition, Cambridge, 1990).

Colin Kidd, *Subverting Scotland's Past. Scottish Whig Historians and the Creation of an Anglo-British Identity c.1689–c.1830* (Cambridge, 1993).

———, 'Religious realignment between the Restoration and Union', in Robertson ed., *A Union for Empire*, pp. 145–68.

Phil Kilroy, *Protestant Dissent and Controversy in Ireland 1660–1714* (Cork, 1994).

Mark Knight, 'London's "Monster Petition" of 1680', *Historical Journal*, 36 (1993), pp. 39–67.

Ned Landsman, *Scotland and its first American Colony 1683–1785* (Princeton, 1985).

———, 'Nation, Migration and the Province in the First British Empire: Scotland and the Americas 1600–1800', *American Historical Review*, 104 (1999), pp. 463–75.

Christina Larner, *Enemies of God: The Witch-hunt in Scotland* (Oxford, 1981).

Bruce Lenman, 'The Scottish Episcopal Clergy and the Ideology of Jacobitism', in Eveline Cruikshanks ed., *Ideology and Conspiracy: Aspects of Jacobitism 1689–1759* (Edinburgh, 1982), pp. 36–48.

———, 'The poverty of political theory in the Scottish Revolution of 1688–90', in Lois Schwoerer ed., *Changing Perspectives on the Revolution of 1688–89* (Cambridge, 1992), pp. 244–59.

————, 'Militia, Fencible Men, and Home Defence, 1660–1797', in Norman Macdougall ed., *Scotland and War A.D. 79–1918* (Edinburgh, 1991), pp. 170–92.

Brian P. Levack, 'The Great Scottish Witch-hunt of 1661–1662', *Journal of British Studies*, 20 (1980), pp. 90–108.

John Gibson Lockhart, *The Life of Sir Walter Scott*, 10 vols. (London, 1902–3).

Harold Love, *Scribal Publication in Seventeenth-Century England* (Oxford, 1993).

Michael Lynch, 'Response: Old Games and New', *Scottish Historical Review*, 73 (1994), pp. 47–63.

Thomas B. Macaulay, *The History of England from the Accession of James II*, 2 vols. (London, 1849).

Iain MacIvor and Bent Petersen, 'Lauderdale at Holyroodhouse, 1669–70', in David J. Breeze ed., *Studies in Scottish Antiquity, Presented to Stewart Cruden* (Edinburgh, 1984), pp. 249–68.

Æ. J. G. Mackay, *Memoir of Sir James Dalrymple, First Viscount Stair* (Edinburgh, 1873).

Aonghus MacKechnie, 'Housing Scotland's Parliament, 1603–1707', *Parliamentary History*, 21 (2002), pp. 99–130.

D. F. Mackenzie, 'Speech-Manuscript-Print', *Library Chronicle*, 20 (1990), pp. 87–109.

W. C. Mackenzie, *The Life and Times of John Maitland, Duke of Lauderdale (1616–1682)* (London, 1923).

D. Maclean, 'Roman Catholicism in Scotland during the Reign of Charles II', *Records of the Scottish Church History Society*, 3 (1929), pp. 43–54.

E. J. MacRae, 'Charles II. Statue, Parliament Square', *Book of the Old Edinburgh Club*, 17 (1930), pp. 82–90.

Alastair J. Mann, 'Book Commerce, Litigation and the Art of Monopoly: The Case of Agnes Campbell, Royal Printer 1676–1712', *Scottish Economic and Social History*, 18 (1998), pp. 132–56.

————, *The Scottish Book Trade 1500–1720. Print Commerce and Print Control in Early Modern Scotland* (East Linton, 2000).

John Marshall, 'The Ecclesiology of the Latitude-Men 1660–1689: Stillingfleet, Tenison and "Hobbism" ', *Journal of Ecclesiastical History*, 36 (1985), pp. 407–27.

Roger Mason, 'Scotching the Brut: Politics, History and the National Myth of Origin in Sixteenth-Century Britain', in Roger Mason ed., *Scotland and England 1286–1815* (Edinburgh, 1987), pp. 60–84.

————, ed., *Scots and Britons. Political Thought and the Union of 1603* (Cambridge, 1994).

————, 'George Buchanan, James VI and the presbyterians', in Mason ed., *Scots and Britons*, pp. 112–37.

W. Matthews, 'The Egyptians in Scotland: The Political History of a Myth', *Viator*, 1 (1970), pp. 289–306.

Henry W. Meikle, *Some Aspects of Later Seventeenth Century Scotland* (Glasgow, 1947).

Friedrich Meinecke, *Machiavellism. The Doctrine of Raison d'Etat and its Place in Modern History*, Douglas Scott trans. (London, 1984).

Stan Mendyk, 'Scottish Regional Historians and the *Britannia* Project', *Scottish Geographical Magazine*, 101 (1985), pp. 165–73.

J. N. Moore, 'Scottish Cartography in the later Stuart era, 1660–1714', *Scottish Tradition*, 14 (1986–7), pp. 28–44.

Howard Nenner, *The Right to be King: The Succession to the Crown of England 1603–1714* (Basingstoke, 1995).

Jane Ohlmeyer ed., *Political Thought in Seventeenth-Century Ireland* (Cambridge, 2000).

Hugh Ouston, 'York in Edinburgh: James VII and the Patronage of Learning in Scotland 1679–1688', in John Dwyer, Roger Mason and Alexander Murdoch eds., *New Perspectives on the Culture and Society of Early Modern Scotland* (Edinburgh, 1982), pp. 135–55.

———, 'Cultural Life from the Restoration to the Union', in Andrew Hook ed., *The History of Scottish Literature. Volume 2: 1660–1800* (Aberdeen, 1987), pp. 11–32.

John Patrick, 'The Scottish Constitutional Opposition in 1679', *Scottish Historical Review*, 37 (1958), pp. 37–41.

———, 'The origins of the opposition to Lauderdale in the Scottish Parliament of 1673', *Scottish Historical Review*, 53 (1974), pp. 1–21.

A. Philp, 'Dr. Canaries: A Vicar of Bray', in A. Philp, *The Evangel in Gowrie* (Edinburgh, 1911), pp. 151–63.

Steve Pincus, ' "Coffee Politicians Does Create": Coffeehouses and Restoration Political Culture', *Journal of Modern History*, 67 (1995), pp. 807–34.

J. G. A. Pocock, 'British History: A Plea for a New Subject', *Journal of Modern History*, 47 (1975), pp. 601–28.

———, 'The limits and divisions of British History', *American Historical Review*, 87 (1982), pp. 311–34.

———, 'Texts as Events: Reflections on the History of Political Thought', in Kevin Sharpe and Stephen Zwicker eds., *Politics of Discourse: The Literature and History of Seventeenth-Century England* (Berkeley, 1987), pp. 21–34.

———, *The Ancient Constitution and the Feudal Law. A Study of English Historical Thought in the Seventeenth Century* (2nd edition, Cambridge, 1987).

———, 'Two kingdoms and three histories?: Political thought in British contexts', in Mason ed., *Scots and Britons*, pp. 293–312.

———, ed., *The Varieties of British Political Thought 1500–1800* (Cambridge, 1993).

———, 'Empire, state and Confederation: The War of American Independence as a Crisis in Multiple Monarchy', in Robertson ed., *A Union for Empire*, pp. 318–48.

Thomas I. Rae, 'The Origins of the Advocates' Library', in Patrick Cadell and Anne Matheson eds., *For the Encouragement of Learning: Scotland's National Library 1619–1989* (Edinburgh, 1989), pp. 1–22.

Alexander Robertson, *The Life of Sir Robert Moray. Soldier, Statesman and Man of Science (1608–1673)* (London, 1922).

John Robertson ed., *A Union for Empire. Political Thought and the Union of 1707* (Cambridge, 1995).

M. Rooseboom, *The Scottish Staple Port in the Netherlands* (The Hague, 1910).

John L. Russell, 'Cosmological Teaching in the Seventeenth-Century Scottish Universities', *Journal of the History of Astronomy*, 5 (1974), pp. 122–32 and 145–54.

J. H. M. Salmon, *The French Religious Wars and English Political Thought* (Oxford, 1959).

Lois Green Schwoerer, 'The Shape of Restoration England: A Response', in Howard Nenner ed., *Politics and the Political Imagination in Later Stuart England* (Rochester, NY, 1997), pp. 197–221.

Paul Seaward, 'Constitutional and Unconstitutional Royalism', *Historical Journal*, 40 (1997), pp. 227–39.

J. A. Sharpe, ' "Last Dying Speeches": Religion, Ideology and Public Execution in Seventeenth-Century England', *Past and Present*, 107 (1985), pp. 144–67.

A. D. C. Simpson, 'Sir Robert Sibbald – The Founder of the College', in R. Passmore ed., *Proceedings of the Royal College of Physicians of Edinburgh Tercentenary Congress 1981* (Edinburgh, 1982), pp. 59–91.

Allen Simpson, 'John Adair, cartographer and Sir Robert Sibbald's Atlas', *The Map Collector*, 62 (1993), pp. 32–6.

Grant G. Simpson, 'The Declaration of Arbroath revitalised', *Scottish Historical Review*, 56 (1977), pp. 11–33.

Murray Simpson, 'Some Aspects of Book Purchasing in Restoration Scotland: Two Letters from James Fall to the Earl of Tweeddale, May 1678', *Edinburgh Bibliographic Society Transactions*, 6 (1990), pp. 2–9.

A. Maclean Sinclair, *The Maclean Bards. Volume I* (Charlottetown, 1908).

Quentin Skinner, 'Meaning and Understanding in the History of Ideas', *History and Theory*, 9 (1969), pp. 1–69.

Adrienne Skullion, ' "Forget Scotland": Plays by Scots on the London stage', *Comparative Drama*, 31 (1997), pp. 105–28.

Iain M. Smart, 'The Political Ideas of the Scottish Covenanters 1638–1688', *History of Political Thought*, 1 (1980), pp. 167–93.

David L. Smith, *Constitutional Royalism and the Search for Settlement c.1640–1649* (Cambridge, 1994).

David Nichol Smith, *Dryden* (Cambridge, 1950).

J. Smith, 'Dalry House: Its Land and Owners', *Book of the Old Edinburgh Club*, 20 (1935), pp. 26–66.

T. C. Smout, 'The Road to Union', in Geoffrey Holmes ed., *Britain after the Glorious Revolution* (London, 1969), pp. 176–96.

Jim Smyth, *The Making of the United Kingdom 1660–1800* (Harlow, 2001).

John Spurr, 'Latitudinarianism and the Restoration Church', *Historical Journal*, 31 (1988), pp. 61–82.

———, ' "Rational Religion" in Restoration England', *Journal of the History of Ideas*, 49 (1988), pp. 563–85.

———, *The Restoration Church of England, 1646–1689* (New Haven, 1991).

David Stevenson, ' "The Letter on Sovereign Power" and the Influence of Jean Bodin on Political Thought in Scotland', *Scottish Historical Review*, 61 (1982), pp. 25–43.

———, 'Masonry, symbolism and ethics in the life of Sir Robert Moray FRS', *Proceedings of the Society of Antiquaries in Scotland*, 114 (1984), pp. 405–31.

———, *The Origins of Freemasonry. Scotland's Century, 1590–1710* (Cambridge, 1988).

———, 'Twilight before night or darkness before dawn? Interpreting seventeenth-century Scotland', in Rosalind Mitchison ed., *Why Scottish History Matters* (Edinburgh, 1991), pp. 37–47.

D. Stewart, 'The Aberdeen Doctors and the Covenanters', *Records of the Scottish Church History Society*, 22 (1984), pp. 35–44.

Gerald Straka, *Anglican Reaction to the Revolution of 1688* (Madison, 1962).

James Sutherland, *The Restoration Newspaper and its Development* (Cambridge, 1985).

Martyn P. Thompson, 'The History of Fundamental Law in Political Thought from the French Wars of Religion to the American Revolution', *American Historical Review*, 91 (1986), pp. 1103–28.

Richard S. Thompson, *Islands of Law: A Legal History of the British Isles* (New York, 2000).

Terence Tobin, 'Plays presented in Scotland, 1660–1705', *Restoration and Eighteenth-Century Theatre Research*, 12 (1973), pp. 51–9.

———, *Plays by Scots 1660–1800* (Iowa, 1974).

Hugh Trevor-Roper, 'George Buchanan and the Ancient Scottish Constitution', *English Historical Review Supplement 3* (1966).

———, 'The Scottish Enlightenment', *Studies on Voltaire and the Eighteenth Century*, 63 (1967), pp. 1635–58.

James Tully ed., *Meaning and Context: Quentin Skinner and his Critics* (Cambridge, 1988).

H. Turnbull, 'Early Scottish Relations with the Royal Society', *Royal Society Notes and Records*, 3 (1940–1), pp. 27–38.

Brian Vickers ed., *Public and Private Life in the Seventeenth Century: The Mackenzie-Evelyn Debate* (New York, 1986).

Alan Watson, 'Some Notes on Mackenzie's *Institutions* and the European Legal Tradition', *Ius Commune: Zeitschrift für Europäische Rechtsgeschichte*, 16 (1989), pp. 303–13.

Sheila Williams, 'The Pope-Burning Processions of 1679. 1680 and 1681', *Journal of the Warburg and Courtauld Institutes*, 21 (1958), pp. 104–18.

Arthur H. Williamson, *Scottish National Consciousness in the Age of James VI: The Apocalypse, the Union and the Shaping of Scotland's Political Culture* (Edinburgh, 1979).

Robert Willmann, 'Blackstone and the "Theoretical Perfection" of English Law in the Reign of Charles II', *Historical Journal*, 26 (1983), pp. 39–70.

Charles W. J. Withers, 'How Scotland came to know itself: geography, national identity and the making of a nation 1680–1790', *Journal of Historical Geography*, 21 (1995), pp. 371–97.

———, 'Geography, Science and National Identity in Early Modern Britain: The Case of Scotland and the Work of Sir Robert Sibbald (1641–1722)', *Annals of Science*, 53 (1996), pp. 29–73.

———, *Geography, Science and National Identity: Scotland since 1520* (Cambridge, 2001).

Jenny Wormald, *Lords and Men in Scotland: Bonds of Manrent, 1442–1603* (Edinburgh, 1985).

G. M. Yould, 'The Duke of Lauderdale's Religious Policy in Scotland, 1668–79. The Failure of Conciliation and the Return to Coercion', *Journal of Religious History*, 11 (1980), pp. 248–68.

R. M. Young, 'News from Ireland: Being the Examination and Confession of William Kelso, 1679', *Ulster Journal of Archaeology*, 2 (1895), pp. 274–9.

Unpublished Dissertations

Kathleen M. Colquhoun, ' "Issue of the Late Civill Wars": James, Duke of York and the Government of Scotland 1679–1689' (University of Illinois at Urbana-Champaign, Ph.D. dissertation, 1993).

Georgina J. Gardner, 'The Scottish Exile Community in the United Provinces, 1660–1690' (University of Oxford, D.Phil. dissertation, 1998).

G. W. Iredell, 'The Law, Custom and Practice of the Parliament of Scotland with particular reference to the period 1660–1707' (University of London, Ph.D. dissertation, 1966).

Ronald Lee, 'Government and Politics in Scotland 1661–1681' (University of Glasgow, Ph.D. dissertation, 1995).

Roy W. Lennox, 'Lauderdale and Scotland: A Study in Politics and Administration 1660–1682' (Columbia University, Ph.D. dissertation, 1977).

J. Maclean, 'The Sources, particularly the Celtic Sources, in the history of the Highlands in the Seventeenth Century' (University of Aberdeen, Ph.D. dissertation, 1939).

Christine M. Shepherd, 'Philosophy and Science in the Arts Curriculum of the Scottish Universities of the 17th Century' (University of Edinburgh, Ph.D. dissertation, 1974).

Margaret Steele, 'Covenanting Political Propaganda 1638–89' (University of Glasgow, Ph.D. dissertation, 1995).

Index

Habeas Corpus, writ of, 132
Halifax, marquis of: see *Savile, Sir George*
Halyburton, Thomas (1674–1712), 177
Ham House, Surrey, 80, 177
Hamilton, James, Bp. of Galloway (1610–74), 109
Hamilton, John, 2nd Lord Bargeny (d.1693), 144
Hamilton, John, 2nd Baron Belhaven (1656–1708), 150
Hamilton, Robert, 67–8, 136–7
Hamilton, Robert (1650–1701), 71
Hamilton of Preston, Sir Thomas (d.1672), 85
Hardy, John, Gordon minister, 161–2
Harris, Benjamin, 33
Hay, Alexander, Kilconquhar minister, 214
Hay, Jean, countess of Tweeddale, 40
Hay, John, 2nd earl and 1st marquis of Tweeddale (1626–97), 39, 78, 80, 90, 92, 115, 149, 194, 207
Hay, John, 2nd marquis of Tweeddale (1645–1713), 194, 205, 207, 208
Henry VIII, King (1491–1547), 116, 117
Henry, Prince of Wales (1594–1612), 83
Hickes, George (1642–1715), 42, 74, 86, 99, 119, 141, 144, 146
'Highland Host' (1678), 143
Hobbes, Thomas (1588–1679) and Hobbesian ideas, 62 n.85, 67, 70, 102–3, 142, 147, 164, 176, 177–9, 181, 187, 188, 203
Holland: see *United Provinces*
Holyroodhouse, Palace of, 17, 18, 43, 52, 53, 65, 180, 202, 218
Honyman, Andrew, Bp. of Orkney (1619–76), 7, 44, 45, 55, 58, 61, 62, 63, 111–12, 113, 125, 137, 145, 148, 164, 171, 205
Hotham, Sir John (1632–89), 97
Howell, James (?1594–1666), 31
Huber, Ulrich (1636–96), 56
Hume, David (1711–76), 3, 209 n.79
Hume of Polwarth, Sir Patrick, 1st earl of Marchmont (1641–1724), 161
Hyde, Edward, 1st earl of Clarendon (1609–74), 32–3, 47, 74, 76, 77, 107, 93 n.91, 114

Indulgences (ecclesiastical), 118, 120
Ireland, 5, 6, 34, 46, 55, 56, 79, 137 n.31, 194, 205, 206, 207, 208, 211
Irvine, Christopher (fl. 1638–85), 31
Israel, Jonathan, 6

Jacobite ideas and Jacobitism, 53, 121, 192, 206, 208–15
Jaffray, Alexander (1614–73), 147
James VI & I, King (1566–1625), 17, 25, 48, 50, 52 n.34, 54, 56, 60, 63, 65, 66, 83, 86, 87, 89, 101, 133, 135, 136, 138, 169, 196, 207, 218
James VII & II, King (1633–1701), 1, 3, 12, 16, 17–18, 20, 21 n.32, 24, 30, 33, 35, 36, 38, 41, 43, 46, 49–50, 52 n.34, 54, 58, 71, 74, 79, 96, 98, 114, 117, 123, 127, 128, 132, 135, 138, 144, 155–62, 172, 192, 193–215, 219, 220
James 'VIII & III', 'The Old Pretender' (1688–1766), 191, 200
Jameson, John, Eccles minister, 15, 148
Jeffreys, George (1644–89), 153
Johnson, Samuel (1649–1702), 36, 194
Johnston of Wariston, Archibald (?1610–63), 41, 42, 189
Justinian I (482–565) and Justinianic ideas, 139–40, 211

Kennedy, Lady Margaret (?1630–85), 40
Kennedy, Robert, 18
Kenyon, John, 202
Kerr, William, 3rd earl of Lothian (1605–75), 149
Kidd, Colin, 3
Kincaid, Thomas, 11
Kincardine, 2nd earl of: see *Bruce, Alexander*
Kirk, Robert (?1641–92), 32, 113, 135, 150, 166, 167 n.18, 168, 171, 188, 202
Kirkton, James (?1620–99), 14, 98, 106, 114
Koelman, Jacobus (1632–95), 38

Laud, William, Abp of Canterbury (1573–1645) and Laudian ideas, 66, 74, 107, 122, 146
Lauder of Fountainhall, Sir John (1646–1722), 21, 24, 25, 35, 38, 44, 52, 71, 79, 83, 90, 97, 98, 116, 119, 127, 134, 141, 146–7, 151, 155, 158–9, 160
Lauderdale, duchess of: see *Maitland, Elizabeth*
Lauderdale, 2nd earl and 1st duke of: see *Maitland, John*
Lauderdale, 3rd earl of: see *Maitland of Hatton, Charles*
Law, 7, 12, 19, 25–7, 38, 41, 45, 48–9, 51, 54, 56, 59, 60, 62–4, 67, 72, 73–4, 76–8, 82–7, 90–1, 94, 99, 101–3, 105–6, 108–9, 111–12, 115, 131–2, 135–44, 148, 151–3,